HUD

1st

395

LAFAYETTE

LAFAYETTE AS A YOUNG MAN

Portrait owned by Stuart W. Jackson.

LAFAYETTE

W. E. WOODWARD

Illustrated

FARRAR & RINEHART, INC.
NEW YORK   TORONTO

CONTENTS

LIST OF ILLUSTRATIONS

A LETTER TO MY READERS

A BIOGRAPHER works in a tightly closed ring of limitations. Compared with him a writer of novels is as free as a bird. The novelist creates his own characters. They are products of his imagination, yet it is true that there are some restraints on his exuberant fancy. He must portray his people in such fashion that they will be recognized as members of the human race; he must bring them together in a plausible narrative which has an underlying theme, and his story should develop through emotional or moral stress into a climax. The dialogue must fit the characters, and the writer must be sufficiently skilled in writing to hold the attention of his readers. Outside of these few restrictions the novelist has full liberty to do whatever he pleases.

A writer of biography faces an entirely different problem. He finds his characters already created. The action has occurred; the events have taken place; the people have lived and passed away. There they stand—Characters and Events—immutable, unchangeable, like figures cast in bronze

> "The Moving Finger writes; and, having writ,
> Moves on: nor all your Piety nor Wit
> Shall lure it back to cancel half a Line,
> Nor all your Tears wash out a Word of it."

The static quality of the Past is in curious contrast to the unceasing change that pervades the universe. Heat, light, energy, motion are discernible in the most distant stars as well as in our compact little solar system. On Earth the human race is in constant movement. Things happen. Then, one by one, men and women disappear into the past, and there nothing ever happens.

The business of the historian and the biographer is to make the people and events of the past live again in the minds of readers. There is a good deal more to life than names and dates. As a matter of information, for instance, it may be worth remembering that James Stuart, king of Scotland, succeeded Queen Elizabeth—in 1603 —on the throne of England, and that he had a "royal progress" of thirty-two days from Edinburgh to London. That is as helpful as an inscription on the marble façade of a tomb. But it is much more interesting, and also more informative, to learn that James I kept his mouth open all the time, and probably had adenoids; also that on his royal progress from Scotland to London he conferred the order of knighthood on two hundred and thirty-seven gentlemen, most of whom he had never seen before; and that he said, "Kings are not only God's lieutenants upon earth and sit on God's throne, but even by God himself are called gods." These three facts alone give us a better knowledge of James I than any number of dates.

We read the daily newspapers because we want to find out what is happening throughout the world. Only a few of the stories displayed in such prolific fashion on their pages have any intimate, personal relation to the average reader. With intense curiosity he reads and thinks about the actions of strangers, and the basis of his curiosity is that the news is mainly about people.

History is news from the past, and its subject matter is people and their doings. One may write a history of ideas, but ideas do not and cannot stand alone; they are bred like babies; they must have fathers and they are born from pregnant minds.

All news is not history. Most of it is entirely negligible. A suicide who leaps from a window does not make history except for his family and friends, yet the incident has a news value. The weeding-out of unnecessary facts, episodes and characters is one of the primary and unescapable tasks of historians.

But if ten thousand people should jump from windows and kill themselves in a single week that would find a place in history, undoubtedly, and would probably be called the Great Suicide Craze of the Year So-and-so.

Biography is definitely a study of character. A biographer must be—or, at any rate, should be—competent to develop the shadowy and dim psychological motivations of his subject; for these, despite their obscurity, are often the determining factors of a man's life.

We must try to know not only *What* our subject did but also *Why* he did it. Then we set forth the consequences, if we can determine what they were.

A man without a background is just a stranger. It is impossible to know him well, for in studying him you have no map or plane of reference.

To my way of thinking, the background of a man's life is of great importance in the formation of his character. The community in which he was brought up, the social and economic status of his parents and relatives, his youthful companions, the things and people around him—all these leave an impress on his personality as sharp and clear (if you know how to look for it) as the stamp of a die on the face of a coin.

My purpose in giving so much space to the feudal regime in France is to build up a background for Lafayette. I wanted to see him among the people of his time. That enables us to observe him clearly and to know him better by contrast with his surroundings.

To acquire an understanding of that epoch I relied more on memoirs and letters and official documents than upon the works of historians. One may ask why. The reason is that the historians present a finished picture of the times and the people as they see them, while I want to form my own conclusions. The discovery of motive stands at the center of my biographical research, and I prefer to ascertain the motives myself and not take somebody else's word. In other words, I think a good biography ought to be a thesis in psychological interpretation.

The newspapers of a vanished era are always very helpful. Much of their contents are mere gossip, or plain lies; therefore they can be rarely quoted, but even if they are untrue as to facts they do reveal the spirit of the times. When I was writing my biography of General Grant I spent many days poring over a file of Confederate newspapers printed in the fall of 1864 and the spring of 1865. I learned more of definite value about the state of mind of the southern people in the last year of the Civil War from those ragged and inky newspapers than I ever learned from the tomes of history.

History is not a science, nor is biography. Science is mechanistic. Given the same conditions the results should be the same. But that is not so in the field of history. The future is unpredictable. Something that is completely unexpected may appear. The chance element has an important part in human affairs. It is often productive of momentous consequences.

Lafayette's coming to America was determined largely by chance. If he had not come he would not have met George Washington, who became the most potent influence in Lafayette's life. There we have the random element in history.

In writing of the past I try to put myself in the place of an observer traveling in a foreign land. He is quite objective, what he sees is none of his business, but he listens and gets around and meets people, and then he writes letters and tells the home folks about the conditions and personalities he has encountered. One may travel in the past just as one goes to France or India today, and traveling in the past is not nearly as inconvenient as traveling in the present. You do not need passports, nor steamship tickets, and there are no hotel bills.

I like to write about Lafayette. He is such a pleasant person, not too wise and profound. He is not at all oppressive, and when you say good-bye to him and depart you do not feel like a worm crawling away from the Great Presence. In other words, he is a likable human being.

I agree with Andrew Lang that dullness is the only unpardonable literary sin. If any of my readers find this book dull and boresome I offer them my sincere apologies.

W. E. WOODWARD

New York City
August 15, 1938

P. S. I take this opportunity to express my gratitude to Judge Walter P. Gardner, John Gough and Stuart W. Jackson for their kindness in lending me valuable documents and letters from their collections of Lafayette material. Also to René de Chambrun, of Paris, for his data on the genealogy of the Lafayette family. Mr. de Chambrun, who occupies the unique position of being a citizen of both France and the United States, is Lafayette's great-grandson.

LAFAYETTE

CHAPTER I

LAFAYETTE ARRIVES

I

THE *Victoire*, wide-beamed and clumsy, was a slow sailer. She crept over the ocean like a man crawling on all fours. Fifty-four days at sea had terribly bored the young marquis and his companions, but all voyages come to an end at last. On June 13, 1777, the green and white coast of South Carolina was in sight. Green trees and a glittering white beach with the surf breaking into foam against it. There were no houses—only the beach, the surf, and the dark-green palmettos.

The Marquis de Lafayette, who was then a youth of nineteen, owned the ship. He had bought the vessel and was sailing in her to join the struggling American revolutionary army as a volunteer officer. The original destination of the *Victoire* was Charleston, but those on board learned from a passing American vessel that the port was blockaded by a British squadron. The blockade was not very effective; the British ships were frequently away from their stations for three or four days at a time. Lafayette did not know this until he and his party had landed.

Besides Lafayette there were fifteen officers aboard. Among them was Baron De Kalb, a soldier of experience and ability. He was in his fifty-sixth year; all the others were young. All of them were guests of the marquis, and their voyage had cost them nothing. He had known some of them for years; others were almost unknown to him. They had appeared with letters of introduction and said they wanted to accompany the expedition. After a sketchy examination of their credentials they were invited aboard. The marquis cared nothing for expense. He was—at that time—so rich that he did not know the extent of his fortune, and he was accustomed to spending money with generous abandon.

Not one of them, so far as we know or the record shows, cared anything for the democratic notions of liberty and equality for which the Americans were fighting. Not even Lafayette. Their motives were mixed. The young marquis wanted to distinguish himself as a soldier. He hoped to show his father-in-law, all of his relatives, and the court at Versailles that he was somebody after all, and not a mere dawdling time killer, as they thought he was.

Besides, he had another motive—a lesser one. He detested England and the English. Victors in the confused Seven Years' War, the triumphant English humiliated France and had taken away the French dominion of Canada. Lafayette had all the martial pride that a Frenchman is expected to have—and even more. He wanted to see England get a beating; he wanted her to lose her American colonies and he had come to help the Americans win, gain their independence, and lower the pride of the insolent English nation.

De Kalb's reasons for coming are clear enough. He was an officer of distinction, but because he was a fictitious noble—and not a real one—he could never attain high rank in the French army. He sought advancement and money. Moreover, he had been entrusted with a secret mission by his patron, or "boss"—the Comte de Broglie—who desired nothing less than to supersede Washington and be made commander in chief of the American army.

The rest of them were either military adventurers, who are attracted to any war for the excitement of it, or ne'er-do-wells who simply wanted to get on the American army's payroll. Among them were the Vicomte de Mauroy, the Chevalier du Buysson, de Lesser and de Valfort—they ranked as colonels—and de Fayolles and de Franval, who were lieutenants.

On June 13th the *Victoire* poked her nose cautiously into North Inlet, which is about fifty miles north of Charleston. It was not only the thirteenth day of the month, but also a Friday. I do not know whether the superstition of bad luck hovered in that era around the combination of Friday and the thirteenth. Anyway, Lafayette says nothing of it, nor does anyone else. It was certainly a good luck day for the marquis. From that Friday—the thirteenth—must be dated his great celebrity. Until then he had no place in the solemn halls of history and was not expected to have any by those who knew him.

Further on I shall relate his exciting adventures in getting away from France, but I may say here briefly that his departure was in the nature of an escape. He was not the first French officer who had gone to America to join the American revolutionists, by any means, but he was the most conspicuous one. The others who had gone before were small people, minor figures in French life. Nobody cared very much whether they went to America or stayed in France. The French Foreign Office could always shrug its shoulders and tell the British ambassador that it had no control over unimportant people who wanted to leave. What difference did it make?

But the case of the Marquis de Lafayette was another matter. He was a wealthy noble of long descent; he belonged to the court at Versailles; he had married Adrienne, daughter of the Duc d'Ayen, and was thus related by marriage to the great house of Noailles. The French government was supposed to keep track of him—as of all shining lords—and his going to America to fight England, with whom France was then at peace, would require a lot of explanation and diplomatic subtlety. And there was his wife's family. The Duc d'Ayen looked upon his proposed voyage to America as a foolish exploit and ordered him emphatically not to go. It may be said here that, according to the available evidence, Lafayette's father-in-law considered him a harum-scarum fool by nature and had a sort of contempt for him.

What about his wife? Well, she was pregnant and expected to have a child in July. Lafayette ran away from them all. He did not tell even his wife good-bye, but left a letter to be sent to her after he had sailed.

2

At last there was land in sight. Probably no one aboard the ship knew where they were exactly, nor did anyone care so long as they did not fall into the hands of the British. All the passengers were tired of the long and eventless voyage. The salty little vessel, with its boxed-in spaces and its tiny cluttered deck, was not at all to their liking, and its discomforts could have been endured only with the aid of a glowing military ardor—of which there was a plentiful supply aboard. But at that time there was nothing in the world they wanted so much as to put their feet on dry land.

Lafayette, De Kalb, Brice and some sailors rowed ashore. They came across some negroes, in a large canoe, grappling for oysters. These negroes said they were servants of Major Benjamin Huger, an officer in a South Carolina regiment. His plantation was some miles up the river. Lafayette decided to call on him.

In the boat with the marquis were some sailors and De Kalb and Edmund Brice.* It was nearly midnight when Lafayette and his two companions arrived at Major Huger's plantation. The first thing the ardent young marquis did, on stepping ashore, was to raise his hand and swear to live or die by the American cause. It was a dramatic gesture, one may be sure, and very French.

The Huger family had gone to bed, and the night was pitch dark. In the warm southern air there was a scent of magnolias. Dogs barked, lights appeared. The puzzled family, who thought at first that it was a British raid, soon learned that their nocturnal visitors were peaceful folk, and invited them into the house. De Kalb could speak English well, and it was Brice's native tongue. They expected to interpret for the marquis, who had only a slight knowledge of the language.

To their surprise, they learned that the Hugers spoke French and during their two days' stay at the Huger plantation the French language was the medium of conversation.†

The Hugers were much impressed by the poise and Old World urbanity of their guests. And Major Huger (the name is pronounced "Hugee") thought them astonishing. Courageous and able men who came across the ocean at their own expense, in their own ship, to fight for the colonies. He could not keep his own local South Carolina battalion together, because of evaders and deserters, yet his men-at-arms were his neighbors, men who should have their hearts in the cause.

The servants were awakened and soon a southern midnight supper appeared. Among the Hugers was a little boy, about three years old, who stared at the visitors with wide-open eyes. Years later, as a young man, he was to play a part in one of the most exciting episodes of Lafayette's career.

* Brice was an American who lived in France. He was sent by the American diplomatic agents in Paris to accompany Lafayette as an aide. On the ship's list of passengers Brice, for some unknown reason, put himself down as Leonard Price, and so his name appears in nearly all the accounts of Lafayette's voyage. Gottschalk, *Lafayette Comes to America,"* p. 163.

† My authority for this statement is the late Alfred Huger, of Charleston, who was a descendant of Major Benjamin Huger. French Protestants, called Huguenots, had emigrated in large numbers to South Carolina around the close of the seventeenth century. They kept their language alive as a means of daily intercourse for several generations thereafter.

On Saturday, June 14th, after a prodigious ham, egg, hominy and fried chicken breakfast Lafayette and De Kalb went out in a boat to the *Victoire*. She was standing there in the inlet, awaiting orders. The marquis thought that she should sail to Charleston by the first favorable wind, and try to get past the English blockading war vessels. The captain agreed. Lafayette was going by land, and he gave his fellow travelers the choice of traveling with him or going by sea. In the end Lafayette, De Kalb, the Chevalier du Buysson and four others, with their servants, were rowed back to the Huger plantation. The *Victoire* got ready to run the blockade.

It must have been embarrassing to Major Huger when seven officers returned from the ship and declared that they would ride to Charleston. He had only three saddle horses. Lafayette, his servant, and De Kalb left on the horses Sunday afternoon and the others were told to find their way on foot.

The marquis and the Baron De Kalb got to Charleston on Tuesday. They had been on the way two full days. In our time you can make the trip by motor, over fine roads, in about two hours. Those who walked did not arrive until Friday, and they were so ragged and dirty that the common people hooted at them in the streets of Charleston. The weather was so hot that they had thrown away their military boots. Then they discarded their luggage; it was too heavy to carry. Their coats went next. Have you ever tried to walk through a South Carolina pine barren in June? Your foot sinks six inches in the torrid sand, and slips. One can make about a mile an hour.

The *Victoire* arrived the next morning after Lafayette reached Charleston. She had sailed on Monday, with a do-or-die resolve on the part of her passengers and crew to run the blockade, but when they arrived at the entrance of the harbor they found that there was, at the moment, no blockade. A strong offshore wind had blown away the British fleet for the time being, so the marquis's vessel sailed in and dropped anchor.

In 1777 the gracious city of Charleston was not particularly enthusiastic over the coming of Frenchmen. There were plenty of them there already. It seemed that every governor, judge and commandant of the French West Indies who wanted to get rid of a rascally official deported him to Charleston with a glowing letter of praise in which the colonial authorities were urged to take him into their service that he might have an opportunity to "fight for the cause of liberty." The town was full of shabby Frenchmen who begged or borrowed money, and who were wholly incompetent.

But the youthful marquis was obviously a different kind of Frenchman, a young man of substance who had come in his own ship. And, of course, the intelligentsia of Charleston had heard or read of the distinguished French family of Noailles, to which Lafayette belonged by reason of his marriage to a daughter of the Noailles clan.

3

The marquis and his companions remained in Charleston about ten days, and the town spread itself to show them every possible attention. For the first time in his life Lafayette found himself in the center of the stage, and that almost turned his young head. He had hardly an hour that he could call his own. The bands played; fair ladies tossed flowers in his direction; the dignitaries called and made speeches of welcome; there was a grand banquet at which he was the guest of honor.

At the banquet he must have been dismayed at the colonial custom of drinking toasts. It was understood that any guest at these dinners had the social right to get up and propose a toast to anybody from Christopher Columbus, or the spirit of Moses, down to "the ladies—God bless 'em." This last-named toast was invariably given, also one to General Washington (during and after the Revolution). As for the rest, they ran in a bewildering variety. Everyone was expected to drink his liquor down at every toast, and sometimes there was an incredible number of them. How they managed to do it and walk out on their own feet at the conclusion of the ceremonies is still a mystery.

Then, as now, Frenchmen drank a few glasses of wine at dinner. The American habit of heavy drinking at convivial dinners is mentioned in nearly all the memoirs written by French officers who served in America. At the Charleston banquet toasts were drunk to the Marquis de Lafayette, to General De Kalb, to the king of France, to the queen of France, to all who had come in the *Victoire*, to General Washington, to General Moultrie, and to many other persons.

Lafayette rose, and in slow, stammering English proposed a toast to American independence. The people at the banquet saw a slender, erect, young man with reddish hair, blue-gray eyes, and a forehead pushed back in line with his nose, a slanting head.* Yet he was impressive because he was nonchalant and sure of himself. The Charlestonians clapped their hands and called for more. He did not know enough of the language to venture on a long discourse, and said so. They cheered him again.

That same evening, probably very late, he wrote to Adrienne— his wife. He gives his impressions of America; he had been here only a week. He wrote:

I am now going to speak of the country, my dear heart, and of its inhabitants. They are as kind as my enthusiasm has been able to represent them; the simplicity of manners, the desire to please, the love of country and of liberty, the delightful equality that reigns everywhere here; the richest man and the poorest are on a level, and while there are many fortunes in the country, I will defy anybody to find the least difference between their respective manners one for the other.

Well, this is just another example of the folly of writing about things of which you know nothing. The folly still exists. It did not come to an end with Lafayette. He was one of a long line of Frenchmen and Englishmen who have depicted social and economic conditions in the United States after having been here three weeks.

The young marquis writes of "delightful equality." He is wrong. The "richest man and the poorest" were not on the same level, by any stretch of the imagination. A white carpenter, for instance, had to compete with slave labor. The owners of slaves had their negroes trained to do such work, and they hired out these trained menials at wages which were below any possible scale of decent living.

What pleases me most is that all the citizens are brothers. In America there are no poor people, not even what may be called peasants. Every citizen has his own property and all have the same rights as the wealthiest landowner in the country. . . .

No poor people! There were thousands of people in South Carolina who were not able to buy a clock to know the time, nor a pair of shoes. They drank water from gourds and their dishes were wooden

* The marquis is usually described as "tall," but his height was only five feet, nine inches. His hair was described as "sandy" by some of his American acquaintances; others wrote that he had red hair. He stood perfectly straight, and walked with soldierly vigor in his youth. When he was much older one of his legs was broken in an accident, and thereafter he limped and used a cane. His most noticeable feature, from my point of view, was the sharp backward slope of his forehead.

platters. Tea and coffee were unknown to them. They had hardly any furniture in their homes, they slept on the floor; they lived in hovels, just as did the peasants in France.

But the marquis knew nothing of that. He did not understand poverty, and always wanted to get rid of it by uttering a phrase. He had the best of intentions, yet economics was a mystery to him to the end of his days. When he wrote about the rich and poor in South Carolina he knew almost nothing of the rich and poor in France. He had only a vague idea of how his own peasants managed to live. All that was left to his business agents and he took the income as it came in.

As to myself, I have been welcomed in the most agreeable manner by everyone here. I have just this moment returned from a grand dinner that lasted five hours, given by a gentleman of this city in my honor. . . . We drank many healths and [I] spoke bad English which language I am beginning now to use a little. . . .

I finish because I have no more paper and no more time, and if I do not repeat ten thousand times that I love you, it is not because I have no more sentiments, but truly because of modesty. I confidently hope that I have persuaded you of it. It is very late at night, the heat is frightful, and I am devoured by small gnats which cover one with great blisters, but the best countries have, as you see, their inconveniences. Adieu, my heart, adieu!

Gnats? It was his first experience with mosquitoes.

In the course of his ten days' stay in Charleston he was taken by his hosts to Sullivan's Island, at the entrance to the harbor. The fort was built of palmetto logs. About a year before Lafayette's coming a British fleet had attempted to batter it down and take the town of Charleston. Their assault failed miserably. Palmetto logs are soft and spongy; they absorbed the British cannonballs, and in the end the fort was stronger than it had been in the beginning because of the amount of iron introduced into its system. Meanwhile, the American gunners—with a surprising accuracy of aim—had riddled the British ships.

Lafayette went over the fort with all the curiosity of a young and ambitious soldier. He met General William Moultrie, its tough and hard-faced commandant. Then the troops were drawn up for his inspection. He was shocked. There was not a decent garment among them. Most of them were barefoot; some had no coats or hats. He had never seen such soldiers in France.

Before he left Charleston for Philadelphia he presented Moultrie with enough money to buy clothing and arms for one hundred men.

4

Charleston was only a stopping place on the road to Philadelphia, where the Continental Congress was in session. In his pocket the marquis had a commission as a major general in the revolutionary army, and the field of glory was as wide as the horizon.

The major general's commission was devoid of validity, but the marquis did not know that. The appointment had been made by Silas Deane, a Connecticut merchant who was in 1777 the American agent in France. Deane had no authority to give commissions to foreign officers, though Lafayette thought he had, and probably Mr. Deane thought so too.

There was the question of money; one needs cash even in the most friendly surroundings. Lafayette expected to sell the ship and use the proceeds to defray the expenses of himself and his companions on their journey to Philadelphia. But when the time came to sell it Le Boursier, captain of the vessel, presented a note for forty thousand livres, representing money still due on the ship's purchase price. The young marquis had signed the note in Bordeaux—where the ship was bought—evidently without knowing what he was doing. Let us keep in mind that he had very little money-sense—then, or ever. Throughout his life he was a mere child in financial dealings of any kind. The former owners of the *Victoire* had entrusted the note to the captain with instructions to collect the money or bring the ship back to France.

This turn of events took the youthful adventurer by surprise, and he hardly knew what to do. He had to borrow money in Charleston, and he soon learned that social amenities and moneylending do not usually go hand in hand. But he did manage to borrow some money, at usurious interest. In payment he gave a note, or draft, payable by the trustees of his estate in France. The borrowed money was a mere trifle to the marquis, but the moneylenders were not sure of that, or of him. At any rate, he got the money.

The *Victoire* had bad luck. Soon after the money business was arranged she set sail for France, and was wrecked on the bar at the entrance of Charleston harbor. According to Lafayette, the ship was not insured on her return voyage and was a total loss. In a long statement made in 1810, of his losses over many years, the marquis says that the *Victoire "périt au retour avant qu'on ent le temps de le faire assurer."* But Lafayette's memory of financial transactions was often at fault. Gottschalk says, quoting du Buysson, in his *Lafayette Joins the American Army* (p. 8), that the *Victoire*, on her return, was insured by an American firm, and that Lafayette "could expect to collect insurance on both the vessel and her cargo of rice."

This incident is of slight importance, but it does show in its small way how biographers and historians are pestered by the conflicting memories of people who have long ago passed out of life. In such cases the historian must rely on his knowledge of human conduct. With that as a guide, I am convinced that the *Victoire* was insured, and Le Boursier, her captain, would have never sailed without an insurance policy covering both ship and cargo.

The loss of the ship made no difference to Lafayette. He started to Philadelphia on June 25, 1777, in four carriages, with a number of people riding on horses. The distance from Charleston to Philadelphia is about six hundred and fifty miles. They made it in one month and two days. Imagine the roads hub-deep in mud, the cowpaths where no road was visible, the clearings of roads over the stumps of trees, the bad inns, the poor food. "In four days," says the Chevalier du Buysson, "some of our carriages were reduced to splinters; several of the horses, which were old and unsteady, were either worn out or lame, and we were obliged to buy others along the road. This outlay took all our money. We had to leave behind us a part of our luggage, and part of it was stolen. We traveled a great deal of the way on foot, often sleeping in the woods, almost dead with hunger, exhausted by the heat, several of us suffering from fever and dysentery."

That sounds pretty bad, but the marquis took it all in good spirit. Unconquerable youthful heart! For the first time he was living his own life, outside and far away from the formalized pattern of the Parisian aristocracy. Du Buysson says:

We were encouraged by the bright prospect of the reception we counted upon from the people there [Philadelphia], and I can say with truth that this thought would have induced us to undergo much greater hardships with the same willingness and the same lightness of heart that I felt after once I had made up my mind. We were all animated by the same spirit. The enthusiasm of Lafayette would have incited all the rest of us, if anyone had been less courageous than he.

The dilapidated Lafayette caravan arrived in Philadelphia on July 27th. Congress was in session and they went at once—after a little brushing up at their inn—to present themselves. They were received by John Hancock, the president of the Continental Congress at that time, in a manner that may be accurately described as frigid. Most of the volunteer officers who had come before Lafayette, nearly all of them in fact, were incompetent. Du Buysson says the president of the Congress sent them to see "M. Moose" (it may have been Robert Morris) who made an appointment to meet them the next day at the door of the Congress—and, "in the meantime our papers were read and examined." They were there promptly the next day, standing in the street before the door. Du Buysson says:

Finally M. Moose appeared with another member, and said to us, "This gentleman speaks French very well, and he is entrusted with the matters that concern people of your nationality; hereafter your communications will all be with him." He then went in and the other member M. L—— [he was probably James Lovell, who was then the head of the Committee of Foreign Affairs] talked with us in the street, where he left us, after having treated us, in excellent French, like a set of adventurers. He ended his speech by saying, "Gentlemen, have you any authority from Mr. Deane? We authorized him to send us four French engineers; but, instead of that he has sent us Mr. du Coudray and some men who pretend to be engineers but are not, and some artillerists who have never seen service. We then instructed Mr. Franklin to send us four engineers and they have come. It seems that French officers have a great fancy to enter our service without being invited. It is true we were in need of officers last year, but now we have experienced men and plenty of them."

Mr. Lovell then gave them a curt good-bye and went back to the halls of Congress, leaving Lafayette and his friends in the street. Du Buysson says they were stupefied at this reception and I can well believe they were. There they stood, in the hot sunshine, looking at the red brick front of Independence Hall, the demure Quaker houses, with their white marble doorsteps, on the other side of the street, and beyond Independence Hall the shady green trees of the park.

CHAPTER II

WASHINGTON MEETS THE MARQUIS

I

THE sore disappointment of Lafayette and his fellow travelers may be well imagined. They had come so far, their hearts filled with enthusiasm and courage, only to meet with an icy reception. They were not only disappointed; they were also angry. Their rejection was without dignity; they had been turned away with the nonchalance of a householder driving peddlers from his door. A return to France after such an unceremonious dismissal would have made the bold young marquis a laughing stock of the Paris salons.

But let us look at the American side of the affair. For a year or more Congress had been bedeviled by nondescript French officers who had come without invitation, for the most part, to enter the American service. These volunteers were usually self-assertive and almost ready to burst with a sense of superiority over everything in sight.

None of these vagrant visitors from across the sea ever volunteered to serve as a private in the ranks. They all demanded commissions of a higher status than they would ever be likely to achieve in France; and all of them were voracious in the matter of pay. As a rule they could not speak English, and some of them were imposters, pure and simple. Among those who wangled commissions only a few turned out well.

The effect on the American army was deplorable. Native-born officers who had served from the beginning and had endured innumerable hardships, including poor pay and semistarvation, certainly could not be expected to look with satisfaction at the appointment of foreigners to places of high command.

Then there was the du Coudray affair, which was still reverberating when Lafayette and his companions arrived in Philadelphia. Tronson du Coudray was an artillery officer in the French army. He got a leave of absence and persuaded Silas Deane to promise him the rank of major general and chief of artillery on his arrival in America. His pay was to be thirty-six thousand livres a year, and he was to receive, in addition, three hundred thousand livres as a bonus after the war.

As I have said before—in the preceding chapter—Deane was not authorized to make appointments in the military establishment. Only Congress had the power to do that. Yet it appears that, in his conferences with du Coudray, Lafayette, De Kalb, and others, he made it appear that he could confer commissions and arrange the rates of pay, and that the ratification by Congress was only a formality. But Deane was not wholly to blame. He could only recommend the employment of officers sent by him to America; nevertheless, his authority in these matters was extensive, and he was led to believe that his recommendations would be accepted.

Du Coudray came to Philadelphia in June, 1777, about six weeks before Lafayette got there. He knew of the young marquis's expedition, and could have sailed with him but he preferred to come on an earlier vessel. From the knowledge of his character that we now possess it seems rather obvious that his purpose in going ahead of Lafayette was to be first on the ground, so that he would stand out as a more impressive figure than would have been possible if he had arrived as one of a group of sixteen.

Congress was aghast at Deane's arrangement with du Coudray. It would mean the turning over of one of the most important branches of the military service to an unknown foreigner. As soon as the news was known, Generals Greene, Knox and Sullivan sent in their resignations, to take effect if du Coudray was made a major general.

While the discussion was going on, du Coudray swaggered about Philadelphia, putting on lordly airs. He declared that he was a nobleman of high rank, which was not true; he was really the son of a bourgeois wine merchant. Would the American yokels know that? He thought not, but they did. Some Americans—and among them were members of Congress—had correspondents in France. Also he declared that the secret aid in the way of money that the French treasury had given to the colonies was due wholly to his influence at the court of Versailles; and that was not true either. He had no influence at Versailles; he was merely a *chef de brigade d'artillerie*. When Congress declined to ratify Deane's agreement

du Coudray blustered and threatened, and the argument sank to
the level of an ill-tempered dispute. In the midst of it Lafayette
reached Philadelphia.

The du Coudray episode came to an end in a dramatic and
tragic manner. Du Coudray got on a ferryboat, riding a horse. He
did not dismount but stayed on the animal's back. The horse was
frightened at something, leaped into the river, and du Coudray,
caught in spurs and entanglements, was drowned.

It seemed as if the gallant marquis had come at precisely the
wrong time, but he had no intention of turning back just because
a man whom he had met on the doorstep of the hall of Congress
had told him that French officers were not wanted.

On the evening of the day when Mr. Lovell, of the Foreign
Affairs Committee, had treated him and his friends in such a boorish
fashion he took pen in hand and composed a letter to Congress. It
was an epistle of appealing directness and simplicity. Among other
things he said:

After the sacrifices that I have made in this cause I have the right to ask
two favors at your hands: the one is to serve without pay, at my own
expense; and the other that I be allowed to serve first as a volunteer.*

That sentence caught the attention of every man in the Congress when the letter was read. It was the first time any foreigner
was willing to serve without pay. Lafayette stood in a class by himself. It is probable—or possible, at any rate—that his case had not
been brought before Congress and that his dismissal by Mr. Lovell
had been done entirely on that individual's initiative in carrying out
the policy that no more foreign officers were desired.

Congress was eager for French loans or gifts of money, also
for recognition by the French government. These incentives were
strong enough to swing Congressional opinion in favor of Lafayette,
though Congress, naturally, was reluctant to give him the rank of
major general. He was only a nineteen-year-old boy, without any

* It may be worth noting here that Lafayette never—to the end of his days—
learned to spell English correctly, and his grammar was always defective. He spoke
with a pronounced foreign accent.

His early American biographers, with the best of intentions, we may presume,
rewrote his letters and fixed up the spelling and grammar before reproducing them. In
doing this they destroyed the peculiar flavor of his English epistolary style. He wrote
of "nacked soldiers" (meaning "naked"), "oppened field" (meaning "open"), "beggin-
ing" (meaning "beginning"). "Shall" was always spelled "schall"; and "spoken" was
spelled "spocken."

experience in warfare, without knowledge of American ways, and he spoke English very imperfectly. On the other hand, he was wealthy and generous—the story of his gift of clothing to Moultrie's men had reached Philadelphia; he belonged to one of the great noble houses of France; and, moreover, he did not want any pay for his services.

On July 31, 1777, to his great joy and elation, he was made a major general. That the appointment was a purely honorary one seems to have been definitely understood in Congress. It appears, however, that the marquis did not so understand it. He expected to go into active service at once.

Early in August a letter came to General Washington from Benjamin Franklin, then in Paris.* He wrote:

The Marquis de Lafayette, a young nobleman of great family connections here and great wealth, is gone to America in a ship of his own, accompanied by some officers of distinction, in order to serve in our armies. He is exceedingly beloved, and everybody's good wishes attend him; we cannot but hope he may meet with such a reception as will make the country and his expedition agreeable to him . . . we are satisfied that the civilities and respect that may be shown him will be serviceable to our affairs here, as pleasing not only to his powerful relations and the Court but to the whole French nation. . . .

In that period of our history Franklin was looked upon as the greatest of Americans, and every communication from him carried weight.

William Duer, a member of Congress who spoke French, had some long talks with Lafayette while the discussion over accepting his services was going on. Duer says that Lafayette told him that he did not expect to remain long in America; that he came for glory and adventure; that he desired to serve under Washington for a short time. Then he would make a sensation on his return to France.

2

What about the officers who accompanied the marquis?

Congress was equally decisive on that point. They were to be sent home, with their expenses paid.

* Silas Deane was the sole American commissioner in Paris until near the end of 1776. Congress decided to have a three-man commission there, as it had become distrustful of Deane's ability and influence. Late in 1776 Franklin and Arthur Lee arrived in Paris to serve on the commission.

Lafayette's fellow voyagers were indignant. The youngest stripling among them had been given the rank of major general while the rest of them were dismissed with a little travel money. Du Buysson wrote that Lafayette was so completely dazzled by his sudden elevation, and by the attentions paid to him, "that he forgot us for a moment. But I do him justice. He has too good a heart for that forgetfulness to last long."

No, he had not forgotten them. In his letter to "M. Hancok, [*sic*], president of Congress," he said:

It is now as an american that I'll mention every day to congress the officers who came over with me, whose interests are for me as my own, and the consideration which they deserve by their merits, their ranks, their state and reputation in france.

Lafayette's appeal had little effect, apparently. He was informed that he might select his aides from those who had come with him, but beyond that Congress would do nothing. De Gimat and de La Colombe remained on his personal staff, and for some reason unknown to me de Bedaulx was given a place as brevet captain. Capitaine du Chesnoy, a competent topographical engineer, was also retained in the service.

Baron De Kalb was greatly disappointed by this turn of affairs. Before leaving Philadelphia to embark at some southern port he wrote a scathing letter to the president of Congress in which he said—in part: "I do not think that either my name, my services, or my person are proper objects to be trifled with or laughed at. I cannot tell you, sir, how deeply I feel the injury done to me, and how ridiculous it seems to me to make people leave their homes, families, and affairs to cross the sea under a thousand different dangers, to be received and to be looked at with contempt by those from whom you were to expect but warm thanks. . . . I should be sorry to be compelled to carry my case against Mr. Deane or his successors for damages. And such an action would injure his credit and negotiations, and those of the state at Court."

Congress was in a quandary, and hardly knew what to do. That august body, as well as General Washington, was embarrassed by Deane's contracts and the presence of these officers. Finally, they solved the problem by disavowing Deane's arrangements and—immediately thereafter—they gave Baron De Kalb a commission as major general. Swift riders were dispatched to overtake him. He came back. Then he insisted that Lafayette's commission should not antedate his. "It would seem very odd and ridiculous," he wrote to the president of Congress, "to the French ministry and all experienced military men to see me placed under the command of the Marquis de Lafayette." Congress agreed, and the baron's commission was dated as of July 31st.

I think there can be no question that De Kalb had a low opinion of Lafayette's ability. One must take into account the fact that De Kalb was a veteran of the wars, a man who had lived in armies all his life, and—on the other hand—Lafayette had never been in a battle, had never seen dead and wounded men, had never fought his way out of a ring of enemies. De Kalb had been through all that. His inner convictions could not justify the appointment of a youthful playboy—as Lafayette then was—to a major position in the American military establishment while De Kalb himself was sent away. Yet such things happen and must be met with as good grace as possible.

From a practical, common-sense point of view Congress was quite right in giving preference to Lafayette. The connection of the marquis with our affairs served to lift the American Revolution into the Social Register, so far as France was concerned.

3

The worthy De Kalb was an embodiment of one of the many curious contradictions that run through the history of the eighteenth century. He was the son of a German peasant and his real name was Johann Kalb. Although by custom and tradition nobody without noble birth could become an officer in any army on the continent of Europe, Kalb was nevertheless an officer, and a distinguished one; and in spite of the rules he was not the only officer of common origin.

He ran away from home at the age of sixteen and got a job as a waiter in an Alsatian inn. There he learned French and, moreover, he learned how military officers behave, from the many who came to eat and drink. He saved his money and bought a lieutenant's commission in the French army. (In those days commissions were sold, but they were seldom sold to commoners.) As nobility was essential for advancement to the higher posts in the French army, Kalb made himself a noble by the simple process of putting "De" before his name. Everybody who took the trouble to look into the matter knew of this deception but apparently nobody cared so long as he remained in the lower rank of officers. During the Seven Years' War he made a name for himself as an officer of ability. After the rout of the French at Rossbach he saved the Comte de Broglie's transport and rear guard from destruction. De Broglie took him on as an aide—a henchman, or whatever one may call it—and managed his advancement to the position of lieutenant colonel, which is about as far as he could ever go in the French service. In the meantime De Kalb married the daughter of a wealthy Dutchman.

When the Duc de Choiseul was the head of the government in France, in the 1760's, he sent De Kalb to America to report on conditions in the colonies and the attitude of the colonials toward England. He traveled all over the country, learned a great deal about it and acquired a fluent knowledge of the English language.

De Kalb could not attain a higher place in the French army through the regular method of advancement, but there was a rule that any officer who had served in another army, with promotion, should be given the same rank in the French army when he came home. The only hope, therefore, for De Kalb was to go abroad and be a major general.

From his patron, the Comte de Broglie, he brought a most extraordinary proposal. It was simply this: De Broglie was willing to come over to America and win the Revolution by the exercise of his superior administrative, diplomatic and military talents, provided the American people would give him a free hand. His title was to be Stadtholder, and his authority, while the war continued, was to be supreme, above that of Congress, Washington and everybody else.

That an intelligent man could conceive such a proposal is an illustration of the ignorance of the American situation then prevailing in Europe. To even well-informed Europeans our revolutionists were a flock of dull-witted children who were struggling against English tyranny. As soon as De Kalb had learned the true state of affairs he

LAFAYETTE'S MOTHER, WITH LAFAYETTE AT HER SIDE

The picture in the frame is that of one of Lafayette's young cousins. Lafayette was about seven years old when this painting was made. The name of the artist is unknown.

LAFAYETTE AS A YOUTH

In this painting by an unknown artist Lafayette is shown as he appeared at about the age of fourteen. The picture is owned by M. Xavier de Pusy, a great-great-grandson of the Marquis.

wrote to the Comte de Broglie that "it is impossible to execute the great design I have so gladly come to subserve." *

Washington was displeased at the action of Congress in giving a major-generalship to a French youth who was hardly old enough to be a lieutenant. He was annoyed and not at all reluctant to say so. The members of Congress with whom he discussed the matter assured him that the appointment had been made as a good-will gesture toward France, and it was, in effect, nothing more than an honorary title. The commander in chief, they said, need not put the marquis in command of troops or employ him at all, but merely keep him as an ornament to the headquarters staff. Washington understood that, but he did not like the appointment anyway. It would discourage the whole body of American officers.

Perhaps it is just as well that none of us can foretell the future; we would all go raving mad at its surprising revelations, most of them utterly contrary to our expectations. Lafayette was destined to become one of the few people on earth for whom Washington acquired a profound affection.

Lafayette's admiration for Washington grew until it was on the borderline of worship. He adopted Washington's military ideas, his mannerisms and his political philosophy. During the French Revolution the persistent attempts of Lafayette to turn France into a republic of the American type—with a king, however, like England —and with himself as a Gallic Washington, ruined his career and almost caused him to lose his head under the guillotine.

The marquis saw Washington for the first time at a dinner given in honor of the commander in chief on August 1, 1780—the day after Congress had agreed to accept his services. Lafayette says in his *Mémoires* that he recognized Washington by "the majesty of his countenance and his tall form."

The marquis was a very self-possessed person, an aristocrat of excellent manners. One got an impression, in looking at him, of a smashing boldness held in quiet reserve. He was never ready with repartee, nor with quick, brilliant answers. Washington was not, either.

When the dinner was over Washington drew Lafayette to one

* De Kalb never saw Europe again. He became one of the most valued officers in the American army and died heroically in the battle fought at Camden, South Carolina, on August 16, 1780.

side and talked with him awhile. There is no adequate record of their conversation but I am sure that it was carried on in Washington's usual courteous, cool and detached manner. He spoke no French, and Lafayette could speak but little English, so I fancy that the marquis did most of the listening. Washington invited him to witness a review of the troops the next day.

The appearance of the American army probably surprised the ardent young Frenchman, although he was prepared for almost anything. Eleven thousand ragged, disheveled men, many of them barefoot, and hardly a complete uniform among them.

Washington, knowing that his youthful friend was half-stunned by the look of the army, said:

"We are rather embarrassed to show ourselves to an officer who has just left the army of France."

"I am here, sir," Lafayette replied, "to learn and not to teach."

It was an apt and courteous reply, and not a bit like the comments usually made by French officers on beholding Washington's disorderly and shabby army.

4

The marquis, on the general's invitation, lived at headquarters, and became an unofficial member of the staff. But that did not suit him; he wanted to command troops. The idea was nothing less than preposterous. He did not know the language well enough, nor the country, nor the army. But when he wanted anything he asked for it, and kept on asking. Washington was annoyed by his persistency, and he wrote a letter to Benjamin Harrison, chairman of the military committee in Congress, in which he said:

What the designs of Congress respecting this gentlemen were, and what line of conduct I am to pursue to comply with their designs and his expectations, I know no more than a child unborn, and beg to be instructed. If Congress meant that his rank should be unaccompanied by command, I wish it had been sufficiently explained to him. If, on the other hand, it was intended to invest him with all the powers of a major-general, why have I been led into a contrary belief, and left in the dark with respect to my conduct towards him? . . . Let me beseech you, my good Sir, to give me the sentiments of Congress on this matter, that I may endeavour, as far as it is in my power, to comply with them.

Harrison replied that Congress considered Lafayette's appointment as honorary but intimated that Washington might use his own judgment. Washington did that, and for some time Lafayette had no independent command.

Yet, in spite of the nagging, Washington liked him more and more as the weeks went by. There was something about him that reminded Washington of himself when he was a youth. In the fall of 1777 Lafayette was twenty and Washington was forty-five.

CHAPTER III

YOUTH AND MARRIAGE

I

NEARLY all Lafayette's male ancestors were soldiers with a remarkable talent for getting killed. For this they gained much distinction, for being killed in battle was then, as now, looked upon as a highly creditable way of dying, regardless of the cause of the war or its ultimate effect on the human race.

The family name of the Lafayette line of nobility was Motier. In the twelfth century the Motiers owned, lived in and ruled a place called Villa Faya, which evolved eventually into Lafayette. There were two branches of the family, and our Lafayette belonged to the younger, or cadet, branch. One of the Motier women married a gentleman named Champetière, and until around the end of the seventeenth century Lafayette's forebears were called Champetière. Then, by reason of an intricate will and a corresponding transfer of property, the Champetières were authorized to call themselves Lafayette.

Our Lafayette's father was a colonel in the French army. In 1754, when he was twenty-two, he married Mlle. Julie de La Rivière, a wealthy heiress. Their son, and only child, was born on September 6, 1757. He was christened Marie Joseph Paul Yves Roch Gilbert du Motier. This string of words came from the old French custom of tacking on to a child the names of many of his ancestors. The family called him Gilbert—pronounced, of course, "Jeelbare," in the French fashion.

The boy had no memory of his father, who was killed in the battle of Minden, which was fought on August 1, 1759, when Gilbert was not quite two years old. In connection with this event Lafayette in his *Mémoires* perpetrates a curious error. He says,* *"Ma naissance, qui suivit de près la mort de mon père à Minden."* (My birth, which came soon after the death of my father at Minden.) Certainly anyone is expected to know the date of his own

* *Mémoires de ma Main,* Vol. I, p. 6.

father's death, but evidently Lafayette's knowledge was deficient in that respect. It is almost incredible.

Charlemagne Tower, in his ponderous two-volume work, *The Marquis de Lafayette in the American Revolution,* says (vol. I, p. 9) that, "His father, Colonel the Marquis de Lafayette, was dead when this son was born, having fallen at the head of his grenadiers in the little battle of Hastenbeck, on the 26th of July of that same year, 1757, when he was not as yet twenty-five years of age." Tower thinks that Lafayette, when writing his Memoirs, was not mistaken as to the time, but as to the battle, so he follows Henri Doniol, a French authority on the participation of France in the American Revolution, and places Lafayette's father's death at Hastenbeck.

As a matter of fact he was killed at Minden in 1759, of which there is abundant proof, and no doubt whatever.

None of this is of much importance except to show how factual errors slip into biography and history.

Our marquis was born at Chavaniac in Auvergne. You will not find Chavaniac on your map unless you have a large scale French map. But you can find Le Puy on almost any map of France. It is a town of twenty thousand inhabitants and is about seventy-five miles southwest of Lyons. Chavaniac is twenty miles—or thereabouts—from Le Puy.

The land around Chavaniac is of ancient volcanic origin—a black country—with jutting peaks here and there. The château still exists. Approaching it, one may see its towers and its roof over the tops of the trees. There is nothing in its form that makes it beautiful, or even impressive, as a building, but it stands on high ground and the view from its terrace and its windows has the poetry of distance. It seems to exist in a land of quiet and lovely dreams, of pleasant hills and quiet valleys. Far away, on clear days one may see the towering mass of Puy-de-Dôme.

The château has many rooms—most of them large—and in the profusion of historical relics and paintings it is, in effect, a Lafayette museum. Thirteen of the bedrooms carry the names of our thirteen original states. One is surprised, on visiting the château, at the sunlit brightness of the rooms.

In 1916 Chavaniac was offered for sale. It was purchased by an American association known as the "Lafayette Memorial Fund." The château was slowly going to decay at that time. The floor boards were so rotten that they gave way under one's feet. The stairs were unsafe; there was nothing in the place that might be described as "modern conveniences."

That has all been changed by the funds generously supplied by the Lafayette Memorial Fund. Now there are modern kitchens, electric light, refrigerators, and bathrooms with running water. The interior of the great house is well-kept and attractive.

During the World War Chavaniac—after its purchase by the American association—was used as a convalescent home for wounded French soldiers, and for some years thereafter it was an orphanage for the children of those who had lost their lives in the war. Today it is a Lafayette memorial all the year round. During the summer the grounds, with the buildings erected on them, are used as a boys' camp.

The village of Chavaniac, and all the land thereabout, belonged to the Lafayettes. They were the feudal lords, the seigneurs, of that community. But the income did not amount to a great deal; as nobles they were considered rather poor, though the mother of the young marquis would inherit a great fortune on the death of her father. The village today lives in the backwash of time. The houses are small and weather-stained. There are a few dark little shops. Women sit before their doors knitting and sewing. The place is quiet, and without bustle or animation.

Lafayette's mother, who was a young woman at the time of her husband's death, could not stand the stale monotone of Chavaniac. She went to live in Paris with her father, the wealthy Marquis de La Rivière, and the infant Gilbert was left to be brought up by his grandmother and his two aunts. He hardly knew his mother. She came to Chavaniac for a month or two in the summer when the Paris social season was over. His only playmate was his cousin—a little girl—the daughter of his aunt Louise Charlotte.

We had better get the family relationship straight right here. The grandmother of Lafayette was Marie Catherine du Motier. She was the chatelaine of Chavaniac and general manager of the neighborhood. Her son was Lafayette's father. She had an excellent head for business and knew how to make a feudal estate profitable. She was the kind of person who is beyond all disputes, or even mild arguments. She did not care what you wanted to do; she told you what you ought to do. The people of the district held her in great esteem. They had a high opinion of her and her wisdom, probably because when she was available as a counselor they did not have to do any thinking at all.

To nine-tenths of the human race, at least, thinking is looked upon as a calamity which has about the same opprobrious standing in relation to the mind that scarlet fever has in relation to the body. While grandmother Marie Catherine du Motier was alive, Chavaniac and the outlying districts were spared that scourge.

She had two daughters. One of them, Marguerite Madeleine, had never married. She assisted her mother in the conduct of the property. Another daughter, widowed at an early age, was Louise Charlotte Guerin, Baroness of Montéloux. Her little daughter Louise Charlotte was about the age of young Lafayette.

In 1768—he was then eleven years old—he went to Paris with his mother to be trained in the culture and manner of an aristocrat. His mother and her father were among the tenants of the Luxembourg Palace. The boy lived with them.

2

The Luxembourg is now the meeting place of the Senate of France. Its brownish front faces the Rue de Vaugirard, and behind the palace are the Luxembourg Gardens, formalized in the French fashion, where children roll hoops and quiet pools mirror the trees in their still waters.

Away back in time, before the French Revolution, the Luxembourg was a kind of apartment house for the *noblesse*. Maybe it was a comfortable place to live in, but an exercise of the imagination is needed to build up a picture of its desirability. The rooms were large and gorgeous. But it had few closets, and no conveniences. It was probably cold in winter. Like the great palace at Versailles, and many of the châteaux, it was designed as a show place rather than as a residence. There could be no privacy. The occupants of these magnificent rooms dressed and undressed before a crowd of friends, acquaintances and casual callers. When they took a bath or went to the toilet they were usually attended by servants and retainers.

The education of the young marquis was conventional and classic. Soon after his coming to Paris he was entered as a student at the Collège du Plessis, an aristocratic school. The college was on the Rue Saint-Jacques, near the Luxembourg, and almost exactly opposite the Sorbonne. The Lycée Louis-le-Grand now occupies the site of the college. The study of Latin seems to have taken up most of the students' time. Lafayette acquired enough of the ancient tongue to win a prize for Latin composition. Not only that—he learned to speak the language in a fashion. Many years later he could converse in Latin if the occasion required it.

Notwithstanding his aptitude as a Latin scholar his education was extremely defective according to modern standards. He learned only a little history, most of which was false. Economics was neglected, the course in geography was sketchy, and the school's instruction in mathematics was of the most elementary kind.

He lived at the college in a little room on the top floor. On holidays and Sundays he would go over to the Luxembourg to visit his mother.

The students, all between the ages of ten and fifteen, must have looked like little manikins. Their hair was slicked down by pomade and powdered; they wore embroidered coats, small swords, silk stockings and silver buckles on their shoes. The strenuous games were unknown to them. At the age of twelve a young noble was expected to have courtly manners. Nearly all the students were intended for military careers—or, if not, they were to be statesmen or diplomats.

Lafayette had no intimate friends among them. I do not know why this is so, but merely accept the fact. In his later life he mentions none of them in his writings.

3

The mother of our marquis died on April 3, 1770. She was still a young woman, not thirty-three years old. Her father, the Marquis de la Rivière, died a few weeks later, and it was said that grief over his daughter's death killed him. That may not be true; grief seldom kills anyone, but loneliness frequently does. However, he died and the thirteen-year-old Lafayette inherited his great estates in Brittany and Touraine.

The young orphan's affairs were managed by trustees and a lawyer. His income from his father's estate was around 25,000 livres a year. This was greatly increased by the inheritance from his grandfather. He could expect, on his majority, to have the use of 120,000 livres a year.* He was a rich little boy.

In considering the influences that shaped his character we must not overlook the Lafayette family traditions, the legends of chivalry which glowed around the name. The tenor of the fables was that the Lafayettes had always been valiant warriors in search of a Holy Grail of some kind or other—soldierly adventurers in foreign lands, defenders of virtue and innocence, slayers of the dragon. One of the Lafayettes had ridden by the side of Joan of Arc and fought against the English; another had distinguished himself in the German wars; another had fought fantastic duels in a mood of laughter. Men riding like mad, to save this and that; the gaiety of bloody battles; the courage that it takes to stand on the sky line of a hill and be shot at by enemies who have no regard for sky lines or bold personalities; the desire to be unusual and extraordinary. All these legends and stories, some of them false and some of them true, entered the mind of the boyish marquis with the sharpness of sunlight falling on the sensitive plate of a camera.

The guardians of young Lafayette intended that he should follow the profession of arms, as a matter of course. In April, 1771, while he was still a schoolboy, they obtained for him a commission as subofficer, or cadet, in the famous regiment of the Black Musketeers. Almost bursting with pride, he attended reviews and parades in full uniform, and on those big days he was excused from attendance at the college.

4

During the summer holidays he went back to his native Chavaniac. Dark Chavaniac, with its black hills and the lava dust underfoot. The quiet house, with its spacious rooms, and its portraits of ancestors, was lonely and sad. No cheerful groups of boys, invited

* The livre was roughly equivalent to the modern franc before its devaluation after the World War; that is to say, it represented about twenty cents in silver. But this metallic valuation gives no idea of its purchasing power translated into modern terms. Gottschalk's estimate is that the livre—before the French Revolution—was worth approximately $1.20 in terms of today. I cannot agree with him. I think his estimate is too high. The studies that I have made of living costs, rent, food, clothing and so on compared to wages in that period have led me to accept the livre as the equivalent of the modern American dollar. In this I may be in error, but if so the error is not a great one.

down from Paris, to romp around the place. Only his grandmother, his aunt Mademoiselle du Motier, and his aunt Louise Charlotte and her slender daughter. When the little marquis drove through the village in his glittering carriage the men took off their hats and bowed to him, and the women, sitting at the doors, arose and made a curtsy.

On his return to Paris in the autumn of 1772 he learned that his great-grandfather, the Comte de La Rivière, had arranged a marriage for him.*

His prospective bride was Adrienne, the second daughter of the Duc d'Ayen. That influential nobleman had five daughters and no sons. Daughters were something in the way of an incumbrance. There was no career for them except marriage or a convent, and the Duc d'Ayen naturally wanted to get good husbands for them—and that meant wealthy nobles.

The negotiations, as one reads of them, sound like the dickering over the sale of a herd of cattle. The aged Comte de La Rivière, the Abbé Murat, and Jean Gerard—attorney for the Lafayette estate—represented the Lafayette family. The Comte de Lusignem and his wife also had something to do with it. Mme. de Chavaniac, the maternal grandmother of the marquis, who lived in faraway Auvergne, took no part, but turned it all over to the committee in Paris. On the other side were the numerous Noailles people and their lawyers and notaries. Before the deal was concluded almost everybody in both families had a hand in it, except the boy and the girl, who knew nothing about it.

Adrienne had not then reached the age of thirteen and the young marquis was fifteen. The girl's mother, the Duchesse d'Ayen, held up the negotiations for months. She thought both her daughter and Lafayette were too young; that they ought to wait and decide for themselves. That was, of course, the modern point of view but it was not popular with the French nobility. All marriages among the aristocracy were arranged by the families of the parties most intimately concerned. It was the accepted fashion.

Eventually the Duchesse d'Ayen was persuaded, or convinced, and the papers were signed. Formidable documents with ribbons and

* The reader will recall that Lafayette's grandfather—the Marquis de La Riviere —had died in 1770. The Comte de La Riviere was the father of his grandfather. I know it is an intricate relationship, great-grandfathers living longer than fathers and grandfathers, but that is the way it was.

dangling wax seals. It appears that the king's consent was required. He was very gracious about it and said he would approve the contract when it was presented to him. Adrienne was to bring her husband 400,000 livres as a *dot*. (For some reason only half this sum was ever paid.) It was also arranged that the young marquis was to live with the Noailles family. School days were over.

The consent of Adrienne's mother was gained only on the condition that the marriage be deferred until the spring of 1774, when the bride would be more than fourteen, and the marquis would be in his seventeenth year.

While the boyish marquis and his child fiancée were living in the same house at Versailles they fell in love with each other, fortunately. In the vast Noailles hôtel * at Versailles Lafayette had his own separate apartment, where he was attended by servants, and by the Abbé Fayon and a former army officer named Margelay. These were his tutors; they carried on his education. However, they did not teach him a great deal.

He took riding lessons at the royal riding academy. There he met many young noblemen of high degree; also the Comte d'Artois who, years after Napoleon's time, was king of France as Charles X (1824-1830). Lafayette, who had shot up in height as a weedy youth, was awkward and clumsy, the kind of boy who falls over his own feet on entering a room. The skillful art of repartee was unknown to him. He was laughed at, and was the subject of many jokes among the young *noblesse* of the riding academy.

The wedding of the marquis to Adrienne d'Ayen took place on April 11, 1774. It was a splendid affair—the Noailles family would see to that. The chapel of the Noailles in their hôtel at Paris was packed with aristocrats, flowers, perfume and incense. But worms are gnawing on the most impressive occasions. The worm in this case was the genealogist of the court at Versailles. He had thumbed the *Dictionnaire de la Noblesse* and found the Marquis de Lafayette was not in it. So, businesslike and in a clerical fashion, he wrote to the young man and asked him to furnish evidence to prove his claim to titles and nobility. There were many imposters among the so-called

---

* Perhaps it is unnecessary to say that the word "hotel" has been greatly changed in meaning since the eighteenth century. At that time it was defined as a *demeure somptueuse d'un haut personnage* (the sumptuous dwelling of a high and mighty person). In the country the residences of the nobility were called châteaux; in the city they were called hôtels.

noble families of France. Lafayette was offended by the letter from
the genealogist, yet it was not intended to be offensive. It was just
a part of office routine. Lafayette wrote indignantly that he would
furnish no information, that his family was well known, which was
quite true. Anyone who wears a hard shell would have never given
it another thought. But the marquis was an extremely sensitive
person who had a tendency to make a drama of any insignificant
doing that affected his pride and vanity.

He was soon to learn that his father-in-law had brought about
the marriage solely because the young marquis was rich.

5

Something had to be done for him in the way of military advancement. It was not seemly for the haughty Noailles clan to have
a son-in-law who was only a cadet officer in the Black Musketeers.

There was the Noailles regiment of cavalry. I must explain
here, parenthetically, about the proprietary regiments, of which
there were sixty in the French army at that time. In the age of
feudalism the king was, by custom and authority, only the chief
of a large and powerful group of semi-independent nobles. When
he went to war he summoned these henchmen to support him, and
they came with their bands of fighting men whom they fed and
clothed. As the feudal system decayed, more and more power went
into the hands of the royal government. The warrior bands became
regiments in the service of the king, but the *seigneurs* who had created them still retained a sort of symbolic authority over them.

In this sense the Noailles regiment was controlled by the family
of Lafayette's father-in-law. The Duc d'Ayen had his young son-in-
law made a captain, over the protest of the minister of war, who
considered him too young. It was agreed, however, that he would
not take command of a company until he had reached the age of
eighteen. Until then he was to serve as a lieutenant although he had
the nominal rank of captain. It was also stated that he was to become colonel of the regiment at twenty-one.

This command was stationed at Metz, and to that dull place
the marquis went in the early part of 1775, leaving his child wife
at her father's home in Paris.

The town house of the Noailles family was large and spacious.

It stood on the Rue Saint-Honoré. Part of it still remains and is now the Hotel de Saint James et Albany. At that period the Rue de Rivoli did not exist, and the gardens of the great houses on the Rue Saint-Honoré ran back to the Tuileries. The Hôtel de Noailles was a stately mansion, filled with priceless paintings, tapestries, huge mirrors, vases, statues. There was an air of an art museum about it, as there was about all the hôtels and châteaux of the wealthier nobility.

To this ménage Lafayette, who was in the position of a paying guest, contributed eight thousand livres a year to defray his share of the *pension alimentaire* of himself and his wife. But that was not all the expense, apparently. It included only food—pension alimentaire. In his voluminous account of his finances he says, or an auditor says for him:

Pension alimentaire...................... 8,000 livres
Dépenses de toute la maison y compris M. de
    Lafayette pour mille louis and Madame
    pour 10,000......................... 78,000 "
                                         86,000 livres

That was, and is, a lot of money. It would seem, according to the auditor's statement, that he was living at the rate of 86,000 livres a year for board and lodging and entertainment in his father-in-law's house. It may have been worth it. As to this I have no way of knowing. The expenses of a separate establishment for himself and his wife might have been more.

6

Adrienne de Lafayette is not mentioned by contemporary writers as one of the beauties of the day. Her portraits, in spite of their idealization, show her as a plain-looking, wholesome young woman. She had a reputation for sedateness and virtue. But she was courageous and her tongue was sharp. She did not hesitate to speak her mind when her feelings were aroused.

There were some queer persons in the Noailles family. Adrienne's aunt, Mme. de Tessé, was a sort of atheist and a friend of Voltaire. She was looked upon as a horrible example by her sister-in-law—Adrienne's mother. Her opinions on all subjects were violently dogmatic, and she had a language of her own which could be understood by only a few people. In short, she was eccentric and talkative. As she conversed her mouth made startling grimaces now and then, and it took her listeners some time to get used to them. Nevertheless, Thomas Jefferson—when he met her—was much impressed by her intelligence and sound sense of values. In his letters he refers to her frequently with respect and admiration.

The Duc d'Ayen and his duchesse were themselves a peculiar couple. A worldly-minded man with a reputation as a wit, he associated with a fashionable set and dabbled in the philosophies and sciences. His wife, on the other hand, was almost a recluse and religious to the point of saintliness.

The old Maréchale de Noailles, mother of the Duc d'Ayen, was a kleptomaniac of articles supposed to be holy. She had to be watched carefully when in church to prevent her from stealing something. She corresponded regularly with the Virgin Mary. Her letters to the Holy Virgin were placed in a receptacle, and the family chaplain took them out and replied to them. She grew indignant at one of the letters from the Virgin, who had addressed her familiarly as "Chère Maréchale." She spoke of Mary as that impudent little bourgeoise of Nazareth. "But," she concluded, "I must remember that she is my Savior's mother."

CHAPTER IV

THE GREAT ADVENTURE BEGINS

I

THE DUKE OF GLOUCESTER, brother of King George III of England, was traveling on the Continent in the summer of 1775. He had incurred his brother's displeasure because he had married Horace Walpole's niece, who happened unfortunately to be of illegitimate birth. The duke was, for the time being excluded from the English court and all its doings. For that and perhaps other reasons, he was vehemently opposed to the policies of George III. In the course of his travels with his wife he came to Metz.

The Comte de Broglie, who commanded the French army in that region, invited the Duke of Gloucester to dinner. Among the guests—all of them officers—were the young Marquis de Lafayette, the Comte de Noailles (who had married Louise, a sister of Lafayette's wife), and the Comte de Ségur, who was one of Lafayette's most intimate friends.

His Grace, the Duke of Gloucester, discussed with animation the shortcomings of his royal brother. The war in America was all wrong, he said. Fighting the colonies was senseless; it could only lead to disaster. The colonials were Englishmen; they had their rights; and England and its king should respect them. Everyone who heard him listened with close attention; everyone there was a bitter foe of England and would welcome with applause a catastrophe to the British Empire. The Duke of Gloucester probably knew that, and did not care.

According to the generally accepted Lafayette legend the marquis made up his mind then and there to go to America and fight for American independence. It will sound disappointing, I am sure, but the plain fact is that there is no contemporaneous evidence to support this view of the matter. His *Mémoires de ma Main*—that is, his autobiography—is not to be trusted, for the reason that he wrote it in a slapdash fashion when he was much older and put in it ideas which he did not have in his youth. After its first publication he kept on revising it for successive editions. He was unable to carry himself back in memory to his early days and re-create the ideas which he had at that time.

This lack of historical sense is not at all uncommon. Most people, at the age of fifty, have only a dim notion of what they were at the age of twenty. They may tell you all about it, but what they say is likely to be only an afterthought.

Jared Sparks, in his *Writings of George Washington,* says that Lafayette told him the dinner to the Duke of Gloucester was in 1776. Gottschalk, careful fact-handler, suggests that Lafayette, when he saw Sparks, in 1828, had forgotten the date of the dinner, and had "begun to believe the legend that had grown up around his departure for America." † Andreas Latzko, in his fantastic biography of Lafayette—fantastic because of its astounding errors of fact— says that while the duke, with a group of officers, was inspecting fortifications of Metz, a messenger, dusty with hard riding, arrived and handed the duke a sealed letter. The duke broke the seals, read the letter and its attached document, which was a copy of the Declaration of Independence.‡ It is pure fiction, though it sounds dramatic. Gloucester's visit to Metz was in August, 1775, and the Declaration did not appear until July, 1776.

Lafayette himself, in his confusion of memory, actually sets forth this supposed incident in his autobiography, and declares that "his heart was captured" when he heard the Declaration read aloud by the Duke of Gloucester.

2

In December, 1775, the marquis was back in Paris; and, on the fifteenth of that month, his wife presented him with a daughter who was given the name of Henriette.†

There were long absences from the army in Lafayette's scheme

---

* Gottschalk, *Lafayette Comes to America,* p. 50.

† Andreas Latzko, *Lafayette, A Life,* p. 25. Latzko swallows the story whole. On the same page he declares that the Duke of Gloucester expressed his indignation at the hiring of German mercenaries by his royal brother. The fact is that the contract with the German princes under which they furnished troops for service in America was not made until February, 1776, and it was months after that before any of these mercenaries were sent across the Atlantic.

‡ A sickly child, she died while her father was in America.

of life. He was intolerably bored by inactive garrison duty in the dull town of Metz; and he was equally bored by the courtly life of Versailles and Paris.

A high-class cabaret, called the Epée de Bois (The Wooden Sword), stood in the suburbs of Porcherons, which was a village at the foot of the Montmartre hill. Both the village and the tavern have long since disappeared in the growth of Paris. The tavern was a favorite resort of young, roistering nobles. Lafayette belonged to that set, and so did the Comte de Provence and the Comte d'Artois, brothers of King Louis XVI. They formed a sort of informal club, the Société de l'Epée de Bois, which devoted much time and laughter to ridiculing the elder statesmen, and the absurdities of court etiquette. These cabaret companions considered themselves the smartest and most daring young men in Paris.

But Lafayette himself was not a jolly person, though he was certainly far from gloomy. His mind was too slow in movement to be witty. No doubt his wealth and his relation to a high and mighty family gained his admission to the exclusive and foolish Society of the Wooden Sword. He was in about the same position as a rich country squire would be in the night clubs and social doings of London's Mayfair.

At the court of Versailles he was not a success. Queen Marie Antoinette laughed at his awkwardness in dancing. The Comte de Provence condescendingly tried to patronize him, and was promptly insulted. And the Comte de Provence—like all the Bourbons, who "never learned anything nor forgot anything"—remembered Lafayette's moment of insolence for forty years.*

There was an air of frustration about the young marquis. He realized—apparently—that he did not fit in anywhere. He loved his wife—very much, indeed—according to his own letters and all available evidence. But it happened in his case, as it often does in other cases, that a sincere domestic attachment did not prevent him from having love affairs.

Lafayette was elaborately in love with someone in 1776. His friend, the Comte de Ségur, says in his *Mémoires* that Lafayette's lady friend at that time was the Comtesse d'Hunolstein. This noble gentlewoman was supposed to be one of the mistresses of the Duc

---

* With the downfall of Napoleon and the Bourbon restoration the Comte de Provence, then fifty-nine years of age, became king of France as Louis XVIII.

de Chartres. Her husband was the colonel of the cavalry regiment de Chartres, and the comtesse herself was a lady in waiting to the Duchesse de Chartres, her lover's wife. Whether Lafayette really got anywhere with her at that time is still unknown, but after he came home from the American Revolution it was commonly reported in Paris that he was the accepted lover of the Comtesse d'Hunolstein.

It was also said—in Parisian gossip—that Lafayette, when he went eventually to America, had gone because of disappointment in respect to the comtesse. I doubt that, and do not attach much importance to it. From my knowledge of him I do not believe he would have gone anywhere because of a disappointment in love.

His driving ambition was to win fame, popularity, distinction. He belonged to that strange race of beings who are willing to go to any extreme, to suffer and die just to shine before the public, to get on the front page of the newspapers, to be mentioned and pointed out as important people. Lamartine, who knew Lafayette, said that he had "an instinct for renown." Thomas Jefferson, who also knew him, used a more vulgar phrase. In a letter to Madison—just before the French Revolution, when Jefferson was the American minister to France, he said that Lafayette had "a canine appetite for popularity." Lafayette himself wrote that, from his earliest youth, his great desire was to go to foreign lands and have a career of glory. But glory is likely to perish. The years eat into it with the readiness of a biting acid destroying a copper coin.

But the way to glory was not yet clear and for the greater part of the year 1776 the marquis ran about Paris enjoying himself. It was easy enough to get prolonged leaves of absence from his post in the Noailles regiment.

3

The fortune of the marquis was increasing as time went on. His affairs were ably managed by Jean Gerard, a shrewd middle-class lawyer. The young man had never seen his estates in Brittany and Touraine; they were in charge of intendants who made their reports to M. Gerard. After the death of his grandmother in 1772 the Chavaniac estate was in charge of one of his aunts, Mlle. du Motier.

Gottschalk says that Lafayette's income rose during his minority from 120,000 to 146,000 livres (or francs). He takes these figures from the *Compte rendu sur la fortune de General Lafayette*, and they are probably correct. Sixty thousand francs came from the lands in Brittany; 13,000 francs from Touraine; 15,000 francs from Auvergne; and there was an income of 58,000 francs from other properties and investments.*

Around the end of 1775 the Comte de Saint-Germain became minister of war. He was a real soldier who had fought his way to the top of the army. A hard-bitten, curt official, he had no patience with lackadaisical officers and stale regiments. He set out to reform the service and, in the course of reform, he dropped many young noblemen without regard to the protests of their families. Lafayette was relieved from duty in June, 1776, and put on the reserve list. This was a great blow to the self-esteem of the youthful marquis. He found himself without a serious occupation, but he was busy in a number of trivial ways.

The Comte de Ségur, the young blade who was one of Lafayette's friends, wrote many years later in his *Mémoires* that Lafayette wanted to fight a duel with him in 1776 over the Comtesse d'Hunolstein. The marquis remained in his friend's room all night, arguing with him, and insisting on the duel. De Ségur, who had little interest in the lady, but a warm fondness for Lafayette, laughed off the matter, treated it all in a spirit of levity, and refused to fight.

Obviously, this incident indicates an almost puerile immaturity on Lafayette's part and also a general lack of common sense. Like an adolescent boy saturated with adventure stories and thrilling motion-picture plays he wanted to shine at all cost, to be somebody—even if he had to fight his friend.

Poor confused youth! Do not be impatient. Your day is coming. The angels of Destiny are fluttering over your head. Your name is to resound throughout the world, and long after you have departed this life men will speak and read of you and a great nation across the sea will hold you forever in its loving memory.

* These figures and, indeed, a complete analysis of Lafayette's fortune, may be found in Gilbert Chinard's *Letters of Lafayette and Jefferson,"* p. 303.

4

Let us consider now the Comte de Broglie. In 1776 he was fifty-eight years old, an able soldier, a man of vast worldly experience and high ambitions. He had commanded armies and had been employed on the secret side of French diplomacy.

In his head he carried mysterious, majestic schemes which were too grandiose ever to be realized. One of them was a new war with England, with an invasion of the British Isles. Among the ruling class in France—since the disastrous Seven Years' War—hatred of England had grown and revenge had become a secret national policy.

De Broglie persuaded the king and the ministry to accept his views. On his recommendation Johann Kalb—better known as "Baron De Kalb"—was sent to England to study the land with the idea of a French invasion. Later on—in 1767—De Kalb was dispatched on a secret mission to America to investigate the dissatisfaction with British rule that was taking form and substance in the colonies.

Nothing came of these ideas and excursions in the 1760's, but as soon as the American colonials began their revolt in 1775 de Broglie opened up the subject again. It may be said here that he was always in secret communication with the king's ministers at Versailles. Behind the outward, imposing front of the French government there had existed for centuries a secret system which included a strange mixture of personalities and ideas—mistresses of the king, great nobles, bankers, common spies, generals in the army, archbishops and listeners at keyholes.

The government did not have to make any sort of report to the nation of its income and expenditures; there was no parliament or congress. In theory, but not in practice, the whole of France was the personal property of the king. In such circumstances intrigue thrives and eventually becomes unmanageable.

The French government, acting with great caution, gave financial aid covertly to the colonies through an involved method. De Broglie's idea was to send them competent officers including, of course, himself. He was to be the viceroy, or Stadtholder—the big man—and he would help them win their war. De Broglie called on Silas Deane, the American commissioner, and introduced De Kalb, whom he wished to send to America as his representative. Deane was impressed greatly by de Broglie and De Kalb, and he promised De Kalb a commission as major general in the American army. They did not tell Deane the whole story. De Kalb, he was informed, wanted to go to America to fight for liberty and equality. It is one of the vices of language that men may use words to conceal intentions. If de Broglie and De Kalb had really wanted to strive for liberty and equality, there was plenty of opportunity to exercise their talents at home. At that time neither liberty nor equality existed in France.

Before calling on Deane the Comte de Broglie had seen Vergennes, head of the French Foreign Office, and through his mediation had managed to get De Kalb a two years' leave of absence from the army. De Kalb's contract with Deane was dated November 7, 1776. The Vicomte de Mauroy, another of de Broglie's friends, got a contract to be a major general as of November 20th. There were others, too, friends or supporters of de Broglie.

All this was done in dead black midnight secrecy, which meant that it became generally known in a few days, for Paris was a whispering gallery. Everybody gossiped, and the purposes and plans of people were usually discussed even before the principals had decided as to what they wanted to do. Also the English ambassador had spies, some of whom were in the intimate circles of the court.

Despite Lafayette's statement that he wanted to go to America to aid the colonies in 1775, after he had heard the discourse of the Duke of Gloucester, the evidence seems to show that he was not really interested in the matter until a year later. He was stirred to the bottom of his emotional heart by the plans of de Broglie and De Kalb. He wanted to go too, and he talked of his intentions to his friends, the Vicomte de Noailles and the Comte de Ségur. They were in accord with this project of adventure; all three of them made up their minds to go. Lafayette and Noailles went to see their father-in-law, the Duc d'Ayen, to tell him about it. His comment was an emphatic "No," and that settled it with Noailles and Ségur —and, for the time being, with Lafayette.

But the marquis went to de Broglie, who had been his commander in the army, and told him all about it. De Broglie saw at once that this wealthy young man, with his powerful connections, might be a great help in the web of scheming which de Broglie was spinning. So, in his own subtle fashion, he encouraged Lafayette's desire while—also in characteristic fashion—he went on record against it. And, in the course of these devious subtleties, he sent the marquis to Baron De Kalb.

The spurious baron was a man of uncertain status in France. He was afraid of the Duc d'Ayen and would not have encouraged Lafayette if he had known that the powerful father-in-law of the marquis was opposed to his escapade. But Lafayette was not frank with De Kalb; he led him to believe that his family approved of his proposed adventure. So De Kalb took the youth to Silas Deane, and after some conversations interpreted by De Kalb, and extended over several days, Lafayette also got a contract as a major general in the American service. It must be said for Deane that he did not want to approve of such a high military rank for a mere lad, but Lafayette argued that his place in French society—when he was away on his voyage and the news was known—would cause a reverberation at the court of Versailles that would be favorable to the American cause.

Then came a formal note from the French Foreign Office, forbidding Lafayette to go to America. Vergennes, the minister for foreign affairs, was a diplomat of foxlike cunning. A copy of the note would be handy to show the British ambassador in case the young man left anyway and in defiance of orders.

The marquis did not know what to do. His habitual indecision, which always curdled into a muddleheaded vacillation unless it were sharply called into a definite resolve by a superior mind or by circumstances, lay heavily within him.

While these mental disturbances were going on De Kalb said, rather casually, to Lafayette that he and a number of officers under contract for American service expected to sail within a few days from Havre.

The marquis was dumfounded; he had expected to go with them. De Kalb and his friends left, but in a week they were back again. Lord Stormont, the British ambassador, having learned that the ship carried arms and officers destined for America, had made such a strong protest at the Foreign Office that orders were sent from Paris to prevent the sailing of the ship.

There was a conference with De Kalb and Lafayette present, among others. This was in December, 1776. How were they to get to America? Well, they might buy a ship secretly and depart for a false destination, yet land at an American port. That suggestion sounded feasible, but who was going to furnish the money? Everyone turned to Lafayette, and the young man said eagerly that he might be counted upon to provide the vessel.

Dubois-Martin, brother of de Broglie's secretary, knew something of ships and shipowners. He was dispatched to Bordeaux, with the credit of the marquis behind him, for the purpose of acquiring a ship that would take them across the Atlantic. He bought the *Victoire* at a price of 112,000 livres. Lafayette paid down 40,000 livres and owed the balance. It was decided that the group would sail from Bordeaux, but their departure had to be deferred, as the vessel needed overhauling, and would not be ready until the middle of March.

5

The preparations for sailing were supposed to be strictly secret, and it is possible that Lafayette thought they were, but without a doubt many people in Paris knew what was going on.

The young man assured all the important dignitaries, including his father-in-law, that he had given up his idea of going to America. Thereupon, to show that he meant what he said, he went to London to visit the Marquis de Noailles, the French ambassador in England. De Noailles was Adrienne de Lafayette's uncle. He stayed in England nearly a month, was presented at court and dined with many persons of high rank. The *Victoire* was to be ready for sailing from Bordeaux on March 15th, so the marquis cut short his visit to England, much to the surprise of his uncle-in-law, who urged him to remain longer. His intention was to go straight to Bordeaux from Havre, avoiding Paris. But right there a difficulty arose. The ambassador would be sure to write to the Duc d'Ayen that he had enjoyed the young man's visit and was sorry that he had returned to France so soon.

To get around that contingency the marquis told de Noailles that he intended to be in Paris only a few days and would then come back to London. He let it be inferred that he was going to be with an attractive woman—secretly—while in Paris and he wanted no one else to know he was there. The ambassador agreed to keep his secret. If the family wrote and inquired about him he would reply that the young gentleman was a little indisposed and was taking a rest at the embassy.

Upon arriving in Paris he went to De Kalb's house and hid himself. In a few days he and De Kalb set out for Bordeaux, where they arrived on March 19th. The ship was not ready. While they were waiting Lafayette—after all his secret maneuvers in getting there—called on relatives who lived in Bordeaux and gave a dinner to a number of the young lordlings of the town. Of course, his presence caused much talk and conjecture, and soon his destination was no longer a secret.

The port officials had standing orders not to permit the sailing of ships with supplies, or officers on board, for the American colonies. But these orders were a mere pretense. At that very time the French government itself was sending cargoes of munitions, arms and clothing to the colonial rebels. The ships were cleared for some South American port, and their destination was changed at sea.

The *Victoire* was supposed to sail for San Domingo. There was no certainty that the evasion would be permitted in this particular case, however. The young marquis was an important person, and it was likely that the British ambassador would make a great fuss over the incident. De Kalb, cautious and doubtful, feared that emphatic orders might come from Paris any day to prevent the sailing. He induced Lafayette to send the *Victoire* to the mouth of the river, where there would be a better chance of getting away.

It might as well be said here that De Kalb had been deceived all along as to the attitude of Lafayette's family. When they first discussed the project of going to America the young man told him that he had his father-in-law's approval. That was not true, and De Kalb eventually found it out. He was disgusted and worried. De Kalb could not afford to offend the French king or any of the great families, and he thought, naturally, that they would probably accuse him of leading the marquis into unwarranted adventures. But it was too late to turn back.

On March 24, 1777, the cargo and all the passengers—except the marquis—were on board, and the ship dropped down the river. Lafayette, several days before, had dispatched a "Dear Papa" letter by a swift courier to the Duc d'Ayen, in which he had set forth what he intended to do. He asked the sanction and blessing of his father-in-law, and he remained in Bordeaux awaiting a reply.

Strange to relate, he wrote no good-bye letter to his wife, nor had he written her while he was in London; and he had passed through Paris without seeing her.

Le Boursier, captain of the ship, was evidently not informed as to its destination. He brought aboard secretly a lot of merchandise which he intended to sell in San Domingo on his own account. After the *Victoire* got finally to sea there was some angry argument between the captain and the marquis, for Le Boursier wanted to take the vessel to San Domingo where it was bound, according to its clearance papers. Lafayette settled the dispute by purchasing the captain's stock in trade for the equivalent of eight thousand American dollars.

Lafayette was on his way to embark on the ship, having given up the hope of an answer from the Duc d'Ayen, when he received a letter from a friend in Paris. His escapade was known all over the place; everybody was talking about it; the Duc d'Ayen was furious. Moreover, his father-in-law was urging the king to stop the ship's sailing.

Sadly depressed, he went on board the *Victoire,* and in a short time the little vessel was on its way to the Spanish port of Los Pasajes, which is a few miles from San Sebastian. Outside of French territorial waters the marquis intended to await developments.

Why did he tarry in the little Spanish harbor? He was on his way; why not go on?

The answer may be found, I should think, in Lafayette's psychological make-up. The delay and loitering expressed his habitual indecisiveness.

While the ship was riding at anchor in the port of Los Pasajes a courier came with a stern letter from the French government. He was ordered to abandon the expedition and go to Marseilles where he would meet his father-in-law and Adrienne's aunt, the Comtesse de Tessé. They were on their way for a long tour of Italy. He was told that he must accompany them.*

* Some of Lafayette's biographers—Brand Whitlock among them—call this epistle from the government a *lettre de cachet.* It was not. A lettre de cachet was a warrant of imprisonment or permanent exile, signed by the king.

6

Completely upset, and at a loss as to what to do, Lafayette left at once for Bordeaux. His purpose was to persuade his kinsman, the Maréchal de Mouchy (who had an important official position in Bordeaux), to intercede for him. He soon learned that de Mouchy could not—or would not—do anything in his behalf, and he was advised to go on to Marseilles according to orders. He agreed to do that.

But just at that time the Vicomte de Mauroy, friend of de Broglie and of Lafayette, reached Bordeaux. His intention in coming was to accompany De Kalb and the young marquis to America. De Mauroy said that all Paris was acclaiming Lafayette for his courage and initiative; that the ministers never would have sent the peremptory letter to him if the Duc d'Ayen had not persistently urged them.

The marquis was pleased; he decided to go ahead with the expedition. On the pretext of going to Marseilles he and Mauroy procured a post chaise and started on the road. When they were out of the city they made a detour and Lafayette dressed himself in the clothes of a servant.

It was a romantic adventure, and he made the most of it. He was an actor at heart; throughout his long career he dramatized his actions.

At an inn near the border he was resting—while the horses were being changed—on a pile of straw in the stable. (Were the stable and the straw really necessary?) During his siesta a squad of cavalry dashed up and inquired of a servant maid if she had seen a tall young nobleman traveling toward Spain? She replied no, she had not; but it turned out—as a pretty rounding of the story— that she knew the man lying on the straw was the young marquis. She had seen him in his fine clothes, and had served him, two weeks before, when he was on his way to Bordeaux. He had no further trouble in returning to his ship.

It seems that there is some considerable exaggeration in this story of his escape. The evidence now available indicates that the government connived at his proceedings, and that the attempt to stop him was only a halfhearted effort intended to look well on the record. There is no question that he could have been detained if the ruling powers at Paris had really wanted to do so.

The *Victoire* set sail for Charleston on April 20, 1777, and arrived off the South Carolina coast on June 13th.

On shipboard he wrote several letters to Adrienne. They are full of love and tenderness. In one of them he wrote, in part:

You must admit, my heart, that the occupation and the life that I am going to have are very different from those that they arranged for me on that futile journey.* Defender of that liberty which I adore, coming of my own free will as a friend to offer my services to that most interesting republic, I bring only my sincerity and my good will; no ambition, no selfish interests. In striving for my glory, I strive for their welfare. I hope for my sake you will become a good American. It is a sentiment meant for all virtuous hearts. The welfare of America is intimately bound up with the happiness of humanity. She is going to become a cherished and safe refuge of virtue, of good character, of tolerance, of equality and of a peaceful liberty. . . .

With penetrating insight Gottschalk says in his comments on this letter (*Lafayette Comes to America,* p. 135):

Here was a young man who had left a loving wife and family and had spent money recklessly in order to go off on an adventure that . . . might end in a British prison, only for the incredible purpose of bringing help to rebels. How could the young marquis tell them [his wife's family]—and especially his wife—that he was tired of their patronage and their condescension? How could he explain that though he considered himself a failure in everything so far attempted he still hoped for success somewhere?

He wanted to achieve distinction, renown, glory, and, as Gottschalk says further on, "He knew that glory was good, at least for for him, and since glory was to be found on the side of liberty and equality, they must be good too, especially since so many brilliant people were said to believe that they were . . . Thus, out of a few catchwords which the American agents in Paris had exploited and the necessity for finding a rational explanation of his own extravagant conduct was born the liberalism of the foremost European exponent of the liberal creed in the two succeeding generations."

* He means the tour of Italy with his father-in-law and Adrienne's aunt.

CHAPTER V

BULLETS ARE FLYING

I

THE GALLANT but impatient marquis, eager to take the field, to be under fire and show his courage, had to bide his time. The Revolutionary War was in one of its stale periods during the hot August of 1777. There was not much to do, and the camp drowsed in the sunshine. General Washington sat day after day at his long table writing letters; the headquarters staff fussed around with muster rolls and army documents; the line officers drilled their ragged regiments.

No duties had been assigned to Lafayette. He spent his time trying on his new uniforms, learning English and testing it for grammar and pronunciation on generals, colonels, captains, sergeants, corporals and privates. Every now and then—at polite intervals—he urged Washington to give him the command of a division or a brigade. Was he not a major general, and who ever heard of a major general sitting around headquarters without a command?

It was pretty dull, but the Fates with their customary thoughtfulness in respect to human affairs, were shaping some rather big events for the near future.

The British General Howe had sailed away from New York with an army on board, a fleet of more than two hundred vessels. Destination unknown to anybody at American headquarters. Perplexity. Washington thought perhaps Howe was bound for Charleston. If so, it was too late for him to do anything about it. The American army, camped near Philadelphia, could never arrive in time—marching over hundreds of miles of bad roads—to save the distant state of South Carolina. But Howe might land in Maryland, or in Virginia. With these possibilities and conjectures in mind the commander in chief decided to remain where he was, awaiting the turn of events.

Far north, on the Canadian border, another movement of major

48

importance was developing. General John Burgoyne, at the head of a British army, was coming down from Canada. His route lay along Lake Champlain. Obviously his intention was to fight his way to New York City. If that could be accomplished the whole length of the Hudson River would be in British hands, and New England would be cut off from the rest of the colonies.

But why had Howe sailed away from New York just at the time when he was in a position to render great assistance to Burgoyne? He could have marched up the Hudson and met the Canadian army halfway. Their combined forces would have been much superior to any opposition the Americans could bring to bear. It was all very puzzling to the officers at American headquarters. On July 30th Washington wrote that the abandonment of Burgoyne by Howe was "unaccountable."

In front of Burgoyne there was an American army commanded by General Horatio Gates. His force, small at first, was being rapidly increased by New England volunteers and by reinforcements sent by Washington.

The mystery of Howe's destination was solved near the end of August, when his fleet came up the Chesapeake and his army landed at the head of the bay, about fifty miles from Philadelphia. It was clear that he intended to take the colonial capital.

Howe was a dull-witted general who had an incorrigible habit of doing things in a queer involved fashion. Philadelphia is only ninety miles from New York. He could have put himself in striking distance of it within five or six days by marching straight across country. But instead of doing that he spent weeks at sea, going all around the barn just to reach the barn door, and after his army landed it was still fifty miles away from its objective.

2

Now the drumming guns are going to speak.

Exhilarated and energized, Lafayette went about the camp aiding in the preparations. The tall, cool and self-possessed commander in chief had given him some small duties. The army was astir. Within twenty-four hours it would be on its way to meet the British.

Through Philadelphia the army marched with drums beating, and all Philadelphia looked on. The ragged soldiers had sprigs of

green in their hats to give the ranks a touch of sprightliness. Some
of the men were in British uniforms, stripped from the dead. Washington and his staff, and all the generals and field officers, wore
splendid uniforms and sat superbly on their sleek horses. The young
marquis rode by Washington's side. One may imagine his exaltation
of spirit. The dominant actor-quality of his personality was on the
crest of the wave. He was playing a great role in public, with the
people on the streets and at the windows pointing him out. He was
on his way to a battlefield, and his fighting ancestors were coming to
life within him. He was determined to live up to the traditions of his
race.

The army encountered the British at Brandywine Creek on
September 11th in that memorable year of 1777. Washington
thought Howe would attempt to cross at Chadds Ford, which was
directly in front of the American position, and his plans were laid
accordingly. But the British, while making a display of force at
Chadds Ford, amid the crash of artillery, sent a strong column to
another crossing and turned Washington's right flank. They were
soon in the rear of General Sullivan's troops, on the extreme right,
and Sullivan's command began to break up into a disorderly rout.

Lafayette was sent by Washington to do what he could, and
it was there that he won his first military distinction. He deserved
it for his coolness and bravery. You can see the picture—a horde
of terror-stricken men in a panic; the confusion and yelling; bewildered officers; blood flowing; rearing horses; bullets zipping by.
No one on earth could have stopped the rout; it was beyond human
control. Lafayette was within twenty yards of the advancing British
when he was shot. It was only a flesh wound in the leg and he did
not know he had been hit until somebody told him that his blood
was dripping to the ground. He grew faint from bleeding eventually,
and his aide, Major Gimat, rode at his side and supported him on
his horse.

By that time the whole army was in retreat. Washington came
up and ordered Lafayette to retire and have his wound dressed. To
the surgeons Washington said, "Treat him as though he were my
son."

For a few days he lay at Philadelphia, but as the British advanced, and it was obvious that the Americans could not hold the

place, he was taken to Bethlehem, which was then a quiet Moravian settlement. The Moravians of Bethlehem were a pious industrious people of German descent—the so-called "Pennsylvania Dutch."

Lafayette was confined to his bed only a few days, but several weeks passed before he could walk easily or mount a horse. He wrote to Adrienne and told her all about it. He said that the Americans "after having held their ground for a fairly long time" were defeated, and that while he was trying to rally them "messieurs the English paid me the compliment of wounding me slightly in the leg." It takes a Frenchman to put it that way. An American or an Englishman would say simply, "I got a bullet in my leg."

While he was convalescing at Bethlehem he lived at the home of a prosperous farmer named Boeckel. He occupied the entire top floor of the house, with his valets, nurses and aides.

In the underground gossip of the period there is a story that he had a brief love affair with Lisa Boeckel, the farmer's daughter. Maybe he did—I don't know—and I am quite willing to believe that he did or did not. Sexual virtue is a slippery quality which cannot be depended upon with any definite conviction of assurance.

Many persons called on the marquis to pay their respects during his convalescence. Members of Congress and generals of the army. On October 6th he wrote in his amiable manner to the dear little marquise in Paris and said—in part:

At present, as wife of an American general officer, I must teach you your lesson. They will say to you: "They have been beaten." You will reply: "That is true, but between two armies equal in numbers and on the plain, the old soldiers always have an advantage over the new; besides they had the pleasure of killing many, indeed a great many more of the enemy than they lost themselves." After that, they will add: "That is all very well, but Philadelphia, the capital of America, the bulwark of liberty, is taken." You will reply politely: "You are fools. Philadelphia is a miserable city, open on all sides, of which the door was already closed; that the seat of Congress made it famous, I do not know why; that is all there is of that famous city, which we shall make them give back before long."

The thought of being a general was evidently of the most overwhelming importance. But why? The rebellious colonies were packed with generals, some of whom had never commanded more than three hundred men. Nevertheless Lafayette was a general of weight and substance, regardless of his youth and lack of military knowledge. Great invisible issues of statecraft stood around him, their faces veiled. In the letter to Adrienne he said further:

Just think, my dear heart, I have only received news of you once—by Count Pulaski. I have had frightfully bad luck; and I am cruelly unhappy about it. Judge of the horror of being far from all that I love, in such desperate uncertainty; there is no way to endure it, and yet I know that I deserve no pity; why was I so mad as to come here? I am well punished for it.

"Why was I so mad as to come here?" That statement of remorse may have been rhetorical, a figure of speech to please his wife, and judging from what I have learned of him I think it was. He wanted to be here; he loved it. Adventure, freedom, fighting men. If he lived today he would be a motion-picture star, depicting a hero in strange lands, a champion of virtue, honesty and truth.

In his letter to his wife the marquis said:

Be at ease about the treatment of my wound, for all the doctors in America are aroused in my behalf. I have a friend who has spoken to them in a way to insure my being well cared for, and that is General Washington. That inestimable man, whose talents and virtues I admire—the better I know him the more I venerate him—has been kind enough to become my intimate friend.

His tender interest in me quickly won my heart; I am established in his household * and we live together like two devoted brothers in mutual intimacy and confidence. This friendship makes me most happy in this country. When he sent his chief surgeon to me, he told him to care for me as though I were his son, because he loved me as much as a son, and, having heard that I wished to join the army too soon, he wrote me a letter full of tenderness in which he urged me to wait until I was entirely cured. . . .

3

Philadelphia was taken and occupied by the British. But their victory was a fruitless one, with little or no bearing on the final outcome of the war. The occupation of the town required a garrison of troops who were thus rendered static and unable to take part in field operations.

The mental effect on the colonies, which was naturally disheart-

* In writing "household" he means Washington's staff. In those days a general's staff was called his household or family.

MADAME de LAFAYETTE, WIFE OF THE MARQUIS

CHAVANIAC

ening, did not last long, for before the month of October had come
to an end fast riders from the north, mud-splashed and breathless
with news, were carrying to every village and town the story of
Burgoyne's surrender. Bonfires blazed and bells pealed. In the
streets and on the village greens the people sang patriotic songs and
some of them got drunk in the way of celebration.

Burgoyne had got as far south as Saratoga before he gave up
the struggle. On October 17th he surrendered his entire army with
all its guns, munitions and stores, to General Gates and his Americans. It was the first time a British army had surrendered on the
field in many years. Gates deserved little credit for the victory.
His generalship was execrable, but he had an army of twenty thousand men while Burgoyne had only five thousand, and numbers
prevailed.

But Gates was no blushing violet. He claimed all the credit
personally, and right on the heels of Burgoyne's surrender he became the center of a conspiracy to deprive Washington of his place
as commander in chief.

Lafayette, the next day after the surrender at Saratoga, left
Bethlehem and rejoined the army. He was tremendously proud—
in a boyish way—of the part he had played at Brandywine, as he
certainly had a right to be. He had proved himself to be a man
among men and not merely a pampered *mangeur de soufflés* in Parisian high society.

But the army was full of fighters. Washington's outfit was a
hard lot—inured to wounds, starvation, cold, rags, defeat and disaster in general—and they held together and could put up a stiff
fight. They were not much impressed by Lafayette's experiences. A
little flesh wound in the leg, but what of it? Slightly wounded, and
then nurses, clean beds, officers in attendance, good food, pretty
ladies.

Lafayette thought of going back to France. The commander in
chief was still reluctant to give him a command. Winter was coming
on; its chill breath was in the air. The marquis wandered around
the forlorn camp and watched the officers play their interminable
card games. The army chest was bare; the men had no winter
clothes. In his despondent state he would go back to headquarters
and see the serene commander in chief, and his faith and confidence
would come back to him.

Both Washington and Lafayette were fatalists. They believed that what is to be will be, though neither of them ever uttered this belief in any definite way to the best of my knowledge. Occasionally Lafayette, in his letters to his wife, refers to "my star," meaning his destiny. Washington never said anything about his "star," but the psychological aspects of fatalism are clearly discernible in the careers of both of them.

Their fatalism is not as formidable as the word sounds. It meant simply an unconquerable belief in a life pattern. The fatalist says, "I am going to do this because I cannot help doing it even if I tried. It is in accord with my being, my life design. The result may turn out splendidly for me, or it may turn out badly, yet in either case I shall stand by it, and go my way."

I grant you that this inflexible determination does not seem at once to be in harmony with Lafayette's indecisiveness, but his lack of decision was always temporary. At times he did not know where his "star" pointed, but when he caught the course of his life design he went ahead, often foolishly, regardless of consequences. On the other hand, there was no indecision about Washington, except in minor matters. His character was fixed, inflexible, and powerful. To such men hell and damnation may come in an avalanche, yet they will be themselves, serene and cool. If they happen to be overwhelmed by disaster, then that is what has to be. It is fate.

In that last week of November the young marquis was put in charge of about a hundred men and sent to attack a British outpost on the New Jersey side of the Delaware River. His conduct was excellent in that small affair. Washington—who had already developed an affection for him—was impressed by his soldierly bearing. On December 4, 1777, he gave Lafayette the command of a Virginia division. He was then just past his twentieth birthday, and the youngest general in the American service.

To father-in-law d'Ayen he wrote:

Our general is a man truly made for this revolution, which could not be successfully accomplished without him. I see him more closely than any man in the world and I see that he is worthy of the adoration of his country. His tender friendship and his entire confidence in me in regard to all military and political subjects, great and small, that occupy him, place me in a situation to judge of all that he has to do, all that he has to conciliate and overcome. I admire more each day the beauty of his character and of his soul.

In December of 1777 the American army went to Valley Forge for the winter. On the way Lafayette received a long-delayed letter from France which told him of the birth of his second child—a daughter—who had come into the world on July 1st. She was named Anastasie. For the moment the marquis was depressed because Adrienne's second child was not a boy. He wrote a loving letter to her in which he managed to say, in the spaces between sentiment and affection, that it is "absolutely necessary" to have a boy the next time, as if she were able to choose the sex of her children.

Henriette, the first daughter, had already died, but her father did not learn of her death for months.

In the history of nations one encounters many amazing spectacles. I am willing to put the fact that Washington's army survived the winter at Valley Forge high on the list of extraordinary achievements. It was—and is, in retrospect—an astounding thing. The whole country seemed to have forgotten Washington and his forlorn and shivering army in its log huts. You understand, of course, that the statement I have just made is not literally true, but that is how it looked to the officers and men at Valley Forge.

One of the reasons for Washington's selection of Valley Forge —within twenty-five miles of Philadelphia—as winter quarters was its location in a fruitful agricultural country—a land full of prosperous farmers, cattle, bread and meat. This reasoning looks sound enough as seen from a front, or full-face, view. Its aspect in the rear, however, caught as it passes over the hill of history, is not so pleasing. There was plenty of food in the Valley Forge country, but the Quaker farmers seem to have been lacking in the more impulsive qualities of patriotism. They refused to accept the Continental paper money, which is all that Washington had to give them, and sent their produce to Philadelphia to be sold to the British, who paid for it in gold. This traffic was treasonable, but it was difficult to catch them at it.

There were times when the soldiers at Valley Forge had no bread for days. Washington's own Christmas dinner of that year was served without bread, sugar, tea, coffee or milk. By February of 1778 the army was on the point of dissolution. Congress, sitting at York—after its flight from Philadelphia—authorized Washington to seize food from the farmers and force them to accept payment in Continental currency.

Clothing was even more difficult to obtain than food. Before the war textile fabrics, shoes, stockings, blankets—and almost all other manufactured articles—were brought from England. During the war supplies of clothing and arms were sent from France, but these shipments were uncertain and subject to the hazards of the British blockade. More than three thousand men, or one-third of Washington's army, deserted in the winter of 1777-78. They were simply unable to endure the destitution of their camp.

4

In February, 1778, Baron von Steuben, a former Prussian officer who had served many years in the armies of Frederick the Great, entered the American service. It was his job to reorganize the army in a technical sense and to teach military evolutions and plain, simple drill-ground tactics. He was good at it. On the sky line of history he stands by the side of Lafayette. The connection of the marquis with our wavering fortunes, had, without a doubt, some significance in international politics and diplomacy. But Lafayette was not a drillmaster or an organizer. He was a symbol of the friendship of France, or at any rate he was so considered. Von Steuben, on the other hand, had no influence in Europe. He was a rough, good-humored working soldier, and he knew armies in about the same way that a competent garage mechanic knows automobiles. He was a typical eighteenth century mercenary, which means that he was willing to fight for anybody who paid him. His highest post in the Prussian army had been that of captain, and Frederick the Great had dropped him from the army list after the Seven Years' War. For years he had wandered around Europe, evading his creditors, serving a little here and there, and living at inns. General Palmer,* who is an authority in this matter, says that von Steuben's coming to America was engineered by Beaumarchais. The former captain was introduced to Benjamin Franklin

* The best biography I know of von Steuben is the one written by John McAuley Palmer, a retired general of the American army, who spent years in running down the facts and the legends concerning this Prussian officer. His book was published in 1937.

by clever Beaumarchais, and was represented to be a lieutenant general in the army of Frederick the Great, friend of the Prussian king, and owner of large landed property which he was losing as a forfeit for leaving the king's service. General Palmer says that the expenses of his voyage to America were paid by Rodrique Hortalès et Cie., the dummy concern that Beaumarchais had set up to carry on a secret traffic in arms with the Americans. I can well believe it, as it sounds precisely like one of Beaumarchais's melodramatic plots.

At any rate, von Steuben, whatever the pretense of his coming may have been, was a most capable officer. Upon looking over the disorderly herd of men at Valley Forge he was aghast with astonishment. It was not an army at all; it was just a mob. In describing the situation he wrote much later:

... the words company, regiment, brigade and division were so vague that they did not convey any idea upon which to form a calculation, either of the particular corps or of the army in general. ... I have seen a regiment consisting of thirty men, and a company of one corporal. ... No captain kept a book. Accounts were never furnished nor required.

The description of the dress is easily given. The men were literally naked, some of them in the fullest extent of the word. ... I saw officers mounting guard in a sort of dressing gown, made of an old blanket or woolen bed-cover. With regard to military discipline, I may safely say no such thing existed. In the first place, there was no regular formation. A so-called regiment was formed of three platoons, another of five, eight, nine, and the Canadian regiment of twenty-one.*

He says further that the drill consisted only of the manual of arms. "Each colonel had a system of his own," von Steuben wrote, "the one according to the English, the other according to the Prussian or French style. ... The greater part of the captains had no roll of their companies, and had no idea how many men they had under their orders."

Certainly it is a sad picture; nevertheless, this half-starved mob managed to keep together and to win minor engagements now and then. Von Steuben accomplished a great deal in turning an undisciplined crowd into an army, and for this the American nation has always been grateful.

Lafayette adapted himself, without the least trouble, to the hardships of the Valley Forge atmosphere. Why not? It was all a

* Kapp, *Life of Steuben*, p. 115.

play, a drama, an episode to be recalled in later years. He was
hungry for experiences among men of a different breed and type
from those he had known all his life.

At Washington's meager breakfast table he learned to eat corn
hoecake in spite of his dislike of it. He took care, as well as he could,
of his little command, a division of less than a thousand men; he
lived in a log hut which he had to share with other officers; he
adopted American manners.

5

The mind of General Gates, always light and unsteady, had
been turned by his success at Saratoga. That he deserved little merit,
if any, for the surrender of Burgoyne probably never occurred to
him. He thought of himself as the coming man.

There was an active anti-Washington faction in Congress. A
whispering campaign against the commander in chief began soon
after the battle of Saratoga. It ran on this note: Washington, admirable as he is in character and in resolution, has never won an
important battle. A splendid man, but of small military capacity.
He lacks decision; cannot make up his mind without consulting
every general in sight. But Gates is a man of decision; he has a habit
of going straight ahead; he has won the only great victory of the
war. Britain and her statesmen are stunned by Burgoyne's surrender. Why not retire Washington, with honors, let us say, and put
Gates in his place?

No, no, said the anti-Washington League, that would not do.
His standing was too high; he could not be summarily dismissed
without irreparable injury to the Revolution. Among other matters
to be considered there was the position of the Marquis de Lafayette. If Washington were forced out of command Lafayette would
undoubtedly go with him, and what effect would that have on the
French from whom so much was expected?

It may be worth while to say here that Lafayette's influence
in France was always overrated by the Americans. He had really
no personal influence on the decisions of the French ministers, but
his adventure was applauded in the highest circles, as he was a
great noble, and his coming here gave a kind of social standing to
the American cause that it had not had before. But there are strong

reasons for the conviction that France would have come into the war on the American side even if Lafayette had never crossed the Atlantic. He was only a twenty-year-old boy. France, badly as it was governed, had its elder statesmen, men of sagacity and judgment. Suppose one of our young millionaires, of high social prominence, should go to China and enter the Chinese service in a war with Japan. Would we go to war with Japan on that account? Certainly not. Well, that is exactly the way it was. The exploits of our daring young man would attract a lot of attention, as those of Lafayette did in France, but we would not fight over his adventures. There were other reasons, and potent ones, for the entry of France into the American Revolution.

6

The first step of the faction opposed to Washington was to place Gates at the head of the Board of War and give the board enlarged powers of direction and control. This measure went through Congress without much opposition. The effect of it was to promote Gates over Washington's head, and to make the victor of Saratoga the commander in chief in reality, if not in title.

Of course, in carrying out their intention to shelve Washington, it was desirable to break up the Washington-Lafayette friendship and weaken the attachment of the marquis for his fatherly commander. That might be done, they thought, by giving Lafayette a separate command. So an expedition for the invasion of Canada was planned, with Lafayette at its head. As a military adventure it was perfectly asinine, but when the Board of War proposed it Congress approved the idea at once, though it seems unlikely that any man of military experience would have given it a second thought. But Congress was composed of politicians, philosophers, and "hardheaded" persons of one kind or another.

There was no lack of arguments to support the plan. The Canadians were almost entirely French, their language was French and their habits were French. The country had been acquired by conquest, and the British were believed generally in the English colonies to hold Canada by force, which was far from the truth. The Marquis de Lafayette would be hailed as a liberator. The crushing defeat of Burgoyne was known all over Canada, and very likely the French-Canadian awe of Britain's power and majesty had degenerated into something closely akin to derision. That was not true, but it sounded reasonable.

On the other hand, the snow was four feet deep in lower Canada. This was in January, 1778; the Americans would have to fight cold as well as the British. There were not enough men, not enough money and not enough warm clothes.

Surely Gates and his supporters knew all that. But what of it? It was all a part of a scheme to get rid of Washington. Through some unforeseen miracle Lafayette might win; in that case they could point out that the Board of War, with wise General Gates at the head of it, and a twenty-year-old boy in command of the expedition, had driven the British from Canada. But suppose Lafayette was defeated? Then he might be sent back to France, and the French would learn what an addleheaded weakling they had nourished.

The plan was conceived and adopted without Washington's knowledge. Lafayette was astonished when the order detaching him from Washington's command was received by him. He declined to accept unless he could report directly to his commander in chief— and not to the Board of War or to Congress. In making that decision he was not influenced or persuaded in any way by Washington. In the end the anti-Washington faction had to agree to the stipulation. Report to General Washington and send duplicates of your reports to Congress.

The expedition was a complete fizzle. When Lafayette reached Albany on February 17, 1778, he found that instead of three thousand men awaiting him there were only a few hundred. They were shivering in their clothes. No food; no snowshoes; nothing. It was a wild-goose chase. He met a number of the northern generals; they all said that an invasion of Canada, in the circumstances, was out of the question.

He dismissed the militia and came back to Philadelphia, realizing that he had been made a dupe by those who were opposed to Washington. After that experience he understood clearly the drift of events.

CHAPTER VI

A SPIRITED YOUNG MAN

I

T HE CONSPIRACY to displace Washington as commander in chief is known as the Conway Cabal, though there is reason to believe that Conway was only a figurehead, and that Gates was the moving spirit of the intrigue, abetted by a group of politicians in Congress.

Thomas Conway, an Irishman by birth, had been brought up in France and had become a colonel in the French army. He accompanied du Coudray to America and was made a brigadier general, to the great dissatisfaction of a long line of American colonels. Conway thought, and said, that Washington and Congress had not done the right thing by him; he should have been made a major general. Bristling with complaint, he sent carping letters right and left. Washington estimated him correctly as an irresponsible adventurer and trouble maker, and received him coldly.

Lafayette was so ignorant of army politics that he was completely deceived by Conway and Gates—for a while. Conway pretended great admiration for Lafayette, and went around calling himself "Lafayette's soldier," but he wrote privately to Congress that it was a ridiculous procedure to give the marquis the rank of major general—one of those high ranking officers, "who had never seen a line of battle"—while he (Conway) was a brigadier general. Lafayette was, for a time, a stanch advocate of Conway. He wrote to Washington that "General Conway is so brave, intelligent, and active officer that he schall, I am sure, justify more and more the esteem of the army and your approbation." And upon hearing of the surrender of Burgoyne he wrote, from his bed in Bethlehem, an affectionate letter to Gates, assuring him of his lasting esteem. Again, in December of that year (1777), he wrote to Gates, saying in part:

The idea of obtaining your friendship is highly pleasant to me. Be certain, sir, that you can depend upon my attachment forever. . . . The knowledge I got of your character adds infinitely to the pleasure which my heart feels in receiving the assurances of your future affection towards a young soldier who desires it very heartily.

Lafayette was swiftly getting himself involved—ignorantly, of course,—in a conspiracy to discredit Washington, his favorite demigod.

His lack of perception in this affair is very remarkable. When he wrote the letter just quoted above Gates had been already placed over Washington's head as president of the Board of War, and Conway had been given the post of inspector general. Washington knew quite clearly what was going on, and so did every member of Congress, as well as most of the generals in the army. It was common knowledge among the well-informed that the Gates-Conway faction intended to put General Washington on the shelf. How in the world did it happen that Lafayette was unaware of it?

Right here arises a suspicion that the marquis did know of the intent of the anti-Washington group, and planned to switch his allegiance to Gates. I cannot believe it. Lafayette was the very soul and shining symbol of honor; he would never betray a friend, and his affection for Washington was profound. The most satisfactory explanation is that he did not know what it was all about; just pure dumbness of comprehension.

Well, after all, he was only a boy of twenty.

For a while Lafayette and Conway were great cronies, though Conway was attempting to undermine him secretly. Together they planned a harebrained naval and military expedition to capture the British West Indies. Conway, who was a rascal of experience and considerable ability, must have been leading him on and encouraging his foolish ideas. The Americans did not have the ships, nor the men, nor the money, nor the arms, for such an armada. It was certain to fail. Congress would not even discuss it.

The realization of the true import of the Gates-Conway maneuvers evidently occurred to the marquis rather suddenly around the first of the year 1778. He wrote to Washington:

. . . if you were lost for America there is nobody who could keep the army and the revolution for six months. There are often dissensions in Congress, parties who hate one another as much as the common enemy;

stupid men, who without knowing a single word about war, undertake to judge you, to make ridiculous comparisons; they are infatuated with Gates, without thinking of the different circumstances, and believe that attacking is the only thing necessary to conquer.

It appears that he had known Conway only slightly, or not at all, in France. He tells Washington that he has recently inquired into Conway's character, which means, I suppose, that he had asked other French volunteers about him. "I found," Lafayette continues, "that he is an ambitious and dangerous man. He has done all in his power, by cunning maneuvers, to take off my confidence and affection for you. His desire was to engage me to leave this country."

In another paragraph he assures Washington that "I am now fixed to your fate, and I shall follow it and sustain it as well by my sword as by all means in my power."

Conway had the letter-writing habit. He wrote a laudatory epistle to Gates, which that general evidently read to his military family. Major Wilkinson, a member of Gates's staff, got drunk at a dinner not long afterward and said that Conway had written: "Heaven has been determined to save your country, or a weak general and bad counselors would have ruined it." The story reached Washington, who thereupon sent a note to Conway, which contained nothing but these words:

Sir: A letter which I received last night contained the following paragraph: "In a letter from General Conway to General Gates, he says, *Heaven has determined to save your country, or a weak general and bad counselors would have ruined it.*"

This brief letter was signed, "I am, sir, your humble servant. George Washington."

Conway sought Washington and insisted that the quotation was not correct, but he did not supply the correct wording. Then Wilkinson, frightened at his own indiscretion, told Gates it was not he who had revealed the contents of the letter. Pretty soon Gates found out that Wilkinson was a liar, and spoke to him so severely that Wilkinson challenged his commander to a duel. On the morning set for the duel Gates went to Wilkinson and burst into tears— according to Wilkinson—and declared that he had just as soon shoot his own son as to shoot Wilkinson. There could be no duel in the face of such an abject apology. Not long afterward, however, Wilkinson resigned from his position as secretary of the Board of War and wrote to Congress that he had detected General Gates in "acts of treachery and falsehood."

There was not much secrecy about these doings. Congress had learned about the letter writing and the lying, and the duel, and was thoroughly fed up with it. The affair had become ridiculous, and Washington's imperturbable demeanor shone by contrast.

Congress ordered Gates back to the army and Conway was put in command of the insignificant post of Albany. From his obscure corner Conway wrote an impertinent letter of resignation to Congress, and his resignation was immediately accepted. It appears, however, that he did not really want to resign and had hoped that Congress would ask him to stay. After his letter was dispatched he feared that Congress would take him at his word, so he rode a horse almost to death to reach York, in Pennsylvania, where Congress was in session, before his resignation was acted on. He came too late. When he arrived he was already out of the army.

The next thing that happened was that Conway, because of his continued abuse of Washington, had to fight a duel with General Cadwallader. "I have stopped the damned rascal's lying tongue, at any rate," Cadwallader said, as he saw Conway lying on the ground with blood gushing from his mouth.

It was thought that Conway would die, but he recovered. While he was anticipating death he wrote Washington a humble letter of apology. As soon as he could get about he returned to France.*

The policy of the French government, which had been mendacious and secretive in its attitude toward England from the beginning of the war, was changed by the resounding defeat of the British at Saratoga. France came out in the open and declared war against England in February, 1778. On the sixth of that month a formal treaty of alliance between France and the American colonies was signed at Paris.

When the news reached America six weeks later the young mar-

---

* After the war the Society of the Cincinnati was organized by American officers who had served during the Revolution. Lafayette was asked to name the French officers who were worthy of the society's decoration. Conway wanted the decoration, but evidently had small hope of getting it. He said that, of course, he would get no favors from the man who had ruined and abandoned him in America, meaning Lafayette. But to his surprise, and to that of many other people, Lafayette awarded him the coveted honor. This seems inexplicable, for Conway's American career was certainly discreditable. Lafayette wrote to Washington and intimated that he had given Conway the decoration not from a spirit of generosity, but just to close his mouth.

quis bounded into Washington's room at Valley Forge and kissed the grave commander in chief on both cheeks, French fashion.

As soon as the French took up the American cause the entire aspect of the situation was changed. The British found themselves surrounded by momentous difficulties. Within twenty-four hours the theater of action became world-wide.

The directing minds of the British Empire had to think of many things—the gleaming West Indies and their sugar plantations, the long sea route around the Cape of Good Hope, dusky India with its wealth, the narrow English Channel and French Canada.

The reasons which moved the French and sent them on this large-scale military adventure seem puerile and inadequate. They were instigated chiefly by a desire for revenge, but revenge is an empty egg. When you have had your revenge, you crack the egg and there is nothing inside. War costs money, and men, and ships, and there is always the possibility of unexpected and overwhelming disasters. Was revenge worth the risk? There were peaceful French merchant ships on all the seas; they would be the prey of British privateers. The French West Indian islands were highly valuable colonial possessions. Would France be able to hold them? It seemed doubtful.

What did the French hope to get out of the war? Possibly prestige. Also the division of the English-speaking race into two mutually hostile nations. But were these objectives worth the trouble and expense?

The statesmen at Versailles had a vague notion of regaining Canada, but that project was discouraged by the American commissioners in Paris as well as by American public opinion. The Americans preferred the British to the French as overlords of Canada, and did not care to exchange one foreign power for another. To make these matters plain to a twentieth century reader it must be stated clearly that the colonials, although they welcomed the assistance of France, distrusted the French and their motives. Public opinion was opposed to the landing of a French army on this continent. Many people of consequence believed that if a French army came it would never leave.

When Rochambeau's army of Frenchmen arrived at Newport in 1780 they found no bands blaring in the streets, and no committees of welcome. The houses were dark and shuttered, and only a few inhabitants could be seen. It was like a dead town. Nevertheless, in a short time the Rhode Islanders learned that Frenchmen did not have horns and a spiked tail. They also found out that Rochambeau and his officers and men had gold to spend, and they spent it freely. So the shutters were taken down, the girls began to learn French, and there were dinners and dances.

What the American revolutionists wanted from France in 1778 was not troops but money, clothes, guns, munitions. And sea power.

2

Philadelphia was an occupied town, held by the British. Though there were many Tories—friends of the British—in the place, there were also many loyal Americans. Every second man, or woman, was a potential American spy, and some of them were actively employed in espionage. Washington was well informed as to what was going on.

In May, 1778, the news came to Valley Forge that Sir Henry Clinton had superseded Sir William Howe as the British general in chief, and that Clinton was getting ready to evacuate Philadelphia. It was known that a powerful French fleet, under command of the Comte d'Estaing, was on its way to aid the Americans. If the French succeeded in establishing a naval blockade at the mouth of the Delaware—which was obviously the best thing they could do—the position of the British army in Philadelphia would be untenable.

Lafayette was given command of a force of twenty-two hundred men, and sent off with elaborate instructions from Washington, to proceed toward Philadelphia and "cover the country between the Delaware and the Schuylkill . . . to obstruct the incursions of the enemy's parties, and to obtain intelligence of their motions and designs."

A tone of anxiety runs through this letter; Washington was not sure that the marquis would handle the expedition with caution and wisdom, though he had too much tact to say so. Lafayette's military experience was almost negligible, and it was evident to Washington and the other general officers at Valley Forge that there was a good deal of recklessness in his make-up. Washington wrote further:

You will remember that your detachment is a very valuable one, and that any accident happening to it would be a very severe blow to this army. You will therefore use every possible precaution for its security, and to guard against a surprise.

Within twenty-four hours the British had learned about the expedition. They knew the number of men under Lafayette's command and his objective. It was very difficult to keep either American or British military plans or movements secret during the Revolution. There were spies on every hand, in both armies.

Sir Henry Clinton made up his mind to capture "the boy," as he called Lafayette, and to bag his whole detachment. As one may see, the moral effect of such an achievement would have been tremendous, besides the material loss to the American army. Eight thousand men, under command of General Grant, were sent out from Philadelphia to pen the valorous young marquis's twenty-two hundred men between the two rivers. Then they were to be rounded up like a herd of cattle. And Clinton almost succeeded in doing it.

The battle, such as it was—in the records it is called the battle of Barren Hill—occurred on May 20, 1778. Lafayette says in his *Mémoires* that General Clinton and General Howe, who were absolutely sure of their success, had invited a number of ladies and gentlemen to a party in Philadelphia the next day to meet the Marquis de Lafayette, as a prisoner of war.*

It all went wrong, so far as the British were concerned. Their various detachments did not arrive in time, the pincers did not close, and the marquis discovered a ford across the Schuylkill which seems to have been generally unknown. He and his detachment escaped with a trifling loss. On May 24th Washington wrote to the president of Congress and said, "On the night of the 19th the enemy moved out in force against the detachment under the Marquis de Lafayette . . . which made a timely and handsome retreat across the Schuylkill at Matson's ford. Our loss was nine men in the whole. The enemy's loss is supposed to be something more."

The boy had made good. Yet for a few hours his fate, his career, his future hung in the balance. If the British had taken him and all his men into Philadelphia that would have been the end of the Marquis de Lafayette as a figure of importance. The Americans would have forgotten him, the French would have laughed

* *Mémoires de ma Main*, Vol. I, p. 75. I doubt that story. As I have pointed out before, Lafayette cannot be wholly trusted in respect to memory. It is just the kind of fictional element that he would unconsciously bring in to round out the episode.

at him; there would have been no biographies. But he found a ford where his men could wade across. Of such things history is made.

The British evacuated Philadelphia around the middle of June and started across New Jersey on their march to New York. The progress of their army was extremely slow; they had no less than twelve miles of wagons. Washington left Valley Forge and pursued them.

On June 28th—the year is 1778—the Americans overtook the British. In the ensuing battle of Monmouth Lafayette distinguished himself by his coolness under fire and his clear perception of what was required of him and his command. It was a record-breaking hot day, and under the brazen sky the battle was like a combat in an oven. Hundreds of men on each side were prostrated by the heat. Both the British and the Americans claimed a victory. But it was actually a drawn battle. During the night the British went on their way, and Washington pursued them no farther. That night Washington and Lafayette lay on the ground, under the stars, on the general's cloak, and talked for hours.

3

The fleet of the Comte d'Estaing arrived at the mouth of the Delaware River early in July, and, upon learning that the British had left Philadelphia, the fleet sailed northward and hovered around the entrance to New York harbor.

The story of d'Estaing's unfortunate expedition, if told in full, would be a voluminous epic in which the rather disagreeable qualities of Envy, Malice, Ignorance, Bad Temper, Poor Judgment and False Pride would all be personified like the characters in a morality play of the Middle Ages—and the parts would be about equally divided between the French and the Americans.

Lafayette was in transports of joy over the coming of the French fleet. Washington's army had gone into camp in northern New Jersey, about fifty miles, or less, from the position of the fleet at sea. Messengers and aides passed back and forth. Lafayette wrote gushing letters to d'Estaing, who was an Auvergnat and a distant relative.

Let it be made clear that our marquis was then, as always, a sentimentalist—and, like all sentimental people, he preferred abstractions to factual estimates or calculations. His desires were ardent and passionate; his loves and hates frequently exceeded the limitations of their subject matter. He was a gushing person, most distinctly lacking in intellectual poise.

At any rate, he made it plain that he loved the Comte d'Estaing and all other Frenchmen; that he loved General Washington and all his friends. and hated all Englishmen fiercely. "How fortunate it would be," he wrote to d'Estaing, "for me to find at last a chance to shed my blood for my country and to be avowed by her!"

The French fleet was superior to that of the British in New York harbor, and d'Estaing also had a French army aboard his ships. Washington proposed a joint naval and military attack against New York.

D'Estaing agreed with that suggestion, but just then the General Contrariness of Things—a blind and malicious god—took charge of affairs. The French ships were deep-draft vessels; there was not enough water over the Sandy Hook bar for them to enter the harbor. Moreover, the fleet was short of supplies and of drinking water. It could not remain where it was. The project was abandoned.

Washington then proposed that the fleet go to Rhode Island and co-operate with an American army against the British force entrenched there. D'Estaing was informed that he would find plenty of supplies on his arrival. So he sailed for Rhode Island. The American army promised by Washington did not exist; it was to be raised in New England, from the local militia. Nor were the supplies on hand.

Lafayette could hardly contain himself. He wanted to be there too, and fight by the side of the gallant French, his countrymen. Washington gave him the command of twenty-eight hundred men, subject to the orders of Major General Sullivan. The marquis said good-bye to Washington on July 23rd. His troops had been sent on ahead, several days before.

A stream of effusive letters went from him to d'Estaing; he wrote from every stopping place and forwarded his epistles by hard-riding couriers. He hinted to d'Estaing that he desired greatly to command the French troops that would be landed for the attack on Newport. D'Estaing agreed, to the annoyance of his officers. They considered Lafayette an American, an expatriate Frenchman. Why should this lad of twenty-one, with an American title of major general, take command? General Sullivan and the Americans did not like the arrangement either. To them Lafayette was a Frenchman who had become Washington's pet. Now, here he was, not only in command of an American division but also in command of the French landing force. It was perfectly plain to them that the marquis was ready and eager to take all the glory—if any.

But there wasn't any.

Everything went wrong. The raising of the New England army took weeks, and instead of the fourteen thousand men that were promised, Sullivan was able to get together only eight thousand. The smart French officers made fun of the Yankee militia and called them "tailors and apothecaries." In the midst of the growing ill-temper Washington sent General Nathanael Greene, a native Rhode Islander, to share the command of the American troops with General Sullivan. Of course, Sullivan did not like that.

Now comes on the stage the Vice of Small Minds. Sullivan proposed to send the American troops over to the island first, covered by the fire from the ships; then the French should land and reinforce them. Lafayette went up in the air, so to speak. That plan would never do. French troops playing a secondary role! It would be humiliating. So it was agreed that both the French and Americans were to land and attack simultaneously, but at different points.

General Sullivan did not keep the agreement. While the French fleet was coming up the channel he landed his force and when the French got there part of the island was already occupied by the Americans. Indignation among the French officers. It was a breach of faith and most of them did not want to have anything more to do with the affair.

While this point was being argued a British fleet came sailing down Long Island Sound, going in the direction of New York. The Comte d'Estaing and all his vessels went in immediate pursuit. He sent word ashore that as soon as he had fought the enemy he would return and co-operate with the Americans. General Sullivan was furious, and declared that the French had deserted him.

The French fleet soon had its troubles, and they were big ones. D'Estaing had a much stronger fleet than the British and was engaged in battle with them when a storm arose which threatened to destroy both the British and the French. It raged all night, tore the sails to rags and dismasted ships. About a week later the limping, disabled French fleet, on its way to Boston repairs, paused a little while at the entrance to Newport harbor. Sullivan promised, asserted, and took his oath that the ships could be refitted right there. He would furnish carpenters, riggers, masts and sails. But no, d'Estaing would not agree to that. His definite instructions from the king were to go to Boston in case the fleet required repairs, and to Boston he would go. Well, then, said Sullivan, leave the troops here and we shall attack the British. But d'Estaing declared the troops had to go with the ships. The fleet sailed away and Greene and Sullivan—and Lafayette—were left to their own devices.

General Sullivan called a council of war and read a long and insulting protest against d'Estaing's conduct. That was too much for the high-tempered marquis to endure. He said vehemently, with blazing eyes:

I would have you all understand that France is dearer to me than America; that whatever France does is always right; the Comte d'Estaing is my friend and I am ready to maintain these sentiments with my sword; it could never be better employed.

While the smoke of that bombshell was in the air the members of the council hastened to explain, in the usual fashion, that nothing personal was meant, and they begged Lafayette's pardon. He refused to accept their apologies and went to his own quarters in angry silence. There he pouted for several days; he would speak no English, and his only associates were the French officers of his staff.

Sullivan put the fat in the fire again by getting up an order of the day in which he criticized the French. This document was read to the troops and was given to the newspapers. The marquis went to headquarters and told Sullivan that he intended to challenge him to a duel. Sullivan said, all right; he would accept the challenge.*

Both of them were men of such impetuosity that their natural inclination was to fight it out first and explain afterward. But Lafayette was troubled by what Washington might think of these rash doings. So he did not send the challenge; instead, he devoted himself to a long inky-fingered epistle to the commander in chief, telling all about the quarrel, and asking advice. In reading it one thinks of a college boy in trouble writing home to his father. "Whenever I quit you," he wrote to Washington, "I meet with some disappointment and misfortune."

* This, by the way, is gossip. I cannot find any reliable evidence that the Marquis actually said he intended to challenge Sullivan to fight a duel. I am inclined to believe the story, however, as it fits in with Lafayette's character.

In the meantime the active General Sullivan fell into an unusual mood of reflection, and in lame, halting words composed a supplementary order of the day in which he toned down the harshness of his previous expressions.

The commander in chief replied to the marquis that the trouble between the French and American generals should be smoothed over, and he begged him to "afford a healing hand to the wound that unintentionally has been made." Lafayette was so completely in the periphery of Washington's influence that he was eagerly willing to carry out his suggestion. Perhaps—besides—he was tired and a little ashamed of the part he had been playing.

At once, upon the receipt of Washington's letter, he rode over to see Sullivan and extend the friendly hand. Sullivan was in a tight place and begged the marquis to go to Boston and get the French troops to come to his aid. Next day Lafayette rode to Boston—seventy miles in seven hours—to ask the Comte d'Estaing to detach the French regiments from his fleet and send them to Rhode Island. The soldiers were doing nothing but eat and get themselves in rows with the inhabitants of Boston. One of their officers had been killed in a fight with the populace. Why not let them go and help Sullivan beat the British? D'Estaing was not adverse to the plan; yes, he would send the troops.

Lafayette rushed back to Rhode Island and learned that it was too late. Sullivan had not been able to stand the pressure and was giving up the island. (The word "island" in this case does not mean the state of Rhode Island but only the island on which the town of Newport stands.)

Not long afterward Lafayette was again in Boston, urging d'Estaing to co-operate with the Americans in a project to drive the British out of Canada. Without a doubt it was a hopeless proposal. It was a venture that the French king and his ministers had not included in the admiral's instructions; moreover, the Americans did not want the French to hold Canada. But the impulsive young marquis had not consulted the Americans. That was to be done later. He had thought of the plan all by himself.

The Comte d'Estaing seems to have been bored by Lafayette, though I am not sure; it is only a conjecture. The marquis, however, was not bored by d'Estaing. With the fading of the project to invade Canada he wrote to the admiral:

In any case I pray you to take me with you, Monsieur le Comte. My heart loves to attach itself to your fortune, and I hope that you will not oppose the attraction that draws me towards you.

At that time the French were considering a plan to invade England. Continuing, Lafayette wrote:

If they went there without me I would hang myself. I would rather be a soldier there than a general elsewhere . . . provided I had the pleasure of seeing a lovely fire at London.

What adoration! What hatred! What a tumult of emotions bubble and seethe in this letter to the unimaginative and stolid d'Estaing!

"My heart loves to attach itself to your fortune." But he had already attached himself to Washington's fate. Did he have the attaching habit? Well, not exactly. His phrases were often rhetorical, and they sometimes got him into such a tangle of misunderstanding that he had great difficulty in extricating himself. We shall see further on that he was attached to the French Revolution until he learned what the Revolution really meant, and then he had a perilous time getting himself detached.

The idea of taking Canada from the British came to nothing. D'Estaing, much aggrieved because Congress was tardy in sending him a vote of thanks, sailed away to the West Indies and the first French expedition to America came to an inglorious end.

4

Vanity, personal pride, self-glorification—these are qualities that are usually condemned by historians and biographers, and perhaps justly so, but we should not be too severe in condemnation, for all of them are simply exaggerations or perversions of the fine and noble quality of self-respect.

Vanity has been, and is, a dynamic force of tremendous power in shaping the progress of civilization. It has led, times without number, to amazing constructive achievements. Consider the explorers, the athletes, the inventors, the heroes, the writers, the artists. And the money-makers as well. Many a man has given all the years of his life to piling up a fortune that he did not need just to show that he could do it.

To say that Lafayette was not vain would be simply a falsification of the record. His love of glory and distinction was one of his most striking traits. He was not the kind of man who goes down in history as the inventor of a laborsaving machine, or as the author of a great book, or as a lawgiver, or as a builder of roads and bridges. The only way he could attain distinction was to be a hero, so he was always dramatizing himself and his actions, and planning heroic events. I do not say this for the purpose of belittling him; the human race needs heroes just as much as it needs builders of roads. But the film star, the road builder, the ingenious inventor and the personal hero all have their limitations. Naturally enough. One cannot do everything. The marquis was a Sir Galahad by instinct, a redresser of wrongs—real or imaginary, a St. George dashing fearlessly at fiery dragons.

In the fall of 1778, soon after his encounter with General Sullivan, he leveled his lance against a fiery dragon which turned out to be only an ironical and slightly amused tame cat named Lord Carlisle.

The noble lord was one of the commissioners sent over to America by the British government in an attempt to conciliate the rebellious colonies. The effort got nowhere, as the commissioners had no power to grant independence, and that is all the colonies wanted.

Lord Carlisle published an address to Congress—and to the American people—in which he accused the French nation of "a perfidy too universally acknowledged to require any new proof."

Lafayette decided to take him up on that assertion, to challenge him to a duel, and to kill him. So the faithful Major Gimat was sent into the British lines with a defiant challenge. After a long delay his lordship replied:

Sir: I have received your letter. . . . I confess that I find it difficult to make a serious reply. The only one, as you must have foreseen, that can be expected of me in my quality of commissioner of the King, is that I consider myself and shall always consider myself as not being obliged to respond to any individual for my public conduct or for my way of expressing myself. . . . I must remind you that the insult to which you refer in the correspondence that has taken place between the commissioners of the King and the Congress is not of a private nature. Therefore I think that all these national disputes will be best decided when Admiral Byron and the Comte d'Estaing meet each other.

CHAPTER VII

THE MARQUIS RETURNS TO FRANCE

I

THERE was an interlude of more than a year in Lafayette's American service. The episode is rather curious. Early in October, 1778, shortly after the row with General Sullivan and the sending of the challenge to Lord Carlisle the impetuous young marquis spent a day or two with Washington. He told the commander in chief that he would like to return to France for a few months, provided his absence would not be detrimental to the service. Washington thought that the army could get along for a while without the young man and appeared willing and even eager to let him go.

Lafayette had become a kind of problem; he was making a fool of himself. I have not the slightest doubt that Washington's ready assent came partly—but not wholly—from that view of the matter. Let him go home and keep out of trouble; he can come back later. Another reason arose from the obvious jealousy of American officers; and still another—probably the most potent one—was that Lafayette in France would be worth more to the American cause, just at that time, than Lafayette in America.

Besides these considerations, Congress was beginning to look upon one aspect of his activities as a nuisance, however much they valued his services in general. He deluged Congress with letters of recommendation for the appointment of Frenchmen for posts in the military service. It was not necessary for a French officer to have any special talent; if he was French, Lafayette was for him and said so emphatically. He wanted Duportail to have a brigade; another officer wanted to be reimbursed for his expenses, coming here uninvited; La Colombe should be a captain. Something important was lost in the sphere of human affairs if Vrigny failed to get a colonel's commission. Capitaine—who had come over in the *Victoire* with Lafayette—was certainly entitled to consideration;

and so on and so on. If the marquis had had his way, most of the higher officers in the struggling revolutionary army would have been French.

On Washington's recommendation Congress granted him an indefinite leave of absence and gave him a vote of thanks for his services. Also Congress instructed Benjamin Franklin, then in Paris, to have an "elegant sword" made for Lafayette and presented to him in the name of the United States. It was what we Americans call "a gorgeous send-off."

Gerard, the French minister at Philadelphia, who was a sour-puss and too worldly-wise to have much admiration for anything or anybody, even wrote to Vergennes that Lafayette was "the idol of Congress, of the army and the people of America." That was putting it a little strong. The wealthy and self-assertive marquis was certainly not the idol of a lot of army officers.

I wonder if many of those who said good-bye to him so effusively really thought that he would ever return? Of course, I do not know the answer to that question, but from the look of things as they stand on the record I have gained a strong impression that few—if any—expected him to come back. Their good-byes were farewells—and God bless you. They were glad he had come, and grateful to him; and also glad that he was going. Washington hoped to see him again; of that one may be sure, for he had a deep personal affection for Lafayette that arose above all political issues.

In my opinion Washington was the magnet that eventually drew him back. If there had been no Washington, the American Revolution would have seen no more of Lafayette.

During his stay he had spent, or given away, far more than his income, large as it was, and was obliged to borrow money. Beaumarchais, then engaged in large financial operations with the American government, instructed M. Francey, his representative at Philadelphia, to advance funds in any amount. As soon as France came openly into the war the French government took over Beaumarchais's concern and liquidated it, as it had nothing further to do. After that Lafayette borrowed from American moneylenders and merchants and gave them drafts on his business agents in France.

The grateful Congress put the American frigate *Alliance*—a new and swift vessel—at his service for the voyage to France. On the way to Boston, where the ship was awaiting him, the marquis was taken sick. He was extremely fatigued when he set forth on his journey, and he rode several days in a cold rain. He was so thrilled and wrought up that he hardly knew what he was doing. Besides all that, the appreciative citizens on his route had given him too much to drink. At Fishkill on the Hudson he collapsed and was in bed for three weeks. His ailment was called "an inflammatory malady." It seems to have been pneumonia. The attending physicians thought he was going to die.

Washington's headquarters were twenty-two miles away, at Fredericksburg. He got daily news from Lafayette's physician and occasionally he would ride over to inquire into the illness of his young friend. Eventually the marquis recovered and, after bidding Washington "a very tender, and a very painful adieu," he cantered off to Boston. Washington's personal physician, Dr. John Cochran, went with him to look after his welfare. The learned doctor seems to have been a jolly fellow, with a decided inclination to stay up all night and spend the time drinking and singing. Lafayette had to wait many days for the boat to get her crew, and the doctor remained with him. Years afterward the people of Boston told stories of the uproar that came into the still night air from the quarters of Dr. Cochran and the marquis. Evidently Lafayette had entirely recovered from his recent illness.

2

The *Alliance* made the trip from Boston to Brest in twenty-six days. She left Boston on January 11, 1779, and arrived at Brest on the sixth of February. In those days that was considered a swift ocean passage.

But she came within a hairbreadth of not getting there at all, and here is what happened. The crew was composed chiefly of Boston jailbirds and deserters from British ships. They conceived the idea of seizing the vessel and sailing her into an English port, where she might be sold as an enemy's ship captured at sea. The marquis was to be turned over to the government as a prisoner of war. The plot was revealed by an American sailor just before the mutiny was to begin. Everyone who was to take a part in it was seized and charged with mutiny.

The mutineers were a sort of problem when the ship reached France. Nobody knew what to do with them. The mutiny had occurred on an American vessel and the French had no jurisdiction. The American commissioners in France had no jail and no court. The mutineers were held in French prisons and eventually exchanged for American prisoners of war taken by the British.

There are men who constantly find themselves in perilous situations; men who attract danger—just as other men attract money or women or poverty or laborious jobs. Lafayette attracted danger. In retracing his life one becomes so accustomed to finding him in peril that one takes it as a matter of course.

The *Alliance* sweeps bravely over the sparkling blue sea into the harbor of Brest, her white sails gleaming, the sea foam rippling around her swift prow, the marquis on the polished quarter-deck, the mutineers chained in the hold, and at her masthead the new American flag. From the forts come the boom and roar of cannon. The French are saluting the flag of their American ally.

With bare head Lafayette stands and looks at the brown hills and the white houses of France. He has been away from home nearly two years—and what a glorious home-coming! He is not yet twenty-two, yet he is a major general and is coming home as a hero. There go the guns, throbbing on the air, and the lily-white flag of France is floating by the side of the American red, white and blue.

It was all wonderful and exhilarating, but there was one little —rather trifling—technicality that annoyed Lafayette. As soon as he arrived at Paris, and almost before he had had time to embrace his wife, the government informed him that he was under arrest for having disobeyed the king's orders by going to America in the first place. That was a stupid procedure, and everybody knew it was, but orders are orders. The French government had come around to Lafayette's side and was at war with England. Nevertheless, the government considered his escapade a kind of insubordination. Such a ridiculous attitude could not be sustained, but—as a matter of form—they kept him under arrest for a week, not in a prison but in the Hôtel de Noailles, with his wife's grandfather, the Maréchal de Noailles, as his jailer. This meant that he simply stayed at home a week and rested. No visitors were allowed except the members of his own family.

The marquis had become a celebrity of the first rank. White-haired, grave and thoughtful statesmen consulted him about American affairs. Just after the week of pleasant imprisonment was over he was summoned to Versailles to relate his story of adventure and to tell the king about Washington and the American Revolution.

At that time the French ministry was contemplating an invasion of England. It was not a visionary project, by any means. The population of France was nearly three times that of England; the French could put greater armies in the field, and the French military personnel—officers and men—was excellent. Only twenty-four miles of sea separated France from England. The French navy was struggling under the management of an incompetent minister of marine, but even so it should have been able to protect a fleet of army transports in the short trip across the English Channel.

Lafayette heard of the plan to strike at the heart of the British Empire, and his dramatic soul was ablaze with the thought of his own role in the invasion. Certainly he would play a part. America was far away, a diminishing landscape, seen through the wrong end of a telescope. He was to appear on a greater field of action.

In May he bought command of the King's Dragoons for eighty thousand francs, and so he was again an officer in the French army. It does not seem likely that he would have done that if he had had any thought of returning to America; but, on the other hand, he might have done it with the idea of taking the King's Dragoons to America with him as an expeditionary force.

He had spent only a month with his regiment—the month of June, 1779—when he was detached and sent to Havre by the Ministry of War to assist in preparations for invading England. He wrote to Vergennes—in his customary flamboyant style: "My imagination often advances into the enemy's country at the head of an advance guard. . . . The thought of seeing England humiliated and crushed makes me tremble with joy. . . . Judge if I ought not to be impatient to know if I am destined to be the first to arrive on that coast and to plant the first flag in the midst of that insolent nation!"

The marquis fumed and fretted in the commonplace town of Havre during the whole summer of 1779. Adrienne was with him; they kept each other company. Everything in connection with the projected invasion was at sixes and sevens. The Spanish were to co-operate in the enterprise, but the Spanish fleet never came, and there was a general lack of enthusiasm on the part of the French. The entire plan went to pieces, but not all at once; it slowly petered out. Around the middle of October Lafayette was ordered back to Paris.

On Christmas Eve, 1779, Adrienne gave birth to a male child. The marquis wrote joyously to Washington that at last he had a son, and the boy's name was George Washington Lafayette.

3

Another great idea was buzzing in the air. The French king and ministry had decided to dispatch a second expedition to America, composed of a strong fleet and an army of about five thousand men.

Since the prospect of invading England had vanished, the marquis was filled with enthusiasm over the American project. He wanted to return at the head of a French army. That would be glorious indeed.

When he came back to France in February he had told Vergennes and the king, in a spirit of frankness, that the American people did not care to have a French army in their midst. What they needed from France was money, clothes, guns, and the manufactured articles which Great Britain had formerly supplied.

In saying that the marquis felt that he had done his duty, and then, at the suggestion of Vergennes he had prepared a memoir called "Some Thoughts on an Expedition in America." France was now about to send a fleet and an army across the sea, regardless of American coolness to the project—and not primarily for the purpose of freeing the colonies, though that was also a desirable objective, but to save French territories and colonial possessions. It was a plan to divert the British and keep them occupied on the American continent.

From Lafayette's point of view he was absolutely, and without any question, the logical candidate for commander in chief of the French expedition. It appears, however, that he was the only person who thought so.

Vergennes and the other ministers were almost swamped with his letters and applications. He pointed out to them that the French commander should "know how to humor the dispositions of Congress and the different dispositions of each state." Well, Lafayette—as he said himself—knew how to do that. Continuing, he wrote:

. . . if the intimate friendship of the general, if the confidence of the army and the people, if . . . my popularity gives me this boldness, supposing that I should command the detachment on land, I stake my head on avoiding even the shadow of jealousy and dispute.

It was absurd and foolish of him to expect the command, or even to have the faintest hope of it. Had it been given to him all the veteran generals, most of them old enough to be his father, would have been mortally offended.

The command went to the Comte de Rochambeau, a soldier of long experience. He had been in military service more than thirty years. Lafayette was sent on ahead in a French frigate to announce the coming of the fleet and army, and to assist in preparations for their reception. He arrived in Boston on April 26, 1780.

The expeditionary force of fifty-five hundred men—accompanied by five frigates and five ships of the line—did not reach America until July 10th. The expedition made its headquarters at Newport, which the British had abandoned.

Lafayette, in the meantime, had written long letters to Rochambeau, to be given to the latter on his arrival. These epistles told the commander just what he ought to do, and were written in the tone of one who knew the whole American situation. The pilot boat that met Rochambeau's fleet carried three of these military essays. Rochambeau acknowledged them on July 12th, but made no comment on them to Lafayette. To Vergennes he wrote:

On my arrival I found letters from the Marquis de Lafayette awaiting me; they are too voluminous for copies to be sent, and they contain a mass of excited and rather incoherent proposals.

4

The marquis, almost bursting with news, projects and gossip, joined Washington at Morristown, New Jersey, on May 10th. There was not much to do at American headquarters except to sit around and talk. Washington was waiting for the British to make a move. He thought an attack on New York by the combined French and

American armies had an excellent chance of succeeding. It seems to us now, as we look back nearly one hundred and fifty years, that Washington's plan was a very good one. Sir Henry Clinton had dispatched a considerable number of troops to the South, and part of his fleet had gone there too.

Clinton's main idea was to subdue the colonies piecemeal, one by one, beginning with the weakest of them. His first effort was made—in that year of 1780—in Georgia and South Carolina. There were many Tories in each of these states—or colonies—and he expected them to give active assistance to the British. Clinton called his southern campaign a pacifying measure; the colonies were to be "pacified" and brought back to peace under British rule. As chief pacifier he named Lord Cornwallis, who was put in command of the southern armies with authority to pacify by hanging, burning houses, seizing cattle, destroying crops, putting civilians in jail, and all other well-known measures of pacification. After Georgia and South Carolina had been pacified Cornwallis was to go on into North Carolina and Virginia and do some more pacifying.

In New York—on Manhattan Island—Clinton decided to remain, and his principal reason was to keep Washington near at hand. Suppose Washington and his army should depart for the South. It was quite possible that they might defeat Cornwallis. Besides, Clinton wanted to keep New York City in British hands. How could he do that with the French in Rhode Island and Washington in New Jersey, if he should send most of his troops and ships to South Carolina?

Lord Cornwallis usually defeated the American forces in the South whenever he met them. At Camden, in South Carolina, he destroyed for all practical purposes the army of General Gates. Nevertheless, and notwithstanding these crushing defeats, the people in the pacified states would not stay pacified. Invisible marksmen shot at British soldiers, and they were first-class marksmen. Detachments sent from the army of Cornwallis to provide food for men and horses sometimes never returned; even today their fate is a mystery. Intrepid American patriots, the so-called "swamp foxes," lived in a bewildering map of land and water; now and then they came forth, slaughtered the British, and disappeared silently in their queer world of sluggish yellow streams and tangled vines.

5

Let us now return to Washington, Lafayette and Rochambeau.

Within ten days after the French expedition had landed Washington sent Lafayette to Newport as his envoy and spokesman. The young man carried a letter from the general to the French commander in which Rochambeau was assured that Lafayette had his full confidence and that "he is perfectly acquainted with my sentiments and opinions. . . . All the information he gives, and all the propositions he makes, I entreat you to consider as coming from me. I request you will settle all arrangements whatsoever with him."

Washington seldom failed in tact, but that was a tactless letter. It would have been much better, in the way of promoting harmony and co-operation, if Washington had sent the marquis simply as an intelligent, well-informed messenger or aide. But he gave him the status of a plenipotentiary with extraordinary powers. That displeased Rochambeau and he did not mind saying so. He had expected Washington to visit him in person, which was the proper thing to do, but the commander in chief—as he explained—felt that he should not leave the army just at that time.

At any rate, Rochambeau had no intention of discussing large-scale military operations with a youth of twenty-three. He would not listen to the project for a joint attack on New York and said bluntly that he would deal with Washington, and no one else.

Washington was disturbed by Lafayette's account of his interview with the testy and thin-skinned French commander. He dictated a letter to Rochambeau and Ternay—the French admiral—outlining his plan for their co-operation. It was explained to them that Washington anticipated some action by the British, that he had to remain with the army, and that he would have the pleasure of meeting the general and the admiral at some time in the not-distant future. However, Washington did not sign this letter. It was signed by Lafayette. Really, it seems to have been an absurdly inept way of handling the situation.

In this undiplomatic communication Lafayette said—or Washington said, through the marquis—that the French, sitting down in Rhode Island, were of no service to the Americans. The reply from Rochambeau to Lafayette was short and sarcastic. "As to your suggestion, my dear Marquis," he wrote, "that the position of the

French in Rhode Island is of no service to the Americans, I shall observe that I have not yet heard it said that it has done any of them any harm."

He went on to say that the position of the French corps probably had something to do with Clinton's withdrawal into New York. Also, "that while the French fleet is being watched here by a superior and assembled naval force, in fact the coast of America is undisturbed, your privateers take valuable prizes, and your merchant marine has full liberty . . . Moreover, I await the orders of my generalissimo [meaning Washington] and I implore him to accord to the admiral and me an interview."

Simultaneously there was also a letter to Washington from Rochambeau. He said that the British fleet was blockading the French fleet in Rhode Island, and that he was expecting both naval and military reinforcements. Until they came he could not co-operate effectively.

The truth of the matter is that Rochambeau had no love for America or the Americans. To the student of history it is quite plain that he did not intend to co-operate actively so long as any grave risk was likely to be incurred. However, he was entirely right in his assertion that the mere presence of the French was acting as a check on the freehanded operations of the British in New England and the northern states.

But the war had been transferred to the South. There the fighting was being done. In the North the British held only New York City and the American, British and French armies remained idle, looking at each other. In the northern states the people went about their occupations in peace. The war had become an echo, a reverberation of distant thunder in the southern sky.

6

Washington and Rochambeau did not meet until September 20, 1780, at an arranged conference in Hartford. With Washington went Lafayette and his French aides; also Generals Knox and Hamilton, besides a group of minor officers and servants. It was a handsome cavalcade that rode across the pleasant Connecticut hills, brown and gold in the early autumn air.

Lafayette had learned a few hard lessons. He had found out,

at last, that both the French and American officers were jealous of him. They did not dislike him as a person, but they thought he was unmannerly in being so positive and self-assertive in the presence of older and wiser men. At the Hartford conference he said little or nothing. Merely listened.

The conference produced a lot of words that sounded well but perhaps meant very little, and that was all. Washington and Rochambeau had met. The French returned to Newport; Washington and his staff rode back to the Hudson over the hilly roads.

Washington wanted to show the fortress of West Point to his officers and friends. Gouvion and Duportail—on Lafayette's staff—wanted to see it again too; they had designed the fortifications. Benedict Arnold, trusted and efficient officer of the American army, was in command of West Point. All of them knew him and his charming wife and they looked forward with pleasure to spending a day with them. But General Arnold was a traitor; he had just sold the plans of the West Point defenses to the British. Major André, a handsome and popular young officer of the British army, was the intermediary. André had been caught within the American lines with the plans of West Point concealed in his stockings. When the news of his capture reached West Point General Arnold was at breakfast. He rose from the table and departed immediately. A British sloop of war was in the river. He managed to reach it and then he had the American crew of his own boat taken on board and kept as prisoners. Mrs. Arnold and her baby were left behind.

Washington and Lafayette arrived soon after the exposure of the treasonable plot and the flight of Benedict Arnold. Imagine, if you can, that eventful day—Mrs. Arnold in hysterics, the cloud of tragedy, the garrison in fear and trepidation, the silence of the river and the encircling hills. That afternoon Washington rode around the fortifications. They were in disrepair; breaches in the walls; guns out of commission; the scene was already prepared for an easy capture by the enemy. Before the sun had set Major John André had been brought in as a captive—a spy—and confined in the guardhouse.

The marquis was a member of the court-martial that tried Major André. He was found guilty, sentenced to death, and was hanged on October 2, 1780.

In December of that year Lafayette got a leave of absence and went around, here and there, with a group of French officers who wanted to see the country and meet the people. It was a gay excursion, despite the bad weather and the hardships of the war. They went to the battlefield of Brandywine; there Lafayette showed them the exact spot where he had received his wound. Also to Barren Hill and its famous ford; and to Philadelphia, where dinners and dances were given in their honor.

Among this company of travelers was the Vicomte de Noailles, who was the husband of Louise, a sister of Adrienne de Lafayette. The reader will recall that Noailles ardently desired to come to America with Lafayette, but was prevented from leaving France by the stern injunction of the Duc d'Ayen.

The Marquis de Chastellux made the trip also. He was a man of literary distinction, a meticulous observer and a born journalist. His mind was a mental pincushion. He traveled extensively in America after the war and his book, *Voyages de M. le Marquis de Chastellux dans l'Amérique Septentrionale*, is the best account I have ever seen of the life and manners of the Americans of that period. Seeing everything, he wrote of all he saw, the most trivial as well as the most profound, yet even his trivial observations were significant.*

Here is his description of a dinner at Washington's headquarters:

The repast was in the English fashion, consisting of eight or ten large dishes of butcher's meat, and poultry, with vegetables of several sorts, followed by a second course of pastry, comprised under the two denominations of pies and puddings. After this the cloth was taken off, and apples and a great quantity of nuts were served, which General Washington usually continues eating for two hours, toasting and conversing all the time.

They were great eaters in those days, and when they sat down at a table they intended to remain there a long time.

About half past seven we rose from the table, and immediately the servants came to shorten it, and convert it into a round one. . . . I was surprised at this maneuver, and asked the reason for it; I was told they were going to lay the cloth for supper.

De Chastellux did not see how he could find room for supper right after the end of a prodigious dinner, so he retired to his room.

* There is an excellent English translation published under the title of *Travels in North America in the years 1780, 1781 and 1782.*

But in a short time a servant came to tell him that the general "expected me at supper."

The supper was composed of three or four light dishes, some fruit, and above all, a great abundance of nuts. . . . The cloth being soon removed, a few bottles of good claret and Madeira were placed on the table.

He goes on then to tell of the almost interminable rounds of toasts, which always seemed appalling to the French officers, though —being polite by instinct and training—they did their part.

The habitual and untiring industry of the Americans made a great impression on these traveling Frenchmen. They were astonished to find that men of wealth were simple in their ways, that even rich people had jobs and kept regular hours, that occupation and industry were dominant notes in American life. There was hardly anything like it in France. Wealthy people there knew hardly anything of their own affairs, which were left to business agents, notaries or intendants.

CHAPTER VIII

CORNWALLIS AND YORKTOWN

I

LAFAYETTE detested inactivity. He wanted to be doing something all the time and preferably something with a streak of danger in it. Settling down in a winter camp and waiting for spring, or for the enemy to make a move, was to his mind a perfect example of human futility. He did not possess the patience of Washington; far from it. But in action he had a large capacity for endurance. He was willing to sustain hardships and face imminent danger so long as there was an opportunity to distinguish himself.

As soon as he came back from the jaunt with his French companions he resumed his place at American headquarters and began to plead with Washington for an assignment that would lead to meeting the enemy in battle.

At that time—in January, 1781—military affairs stood in this pattern: The British held New York City. They held Charleston and Savannah and all of South Carolina and Georgia, as far as the holding of those turbulent states could be done in the presence of American sharpshooters and rebel bands and "swamp foxes." The British also had a hold on North Carolina, where General Nathanael Greene was retreating before Lord Cornwallis.

The French army, under Rochambeau, was still at Newport. It had not fired a shot since its coming on July 10th of the previous year. Washington's army was in northern New Jersey in winter quarters. The Americans held the whole length of the Hudson above New York City. They also held New England, New Jersey, Delaware and Pennsylvania.

The British high command gave Benedict Arnold a commission as brigadier general soon after his escape into their lines and sent him to Virginia to do as much damage as he could. His expedition went by water under the protection of the British fleet. Arnold fell upon the almost defenseless state like the seven plagues

88

of Egypt. He burned houses, took horses and cattle, destroyed crops and seized slaves who were sold by the British in the West Indies.

It would be difficult for a historian to set forth Washington's full opinion of the traitor Arnold in printable words. To capture Arnold—alive, that he might be hanged—was one of the ardent desires of the commander in chief. And, of course, he wanted to do what he could to protect the state of Virginia.

Washington assigned Lafayette on February 20, 1781, to duty in Virginia for the purpose of putting an end to Arnold's depredations, and to take Arnold, if possible. Twelve hundred men constituted his command; and the French were to send, by sea from Newport, about twelve hundred more.

The selection of the marquis for this important command caused much criticism. The young man knew nothing of Virginia; he had never been there, and it was a country of bad roads and bewildering rivers. But there were other American officers of poise and experience who knew a great deal about Virginia. One of the urgent purposes of the expedition was to get the Virginians to defend themselves, to organize their defense, and to get them to furnish food and forage for the troops. Could a twenty-three-year-old foreigner do that?

In reply to a protest against Lafayette's appointment Washington said:

It is my opinion that the command of the troops cannot be in better hands than the Marquis's. He possesses uncommon military talents: is of a quick and sound military judgment; and besides these, he is of a very conciliating temper and perfectly sober—which are qualities that rarely combine in the same person. And were I to add that some men will gain as much experience in the course of three or four years as some others will in ten or a dozen, you cannot deny the fact and attack me on that ground.

That was high praise, indeed, from the cautious and reserved commander in chief. Did he ever say as much for any other officer? If so, I do not recall the officer or the occasion.

2

But the plan did not work out at all. Yet it was not Lafayette's fault; his competency on this particular expedition, and until the end of the war, belongs to the gold-medal class. The snarls and tangles may be seen clearly if we describe the arrangement for the co-operation of the French and Americans in this Virginia anti-Arnold campaign.

Lafayette was to march his force to the head of Chesapeake Bay and put his men on any boats he could find in the neighborhood. Then he was to wait. The French ships, with their twelve hundred men on board, would go to the entrance to the Chesapeake. The French land force would be put ashore and a fighting vessel was to be sent to the head of the bay, some two hundred miles, to escort Lafayette and his command down to the place where the French had landed. Then they were to combine and pursue Arnold.

The American and French high commands agreed to that arrangement with perfect sincerity, but a lot of other people accepted it verbally only and with very serious, silent reservations. The selection of the marquis as the head of the American participation showed bad judgment, or perhaps ignorance, on the part of Washington, who should have known—as many others did know—that the officers in Rochambeau's expeditionary force, with the exception of the Duc de Lauzun, the Vicomte de Noailles (Lafayette's brother-in-law), and a few others, were exceedingly jealous of Lafayette. On the way from France they had asked Rochambeau not to assign them for duty under the Marquis de Lafayette, and declared that they would not serve under him. Nevertheless, Lafayette was designated as the ranking officer on this combined expedition.

Such animosities are small and puerile, but a biographer has to look at them and weigh their effects if he would know the truth. These silly spites and jealousies seem to exhibit themselves more frequently among military and naval men than among any other class of human beings—except people in theatrical life.

The tacit intention of the French officers was to leave Lafayette stranded at the head of the bay, two hundred miles from his destination, while the French fought Arnold alone. They considered themselves entirely able to handle the situation.

Lafayette waited for some news of the French ships. None came. Around the middle of March he took his command, in their flotilla of small boats, down the bay to Annapolis, so as to be nearer the scene of possible operations.

The French fleet, with its military force aboard, was greatly delayed in sailing from Newport. The British, well informed as to their movements, sent forth from New York a naval armament which met the French at the entrance to Chesapeake Bay, and drove them back. The adventure, from beginning to end, accomplished nothing at all.

ᐧ   The marquis and his twelve hundred men were left at Annapolis, not knowing what to do. Orders came from Washington. Lafayette was to march into Virginia and co-operate with General Greene against Cornwallis.

It was a ragamuffin outfit, those troops of Lafayette's. Many were barefoot; some had no shirts or hats; others had no trousers except a bunch of rags gathered about their thighs. The Revolutionary treasury was as bare as a bone. There was nothing in it for anybody; all salaries were unpaid. Lafayette stopped at Baltimore for a few days and borrowed, against a draft on his agents in France, the sum of two thousand guineas which was spent with Baltimore clothing merchants. Every man was provided, at his commander's expense, with a pair of overalls, a hat, shoes, underwear and a shirt.*

After the marquis had attended the dinners in Baltimore, had drunk the toasts, and had kissed the hands of the ladies, the little army went on its way. There were many desertions. Virtually his whole command was made up of men from the North; they believed that if they should go into the South they would die of malaria, of heat, of God-knows-what. Why fight for Virginia, anyway? To them Virginia was a foreign land. The petty, foolish, home-defense notion was one of the delusions that was like a brake—a drag—on the American Revolution. North Carolina, for example, did not care very much about what happened to Connecticut, but "just let the British come here and we shall show them what we can do."

Lafayette handled the matter of desertions in a way that should appeal to any student of psychology. He got his command assembled and addressed the men. He said, not in these words but in substance: "We are having many desertions. Those who desert are afraid to face the enemy. I shall meet the British and I am not afraid. If any man here is afraid and does not want to go on with me let him step out of ranks and say that he wants to leave me. In that case I will let him go. He shall be provided with a pass to go back to his home or to his former regiment." Not one man came

* That expenditure was eventually repaid from the treasury of the United States.

forward and confessed that he did not want to accompany the marquis, who had stated the situation in such a way that anyone who took the other side would admit lack of courage.

Not long after the arrival in Virginia of the marquis and his little army he got a letter, sent under a flag of truce, from Benedict Arnold. It contained a proposal to exchange prisoners. Lafayette declined to receive it or to have any communication with the traitor, but he wrote that he would receive a letter from any other English officer. Arnold was furious and returned an answer in which he threatened to send his American prisoners to the West Indies. He did not do that, however. Not long after the letter episode Arnold was recalled and returned to New York. He was never captured. At the end of the war he went to England and lived there for the rest of his life.

The marquis wrote to Washington that he had refused to accept Arnold's letters, and the commander in chief replied that "your conduct upon every occasion meets my approbation, but in none more than your refusing to hold a correspondence with Arnold."

3

Lafayette and Cornwallis were agile opponents in the cockpit of Virginia during the months of May, June and July. Their armies went crisscross over the state, coming to blows in skirmishes but never in a decisive battle.

A map of their movements looks like an intricate puzzle and would interest no one but a student of military history.

The campaign reflects great credit on Lafayette. In numbers the British had about five times as many men as the marquis, and he was usually running away with Cornwallis in pursuit. But at the right moment he would stop, turn in his tracks, and give Cornwallis a blow—not a deadly one, but one that was heavy enough to hold the British awhile and deflect their course. He wrote to Washington:

Were I to fight a battle I should be cut to pieces, the militia dispersed and the arms lost . . . I am therefore determined to skirmish, but not to engage too far. . . . Were I anyways equal to the enemy I should be extremely happy in my present command, but I am not strong enough even to be beaten.

At that time Lafayette and Alexander Hamilton were friends. To Hamilton the marquis wrote that the enemy was so much stronger than he in every way "that I durst not venture to listen to my fondness for enterprise. To speak truth I was afraid of myself as much as of the enemy." It is, indeed, a distressing situation when a natural-born fighter has to run away from his opponent. But he was not always running. By clever maneuvers he managed to force Cornwallis out of Richmond and to push him down toward the sea.

Cornwallis was in a most uncomfortable position. He was in an enemy country while Lafayette was in a friendly country, which made a great difference. The British general was far from his base of supplies. Roads were blocked before him and behind him. He was not strong enough to conquer the state while Lafayette's small army was in being, nor was he strong enough even to occupy the important towns. Nor did he know how to get out of Virginia. If he had gone northward he would have encountered Washington's army, and probably Rochambeau's, before he could reach New York. Had he turned toward the south to seek the shelter of the fortifications of Charleston that would have meant hundreds of miles of disastrous fighting. And there was Lafayette constantly dodging around him and before him like a toreador in the presence of an enraged bull.*

Eventually Cornwallis and his army drifted, through these puss-in-the-corner tactics, into the squeezed little corner of Yorktown—a peninsula like a bottle, of which Lafayette made himself the cork.

In their pursuit of each other the armies of Lafayette and Cornwallis covered eleven hundred miles.

The British army was penned up in Yorktown in the latter part of August.

In the midst of the campaign the marquis took the time to write a letter to the Vicomte de Noailles, his brother-in-law, who was in Newport, on the subject of a flood of gossip that had drifted over from Paris about the reputed love affair of Lafayette and the Comtesse d'Hunolstein. According to the gossips, the Duc de

---

* It is interesting to note that one of the personal servants of Cornwallis was in the pay of Lafayette, and that copies of the noble lord's important papers, orders of the day, and lists of troops were sent with only a small delay to the marquis. By what method they were sent I do not profess to know.

Chartres was infuriated by Lafayette's fond regard for his mistress, and was seeking revenge. The marquis wrote to Noailles:

I have something to tell you about the spiteful treatment that has been accorded to a person whom I love; the result of that pleasantry will very likely be to render her forever unhappy and to bring me to daggers drawn with a man against whom I can only, in all conscience, half defend myself ... it is rather annoying that they should come to search me two thousand leagues [sic] from Paris to be the hero of the gossip of the hour, and a woman who is two thousand leagues from the coquetries and intrigues of Paris, to make her the victim of some wicked imagination; write me, my dear brother, if they talk to you about it in jest, or if they really make of it a serious scandal.

According to historical tradition, or the trend of legends, Lafayette was a great lover. I do not believe it, but I am willing to admit that the record—or known facts—of the amatory life of any man who has been dead one hundred years is invariably dim and uncertain. There is no doubt, however, that he did have love affairs now and then, which does not prove, by any means, that he was a Casanova. His amatory relation to the Comtesse d'Hunolstein seems to be verified despite his reference to "wicked imagination" in the letter quoted above; and his liaison with Madame de Simiane was well known in Paris for years.

Nevertheless, Lafayette was a man's man. He was of a highly masculine type, and men of that kind seldom amount to a great deal in the field of amours. His great admirations—in America and in France—were for men, and not for women. But do not, for a moment, think that I mean to imply that his liking for men was unnatural and abnormal. He liked men because of their achievements, their courage, their endurance, their hardness, their ability.

The distinguished lovers in history, as well as the great contemporary amorists, invariably have a streak of femininity in their make-up. They not only love women, but they also like them. They are friends of women, and can be in their company without feeling superior or inferior, bold or shy. To such men love affairs are simply a matter of course. They have many and they take them lightly. The women concerned also take them lightly.

He was not a prude, nor any kind of moralist. The point I am making here is that he did not really care very much for women. He went through Paris in 1777 without saying good-bye to his young wife, who was pregnant, nor did he write to her until he was halfway across the Atlantic ocean. She did not receive his letters for months after they were written. Yet he really did love Adrienne, in his way.

But Lafayette was a *poseur*, as all men are, and all women. I have never met a person in my life who did not try to make an impression which was superior and above themselves, and that means everybody from servants to statesmen. St. Francis of Assisi, long ago, when he was invited to dinner with the pope, brought with him a lot of discarded food, or garbage, that he had picked up in the streets, and he ate that instead of the sumptuous dinner that stood before him. That was intended to indicate humility, but it was really an exhibition of vanity. Even thieves and gangsters claim to be more vicious than they really are. The attitude of posing is natural. It is probably the inspiration of human progress. If you pose in any fashion you must live up to your pretense, or try to, at any rate. Among the French nobility a man who amounted to anything at all was supposed to have mistresses, burning love affairs, and play the amorous gallant every day in the year. Consequently many men who cared little for women attempted to live up to the standard of the times.

4

Before Cornwallis had been maneuvered into the bottle neck of the Yorktown peninsula notable events had taken place in the North. The American Revolution was rising from the dead and was destined to walk the earth potently with a sword in its hand.

Washington and Rochambeau had met at Wethersfield, in Connecticut, for a second conference on May 21st. The French, after their long inactivity, were ready to co-operate with Washington. They expected the early arrival of more ships of war from France; also a number of transports with clothing, munitions and other supplies for the American army.

There was information that Sir Henry Clinton's force had been reduced considerably by the sending of troops to the South, and Washington thought the time was opportune for a combined attack on New York. Throughout the war that was his fixed idea, and there can be hardly a doubt that the taking of New York in the summer of 1781 would have put an end tó the war. But the project was involved in great difficulties. The British were strongly fortified on Manhattan Island and their fleet stood in the harbor.

It was Rochambeau's opinion the two armies should go to Virginia and bag Cornwallis. Washington did not want to do that; if the Americans departed for the South, the whole of the northern region would be open to Clinton's operations. Rochambeau did not know the country and its bad roads. It would be a prodigious task to get the armies to Virginia; and suppose Cornwallis and his force had been taken back to New York by a British fleet in the meantime?

The Americans and the French would look very foolish—would they not?—when they got down to Virginia and found themselves facing a general emptiness of opposition. Washington said he thought Lafayette and Greene were able to check Cornwallis. Finally Rochambeau was convinced, and a plan was agreed upon for a siege of Manhattan. The French army moved out of Rhode Island and had reached the Hudson River on July 3rd.

After the French-American conference a plan for the siege of New York had been written out at Washington's headquarters, and a copy of it was sent by courier to Rochambeau. Tories intercepted the bearer and sent the plan to Clinton, in New York. In the long story of historical accidents this event stands in a high place. It prevented Clinton from sending reinforcements to Cornwallis, and it kept the British fleet at New York until it was too late to be effective in the Chesapeake.

The plan had been suddenly changed, and Clinton was unaware of it. The Comte de Grasse, French admiral, with a naval armament much superior to the British fleet in American waters, was about to arrive in the French West Indies. Rochambeau, by a swift vessel, had sent him a letter about the present situation and had asked him to come to the Chesapeake. The admiral had agreed—but he wrote that he could not stay long. Then came the news that Cornwallis was in his fatal pen of Yorktown.

The American and French armies were on their way. De Grasse's fleet reached Hampton Roads on August 30th. There were three thousand infantry soldiers aboard, under the Marquis de Saint-Simon. Lafayette's troops had been increased by Virginia militia; he had about four thousand men in his command, of whom a large number were untrained and were unaccustomed to the soldierly life. It is almost needless to say that all of Cornwallis' six thousand were hardened regulars, inured to battle and to rigorous discipline. Saint-Simon wanted to attack the redoubts of Yorktown immediately, to win them by French valor alone. But Lafayette would not consent. His friend General Washington was on his way, and the marquis made up his mind to wait until the general came.

Everything that had been planned in this campaign worked out with perfect precision, which is the rarest of all phenomena in military affairs. The French naval force got there before the British because Clinton, in remote New York, had pondered too long over the intercepted document which set forth a plan for a siege of New York. Eventually he learned that the Americans and the French were on their way to the South, and he sent his fighting ships hurriedly to the Chesapeake. They got there too late. The Comte de Grasse had already arrived. He met the British fleet on September 5, 1781, and in a naval battle the British were defeated and driven back to New York. After that event Cornwallis was in a hopeless position.

Washington's and Rochambeau's armies got to Yorktown in the last week of September. Siege guns had been landed from the French ships and they roared day and night. They blew the town to pieces and Cornwallis ate his scanty meals in a smoke-blackened house amid the thunder of cannonades. He looked across the bay, hoping to see the ships of the British navy, but there was nothing on the sea line except the tall masts of the French fleet.

What could one do? Nothing at all. It is fate. Cornwallis surrendered on October 19, 1781.

5

The war still continued as an idea, yet everybody—in England and America—was fully aware that it was all over. Nothing remained but the peace negotiations. There were no more battles.

The conduct of the marquis in Virginia had greatly enhanced his reputation among American and French officers. Rochambeau wrote to Vergennes that the Marquis de Lafayette "has conducted himself perfectly in the Virginia campaign."

Washington wrote to Lafayette:

Be assured, my dear Marquis, your conduct meets my warmest approbation, as it must that of everybody. Should it ever be said that my attachment to you betrayed me into partiality, you have only to appeal to facts to refute any such charge.

Lafayette was granted an indeterminate leave of absence from the American army by Congress and was also given a vote of thanks. He sailed from Boston for France on December 23, 1781.

His military service in America lasted altogether about four years. During that time he had expended not only all his income, but seven hundred and fifty thousand francs of his capital. I must confess that I do not know what he did with this vast sum, nor do I believe he knew, or cared. He gave away money right and left; he paid the men in his command when Congress was unable to pay them; at times he entertained his friends and officers on a lavish scale; he supported numbers of indigent Frenchmen.

The boy had grown up. When he came he was an immature youth of nineteen. In four years he had gained more experience than most men acquire in twenty years.

On the day he sailed from Boston he wrote a farewell letter to Washington. He said:

Adieu, my dear General. I know your heart so well that I am sure that no distance can alter your attachment to me. With the same candor I assure you that my love, my respect, my gratitude for you, are above expression; that, at the moment of leaving you, I felt more than ever the strength of those friendly ties that forever bind me to you, and that I anticipate the pleasure, the most wished-for pleasure, to be again with you, and, by my zeal and services, to gratify the feelings of my respect and affection.

To my way of thinking this letter is very interesting, as is all the rest of the correspondence between Washington and the young marquis. It is an expression of affection, and Washington certainly inspired an affectionate emotion in hardly anybody else. People were, as a rule, scared half to death by him. He was so impressive and cold that those who met him were awe-stricken and almost speechless in his presence, and they did not write him affectionate letters. If they had done so he would have resented it. But to Lafayette Washington was a father, and he thought of Lafayette as one thinks of a son.

CHAPTER IX

THE OLD REGIME IN FRANCE

I

ON HIS return to France in 1782 the young marquis—then twenty-four years old—found himself the outstanding hero of the time. His celebrity was greater than that of Rochambeau or de Grasse, or of any other distinguished officer under the French flag.

The king conferred upon him the much coveted Cross of St. Louis and raised him to the military rank of *maréchal de camp*, which was the French equivalent of a brigadier general.

The populace gave him an ovation whenever he appeared in public.

The king and his ministers gave him their earnest attention when he discoursed on America.

His business agents gave him an account of his finances. They were still in a flourishing condition, notwithstanding his prodigious expenditures during the American war.

The Comtesse de Simiane gave him her virtue, or whatever there was left of it.* The aged and tottering Duc de Richelieu, with sixty years of bedroom gallantries in his past—but none discernible in his future—declared that the conquest of Mme. de Simiane was a greater victory than the defeat of the British in America.

The young marquis loved the renown that encased him like a crust of honey. The story of his exploits went far beyond anything that he deserved. He was called "the savior of Washington" and the "liberator of America." The truth is that he did not liberate America, nor did he save Washington, who was quite capable of saving himself. To him, the marquis was just a pleasant, courageous, sensible, lovable young man for whom he had a deep affection.

* Mme. de Simiane was a sister of Charles Damas, a noble who served in America under Rochambeau. He was a close friend of Lafayette. Mme. de Simiane was considered the most beautiful woman at court.

Somebody called Lafayette "a hero of two worlds." It was a phrase that he liked immensely. He acquired an exaggerated air of self-importance, but who wouldn't in the circumstances?

The venerable Benjamin Franklin, who was still in Paris as the chief envoy of the United States in the peace negotiations, patted the marquis on the back, and at times he was delegated by the American mission to call upon the men at the head of affairs in France and ascertain their views.

2

The contrast in social structure, government, habits and manners between the America which Lafayette had recently left and the France to which he had returned was certainly impressive. Yet he says little about it. In his letters to Washington at this time he seldom mentions the striking differences of the two civilizations. It is reasonable to assume that he looked upon them as inevitable and unworthy of comment. He did write, however, that "kings are good for nothing, unless it be to spoil everything, even when their intentions are good." Nevertheless, in spite of these sentiments, he endeavored during the French Revolution to promote a national government on the English pattern with a king at its head.

We cannot understand Lafayette with any sort of clarity at all unless we recognize and accept the fuzziness of his opinions, the pervading indecisiveness of his mind.* In this respect he was certainly no exception, for it is a characteristic of all but a few outstanding individuals of each generation. There are not many clearcut personalities in history, and all of them may be justly classified as fanatics. Peter the Great was one; so were William Lloyd Garrison, and Samuel Adams, and Karl Marx, and Savonarola, and Eugene Debs and Jefferson Davis, and Robespierre. All those whom I have named were one-idea men; their minds were made up; if there was a side to an argument which was in conflict with their own views they did not even want to hear it, much less consider it.

Most people, when confronted by an important problem within a social pattern, are pulled both ways, or several ways. They cannot

* Years afterward Talleyrand said, in speaking of Lafayette: "His ambition, and his efforts to distinguish himself, do not seem his own, but rather to have been taught him. Whatever he does seems foreign to his nature, he always acts as though he follows someone else's advice."

make up their minds, and their attitudes—when decisions must be made—are frequently determined by inessential and negligible factors.

Many of Lafayette's contemporaries considered him insincere; during the French Revolution they declared that they did not know which side he was on. They did not know, indeed, and Lafayette himself was equally ignorant. But he was not insincere—not intentionally.

Certainly he was not lacking in intelligence. The trouble with him was an inability to co-ordinate his ideas and observations and arrange them in a tangible pattern.

He was by birth, instinct and training a *grand seigneur* of France. He was too high in rank and too wealthy to come in personal contact with peasants and workmen; all his dealings with them were carried on through his agents.

Then, in his youth, he came to America. He was stirred to the bottom of his soul by the brave resistance of the colonials against the mighty British Empire. As an ardent fighter in our revolutionary struggle he acquired a fairly complete set of republican ideas. He was Washington's pupil and admirer. But the revered father of our country did not believe in democracies; he was a *bourgeois*, a middle-class landowner.

On his return to France Lafayette took his place again in the tradional pattern of French aristocratic life. He did all that a distinguished noble was supposed to do—had a mistress, attended the fetes and dances at Versailles, lived in spacious luxury and dawdled in the salons of great houses.

Yet all the time he was trying to reconcile his republican notions with the aristocratic tradition, an attempt that was inherently impossible.

3

In the 1780's the old regime was nearing its end. It was still powerful in authority, yet it was senile and vicious in character and it was destined to die violently in a welter of blood and riot. But no one thought so; the French Revolution was as unexpected as a cyclone would be in Massachusetts. People of intelligence knew that something would have to be done, that the system was in urgent need of reform, but they were quite sure that the changes would be made in an orderly manner—and by degrees.

In theory the king was the owner of the kingdom of France, and all that was contained in it. The nation had no constitution, either written or implied. Louis XV said, in 1766, to the Parlement of Paris,* that:

The sovereign authority is vested in my person. . . . The legislative power, without dependence and without division, exists in myself alone. Public security emanates wholly from myself; I am its supreme custodian. My people are one only with me; national rights and interests, of which an attempt is made to form a body separate from those of the monarch, are necessarily combined with my own and only rest in my hands.

This statement of Louis XV, in spite of its astounding egoism and expression of authority, was rigidly correct. He did have the power and the public sanction to send any person in the kingdom to death, or to torture, or to lifelong imprisonment, without giving a reason. And he could seize and hold anyone's property if he cared to do it, even though the subject so deprived had committed no offense at all. He could make new laws and disregard old ones. He alone had the power to tax, and he could spend the national revenue as he saw fit.

But there were intangible checks on his authority. While it was nominally absolute, there were certain immemorial privileges and customs which he was bound to respect.

In considering this state of affairs one should keep in mind that such an extensive and despotic autocracy is quite unmanageable without the delegation of authority. No man ever lived who could spread himself out sufficiently to look into all the problems that might come before him and make the necessary decisions.

Consequently the government was really carried on by groups. of favored courtiers. They constituted what we Americans call a "ring," but it was a ring that was never checked up, supervised or called to account. An ordinary citizen, even if he were highly intelligent and public-spirited, did not know—nor could he find out—the amount of governmental income or expenditure. The treasury did not make public statements of its finances; many even of the

* The *Parlements* had no legislative functions. Farther on I shall say more about them.

great nobles close to the king at the gorgeous court of Versailles had little or no idea of where the money came from or of how it was expended.

The extravagance was incredible, or so it seems to a twentieth century observer. Thousands of highly paid public offices were merely honorary with no duties at all attached to them. Mme. de Taillard, so-called governess of the children of Louis XV, received one hundred and fifteen thousand francs a year for which she did virtually nothing. The head huntsman in the king's forest of Fontainebleau sold twenty thousand francs' worth of rabbits on his own account each year. The king spent thirty-six million francs on Mme. de Pompadour, one of his historic mistresses. Marie Antoinette's daughter, as a baby, had eighty attendants. What in the world could these eighty people find to do around a child's cradle? Their offices were simply well-paid sinecures.

In the palace at Versailles there were two hundred and ninety-five cooks; and in the king's stables there were four thousand horses. Taine says:

The head chambermaids to the queen ... paid 12,000 francs, make in reality 50,000 francs by the sale of candles lighted during the day. Augeard, private secretary, whose place is set down at 900 livres a year, confesses that it is worth to him two hundred thousand. . . . Madame de Lamballe, superintendent of the queen's household, inscribed for 6000 francs, gets one hundred and fifty thousand.*

The eldest son of M. de Machault was appointed "intendant of the classes," whatever that means. At that time no one seemed to know what his duties were, or ought to be. It turned out, however, that all he had to do was to sign his name twice a year. For this he received an annual emolument of 18,000 francs.

Mme. du Barry was one of the many mistresses of Louis XV. She began her career as a milliner, but found that occupation too laborious. Then she became a professional prostitute. An intriguing courtier managed to get her within the range of the king's notice, and he was attracted by her. Until her royal protector died, in 1774, the national treasury paid her three hundred thousand francs a month for her personal expenses.

* Taine, *The Ancient Regime,* p. 68.

4

There were three classes of people in France: the Nobility, the Clergy, and the Third Estate. The Third Estate included all the common people; in fact, it included everyone who was not a noble or a priest, regardless of wealth, intelligence and education.

The number of noble families in the decade before the Revolution is not definitely known, but according to well-considered estimates it would appear there were about thirty thousand of them, or somewhere around one hundred and thirty thousand persons in all. France, at that period, had a total population of about twenty-five millions—and that, too, is an estimate—but it may be accepted as a means of comparison. It seems, therefore, that one person in two hundred, or thereabouts, belonged to the Nobility. Thousands of so-called nobles were imposters, not inscribed on the registers.

In this swarm of nobility there were great variations in personal status, income and intelligence. Many of the nobles were poverty-stricken. This was sometimes due to their own wasteful extravagance or to that of their forebears, but more often it was the result of the system of primogeniture. Upon the death of the head of a family two-thirds of his or her possessions went to the eldest son; the rest was divided among the younger children. In the course of two or three generations—with continued subdivisions—the descendants inherited nothing at all, except a title.

It is worthy of remark, I think, that in France all the children of a noble—male, female, eldest and youngest—belonged to the nobility, even if they did not inherit property. They were a race apart from the common people, and they had certain privileges which continued during the generations. In this respect the system differed from that of Great Britain, where the title is handed down to the eldest son, and, as a rule, the younger sons are classified simply as commoners.

Innumerable communities, rural countrysides and villages were pestered by indigent nobles, for though they might possess little or no property, and were frequently devoid of a sense of justice, they held tenaciously to their inherited privileges. They had a legal right to hunt game, and also a right to trample down the growing crops of the peasants in their pursuit of partridges and rabbits. Peasants were not permitted to own firearms, and in some provinces there was a law which compelled them to chain logs of wood to the necks of their dogs to keep them from chasing game. Only a noble was authorized to own a dovecote, and the doves ravaged the young plants on the peasants' farms.

The Nobles were exempted from some taxes and evaded others. A local *seigneur* had a right to summon the peasants of the neighborhood to labor, without pay, on his land for ten or twelve days a year. This exaction was called the *corvée*, and it was thoroughly detested not only because of its rank injustice, but also because the summons usually came at the busiest season when every man had his own piece of ground to look after.

The peasant must send his wheat to the seigneur's mill to be ground. And here is a bridge that must be crossed in going to the market town. By virtue of long custom, grown into legal right, the seigneur is entitled to collect a toll from everyone who goes that way. The peasant is required to pay a fixed rent on his little patch of land, even if he owns it outright. This is a lingering remnant of the ancient feudal tenure. The rent—called the *cens*—is paid to the seigneur in addition to the taxes levied by the government. There is also another vexatious rent—the *champart*—which is proportional to the produce of the soil. If a peasant wishes to sell his plot of ground he must get the lord's permission, and pay over to him a percentage of the proceeds.

These customs had long outlived their day and the form of civilization in which they arose. In feudal times the peasant needed the protection of his lord, who was usually a fighting bandit settled down as a landed proprietor. The peasant paid for protection, and the seigneur lived among his people. They labored willingly on his land part of the time in return for the peace and shelter that he was able to give them.

But centuries had gone by, and France had become the most peaceable country in Europe. Its government was highly centralized; all authority flowed from Versailles, an artificial city of splendor and tinsel, where the national treasury was entangled in the banalities of a night club and the blazing glory of a world's fair.

Still the ancient habits survived without a trace of reason or common sense. A traveler, on his way from Lyons to Paris, was obliged to pay eight different tolls, or fees, for simply passing along the route, although the entire road was owned by the nation and kept in repair at the national expense.

Why was that? How did it happen?

The explanation is that in the Dark Ages—so called—hundreds of years in the past, the proprietors of the bordering lands, who had acquired them by force of arms, levied tribute on everyone who passed by. There was no use arguing about it; they were powerful men in armor, backed up by groups of their henchmen. They were brutal, harsh, ignorant and devoid of apologies. If the traveler refused to pay the fee they took his goods away from him, and also his life if he continued to expostulate, for they had no compunction whatever about killing people.

Their descendants owned the land still, thousands of acres, and the tolls had survived as a custom sanctioned by practice and law. But where were the scions of the robber barons? Did they come out on the roadway and collect the tolls? Certainly not. That duty was left to bailiffs and underdogs.

You will find the latest descendant—the Marquis or Comte de Something-or-other—at Versailles. He wears clothes of silk; his ensemble is charming. His handkerchief is perfumed, and so is his hair. The lace ruffles on his sleeves are so long that his hands are almost covered by them. At his left side he wears a jeweled sword, an ornament of no practical use. He has nearly as many frills as a woman, but he is not womanish. He is only romantic, and like all romantic people he is living up to something that exists outside himself.

The current wit is on the tip of his tongue, and the latest scandal of high society. He can be amusing, droll, poetic. He has heard of Voltaire, Rousseau, Montesquieu, and has read enough of their writings to talk superficially about them; and he knows something of the astounding Diderot and his *Encyclopedia*. Arithmetic bores him; he cannot keep his mind on the summation of accounts, the total amount of wages paid, the produce of fields and vineyards. These things should be left to bookkeepers.

Versailles has become, under the inspiration of Marie Antoinette, a vast gambling house, so he gambles—for that is the proper thing to do—but he has a cynical contempt for gaming, as for almost everything else. He scatters his golden louis carelessly on the gambling board.

There is the dance music. He dances gracefully, touches the queen's hand in passing and gives her finger tips a light pressure.

Yes, he knows the singular and rather peculiar Marquis de Lafayette. Like Lafayette, he believes in liberty and equality, in the freedom of mankind; it is a fashion and belongs to the same category as the wearing of white satin waistcoats. As to the collection of tolls on his roads, he knows about that, but what can be done? It is a long-established custom, sanctioned by law. Can he change the law, and remake the world because of such a trifling matter?

He accepts the proceeds, whatever they are, after his bailiff has stolen the greater part of them. He is quite aware that his bailiff is a thief, but it would lower his dignity to get into a squabble with a plebeian on that account. Nearly everybody has some dishonest source of income, so why pick on a bailiff? Even the Princesse de Lamballe, the queen's most intimate friend, receives gratuities from those who seek favors.

Suppose the travelers refused to pay the tolls? Suppose his peasants refused to pay the cens, the champart and their other dues? Would he go out personally and force them to pay? Assuredly not; he would not have the faintest notion of what to do, and would play the part of a frustrated lapdog. He is not in contact with reality; he has lived too long in the roseate clouds and dreams of Versailles.

Yet he has plenty of courage. He can look straight into the face of death and smile. But he does not know how to organize his courage, to assemble it, to make it effective. He is wholly devoid of the slam-bang ferocity of his remote ancestor.

He knows there is something wrong, but what of it? One must trust the king's wise advisers; they will straighten it out in time; they always have in the past.

Here you have the picture of a man who is destined to be struck by the smashing, hairy fist of the French Revolution. He will be astonished into speechless confusion; he has no idea that he has been living on the crust of a volcano, or that the valet who brings in his morning chocolate would like to cut his throat.

You shall see him again, standing on the scaffold of the guillotine, and you shall hear him say, politely and coolly: "I beg your pardon, Mr. Executioner, but may I loosen my collar before you slice off my head?"

There existed an instinctive urbanity, a courtesy that had been nourished for generations, a cynical courage that looked upon danger and death with contempt. That is all very well as an exhibition of high-flown dignity, but it is a false sentiment. It is not exactly human to be contemptuous of people who intend to destroy you and have the power to do it.

The social structure was rotten from circumference to center. It was like a house that is going completely to pieces. The foundations are sagging, the roof lets in the rain, the walls are crooked, the chimneys are leaning this way and that, the floor is decayed.

Men and women who have not lost their wits entirely look upon such a house with dismay. They know it can never be repaired; there is altogether too much wrong with it; the house will have to be torn down and rebuilt from the ground up. Within its tottering walls there is music and feasting. The shaky floors quiver under dancing feet. The soft light of a thousand candles falls upon beautiful laughing faces, upon costumes of taste and elegance. Jewels of great price sparkle and glow. In the air floats the harmonious cadence of French speech with its modulated, musical vowels. Gallant, well-bred *chevaliers,* kissing the fair hands of ladies, propose amatory adventures. A prodigious quantity of delicate food and wine is at hand, served by attentive lackeys who are so handsome, well dressed, and well behaved that one, looking upon them, fancies for a moment that they are not real; that they have come out of a golden fable, and are fairy princes in disguise.

The wind rises; the house seems about to fall. The heavy rain comes dripping through the ceiling and splashes the dancers' silks and velvets. They laugh and turn it all into a comedy, for they have the comic spirit. To such people ruin itself may be a comedy. They are bored half to death by the gilded emptiness of their lives.

Versailles was the head and heart of France. A head without contact with realities, ignorant of public opinion; a heart almost wholly lacking in conscience or sympathy. The court attracted the idle and profligate, sycophants and favormongers. But let us keep in mind that there were thirty thousand noble families in France, and in all probability not more than three or four thousand of them ever went to Versailles, or were ever presented to the king and queen.

The regular courtiers—the day-by-day attendants—came from only a few hundred families, yet their influence was enormous. They were on the ground; they saw the king every day, often joined him in his game hunts, attended the ceremonies of the royal bedchamber, flattered the queen, ran here and there eagerly performing little services. Coaxing money out of the royal treasury became a lifelong career of men without talent or principle. They managed to get themselves inscribed on the swollen payroll in official positions which were not only useless but often incomprehensible.

Nobles who did not spend the greater part of the year at Versailles were distinctly outside the royal favor unless they were men of renowned intellectual achievement. "I do not know this man," said Louis XVI, looking over the petition of a provincial noble. "He never comes here; I never see him." The petition was rejected without further consideration.

Taine says:

None remain in the provinces except the poor rural nobility; to live there one must be behind the age, disheartened or in exile.*

His assertion is not entirely correct. There is abundant evidence that many wealthy members of the nobility, and many more who had won distinction for themselves in science or in literature, or as agriculturists, or as soldiers, or as explorers, went to Versailles only when they had business to transact.

There was no typical noble; in these thirty thousand families there were people of every kind, of all characters and temperaments, ranging from the vicious Comte de Charolais—who shot a tiler on a roof for the pleasure of seeing him fall—to the eminent Montesquieu —a member of the *noblesse de robe*—who was a profound philosopher and humanitarian. His *Spirit of the Laws* is one of the great classics of sociological literature.†

Among the nobles were diligent cultivators of the soil, drunken roués, gamblers, dreamers and poets, boorish country squires and learned linguists.

* Taine, *The Ancient Regime*, p. 45.

† They did not know quite what to do with Charolais, who had used the tiler for target practice. To send a noble to the galleys or to execution for killing a workman would have been deeply offensive to the spirit of the regime. Louis XV pardoned him, and said: "Understand me well. I will likewise pardon anyone who shoots you."

There was Condorcet, one of the world's famous mathematicians. At the age of twenty-two he published an *Essay on the Integral Calculus*. Another mathematician was the precocious Clairaut, whose work attracted such favorable attention that he was elected a member of the Academy of Sciences when he was only eighteen.

And there was Marivaux, a distinguished playwright; Lavoisier, one of the founders of the modern science of chemistry; d'Alembert, who discovered the application of algebra to mechanical problems; Condillac, a keen-minded philosopher; Buffon, the celebrated naturalist, who—in his *Natural History*—was one of the first to suggest the theory of evolution and the mutability of species. Buffon was a grand seigneur, of great estate. His château was one of the most splendid in France.

5

Frauds of many varieties were perpetrated at the expense of the court. Some of them were highly amusing.

There, for instance, was the episode of the Prince of Chios. This man, of distinguished bearing and foreign accent, appeared at Versailles soon after the reign of Louis XVI began. His son, a young man, accompanied him.

The prince explained his unfortunate position. He was a Christian and a direct descendant of the Eastern emperors. For centuries his family had ruled the Greek isle of Chios. But now his ancestral domain had been wrested from him by the Turks, and he had become a penniless wanderer on the face of the earth. He expected, however, that the Turkish sultan would eventually restore his private property, which ran into many millions. In the meantime he begged hospitality from the Most Christian King of France. It was freely given. The Prince of Chios was asked if he would deign to accept a generous pension. He replied that he would so deign. His son entered the French service, and was put in command of a regiment.

This state of affairs continued for several years. One day the prince and his son were dining with the Comte de Maurepas when one of the count's valets entered the room. The prince turned pale, declared that he was ill and left the table at once. As soon as he had gone the valet burst into laughter, and upon being demanded by the count to explain, he said, "Why, M. le Comte, that Prince of Chios is nobody but fat Guillot. I recognized him and he recognized me."

"But who is fat Guillot?" asked the nobleman.

The valet said that the Prince of Chios—so called—used to be a clever peasant on the count's own estate in Berry. He went on with so much detail that it became perfectly plain to Maurepas. He had been entertaining one of his own peasants, to whom the king was paying a large pension.

The story ends there. The "Prince of Chios" and his son disappeared immediately, without leaving a trace, and apparently no one ever knew what became of them.

CHAPTER X

THE KING AND THE PEOPLE

I

VERY LIKELY the hardest job in the world is that of an absolute monarch. It is impossible to make a success of it, though the failure may be concealed for a long time by an air of splendor, censorship, ruthlessness, beneficence and cajolery. If the despot rules over more than a few square miles of territory he must necessarily delegate his authority in an extensive fashion to other men. These officials are almost invariably favorites who have acquired their places of power not through ability, but by their skill in the art of pleasing. Flattery is to them a fundamental principle of statecraft.

The despot, the dictator, never learns the truth about social problems. There is nobody to tell him. Those who would inform him, in a frank and honest fashion, are not permitted to get within speaking distance; and there is, of course, no free press or free speech. The suppression of the press and freedom of speech is inevitable. It is interesting to observe that this is the first thing which occurs to even the newest raw dictator. Stop the tongues of people, stop the printed sheets. Censorship. That is what Mussolini did, and Hitler did, and Stalin did. Notwithstanding their air of bravado, and a surrounding atmosphere of uniforms, medals, machine guns and salutes, all three of them are badly scared. If they were certain of their power and popularity they would permit a free and open discussion of the edicts. The absolute monarchs, the sultans, the dictators—all of them lose the priceless contact with public opinion, freely expressed.

A national dictatorship is simply the result of a gangster motive carried out on a national scale.

Louis XVI had the misfortune to inherit a dictatorship which had been sustained by hundreds of years of custom and authority. If he had fought his way to the top he would have lasted longer, undoubtedly, for to have done that he would have had to be a man of force. As it was, he was simply a royal nonentity. He had no discernible capacity for doing anything that required a mentality higher than one expects to find in a small shopkeeper, and his advisers were cunning and selfish. As the absolute ruler of a nation in a state of ferment he was a complete misfit. A fat man, of indolent mind, he fell asleep frequently at the meetings of his Privy Council.

He had a passion for hunting. The weather being right—clear and fair—he spent almost every day in shooting game in the royal forests. His daily killings are recorded in his diary, but not much else. For instance, he writes that August 30, 1781, was a big day. "Killed 460 pieces." In that year of 1781, he slaughtered 20,291 head of game; in fourteen years the meticulous, faithful diary says that the record had run up to 189,251 pieces—meaning that he had shot that many birds and other animals, not counting deer. And, besides, there were 1,254 stags.

On the days when he was not engaged in killing game he spent most of his time in practicing the trade of locksmith. Making locks, repairing them; not for gain, nor with inventive intention, but merely for amusement, *pour passer le temps*. He employed a locksmith, whose name was Gamain, to teach him the trade. This Gamain person was to cause him infinite sorrow in the end. After the revolutionary mob forced the king to leave Versailles and live in the Tuileries in Paris the king and the locksmith built a safe in a wall of one of the rooms. It was so deftly constructed that the wall appeared to be a blank surface. Surely it seemed secure enough. The king put in this safe his secret correspondence with foreign powers—with Austria and Prussia—in which he urged his fellow kings to come in martial array to his aid and defeat his own people.

Gamain, the locksmith, conceived a notion that the royalists were trying to poison him—and maybe he was right—so he went to the revolutionary leaders and told them about the safe. They investigated the matter and found incriminating documents. These papers helped to send Louis XVI to the guillotine.

Without any doubt whatever this unfortunate king was an habitual liar. But his lying was not artistic. There was in his mendacity no subtlety of phrase, no device of pretended misunderstanding. Evidently he believed that a king—an anointed and sanctified being—was not under any obligation to speak truthfully.

While he was subscribing to the republican constitution of a new France, and wearing a red cap of liberty in public, he was—at the same time—attempting, in his crude, awkward way, to create a counterrevolution.

He was greatly influenced by Marie Antoinette, and the effect was poisonous. Her whole career was one long-continued series of frivolities. With only a rudimentary sense of reality, she knew nothing and cared for nothing but amusement. To her life was a musical comedy, an elaborate charade, a masked ball, an amusing tangle of complicated flirtations.

She was an inveterate gambler, and could afford to lose for the simple reason that she had, among her resources and subject to her draft, the entire revenues of the French nation. In one evening she lost a million francs at cards. The young Marquis de Castellane threw away, at the queen's gaming table, his entire fortune at one sitting. Cheating at the game was a common practice, and now and then a noble lord was found to be nothing more than an ordinary card sharp.

2

At the court the most private, personal matters were carried on before an audience. Even the royal bedrooms were populous with courtiers. The queen sat shivering on the edge of her bed in the morning until the chief lady in waiting came to hand her a chemise. It would have been an unpardonable breach of decorum for an ordinary lady's maid to have performed that simple duty.

There was nothing in the way of "conveniences" at Versailles, or at any other of the royal palaces. No water pipes, no central heating. And, although the king himself was a locksmith, there were no locks on the doors. They were not necessary, as the gentlemen of the guard were always on duty in the antechambers and on the stairways.

Every morning the king rose in the presence of twenty people— or more—who had admission to the levée. Some of them were courtiers whose duty it was to be present; others were petitioners with papers in their hands. The first thing the king did was to sit on a commode. Sitting there, he listened to the grievances and petitions of the noble gentlemen.

Then came the ceremony of dressing. He washed his hands in perfumed water brought in a silver basin by a gentleman in waiting. His underwear, his shirt, and the rest of his garments were passed along by one courtier to another until they reached the royal personage. Meanwhile the royal commode had been taken out by two gentlemen appointed for that purpose; for that duty each of them was paid twenty thousand francs a year.

The queen's children were born in rooms crowded with courtiers. That was an old royal custom. The reason for it was that numbers of truthful people would be able to say on oath, if necessary, that there had been no deception, and that the prince or princess actually came from the queen's body. At the birth of Marie Antoinette's first child—a daughter who became, after the Revolution, the Duchesse d'Angoulême—the queen was in real danger because of the number of people in the room. They crowded so closely around her bedside that the attendants could hardly do their work, and some of the courtiers stood on chairs to see better.*

It is a well-attested fact that Louis XVI had not been able to consummate his marriage to the pleasure-loving daughter of Maria Theresa, of Austria, until seven years after their wedding. He was afflicted with a slight physical impediment that prevented sexual relations. An inconsequential operation might have removed it at any time, but he was so alarmed at the idea that he would not permit anything to be done about it until Marie Antoinette's brother— Joseph II, Emperor of Austria—came on a visit to Versailles for the special purpose of persuading the king to get rid of this obstacle.

Thus, for seven years, Marie Antoinette was a virgin queen. The "queen" part of the assertion is indubitably true; the rest of it is beclouded by the mist of history. Certainly her reputation on the eve of the Revolution, as set forth in the bawdy ballads and guttersnipe jokes of the Parisian streets, was nothing less than scandalous. But remember this: By that time the king and queen, the entire entourage at Versailles, and the national administration had lost the respect of nearly everybody. They were on their way out, and in such cases malicious lies and gossip become indigenous, and there is a general competition as to who can tell the most shocking story.

It is difficult to see how a queen of France could have an illicit

* Mme. Campan, *Memories of the Private Life of Marie Antoinette*, Vol. I, p. 201.

love affair without taking a considerable number of people in her confidence, as she lived practically twenty-four hours a day in public. Yet in spite of these kill-joys and hindrances it does seem probable that Marie Antoinette did manage to have one lover. He was Axel de Fersen, a Swedish count in the French military service. In describing him his contemporaries use such adjectives as handsome, tall, intelligent, attractive, pleasant, courageous, modest. Perhaps he deserved them all. I do not pretend to say with any certainty that he was the queen's lover—their attachment may have been platonic and one of sympathy—but, at any rate, he was her confidant, and one of the most intimate kind.*

3

The Clergy was a privileged order whose authority in the nation was not much less than that of the Nobility. The Church owned at least one-fifth of the land in France. The nobles possessed another fifth, and the state was also a landowner on a large scale. More than half the soil was in the hands of the privileged classes.

It was asserted by contemporary writers that the ecclesiastical lands were the best cultivated in the kingdom, and that the Clergy were fair-minded and even generous in the treatment of their tenants. There is much evidence to support these statements, though there are some startling exceptions. For one thing, the village priests lived for the year round on the lands of the Church. They were in daily contact with their peasants and most of them were farmers as well as priests. They were in the habit of dealing directly with the people of their communities.

On the other hand, the great landowning Nobles of high degree clustered around the king and court. They were nine or ten months in the year at Versailles or Fontainebleau or Rambouillet, or wherever the court happened to be. They knew little or nothing of their properties; absentee landlords who took pride in their negligence. Some of them had not visited their estates for years.

Lafayette was an absentee landlord. His first visit to Chavaniac after his return from America was in the spring of 1783; he had then been in France a year. If he ever went to look over the estates

* Jean Axel de Fersen. *Le Comte de Fersen et la Cour de France* (2 vols.). Also, in O. G. de Heidenstam, *Marie Antoinette, Fersen et Barnave.*

in Touraine and Brittany that he had inherited from his grandfather, the Marquis de la Rivière, his visit is not recorded, so far as
I know.*

The upper stratum of the ecclesiastical hierarchy was composed wholly of Nobles. A priest of plebeian origin could never
hope to become a cardinal, or an archbishop, or even a bishop, no
matter what his religious fervor or his mental attainments might be.

Many of the higher clergy were simply dissolute roués; sensual,
depraved and wholly lacking in moral scruples, to say nothing of
piety and religion. Their cynicism is one of the extraordinary features of the decaying regime. We must understand that, in the curi-
ously distorted civilization of prerevolutionary France, the Church
offered a worldly career to aspiring and unscrupulous nobles. Its re-
wards, in emoluments and income, were very large. The abbot of
Clairvaux, for example, received three hundred thousand francs annually. Cardinal de Rohan's income was more than a million francs.
The archbishops lived in a luxurious fashion. The Benedictines of
Cluny had a revenue of nearly two million francs. Although serfdom had been abolished by royal edict the canons of Saint-Claude
continued to own twelve thousand serfs up to the beginning of the
Revolution.†

Life in the wealthier convents was pleasant and often gay.
These houses were the luxurious retreats of the daughters of nobles.
The ladies who inhabited them might leave at any time, go into
society, and even marry. They wore the fashionable dress of the
period.

The abbess of the chapter of Remiremont was a princess of
the Holy Roman Empire. Her dominion extended over two hundred
villages, from which she received both tithes and feudal dues. Her
carriage was drawn by six horses; she was a paragon of fashion
in her apparel; and she frequently went to the theaters.

In addition to their incomes from church property, from the
taxes and the tithes, many of the prelates possessed wealthy abbeys.

* In the six-year period, from 1777 to 1783, five of these estates were sold on
orders from Lafayette to provide funds for his expenses in America. Their sale brought
altogether 609,000 livres, according to an accounting by Gratepain Morizot, who had
charge of the financial affairs of the marquis during this period. The full accounting,
in all its details, may be seen in Professor Chinard's *The Letters of Lafayette and
Jefferson,* pp. 303 *et seq.*

† Exceptions to the laws, or edicts, are so frequently encountered that, after a
while—in any detailed study of the period—they are taken as a matter of course.

Witness the splendor of M. de Dillon, archbishop of Narbonn
wasteful gambler and extravagant man of the world. He had a
income of one hundred and twenty thousand francs besides h
ecclesiastical benefices. One day Louis XVI said to him: "M. Arcl
bishop, they say that you are in debt, and even largely."

"Sire," he replied carelessly, "I do not know, but I shall inquir
of my intendant and inform Your Majesty."

The Archbishop of Rouen had an income of one hundred an
thirty thousand francs; and M. de Brienne, archbishop of Tou
louse, more than one hundred thousand.

In striking contrasts to these clerical fortunes one sees th
lowly curés, the bare convents of the poorer orders of nuns, th
monasteries where the monks live in squalor and semistarvatioi
The tithes which should have gone to the religious orders were taker
in large part, by the higher clergy.

4

The Third Estate, which comprised more than ninety-eight pe
cent of the population of the kingdom, included everybody who di
not belong to the Nobility or the Clergy. Of course, all the commoi
people were in the Third Estate, and also were the middle-clas
and upper-class *bourgeoisie*—the bankers, big and little merchants
factory proprietors, industrialists, brokers. Next to the Duc d'Or
léans and other members of the royal family, the richest individua
in France in the 1780's was M. Necker, who was a plebeian, a
Swiss by birth and a Protestant. As a Protestant he was considered
in theory, an enemy of the state.

But strange things are to be seen in any civilization that is
breaking down because of its dead weight and confusion and in
competency. Necker, although handicapped by his common origii
and his Protestant faith—as well as by poverty—began life as a
banker's clerk and grew to be one of the wealthiest persons ir
France. His great fortune was made almost wholly by speculatioi
on the exchanges of Europe, and by usurious moneylending opera
tions. He seems to have had very little constructive ability.

In the 1780's this member of the Third Estate was looked upoi
as a wizard of finance. He was summoned by Louis XVI to straighter

out the vast tangle of the nation's budget—which, it may be remarked, he did not succeed in doing.

France was then, as now, an agricultural country, and the great majority of those belonging to the Third Estate consisted of peasants, or farm laborers, or small proprietors. In cultivating the soil the system of *métayage* was in common use. This system is familiar to Americans, to whom it is known as share-cropping. The French share-cropper was called a *métayer*. The arrangement between landlord and tenant was similar to that which is now customary in our southern states. The proprietor would rent a piece of land to a peasant in return for a share of the crop, and the landowner's portion was usually one-half of all the produce of every kind. In many cases the proprietor would furnish farming implements and farm cattle.

The prerevolutionary system of *métayage* differed, in some respects, and to its disadvantage, from the American cotton states' method of share-cropping. The American share-cropper seldom pays any taxes at all; he is too poor to be taxable. But the French *métayer*, who was just as poor, was forced to pay a rather formidable assortment of taxes. He had to pay feudal dues to his lord and the tithes for the support of the Church. The tithes were not uniform—nothing in France was—but they ranged from five to ten per cent of the crop, including pigs, chickens, fruits, vegetables, as well as the staple products, such as wheat. There was a tax on each window in the peasant's house; consequently, he and his family commonly lived in a hut without windows. Besides these taxes and dues he was subject to the corvée for ten or twelve days a year.

The local seigneur had the right to hunt game across and over the fields of the peasant, and the game—which the peasant was forbidden to kill—made continual inroads on his growing crop.

The lot of the métayer was a hard one.* In innumerable instances there was nothing whatever left for him at the end of a year. He had lived in naked poverty; he and his family had toiled like slaves; they had simply contrived to exist; and the only prospect in sight was to keep on in the same way.

The peasants, under French law and custom, could own land outright—subject, of course, to the feudal dues—and they might

---

* Métayage still exists in France, though it is not as extensive as it was in the eighteenth century, and many of its hardships have been abolished.

own anything else, for that matter, if they could manage to acquire it. Strange to say, many of them did become landowners. At the beginning of the Revolution about one-third of the farming land in the kingdom was owned by the peasant class. There were millions of peasant proprietors, but their individual holdings were, of course, very small; tiny slices of land wedged in between the great estates of the Nobility and the Clergy. A passion for land was— and is—one of the outstanding traits of French peasants. The French peasant, rather than the British tiller of the soil, is a true yeoman and was one long before the Revolution.

Farming implements and methods of production in general were centuries out of date. Antiquated wooden plows, such as the Romans used in the time of Caesar, neglect of the soil, lack of fertilizer, ignorance of even the elementary principles of productivity—these defects characterized the farming industry of France at that time. Only a few of the great proprietors had much or any interest in scientific agriculture; farming was looked upon as simply the drudgery of peasants. Thousands of square miles of arable land were turned into hunting preserves; other areas were allowed to go to waste and produced only a crop of weeds.

Consequently, in the reigns of Louis XIV and Louis XV famines were endemic in France. The map of the kingdom was spotted with them. There was always a famine somewhere, as there was in Russia until a few years ago. The difficulties of transportation and the absurd customs barriers between the various provinces made the food shortage more acute than it ought to have been. Bread was never cheap in Paris and other cities even in the years of abundant harvest.

During the reign of Louis XVI the potato was popularized as a food. The honor for doing this—and it is a great honor—belongs to Augustin Parmentier. Potatoes were indigenous to America; they were brought to Europe in the sixteenth century, but for some reason too abstruse to take our time the potato was considered an unwholesome food, dangerous and probably poisonous. Parmentier was a pharmacist who did not share the popular belief. He analyzed the potato and found that there was nothing wrong with it. As an experiment he lived and thrived on potatoes for a period of months. He set out to grow a crop of them in the province of Limousin. The people of the neighborhood destroyed his plants.

Then he persuaded Louis XVI to give him a few acres in the sterile plain of Sablon for potato growing. The effort was amazingly successful. Parmentier took a bouquet of potato blossoms to the king. Soon thereafter potato flowers went into fashion. The courtiers wore them. A great dinner was given with potatoes as the principal dish. Franklin and Lavoisier attended the dinner. Potatoes became popular with the Nobility. The peasants were eventually induced to plant them and eat them.

After potatoes had become a staple product of French agriculture there was no longer any danger of famine. The potato plant flourishes in almost any kind of soil and its yield is astonishing. The entire population of the world could live on potatoes and fish.

In the crafts and industries of the towns the guild system was strongly entrenched, and upheld by royal edict. The guilds were not labor unions; they were bodies of master craftsmen; that is to say, the members of the guilds were employers of workmen.

To belong to a guild one had to know the art and mystery of his trade besides being a substantial citizen and an employer. Otherwise he could not get a license to carry on his business. The guilds had an autocratic control over their own particular industries. They were monopolies with a distributed ownership. They fixed the wages of their journeymen, supervised the quality of the product, and established selling prices within certain limits. The system was an expression of a kind of distorted individualism.

The squabbles between the guilds were incessant. There was, for instance, the complaint of the shoemakers against the cobblers because the cobblers sold new shoes besides repairing old ones. Turgot, when he became a minister of state in charge of industry, abolished the guilds, but they were quickly resurrected as soon as he went out of office.

In regulating wages the guilds were resisted by their workmen, who formed organizations corresponding to the labor unions of our time. These unions were secret, however, as such combinations of journeymen were illegal. Nevertheless, strikes did occur and also the sabotage of machinery and processes.

Many of the proprietors developed remarkable methods of efficiency, or invented new devices. It was not at all unusual for them to accumulate money, to become important people within the economic frame of the kingdom. These people lived in spacious and comfortable houses. They were known as the well-to-do bourgeois. Their sons and daughters were given an education. Some of these tradesmen, rising from plebeian poverty, were sufficiently affluent to buy country houses and titles.

But the Third Estate had no voice in legislation, in the shaping of the laws, in the imposition of taxes or in the direction of governmental expenditures. It is true that they had the right of petition and of remonstrance, but these natural rights, such as they were, had little value or effect.

CHAPTER XI

THE LAWS AND THE TAXES

I

THE KING, as the supreme lawgiver, was assisted and advised by his Privy Council, and the four subordinate councils of State, Finance, Dispatches and Commerce.

The scope of the various councils was not clearly defined, and in consequence there was much confusion and overlapping of authority. The councils were administrative, and in the course of time they had evolved into intricate bureaucracies. All decisions were made in the king's name, and in fact every important matter was submitted to him. The members of the councils were appointed by him and they were almost invariably his favorites at court. The councils drafted the laws and submitted them to the king for approval. They were then submitted to the *Parlements* for registration. It will be understood that every new law was simply a royal edict.

The Parlements—despite their suggestive name—had no legislative function. They were judicial bodies, somewhat like our federal courts. Chief among them was the Parlement of Paris, which might be compared—rather remotely—to the Supreme Court of the United States. Do not be misled, however, by the faint resemblance to our chief judiciary tribunal. France had no constitution, and the king possessed the power to expunge any decision of the Parlements.

The edicts were sent to the Parlement of Paris—and to each of the twelve minor Parlements, in other parts of France, for registration. After that they were incorporated into the code of laws. But the Parlements had a right to object, to point out inconsistencies, to argue that the proposed law was unjust. Whenever that was done, and it did happen now and then, the king and his Privy Council reconsidered the matter. Sometimes the new law was altered to fit the views of the Parlement, but the king might—and often did—send back his royal edict with a positive order that it be registered forthwith. The Parlements obeyed, as a rule, though there were historic occasions when they refused.

In such cases there was a great commotion. The members of the recalcitrant Parlement were summoned to a *lit de justice*, a pompous, formal ceremony at which the king reclined on a mass of cushions under a canopy, surrounded by haughty functionaries, guards and nobles. Each member of the Parlement was required to state his reasons for refusing to register the new regulation. If they stubbornly held out in their refusal, the king dissolved the Parlement and sometimes banished those who composed it. Then he appointed in their places a temporary court and the edict was duly registered. The Parlement of Paris was dissolved by Louis XV; it was not restored until Louis XVI became king.

Membership in the Parlements was purchased, or inherited. Astonishing is this fact to an American mind when one first encounters it among the dust and debris of the eighteenth century. A lawyer who aspired to membership in one of the Parlements looked around until he found a member who desired to sell his place, or he might buy from the heirs of a deceased member. The presidency of a Parlement appears to have cost about three hundred thousand francs, but smaller places in the judicial hierarchy were sold at much lower prices.

The members of Parlement were highly respected. Collectively they constituted what was known as the "noblesse de robe." Their incomes were large, as litigants were required to pay heavy court fees to get their cases heard at all. There appears to have been much dishonesty and favoritism in the administration of justice. The French people, as a whole, accepted the idea of bribery as a matter of course. Let us keep in mind that we are dealing with the men and women of another century. Their upbringing, customs, moral standards and outlook were all quite different from ours. We still have bribery of public officials, often on a large scale, but it is generally done in a quiet and secretive manner and not as a matter of course. We have learned to be sly about it, at any rate. Maybe that is an indication of progress, or maybe not.

Torture was an established means of discovering crime. It was administered in various ways such as the application of fire to parts of the body, the use of the rack, of thumbscrews, and the extremely painful distention of the stomach by pouring water down the victim's throat. These were considered legitimate methods of investigation and were used on men and women who had not been tried and convicted, but merely charged with offenses. This preliminary torture was called *supplice préparatoire*.

Preliminary torture, known as the "third degree," has never been abolished in America, though it is illegal and is carried on in secret. In France before the Revolution these tortures were authorized by law and supported by public opinion.

In old France there was also the torture of the condemned, before their execution. The purpose of it was to make the criminal disclose his accomplices. Many of them, of course, had no accomplices, but—to escape from suffering—they often charged innocent persons with having aided them.

Jury trials were unknown, and in certain cases the defendant was tried in secret and not permitted to have counsel. There was no such legal device as *habeas corpus,* either in fact or in principle. Consequently, a person might be arrested, taken away, and completely disappear. There would be no charge on record against him, and everyone in authority would profess ignorance of his fate. This happened again and again, many thousands of times.

Executions were carried out in public. The usual practice was to break the victim "on the wheel." It must have been a hideous spectacle. The condemned was first stretched on a cross, and the executioner broke his bones with an iron bar. Then the dying man, bloody from head to foot, his bones protruding from his flesh, was strapped to a cart wheel fixed on a scaffold and left to die. The victims sometimes lived for a full day, with the populace standing around and watching the ghastly sight.

Poisoners were burned at the stake, as a rule.

The French nation was callous to suffering, was accustomed to bloody executions, to wounds, to starving beggars, to fatal epidemics. It is no wonder that during the Reign of Terror housewives took their knitting with them and sat all day at the place of execution to see the guillotine chop off heads. Made a day's outing of it with a snack of lunch carried in a napkin. But it is worthy of remark that death by the guillotine was the most humane way of executing criminals in France, or anywhere else.

2

The government was a highly centralized bureaucracy. It had all the faults of a bureaucratic regime, which were intensified by its virtual immunity to criticism. There were monumental delays in getting anything accomplished. Useful projects, carefully worked out by competent engineers and economists, were mislaid and forgotten. Capable men who offered their services in the matter of national finance were snubbed.

The kingdom was laid out in thirty-two territorial divisions, called *generalités*. An intendant, who was a direct representative of the national government, supervised each generalité. It was his duty to see that the laws were obeyed, that the taxes were collected, that the roads were kept in repair—and so on. Some of the intendants were nobles, but the greater part of them were lawyers or hard-working businessmen. They were constantly perplexed by conflicting orders. The governmental machine at Versailles was in such a state of obsolescence that it was ready for the scrap heap. It was missing fire; its clutch was slipping; its gears were stripped; its brakes had no hold.

A skidding machine, it careered crazily through the years while mankind looked on and wondered.

Farseeing men in Europe—in England, in Austria, in Prussia, in Holland, and in France—realized that something would have to be done.

But what?

No one knew or professed to know. Optimists thought it would all come out splendidly in time; gradual reforms, a touch here and a touch there, leading eventually to a wholesome change. Very few anticipated a violent revolution. If they did so, they kept quiet; we do not hear their voices shouting through the printed word.

Yet there were pessimists; there always are. Not many in France, but some. They sent their funds to London, to Amsterdam, for investment. No matter what happened, one might rely on bonds and cash in foreign lands.

Lafayette cannot be included among the pessimists. His lack of the sense of premonition was remarkable, not only before the Revolution, but always. Premonition is simply a prophetic assessment of values. The marquis, like all intelligent persons in France, was aware of the chaotic state of affairs. He thought, however, that it would resolve itself into a placid solution like those angry acids that fight and struggle and all of a sudden become as innocuous as olive oil.

3

The system of taxation in prerevolutionary France, if it could be called a "system," was so thoroughly saturated by inconsistencies and unnecessary complications that a detailed description of it would be merely confusing and less informative than an outline sketch of its main features.

The Nobles and the Clergy were exempted from the tax on land.* Some provinces were more heavily taxed—in proportion to their land values—than others. The land tax was called the *taille*. There was the *taille réelle*, that is, a tax on real estate—on the land itself; and the *taille personnelle*, a tax on production. These imposts were levied in a peculiar way. A district, or a village, was assessed a gross sum and the chief men of the community met and apportioned it to every head of a family according to the ability of the family to pay. But it was a joint and collective liability against the whole community. If anybody failed to pay, his neighbors had to pay in his stead.

The common people made a practice of looking poorer than they really were. The villages endeavored to be squalid in appearance. The Marquis d'Argenson wrote in his journal:

An *officier d'élection* has come into the village where my country house is, and has said that the taille would be raised this year. He had noticed that the peasants looked fatter than elsewhere, and he had seen hen's feathers lying about the doors. . . . This is what discourages the peasants.†

Jean Jacques Rousseau, the well-known philosopher, had the pedestrian habit. He walked around the country for days and days on end as a matter of exercise. He says in his *Confessions* that, almost famished, he entered a peasant's house and asked for food; said he would pay for it. The peasant gave him skimmed milk and "coarse barley bread, saying it was all he had. I drank the milk

---

* Note that there were some exceptions to this general statement, as there were to every other rule or procedure in the mechanism of government.

† Marquis d'Argenson, *Journal et Mémoires*, vi, p. 256.

with pleasure and ate the bread, chaff and all; but it was not very restorative to a man sinking with fatigue."

Then:

The countryman, who watched me narrowly, judged the truth of my story by my appetite . . . he opened a little trapdoor by the side of his kitchen, went down, and returned a moment after with a good brown loaf of pure wheat, the remains of a good but rather highly flavored ham, and a bottle of wine. . . . He then prepared a good thick omelet . . .

He refused to take any pay, because, he said, the "commissioners" might find out that he had this store of provisions. "He should be an undone man if it were not suspected he was almost perishing with want."

A poll tax—known as the *capitation*—was levied on all men and women except the very poor. The population was classified in twenty-two divisions, according to their ability to pay. This tax was not heavy on any class. Maidservants paid three francs a year.

There was the income tax, the *vingtième*, a twentieth part of the taxpayer's annual income. It was levied on everyone, including the Nobles—with the exception of the Clergy and the poor artisans, peasants and domestic servants. Early in the reign of Louis XVI it was raised to eleven per cent, and at the time of the American Revolution, when the national treasury was hard pressed to meet the expenses of financing the war in America, it was raised to fifteen per cent.

This income tax was devised in an unscientific manner. Everybody paid at the same rate, whether he had an income of ten thousand or a million francs a year. There were no progressive gradations; no higher brackets.

The Church, which was exempted from taxation as such, was supported and enriched by the imposition of tithes, which varied erratically in amount and method of computation. In some places, wood, fruit and other commodities were exempt. In parts of the kingdom the tithes ran as high as one-tenth of certain kinds of produce; in other parts they did not amount to more than one-fortieth. In general, it is believed that this tax on the agricultural class in France amounted to about one-eighteenth of the gross product of the soil. So far as the peasants were concerned it was the heaviest of all the taxes.

Instead of paying taxes in formal fashion, the Church made "free gifts" to the king. The term is a misnomer, as the amount of the free gift was fixed by the king's ministers. It was always much less than the ecclesiastical body would have been required to pay if it had been assessed in the ordinary way. These ecclesiastical gifts were sometimes accompanied by provisos. In 1785 the Church agreed to make the king a gift of eighteen million francs on condition that the works of Voltaire be suppressed.*

The indirect taxes were usually farmed out to contractors who bought the right to collect them by paying a lump sum into the treasury. Their profit was the difference between what they paid for the privilege of tax collection and the amount actually collected. Of the eight principal sources of revenue five were farmed. These were the customs, or duties on imports; and the taxes on tobacco, salt, wine and cider. The letting of the contracts was done in an atmosphere of rank bribery and graft, as may be readily imagined.

The farmers-general—or *fermiers-généraux*—were between forty and sixty in number. The institution was, in effect, an underwriting syndicate. The profits were enormous, for the reason that the syndicate never paid anything like the full value of the concessions acquired by them. The fermiers were chiefly of low origin—pushing money-seekers who knew how to make their way in the world of finance.

Besides the active members of the syndicate, who were in charge of its administration, there was an indefinite number of outsiders who invested capital in the enterprise. They were known as *croupiers,* and among them were many wealthy nobles, the great dignitaries of the Church, and even King Louis XVI.

The common people held the *ferme*—or syndicate—in detestation. Naturally. The agents of the ferme were the most inexorable taxgatherers in France. They had no pity, and could not afford to have any, as they were badgered continually by their superiors and were expected always to break previous records in the collection of revenue in their districts.

To become a fermier-général was an absolutely certain way to acquire a large fortune. These speculators bought estates, lived in sumptuous style, purchased titles, married their daughters to noblemen. But even their wealth and their labels of nobility did not entitle

* E. J. Lowell, *The Eve of the French Revolution,* p. 28.

them to presentation at court. The tight little group around the king and queen at Versailles was the most exclusive high society of which we have any record in modern history. It was almost completely out of touch with the commercial classes, with the merchants, financiers and traders who had become, by degrees, the real and substantial power in the national life.

When the Revolution swept over France the farmer-generals were marked men; on their faces was the chalky pallor of imminent death. Some of them—many of them, in fact—escaped to foreign countries. During the Reign of Terror they were killed with no more compunction than one would have in destroying a vicious and obscene animal. Even Lavoisier, one of the most notable figures in the history of science, was sent to the guillotine, and the only charge against him was that he had been a farmer-general in a small way; that is, he had been one of the minor members of the syndicate.

But Lavoisier cared little or nothing for money. He had gone into the farmer-general enterprise to procure funds to enable him to carry on his scientific experiments.

4

My readers are aware, I am sure, that the American war with England did not come to an end when Cornwallis surrendered in October, 1781. Nor did the Anglo-French war. So far as America was concerned, military operations on both sides were suspended, but upon Lafayette's return to France in 1782 he learned that the French were planning a combined naval and military expedition—in concert with Spain—against some part of the English dominions.

It was finally decided to attack the British West Indies. The expedition was to assemble at Cadiz, and was to be in command of Comte d'Estaing. The Marquis de Lafayette was appointed the commanding officer's chief of staff, and he joined d'Estaing at Cadiz in December, 1782.

There had been an addition to his family not long before his departure. On September 17, 1782, Adrienne had given birth to a daughter, who was named Virginie in honor of the state of Virginia.

The proposed expedition never left Cadiz, as a preliminary treaty of peace between France and England was signed in February, 1783. There is reason to believe that it was never really intended to be anything but a bluff—a threat which would strengthen Vergennes's hand in the peace negotiations.

In the spring of 1783 Lafayette made a trip to his ancestral home in Auvergne. Adrienne accompanied him; it was her first visit. Mme. de Motier—Lafayette's grandmother—had died, and Aunt Louise Charlotte (known as Mme. de Chavaniac) was living there alone.

Early that year he bought, for one hundred and seventy thousand francs, the seignory of Langeac, a property which was close to his native Chavaniac.* This seignory was a marquisate, which means that it carried the title of marquis to its possessor. But Lafayette was already a marquis, and it was said—as a piece of gossip—that he hoped to become a duke, and was enlarging his estate in Auvergne toward that end.

On his trip to Chavaniac he took formal possession of Langeac. It was a pompous occasion, which was very pleasing, as no one I have ever heard of had a more lively appreciation of pomp and ceremony than the marquis. He rode a white horse, a military troop with flashing sabres and brilliant uniforms was his escort, he was given the keys of the town in a silver box, a Mass was celebrated, and there was the ceremony of drinking wine in honor of the new lord.

About the same time Lafayette purchased a large and splendid house in Paris as a home for himself and his family. Until then he and Adrienne and their children had lived with his father-in-law in the Hôtel de Noailles. Their new home was at 81 Rue de Bourbon, near the corner of the Rue de Bourgogne.† These acquisitions of im-

---

* I use the words "franc" and "livre" interchangeably in relating financial transactions of this period. The franc did not come into existence until the Revolution, but as a silver coin it had the same weight and value as the livre.

† One day I tried to find 81 Rue de Bourbon, without success, but I must admit that my effort was a halfhearted one. I cannot get up any enthusiasm for Lincoln's favorite chair, or for Jefferson's clocks, or for the salon of Marie Antoinette, or for relics of Lafayette. My interest in the past is limited rather narrowly to mental and moral attitudes and their impact on the social fabric.

The taxi driver said, after turning the pages of the little *carnet* which all Parisian taxi drivers carry, that there was no Rue de Bourbon. I got a map and the street was not on it. *"Elle n'existe plus,"* said the taximan. Anyway, we went over Concorde bridge and wandered around awhile. The Rue de Bourgogne runs at right angles to the river and is almost directly in line with the Pont de Concorde. I fancy that the Rue de Bourbon is now called the Rue de l'Université or the Rue de Lille, but as to this I am not sure and I do not want anybody to tell me, as I am already in possession of a large stock of useless knowledge which I do not know what to do with.

movable property surely indicate that Lafayette had no idea of the impending social earthquake. For the Rue de Bourbon mansion he paid two hundred thousand francs, and he spent fifty thousand more to furnish it.

When the family moved in, the marquis placed a large framed copy of the American Declaration of Independence in the entrance hall. There was a wide empty space beside it and when his friends said, "What are you going to put there?" he replied that the blank space was reserved for a "Declaration of French Rights."

On his arrival at Chavaniac in 1783 he found that the harvest of the previous year had been poor and the spring was cold; there was a well-founded fear of another bad harvest. Among the peasants food was scarce. His bailiff showed him over the estate and pointed out that the spacious granaries of the marquis were full of grain. Prices, in view of the scarcity, were rising. The bailiff—a man of business—suggested that the grain be sold. High prices; handsome profit.

"No, no," said Lafayette, "we'll give it away."

And it was given to the poor.

This episode reveals, in a striking manner, his instinctive spirit of generosity. It was one of his most characteristic traits.

5

Let us contemplate the mentality and character of this young man. It is an agreeable picture. He seeks renown and glory, but not at the expense of his fellow mortals. It is his ambition to be known as a benefactor, as an *ami du peuple*. There is not a trace of tyranny in his make-up, though on occasion ordinary horse sense is sadly lacking. He does not know the common people, and never will know them; he is temperamentally incapable of knowing them. Nor does he know the men of commerce; their problems come to him in language that is only half understood. His lack of mental depth is alarming; he is superficial; in a few hours he makes up his mind on matters of controversy that have occupied the attention of serious men for years.

He believes ardently in justice and in human rights. He does not want to conquer mankind with bayonets, although he is a soldier by tradition, training and experience. He has an abiding faith in the simple human qualities of good sense, charity and forbearance. He has forgotten, if he ever knew, that the civilization of France has become so perverted that it is essentially barbarian despite the excellence of manners, the magnificence of the châteaux and the beauty and perfume of the historic gardens. Inflamed, inhibited savageries lie just below the surface; there they bubble and surge, awaiting their day.

In the coming French Revolution—even now rushing down from the future, unknown to the most expert prognosticators—Lafayette will essay the role of pacifier. A compromiser by instinct, he will see the best intentions of nearly everyone and attempt to harmonize and placate. These are not only dangerous but often fatal tendencies at a time when the social state is in volcanic eruption. Only fanatics will be heard during such cataclysms; it is only they who carry weight and authority.

CHAPTER XII

A POOR BOY WHO ARRIVED

I

THE FRENCH social structure, as it was under the old regime, may be represented graphically as a lofty pyramid with steeply sloping sides. To climb it was difficult, indeed, but not impossible. Many intrepid men of low degree tried, and many failed; but others, equipped with an instinct for toeholds and hand-grips, and a mountain-climbing audacity, managed to pull themselves to the higher levels. Certainly not to the top—not to the apex—for there sat the king, the Santa Claus of the aristocrats, the bottomless jam pot of toadying courtiers, and those who circled near the throne made it their business to keep unauthorized persons at a distance.

Lafayette had no need to be a mountain climber. He was born and bred in the higher altitudes. In wealth and social position, and in family connections, he stood near the top of the list. One of the outstanding and astonishing facts about him is that, with all his advantages, he never fulfilled the brilliant promise of his early career.

In following the course of his life one is thrilled by breathless and pleasurable expectations. Destiny seems to be always waiting just around the corner, loaded down with great honors and places of authority, all intended for Lafayette, but by the time the marquis gets there Destiny has strolled away, like a vagrant peddler who has grown tired of waiting for a customer to appear.

Upon his return from America in 1782, and for a year or two thereafter, he was probably the most popular man in France; the youthful hero of the day. I know nothing comparable to it in our time except the reverberating renown of Lindbergh for a while after his solo airplane flight across the Atlantic.

But Lafayette's fame—or, let us say, his high standing with the court—soon began to sag, though he was never an inconspicuous person. Nothing could be truthfully said in derogation of his conduct, or of his ideals, or of his unfailing courtesy, or of his fearless courage.

Celebrity is a tender plant; it must be watered continually by new deeds. If not, it shrivels and dies and is for a long time afterward preserved under a glass case in the museum of antiquities that is called History.

What was the matter with Lafayette? I am not sure that I know, yet there were some few symptoms which even a didactic and incompetent physician might observe. Although he was hungry for distinction he possessed more personal pride, more self-esteem, than a courtier ought to have. He had a way of speaking out his own mind, of airing his opinions regardless of the status or the influence of his listeners, and his views were in some important respects directly at variance with those held by the reigning sovereigns.

All his celebrity had come from his exploits in the American War for Independence, but in a few years the war had lost its luster. Versailles—and, indeed, most of the French nation—remembered it with a noticeable lack of enthusiasm. The reason is that France had gained nothing substantial by the war. The most lasting result was an enormous increase of the French public debt, with a corresponding increase in taxes. Even the growth in trade with the American states, which was so confidently anticipated, failed to materialize. Great Britain still continued to be the great overseas storekeeper for American importers. Anglo-American trade grew, while that between France and America declined to one-half its former volume.*

The young marquis became, by degrees, the hero of a historical past which was not at all popular in his native land.

Yet even so, it is really remarkable that—with the influence of the powerful Noailles family behind him—he was not summoned to serve as one of the official advisers of the king; as minister of war, let us say. Such an appointment would have pleased him and one has no doubt that as a war minister he would have been efficient and successful.

The queen distrusted him; he was not the kind of person she could admire. Why not? Well, he was much too serious, and she

* Channing, *History of the United States*, Vol. III, p. 416.

was alarmed by serious people. They had objectives in mind which always turned out, in the end, to be disagreeable. He was argumentative without being witty. He was decidedly lacking in cleverness at a time when cleverness was considered one of the finest of human qualities.

2

Now, for a little while, we shall turn aside from the lovable and high-minded marquis, the humanitarian, the paragon of civic virtues, the quixotic crusader, and see what could be done by a climber of humble origin.

I am presenting this picture for the sake of contrast.

There is a profusion of notes lying here—the life stories of moneylenders, so-called bankers, who were really magnified pawnbrokers; the owners of the shipping fleets; prosperous merchants, such as the Boehmers—jewelers of splendiferous fortune—the Cartiers or Tiffanys of that era; and the farmers-general, to whom money poured in an unending stream. But all these were as dull as an ash tray, men without humor or vividness, the sense of money—the desire for profits—having beaten down all humanly entertaining traits. It is not worth while to write of them in detail; their biographies would be tiresome.

But there was nothing dull about Pierre Augustin Caron. No doubt you have heard of him under the name of Beaumarchais—as the author of the *Mariage de Figaro* and the *Barbier de Séville.* Besides his great talent as a dramatist he had an extraordinary capacity for money-making, for hazardous and profitable speculations, for diplomatic intrigue. It was he who organized, under the secret protection of the French government, the shipping firm which sent arms and clothing to the American armies during our Revolution.

Pierre Caron, the son of a watchmaker, was born in Paris in 1732. The elder Caron was a very good craftsman; he had all the work he and his apprentices could do.

The family lived over the shop, which was in the Rue Saint-Denis. Pierre had six sisters. All of them, like himself, were amateur musicians, singers and dancers. In their rooms there was the sound of flutes and violins and the girls went about their household tasks with dancing steps and swaying hips. They sang all day and made up "wisecracks" and jokes. Now and then they had amateur theatricals and invited the neighbors—but not the customers of the shop, for most of their patrons were nobles who would not have dreamed of going to an entertainment at the home of the man who repaired their watches. Some of the witty plays that the Carons presented for the amusement of their friends were devised by young Pierre and his sisters. The plays were almost impromptu, conceived in the afternoon and born the evening of the same day. The young man was a playwright by nature.

Pierre's scholastic education came to an end at the age of thirteen, and he went into his father's shop to learn the trade of watchmaking. As a watchmaker's apprentice he was not much good. A precocious youth, he spent the greater part of his time in running around Paris, engaged in roistering episodes. Besides this pronounced lack of attention to the watchmaking industry he had a most extraordinary love of music. He lived, ate and worked with the throb of violins, harps, pianos, and the rattle and beat of drums in his mind.

Eventually his father grew sick and tired of it all. He expelled his son from the house with an admonition on the order of "never darken my door again," and other lugubrious expressions. But his mother and his sisters interceded for him, so he came back with a contrite and hangdog air. After that experience he did apply himself to the watchmaking trade, and he learned a little, but not much.

Nevertheless, he got enough knowledge of the craft to justify his father in sending him to Versailles to inspect the timepieces of the king. There he was just where he belonged by nature and inclination. He went to the royal palaces much more frequently than was necessary, and he made a remarkably pleasant impression, especially with the aristocratic ladies of the court. He was a novelty, and an agreeable one. The only watchmakers they had ever seen were elderly men with stooping shoulders, bad breath and a humble manner.

The youthful Caron was tall, straight, good-looking and well-mannered. He was witty and smiling; he knew all the clever answers, and his sayings were repeated, even to the king. He dressed like a noble and was considered a clever upstart—an admirable quality in a rich community that is almost ready to die of sheer boredom.

The aristocratic young men at the court had a secret desire to push him downstairs and out of the place. But many of the ladies had a secret desire to push him upstairs and in.

So here we see this aspiring young man—so unlike Lafayette—standing at the threshold of a career. He had no fortune, no ancient descent, no property, no title, but he lived in a land where all these attributes were highly valued.

Well, what did he have?

The answer is that he had a sharp, vivid, quick mind which perceived the *inside* of events. In his personality there was not even a chemical trace of principle, or of ethics, or of morality, so he was relieved of a great burden which bends down the shoulders of most men and women and sends them stumbling and groping through life.

His aversion to work was profound and unshakable. But what can an ambitious man do if he refuses to work? The only answer is that he must live on his wits or starve. Pierre had no fear of starvation. His confidence in himself was superb.

And he knew how to get along very well.

Thinking of him I am reminded of *Les Bouffons,* a play by Miguel Zamacoïs in which the veteran actress Sarah Bernhardt appeared. She played the part of Jacasse, a court jester who wants a job. The prince has all the aspirants compete for the place and Jacasse appears among the rest. They make speeches and tell what they can do.

The recital by Jacasse of his own accomplishments would have fitted young Pierre Caron with neat precision. Here are some extracts from Jacasse's poetical speech:

> Moi, je me présente à mon tour;
> N'attendez pas que j'avocasse
> Comme ces bouffons d'alentour!
> Votre œil, seigneur, plus perspicace
> Que l'aigle ou l'autour
> Sans référence ou paperasse,
> M'aura vite jugé. . . . Bonjour!
> Je m'appelle Jacasse!
>
> Prolonger ici mon séjour
> Est le souci qui me tracasse;

Quand ceux-la feront demi-tour
Je veux demeurer dans la place;
Je sais pour cela plus d'un tour,
Plus d'un moyen efficace,
Que je sortirai dès ce jour;
    Je m'appelle Jacasse!

Pour contraindre quelque vautour
A s'éloigner d'une carcasse,
Mille corbeaux rangés autour,
Dont chacun bruyamment croasse,
Sont moins bavards dans un labour
Que moi quand ma langue fricasse
Pointe, jeu de mot, calembour. . . .
    Je m'appelle Jacasse!

Plaider le contre après le pour
N'a rien du tout qui m'embarrasse;
Je sais cent beaux contes d'amour,
Cent récits de force ou d'audace;
Je sais comment, dans une tour,
Un géant, par un nain cocasse,
Fut transformé topinambour. . . .
    Je m'appelle Jacasse!

Now here comes Mme. Franquet. She is a lady of the court; the young man had met her there. Her husband is clerk controller of the king's household. In other words, he is the chief auditor of the expenses of the royal establishment. Mme. Franquet enters the Caron shop and says there is something the matter with her watch. Pierre examines the watch; there is nothing wrong with it. He flashes a glance at her; she looks down and blushes. Her device is as old as the Bible. He clasps her trembling hands and holds them. The watch, he says, will be repaired, speedily; will she please come for it herself? Oh yes, she will. *"Oui, monsieur, je viendrai avec plaisir."*

"Merci, madame, et j'espère de vous connaitre comme une amie."

Oh dear! It is going to be more than that. The Fates have played their cards. *La connaissance sera plus intime que l'amitié.* When she left the shop friendship had already been jumped over with the sprightly ease of a greyhound leaping a hedge. Pierre Caron became at once an intimate friend of the family and moved into the Franquet house. M. Franquet was much older than his wife, and she was years older than Pierre.*

The triangular relationship went along very well. The husband was in failing health, and in November, 1755, Mme. Franquet and Pierre convinced monsieur that the best thing he could do would be to turn over his post as auditor to Pierre, who would pay him an annuity as long as he lived. Then monsieur could get out of Paris, away from the turmoil and worry, and reside in a suburban village. Monsieur agreed to that, and the transfer of his office was made accordingly with the consent, of course, of the officers of the king's household. Pierre agreed to pay M. Franquet an annuity for life. So, all of a sudden, this twenty-three-year-old son of a watchmaker became an official of minor importance at the court. Not so minor after all, for the reason that it was his duty to approve or reject the bills of the tradesmen who supplied the king's household. M. Franquet had made a fortune at it.

One of Pierre's duties was to be present when "the king's meat" was served. For this function he wore a splendid uniform with a sword at his side. The king jested with him and was astonished at his cleverness.

The annuity to the husband Franquet threatened to be a rather heavy drain on the young man's income, but M. Franquet died within two months of an apoplectic stroke, and there was nothing more to be paid. Thereupon Pierre married the widow. She possessed a considerable fortune which she settled on her husband in a marriage contract, but owing to some oversight the contract was not recorded—as required by law—and was therefore invalid. The lady died of typhoid fever before she had been married to Pierre Caron a year, and her fortune went to her relatives. During their short married life she had turned over to him a small country estate called Beaumarchais. He adopted the name, and is so known in history.

These unfortunate deaths, coming so close together in the matter of time, caused a good deal of unfavorable comment. It was

* I am taking most of this information about Beaumarchais from Gudin de Brenellerie's *Histoire de Beaumarchais;* and Bachaumont's *Mémoires Secrètes pour Servir à l'Histoire de la Republique des Lettres en France.*

said—in gossip, but not openly—that Beaumarchais had poisoned both the husband and the wife. To support this view there is not a shred of evidence, produced then or since.

Many of the courtiers were much annoyed by Beaumarchais's success. The king liked him and his witty tongue; he was often invited to sit in the royal presence and amuse His Majesty with amusing stories. He could play any musical instrument and before long he became musical instructor to the royal princesses in addition to his other duties.

One day as he was passing through the antechamber of the king, which was crowded with courtiers, he was stopped by a noble who held a watch in his hand. "M. Caron," said this courtier. "No —beg pardon—I mean M. Beaumarchais, will you be good enough as an expert to examine my watch; it is out of order?"

"I am sorry," said Beaumarchais, "but I have become very awkward since I ceased to practice the art."

The courtier bowed and smiled, "But I beg you, monsieur, not to refuse me this favor."

A group of nobles had gathered around.

"Very well," Beaumarchais agreed reluctantly. The watch was beautiful and expensive. "Let me see the watch, but I warn you that I am very awkward."

He took the watch, looked at it casually, and let it slip through his fingers to the marble floor. It was smashed hopelessly. Beaumarchais made a bow and said, "I warned you of my extreme awkwardness." With that remark he went on his way.

Before long came the great opportunity that led to his fortune.

Pâris Duverney, the great banker, had no trouble whatever in obtaining any amount of money. He was at the head of a wealth-incrusted financial house that had grown and prospered for nearly a century. But he had a rather doubtful reputation, unfortunately, just because he was not a noble. A prince, a duke, or a marquis might be a thoroughgoing rascal without anybody at the court caring much about it. If a nobleman's debts—unpaid and unpayable—ran into a vast sum, like those of the Duc d'Orléans, he was even looked upon with envy. It was quite different, however, in the case of a bourgeois—a common person. He was supposed to pay his debts, acquire his money by rigidly honest methods, and watch his step.

Duverney had no debts. He was as free of them as a fox is of feathers. But he was formidable as a creditor, a mortgage forecloser, a lender of money at usurious rates, a speculator in every commodity from food to foreign exchange.

Yet he had his worries, which were not financial. He wanted to be noticed by the king and court, to be respected by high personages, to be acclaimed as a wealthy patron of this or that.

With that end in mind he established a military school which was conducted at his own expense. Many young men were given scholarships in Duverney's *école militaire,* but the school languished and the attendance grew steadily less. It had no recognition, no standing, and was completely disregarded by the army.

Duverney, a solemn and depressed figure, haunted the corridors of the palace at Versailles with a hope of telling about the school to the king, or to the minister of war, or to some other highly placed official. He could never get an interview and received nothing except the sneering comments of courtiers.

But he did meet Beaumarchais, and as the latter came loping along one day, all finery and smiles, on his way to give the king's daughters their jolly hour of music lessons, Duverney stopped him and related his troubles. Beaumarchais was sympathetic; he always was with wealth in distress. He told Duverney to leave the whole matter with him, with reliable Beaumarchais who was never known to fail; he would get the royal approval.

And he did.

Not long thereafter he appeared at the military school, after due notice, with the royal princesses. They were enraptured with what they saw, and they told their father. A few days later Louis XV visited the college in great state. The courtyard of the school was filled with the royal guards, champing horses, officers in resplendent uniforms, nodding plumes, nobles of high degree. Duverney almost swooned with joy. The watchmaker's son did not fail to remind him that Beaumarchais, intelligent, trustworthy, and devoted, was the promoter of it all. The king thought the school was wonderful; he gave it a grant of money. From that day it was recognized as a high-class institution. In the course of time it developed into the great military academy of Saint-Cyr, which is the West Point of France.

Beaumarchais and Duverney got together with the mutual prescience of unfailing intuition. They needed each other, and each had what the other did not possess. Duverney wanted the assistance of wit and cleverness; Beaumarchais was always avidly hungry for money. They were hand in glove in various enterprises. Beaumarchais said of Duverney:

He taught me the business of finance in which he was a consummate master. Under his direction I built up my fortune; on his advice I embarked on numerous enterprises; in a few he supported me with capital and credit; in all with his counsels and experience.

Without any training at all Beaumarchais became a writer of plays and satirical pamphlets. The pamphlet was, in that epoch, a popular form of literature; thousands of them were published. His plays were charming; he had an instinctive feeling for comedy; and his satires were devastating.

In a letter to his father he said:

Truly . . . I laugh when I think how nicely the things of this world fit into each other; how odd and diverse are the ways of fortune; and how, above all, in the whirl of affairs, the mind superior to events rejoices at the clash of interests, pleasures, sorrows, which dash and break against it.

Those are the sentiments of an adventurer who is wholly sure of himself; of a schemer who contrives to set people at loggerheads that he may profit by their dissensions.

3

He lost his place at court. The reason is obscure, but his biographers are inclined to think that he became too free in his manner toward the royal princesses. Probably that was the reason; he was an impudent person, without respect (inwardly) for anybody.

This demotion did not seem to make much difference in his status in the world. He had already become a financier and a celebrated dramatist.

Louis XV died in 1774. His successor, the dull-minded Louis XVI, had a high opinion of Beaumarchais, and said, "M. Beaumarchais is the only person who tells me the truth."

Laharpe says that Beaumarchais in conversing with people of high station "always contrived to convey the impression of being convinced that it was impossible to hold an opinion contrary to his own without having less intelligence than himself, which you may be sure he never for a moment allowed it to be supposed, above all, with those who had little."

In June, 1776, Beaumarchais induced Louis XVI to advance him a million francs—and the Spanish government also put up the same amount—to enable him to set up a fictitious firm under the name of Rodrique Hortalès et Cie. The purpose of this concern was to supply arms, munitions and clothing to the American Revolutionists under the guise of shipping French goods to the West Indies. In return for the supplies our struggling forefathers agreed to pay in tobacco, indigo, wheat, or what-have-you.

The volume of business was enormous; it ran into millions of francs. Beaumarchais's offices were fitted out in the manner of stage settings; his assistants looked like actors, as some of them actually were. The accounts were in the most inextricable confusion—purposely kept so (it has been charged) by Beaumarchais in order that he might make exorbitant claims without the possibility of having them checked up and exposed. Receipts and manifests were lost, or never made out at all. Cargoes sent to America were overvalued; cargoes from America to France were undervalued. For tobacco coming from Virginia he refused to allow more than half the current price. American officers complained unceasingly of the inferior quality of the arms and ammunition consigned to them. Over and above this vast tangle of claims and counterclaims the voice of Beaumarchais could be heard bewailing his losses. *Mille corbeaux dans un labour, dont chacun bruyamment croasse, étaient moins bavards que* Beaumarchais. Destitution and bankruptcy faced him—so he said—but he continued to go about in a magnificent coach, to entertain luxuriously.

When his operations were concluded he claimed that the American government owed him two million five hundred thousand livres. The accountants employed by Congress to look into the matter gave it up as a hopeless task and dazed finance committees stared dumbly at a bewildering lot of figures.

The controversy was not settled until 1835, when the American Congress voted eight hundred thousand francs to the heirs of Beaumarchais in full settlement of their claims.

After the war he built one of the finest residences in Paris. It stood facing the Bastille.

He was Lafayette's banker during the service of the marquis in America. M. Francey, who represented Beaumarchais at Philadelphia, was instructed to advance any amount of money to Lafayette on request. These loans were repaid.

For years he was employed on secret diplomatic missions by the French government. He was precisely fitted for the part, for he looked upon life as a sort of mystery story. He dramatized everything—even the most sordid and commonplace things—and all human activity came to his mind with the air of a dime-novel conspiracy.

Sent to London with funds to purchase and destroy the entire edition of a scurrilous book about Marie Antoinette—written by a renegade Frenchman—and also to bribe the author not to write any more about the queen, he succeeded admirably. The edition was bought and burned, and the author was duly bribed.

The evidence, as it appears now, leads one to believe that he split the bribe with the author, and then encouraged him to produce another libelous book under a Jewish name, so Beaumarchais might come over to London with another bribe.*

4

Beaumarchais's name will live in literary and dramatic annals as the author of the *Mariage de Figaro* and the *Barbier de Séville*. They are both biting and bitter satires, wearing the disguise of comedy.

Figaro is a comic servant—impudent, unscrupulous, plausible. He is, in fact, Beaumarchais himself. This laughable character says: "I was spoken of, for an office, but unfortunately I was fitted for it. An accountant was needed, and a dancer got it."

In another place, he says: "They tell me that if in my writing I will mention neither the government, nor public worship, nor politics, nor morals, nor people in office, nor influential corporations,

* The full story of these transactions is very amusing. It may be found in John Rivers's *Figaro: The Life of Beaumarchais*.

nor the Opera, nor the other theaters, nor anything that belongs to anybody, I may print everything, subject to the approval of two or three censors."

And again, he says that he would like to get hold of a censor and give him a piece of his mind. "I would tell him that foolish things in print are important only where their circulation is interfered with; that without freedom to blame no praise is flattering, and that none but little men are afraid of little writings."

The *Mariage de Figaro* was read to Louis XVI and to Marie Antoinette by Mme. Campan. The King indignantly forbade its appearance on the stage. Beaumarchais was invited to read it aloud at several noble houses; and all of a sudden everybody was talking about it. The Comte de Vaudreuil had it enacted by a full cast of amateur players at his château.

Eventually, Marie Antoinette used her influence to have the play presented at the Théâtre-Français, and here it first appeared in public in April, 1784. It was the most popular play that had been produced in France in more than a hundred years.

Beaumarchais managed to get through the French Revolution and its Reign of Terror without losing his head. For a while, during that time of fear and confusion, he was the chief negotiator in the purchase of arms in other European countries for shipment to France to be used by the revolutionists. To accomplish this his transactions were as intricate as the moves in a chess game. While Holland was at war with France he contrived, in some manner, to buy guns and munitions in Amsterdam. In the end, however, he exhausted the confidence of the revolutionary committees. They accused him of playing on both sides, and he was thrown into prison. His destination and final stop was to be the guillotine, but he escaped that fate through the intervention of one of his mistresses, and got away to England. After the Terror was over he returned to Paris, recovered his property and lived happily thereafter. He died in 1799. His career, like that of Necker, proves that even in the caste-bound France of the old regime clever men might accumulate fortunes and attain distinction. But there were not many who could do it.

CHAPTER XIII

THE MARQUIS HAS A WONDERFUL TIME

I

WHILE a quiescent state of war existed between France and Great Britain the Marquis de Lafayette felt that it was his duty to remain in France, so that he could instantly take his place in the army in the event of renewed hostilities. Though he was not in active service he held a general's commission, and nothing on earth could have pleased him better than to lead a military expedition for the invasion of the British Isles.

But the war petered out in a haze of treaty making. The preliminary articles of peace were signed in the February of 1783; and the final treaty was concluded in September of that year.

As soon as the war had formally come to an end he began making plans for a trip to America to meet his former companions in arms, to visit his beloved friend George Washington, to see our fair land in time of peace. Meanwhile, he circulated around the Parisian salons, an elegant and grave young man whose mind was filled with American notions.

No Beaumarchais was the slim marquis; life to him was real and earnest, and decidedly not a series of witticisms or the proper subject for a farce. He said what he meant, and in forthright fashion. He thought that France should have a constitution; that every man should have the right to vote; that every citizen—noble or commoner—should be taxed in proportion to his ability to pay; that the king should not have unlimited power to draw funds from the treasury of the nation; that a National Assembly, elected by the people, should be called into existence and that it ought to have the power, with the royal approval, to pass on matters of taxation and governmental expenditures.

These ideas seem commonplace to us today, but they were not so considered in the France of the 1780's. Such views were looked upon as alarmingly radical in the court circles at Versailles and by most of the higher nobility and clergy. But not by all. Lafayette was only one of a large group of liberals; he was not a solitary reformer, chopping his way through the tangled jungle of tradition. There were others, as high in rank as Lafayette, and among them were men more determined than he, more settled in their straight-line, dynamic convictions. Lafayette was a theorist, an idealist who strove for the betterment of man in his social environment, but he was not prepared to follow his ideas to their final end.

On the roof of the world these well-meaning reformers stood, walked and debated. Far beneath them, in the tightened silence of the underground, there existed inveterate hates, savage and implacable desires, unreasonable monstrosities—some of them intelligent and some stupid, but all of them malevolent, reckless and explosive. Desperate and untrained forces, the hairy Calibans of the social scheme, they are destined to appear in the coming time, when the mountains are riven and the flames of hell blaze in France.

In the darkness of a cell France is nourishing a giant, unaware of his strength, which is terrific, inhuman and remorseless. He has no place in the pattern of society, as it then existed, except as servitor and contemptible underdog. But he shall smash through the walls and take France to pieces with the nonchalance of an ape plucking the feathers and breaking the wings of a bird. Yet, in this case the lovely bird is not worth saving; it has no vitality, no warmth. Nor is Caliban wholly to be condemned. He means well; he dreams of a better world, yet he is like a cook who throws all the dishes out the window—in a resounding smash of crockery—instead of taking the trouble to wash them.

Congress wrote to Lafayette in 1783 and asked him to do what he could in persuading the French government to establish free ports for American commerce. He was eager to oblige, but he did not know what a "free port" was, so he wrote to Vergennes for information. The minister replied that a free port is one from which exports may be sent, and imports received, freely and without duties or tax. Finally, through the efforts of the marquis and the American commissioners, Marseilles, Dunkerque, Bayonne and L'Orient were made free ports for American merchandise. The idea behind this move was to increase the volume of trade between France and America. It failed to work out successfully. The commerce between

Great Britain and her former colonies continued to grow, and that between France and her former American allies continued to dwindle.

Now a new interest attracted the marquis.

At that time Franz Anton Mesmer—a Viennese physician who founded the art, science, or whatever-you-call-it, of mesmerism— was creating a great stir in France. His brother medicos had made life so miserable for him in Austria that he had gone to Paris and settled. He was in no sense a rascal, as he is often and erroneously depicted. However, he may have been to some extent an unconscious quack, not through intention but because of his overwhelming belief in the efficacy of his own powers. He was really the discoverer of hypnotism, a hypnotist, though he never called his art by that name, nor did he ever realize its limitations. His name for his science was "animal magnetism."

Lafayette became one of Mesmer's most ardent disciples. We must not forget that his mind was undisciplined and untrained in science, economics and philosophy. He had a tendency to adopt mental fads under an impression that he was encouraging progress. In 1783 and 1784 "animal magnetism" occupied much of Lafayette's time and conversation. To Washington he wrote:

A German doctor, called Mesmer, having made the greatest discovery upon animal magnetism, he has instructed scholars, among whom your humble servant is called one of the most enthusiastic.

. . . Before I go [to America] I will get leave to let you into the secret of Mesmer, which, you may depend upon, is a grand philosophical discovery.

Presumably he communicated "the secret" to Washington, but I cannot find any reference to it in Washington's papers, nor in Lafayette's after his return from the United States. He appears to have dropped the subject altogether.*

2

Since his Virginia campaign of 1781 Lafayette had kept up a correspondence with Thomas Jefferson, who had been governor of Virginia when Lafayette entered the state as commander of the

---

* There is an excellent—and most interesting—biography of Mesmer in Stefan Zweig's *Mental Healers*.

American troops opposed to Cornwallis. They became lifelong friends in spite of the fact that they were very different in temperament.

Both of them stood for "unalienable human rights" and a republican form of government, and both of them strove for the betterment of mankind. But Jefferson was a much clearer thinker than Lafayette and was much more skillful in adapting available means to attain a desirable end. When great issues confronted him, demanding a solution, Lafayette often lost his bearings and muddled around in a morass of abstractions and halfhearted measures. Jefferson never did; he knew precisely what was needed and what to do.

Jefferson had a scientific mind, though I am not sure that the word "scientific" is the best term to use in describing his mental processes for the reason that he had had no real scientific training. It would be better, perhaps, to say that he was intensely curious, and curiosity is usually the inspiring motive of scientific investigation. He dug up the bones of extinct animals and attempted to classify them; he invented a more efficient wheelbarrow; wrote a dictionary of the languages of the Indian tribes, revised and simplified the New Testament, analyzed soils, tried to estimate the age of the earth, and devised a machine called a polygraph which enabled him to write a letter and a copy of it at the same time.

All that was completely outside the range of Lafayette's mind and action. Nevertheless, the few qualities that they had in common were so strongly predominant in both of them that they were drawn together by mutual respect and affection.

Lafayette sailed for America on July 1, 1784, looking forward, among many other anticipations, to meeting his friends Washington and Jefferson. But Jefferson had been appointed minister plenipotentiary, in conjunction with Benjamin Franklin and John Adams, for the purpose of negotiating treaties of commerce with European nations, and he departed from Boston on July 5th. Their ships must have passed each other somewhere on the Atlantic.

Jefferson was accompanied by his young daughter Martha, a little girl of school age. On October 11th Lafayette wrote to Jefferson, from America, and said:

My house, dear sir, my family, and anything that is mine are entirely at your disposal, and I beg you will come [go] and see Madame de Lafayette

as you would act by your brother's wife. Her knowledge of the country
may be of some use to Miss Jefferson whom she will be happy to attend
in everything that may be agreeable to her. Indeed, my dear sir, I would
be very angry with you, if either you or she did not consider my house as
a second home and Madame de Lafayette is very happy in every opportunity
to wait upon Miss Jefferson.*

Lafayette reached New York on August 4th of the year 1784.
He had never been in New York City before; during the whole of
his military service in America that city had been held by the
British.

Landing at the Battery, he received what our modern newspapers invariably describe as "a tremendous ovation." Thundering
of cannon; smiling committees of reception; rippling flags, beam-
ing ladies; Gargantuan feasts. In the whole of our history no other
foreigner has ever been loved by the American people as they loved
Lafayette, and still cherish his memory. He stands in a class apart
from all others. In France he was a notable figure, though never
one of the first importance. There he was always overshadowed by
other men. In America, as everyone knows, there were in his time,
and are now, much greater men than Lafayette, but few of them,
in our national life, have been surrounded by such a glowing sheen
of legend and drama—even though they were native Americans.

From New York he went to Philadelphia, accompanied by a
swarm of admirers on horseback. He never appeared to get tired
of having people around him. During his entire life, except for the
years that he was held as a prisoner in Austria, in the 1790's—he
lived and moved among crowds of men and women. In such a career
there is not much time for reflection, and hardly any for reading.
Because of vociferous people at his elbow he made important decisions frequently on the spur of the moment; and his reading was
always sketchy, negligible and ill-balanced.

At Philadelphia there were more dinners, receptions and hand-
shakings. From there he went on to Mount Vernon, and was Washington's guest for eleven days in August. This interval seems to have
been fairly placid. Washington kept an open house; that is, he received everybody who looked respectable, but usually there were not
more than ten or twelve callers in the course of a day, and that meant

* This letter is taken from Chinard's *The Letters of Lafayette and Jefferson*,
p. 13.

a kind of loneliness. Sometimes, however, there were twenty at dinner, for the dinners at Mount Vernon were famous, and people who were on their way here and there just dropped in to eat and then go on.

Late in August the marquis left Mount Vernon and went to Baltimore, where he was the guest of honor at a dinner of three hundred covers. Then to New York again—and there was another banquet.

The custom of after-dinner orations in America was as firmly established in 1784 as it is today. Lafayette liked it; he liked almost all our American ways. He had never been called upon to make a formal after-dinner speech in France. They did not have them. At every banquet in this new country he was called upon, and he responded nobly. He was really a poor speaker—he knew that himself, and frequently said so—but he made an excellent impression on his audiences. In his after-dinner talks he always mentioned Washington and referred to himself as Washington's "adopted son." That brought unlimited applause. It was a truthful statement; Washington and Lafayette did have that intimate personal relation, though it was unofficial. Washington was then fifty-two, and the marquis was twenty-seven. One of them wanted a son, and the other wanted a father.

On to Albany our cheerful pilgrim goes, and from there to see the Oneida Indian tribe, by whom he had been adopted in 1778. His tribal name was Kayewla. The address of welcome was made by a tribesman who spoke Provençal French, to the amazement of the marquis. Inquiry at once. Well, the speaker was not an Indian by birth. He had been a French soldier in the Seven Years' War, had become one of the tribe. Married to an Indian woman, he had children and grandchildren, yet the French speech—after all the years—was still on his tongue.

Wondering at the strange things one encounters in life, Lafayette went back to Albany and on through New England to Boston, where there was a "banquet of five hundred covers"—thus beating Baltimore by two hundred. After a few days in Boston he embarked in a French frigate and sailed for Chesapeake Bay. From Richmond he returned to Mount Vernon to make his final visit. He was going to New York; Washington accompanied as far as Annapolis, and there they parted. They never saw each other again.

Before the sailing of the ship for France the marquis received a letter from General Washington, in which he said:

In the moment of our separation, upon the road as I traveled, and every hour since, I have felt all that love, respect and attachment for you, with which length of years, close connection, and your merits have inspired me. I often asked myself, as our carriages separated, whether that was the last sight I ever should have of you? And though I wished to say No, my fears answered Yes.

While the vessel was still in New York harbor Lafayette replied to the general's letter. He wrote, in part:

No, my dear General, our recent separation will not be a last adieu. . . . I realize that you will never come to France; I cannot hope to have the inexpressible pleasure of embracing you in my house, to receive you in a family where your name is adored; but I will return, again and often, under the roof of Mount Vernon. . . . Adieu, adieu, my dear General, it is with inexpressible pain that I feel that I am going to be separated from you by the Atlantic. All that admiration, respect, gratitude, friendship, and filial love can inspire, unite in my heart to devote it very tenderly to you. I find in your friendship a felicity that words cannot express.

He sailed from New York on December 21, 1784, and arrived at Brest on January 20, 1785. His visit to America had taken a little more than six months of his time.*

Despite his expectation of coming over to the United States every few years the marquis's next visit—and his last one—was not made until forty years had gone by.

3

I have mentioned, in a previous chapter, that Lafayette's popularity at Versailles was on the wane long before the French Revolution. This is a fact of importance as—in one way or another—it had much to do with the shaping of his career.

In the intimate circles of the court there were those who pointed out that, after all, Lafayette—of an ancient noble family—had aided

* During his stay in Maryland the legislature of that state made the marquis and his male heirs citizens of Maryland forever, and thus entitled to all the privileges of citizenship, without the formality of naturalization. This statute was invoked a few years ago by René de Chambrun, who is Lafayette's great-great-grandson. He came to this country and was accepted as a citizen and admitted to the bar as a practicing lawyer.

in the creation of a republic. He had shown—according to these detractors—a contempt for his origin, for the traditions of his class, and had helped to set up a state which offended the accepted standards of Old World civilization; and was not a man to be trusted.

It was also mentioned to the king that the marquis passed much of his time in the company of Thomas Jefferson. Our first great Democrat was received with the courtesy that is accorded everywhere to distinguished and able men. Notwithstanding that, it developed later that the Foreign Office had somebody in Jefferson's house—a servant, apparently—who reported the names of the callers and the import of their conversations with our minister plenipotentiary.

Jefferson wrote to Madison on January 30, 1787:

The Marquis de Lafayette is a most valuable auxiliary to me. His zeal is unbounded, and his weight with those in power great. . . .

Was his weight with those in power really great? There is nothing but Jefferson's word for it and Jefferson was in a foreign country where his perception of the prevailing and intricate influences in the government was necessarily limited.

He has a great deal of sound genius, is well remarked by the King, and is rising in popularity. He has nothing against him but a suspicion of republican principles. I think he will one day be of the ministry. His foible is a canine appetite for popularity and fame; but he will get over this.*

In France as it was in the 1780's "a suspicion of republican principles" was enough to put anyone in disfavor at Versailles.

Jefferson says—as quoted above—that Lafayette was "rising in popularity." He certainly was, in 1787, and Jefferson's observation is true. But his growing popularity was not with the royal family—the Comte d'Artois, brother of the king, detested him—nor with the court, but with the common people. His ideas on freedom, equality and liberty had reached them, and they had begun to think of him as a leader in the cause of the downtrodden.

Lafayette had been in France only a short time after his return from America in 1785 before he set out on a tour of the Continent. With an entourage of army officers—some of whom had

* Randolph, *The Domestic Life of Thomas Jefferson,* p. 94.

served with him in the American war—he went first to Prussia and called on Frederick the Great.

He was an honored guest at Potsdam and, as a foreign officer of distinction, was invited to witness the annual maneuvers of the Prussian army. Amazed at the appearance of the great Frederick, he wrote to Washington that the renowned king looked like—

An old, decrepit and dirty corporal, all covered with snuff, his head almost lying on one shoulder, and his fingers nearly dislocated by the gout. But what surprised me much more was the fire and sometimes the softness of the most beautiful eyes that I ever saw, which give to his face an expression as charming as it can be rude and menacing when he is at the head of his army.*

From Berlin the marquis and his crowd of friends and retainers journeyed to Vienna, where he was presented at the Austrian court—and to Emperor Joseph II, the brother of Marie Antoinette —by Adrienne's uncle, the Marquis de Noailles, then serving as French ambassador.

On September 29, 1785, on his way back to France he wrote a long letter to an unidentified "Cher Prince" who was evidently a Prussian if one may form a conclusion from the context of the epistle. It is a dull letter in the customary flat—though sentimental —style of the marquis, and it deals almost altogether with the drilling and maneuvers of Austrian troops. Apparently the Austrians thought he was a kind of high-class spy, but that is open to doubt; it is Lafayette's own deduction, and he would naturally take the most romantic view of the matter.

But he seems to have encountered a charming and beautiful spy—on the other side, whatever the other side was—whom he dominated without the least difficulty. The first paragraph of his letter tells about it. Here it is:

My dear Prince: On my way back from my Austrian visit and the Potsdam manœuvers I discovered at Berlin the prettiest spy I ever saw; you know that once they are caught, anything you please may be done with these persons; but very unfortunately this spy, although very shrewd, was one of those whom you must respect even though you like them; capitulation was arranged between us and we agreed that I should save her the trouble of writing out my confession, upon condition that I might come to her

---

* Frederick the Great was then seventy-three and near the end of his days. He died the next year—1786.

house to hand over my letter. At any rate, I gained the visit and she profited nothing, because my intention always had been to write to you, my dear Prince, and speaking of my little trip, to thank you for all the kindness you showed me while I was in Silesia.*

The Continental tour lasted nearly six months; they were leisurely travelers in those days. Upon his return to Paris in October, 1785, Lafayette immediately took a part in public affairs. He proposed, and advocated vigorously, the freedom of the Protestants.

It will be recalled that the civil rights of those who professed the Protestant faith were seriously restricted in France. For several decades there had been no open persecution of Protestants, but the laws against them were still in force. Their marriages were illegal, and consequently their children were looked upon as bastards. They were not allowed to practice law or medicine. Their religious meetings had to be conducted secretly, or with a pretense of secrecy, at any rate. The last will and testament of a Protestant had no legal value. However, these restrictions were not actively enforced except in special cases; they existed simply as a threat. Like so many things in France, at that time, they were withered at the root, had become dead statutes, and remained in the code chiefly because nobody had the energy to get rid of them.

A Protestant of enterprise and ability might make a fortune, and some of them did. A few of them—Jacques Necker, for example—rose to high places in the government. The land was full of atheists and infidels, followers of Voltaire, scoffers at any kind of religion. Among the irreligious were numerous dignitaries of the Catholic Church who held their offices simply as political appointments.

Lafayette's campaign for Protestant freedom had no success at the time, and the reason is a rather curious one. Hardly anybody, with the exception of a few Catholic fanatics, was opposed to it. Some of the prelates of the Church declared openly, and in public, that they were in favor of removing the restrictions. But the governmental lethargy that weighed heavily on the nation prevented any definite action. At Versailles it was thought that Lafayette had gone out of his way to tinker with a state of affairs that was no concern of his.

* For this letter I am indebted to Stuart W. Jackson, who is one of the vice-presidents of the society known as "The American Friends of Lafayette."

The repeal of the restrictions did not take place until 1787, when Lafayette brought up the matter in the Assembly of Notables. But, even then, it was only a halfway measure. It did not give Protestants the right to meet publicly for worship nor to hold office in the government service.

The abolition of slavery was another projected reform that held the attention of the marquis for a while. There were no slaves in France—not in the formal sense, although there were millions of them in the economic meaning of the word—but negro slavery did exist in the French West Indies and other colonies.

The plight of the black slaves in America had aroused Lafayette's deep sympathy while he was in Virginia during the last year of the American Revolution. In the same letter that carried to Washington the news of the ending of the war the marquis wrote:

At present, my dear General, when you are going to enjoy some repose, permit me to propose to you a plan that may become greatly useful to the black portion of the human race. Let us unite to buy a small property where we can try to free the negroes and to occupy them only as agricultural laborers. Such an example, given by you, might be generally followed and if we succeed in America I shall with joy devote a part of my time to make that idea fashionable in the West Indies. If it is a foolish idea I had rather be judged a fool in that way than to be considered wise on account of the opposite conduct.

The revered Father of Our Country was not at all enthusiastic over the liberation of the slaves, so the matter was dropped for a time, but it kept on simmering in Lafayette's mind.

In 1787 he bought—for one hundred and twenty thousand francs—a property in French Guiana called La Belle Gabrielle. This plantation had a flock of slaves which the marquis intended to liberate. In this project he was greatly encouraged by his wife. Neither of them knew anything whatever of the condition of affairs in the French colonies.

Lafayette wrote to Washington about his faraway plantation, and the reason for its purchase. In his reply Washington said:

The goodness of your heart, my dear Marquis, displays itself in all circumstances, and I am never surprised when you give new proofs of it. . . . God grant that a like spirit may come to animate all the people of this country! But I despair to be a witness of it. . . . A sudden emancipation would bring about, I believe, many evils, but certainly it could be, or ought to be, accomplished gradually, and by legislative authority.

In other words, Washington was greatly relieved on learning that his noble friend had decided to try out his emancipation experiment in a South American French colony rather than in the state of Virginia.

Adrienne, whose piety was indeed extraordinary in that cynical land and century, insisted that before the negroes were freed they should be taught "to know and to love God." To that end she got in touch with a priestly seminary at Cayenne in Guiana. The worthy brothers of the order agreed to instruct the slaves in the principles of morality and religion.

The experiment did not work out well in the end. Before the negroes had been properly instructed the Revolution began, and the project was abandoned and lost in the confusion of the time. The slaves were eventually liberated and went their way—their fate unknown to history—and the plantation was confiscated by the revolutionary government.

4

The marquise was not beautiful, nor was her intellect of a high order, yet she possessed all the plain and homely virtues. She not only loved her husband; she adored him. He was not a "home body," by any means; not a sedate *père de famille* who sat around in the evening wearing a smoking jacket and house slippers. He was away for days and nights at a time, without explanation. When he returned unexpectedly Adrienne sometimes swooned at the sight of him—a most disquieting habit, it would seem.

However, let us be considerate and note on the tablets of history that we are dealing with other times and manners. Swooning was rather prevalent among the high-born ladies. Some of them swooned on hearing poems read. Others swooned before beautiful works of art. I have yet to learn of anyone of them who fainted at the sight of a ragged and famished peasant.

The Princesse de Lamballe, high in court circles and the cherished friend of Marie Antoinette, was an accomplished swooner. She had a habit of passing out completely at the sight of a lobster, or even upon looking at a picture of one.

In 1784 Abigail Adams—wife of the distinguished John—joined her husband in France, where he was residing in his capacity of American commissioner. She was not a swooner. Soon after her arrival she met Adrienne de Lafayette. "The Marquise is a middle-sized lady," she wrote, "sprightly, speaks English with tolerable ease and professes great attachment for America. She kissed me on both cheeks and presented me to her mother, the Duchesse d'Ayen, and her sister, the Vicomtesse de Noailles, all of whom were sitting in a bedroom quite *en famille.*" She says further that Adrienne was engaged in knitting a garment.

The observations of Abigail's twenty-year-old daughter are interesting. She accompanied her mother on this visit. In her diary she says, in reference to the marquise:

She received us very civilly and cordially, with great ease and goodness, and very politely apologized for not waiting on us first. She speaks English a little. She is very agreeable and pleasant. I had always heard she was handsome. I do not think so. She was not painted and very little dressed.

Not long after this visit Adrienne was invited to a dinner party at the Adams home in Auteuil. It should be noted that, in high social circles in France at that time, dinner was served around two-thirty in the afternoon. The performances at the theaters, and at the Opera, usually began at six or seven o'clock. After the theater there was supper and dancing. It was not the custom of French ladies to appear at dinners *en grande toilette,* nor did the men wear evening dress. The practice was to dress elaborately *after dinner* for the theater or the evening's entertainment.

The American ladies who were invited to meet the marquise evidently did not understand this custom. Mrs. Adams says they "glistened with diamonds, watch chains, girdles and buckles" and were arrayed from head to foot in a most magnificent fashion.

Abigail wrote that "no lady of our country would go abroad so little dressed as the Marquise de Lafayette." Adrienne, according to Abigail, wore a brown Florence—whatever that may have been—with a petticoat and a fichu of a "plain double gauze handkerchief." Also a "pretty cap with white ribbons." The effect, she wrote, was "very neat."

5

George Washington Lafayette was six years old in 1785. His parents came to the conclusion that too many people were coming and going in their great house in the Rue de Bourbon for the good of the boy. Too much excitement. So they rented for him a small house in the Rue Saint-Jacques. There he lived with a tutor—M. Frestel—and his mother visited him every day. This M. Frestel had been one of the former teachers of the marquis at the Collège du Plessis. He remained with the family for years and years, and was considered one of the most faithful servitors of the Lafayettes.

Young Lafayette learned to speak English very well, and so did the daughters, Anastasie and Virginie.

CHAPTER XIV

THE PHILOSOPHERS HAVE SOMETHING TO SAY

I

IN THE decade of the 1780's France was a land of words, phrases, theories and pamphlets. The few newspapers that existed were under a strict censorship. The bewildered censors did not know what to approve or disapprove amid the flood of philosophic and political notions and proposed schemes for reform. They settled the matter by excluding practically everything that had any bearing on the actual state of affairs, so the newspapers of the day became extraordinary specimens of dullness.

The writers, cranks, philosophers, and reformers evolved into pamphleteers. They had their say in thin little booklets which were printed in Amsterdam or Switzerland and smuggled into France by the thousands. Phrases, supposed to be replete with wisdom and foresight, floated in the air. Many of them were meaningless, nonsensical; others were the creations of wild-eyed fanatics and dreamers devoid of practical sense.

Edward J. Lowell says, in his informative book, *The Eve of the French Revolution:*

The booksellers' shops were crowded from morning until night. . . . One collector is said to have got together twenty-five hundred different political pamphlets in the last months of 1788, and to have stopped in despair at the impossibility of completing his collection.

He says, further:

In most political crises there is but one great question of the hour; but in France at this time all matters of government and social life were in doubt; and every man believed that he could settle them all by the easy and speedy application of pure reason, if only all other men would lay down their prejudices.

The trouble with that point of view is that "pure reason" is virtually nonexistent, except in the exact sciences. All problems of society and its organization have an emotional content. They must be solved in terms of humanity, with a little logic thrown in to make the stew more appetizing.

Probably the most deplorable vice of language is that the same word means different things to different people. Take the word "liberty," for instance. It has at least twenty meanings, many of which are in direct contradiction with others. To one person liberty means a release from jail; to another it means a democratic government; to another it means the possession of enough wealth to live in idleness; to another it means a license to print or utter anything he wants to say; to another it means a divorce from husband or wife; to another it means freedom from moral restraints.

When a political orator speaks of "the people" he seldom means to include everybody. "Privilege" means one thing to one man and something entirely different to another one. The American Declaration of Independence asserts as a "self-evident" truth, that "all men are created equal." How about the negro slaves? Were they created equal? They were slaves from birth. But that may be explained—and has been explained—by a trick of casuistry, and the explanation is that slaves were not considered men but chattels.

The Declaration goes on to say that all men have certain unalienable rights, among which are "Life, liberty, and the pursuit of happiness." The statement is meaningless and untrue. The whole history of the human race shows that men have no "unalienable rights," even in the freest of democracies. Anything, including life and liberty, may be taken from anybody at the will of the people. After endorsing the Declaration of Independence, our forefathers proceeded to make America a hell for the Tories. Large numbers of these Loyalists were inoffensive people; the only thing against them was that they were opposed to secession from Great Britain. They were murdered in their beds, their houses were burned, their land and cattle were confiscated.

Miriam Beard, in her *History of the Business Man*, calls attention to the fact that the slave traders of the prosperous French seaport of Nantes were, almost to a man, resolute opponents of Tyranny, and supporters of the philosophical principles of "Liberty, Equality and Fraternity."

In the vile trade of selling human beings the slavers of Nantes were conspicuous for their meanness and cruelty. The wealthy merchants of that town sent their ships laden with French goods to the African coast. There the merchandise was traded for negroes who were taken over to the West Indies and exchanged for sugar, indigo, tobacco and other products. The slaves were packed in the dark holds of the ships so tightly that they could hardly find room to lie down. The captains were instructed to jam their ships to the utmost capacity. The weaker negroes would die on the voyage, but it would work out all right in the end, as the stronger ones would survive and bring higher prices.

Miss Beard records the delightfully pleasant-sounding names which were borne by some of the vessels. Among them were *Amitié, Bons Enfants, Saint François, Tendre Famille.*

In Nantes the radical pamphlets were widely circulated and the town was a hotbed for the propagation of the doctrine of liberty and equality. The course of the Revolution, from beginning to end, was marked by startling inconsistencies, muddleheaded thinking on all sides, the substitution of vague phrases for realities; and also by a spirit of inveterate savagery.

When we get further along I think I shall be able to show that every controversial issue entangled in the Revolution might have been settled without bloodshed.

2

Let us consider briefly the writing men—the doctrinaires, encyclopedists, philosophers, intellectual rebels. Such men as Voltaire, Rousseau, Diderot, Helvetius, Quesnay and Holbach.

Though this is an estimate, made by contemporaneous observers, it is entirely probable that not more than twenty per cent of the adults in France could read in the decade which preceded the Revolution.

There were no primary schools; the common people were as ignorant as the Russian peasants during the time of the czars. Very few workers on farms had an idea of the world beyond the next village. They knew nothing of geography, history or social forces; and their conception of the nature of the national government was just a mental fog. But the peasant did know that he had to pay taxes or his cow would be taken from him; also that his lord lived in a fine château not far away; that M. le Marquis, in the château, could do anything he pleased; and that in Paris there was a king who ruled everybody, including M. le Marquis. But nobody could ever see the king; he existed like God.

Four out of five of the peasants were share-croppers (métayers), which meant that the business agent of M. le Marquis took a large portion of their produce—usually half. If this drudging peasant, a brother of the ox, had been given the right to vote he would not have had the faintest idea of what to do with it. In all probability he would have gone to the priest for advice, and would have voted, if it at all, as the priest said.

The workmen in the towns and cities were on a little higher level than the peasants, but not much. Very few of them could read, but during the turbulence and unrest that preceded the Revolution those who were able to read the pamphlets did read them aloud to the others.

Labor unions were forbidden by royal edict, yet the workmen contrived to form them secretly. The government paid little attention to the regulation of hours of labor, or to the welfare of the factory worker.

In the royal factory at Saint-Gobain for the manufacture of glassware the men were bound by contract for four years; they were boarded in houses belonging to the factory, from which they could not go more than a league's distance without being fined. They worked from five in the morning until seven in the evening, with two hours for meals. Work did not cease on Sundays or fete days. They might as well have been convicts. For this labor the average pay was three hundred and fifty livres a year, equivalent in purchasing power to about one dollar a day in America at the present time.

Now, for a while, let us turn from the illiterate peasants and workmen and consider the nobles and the bourgeois. All of them could read and write, but very few of them had a real education, for the reason that higher education—as we conceive it today—did not exist in France. The colleges taught little that was of any value in the field of philosophy, economics, history—or even in the field of clear thinking. Their courses consisted of a memorized rigmarole of Latin and classical learning.

Lafayette could read French, English and Latin, but he read very little and his knowledge of the philosophers and their works was extremely sketchy. In the 1780's everybody in the Parisian salons talked about them and discussed at great length their various conclusions. The marquis learned a little by listening to the arguments. Although he was not a reading man in the true sense he did read every book about the United States as soon as it was published. He became an authority on American affairs, and really knew more about the American states and their people than any other Frenchman then living.

The French race was then—and is now—vivid, intellectual, able and courageous. Their intellectual curiosity, meaning the impulse to examine and dissect philosophic and economic concepts, is in my opinion more dynamic than that of any other people in modern history. They are, in effect, the Greeks of the old time in a modern frame.

Anybody who had anything new to say could get their attention. They might not believe him, but they would listen to him. In the generation before the Revolution the upper crust in France— the nobles and the wealthy bourgeoisie—was the most attentive audience in the world. Practically the whole volume of the literary output, as expressed in books, was radical, or semiradical, or liberal. I have not been able to find even one important, widely circulated book of that period that was distinctly in favor of the old regime.

But there is nothing extraordinary about that. It is a phenomenon that has occurred again and again in history. Social systems that depend for their continued existence on force, or money, or inherited privileges do not seem to be able to defend themselves in print with any degree of conviction. The books of their literary advocates are almost invariably puerile in manner, untruthful in respect to facts, unconvincing and dull.

3

Voltaire was without doubt the most distinguished French author of the eighteenth century, though I am not at all sure that he had more influence on the minds of men and women than Rousseau or Montesquieu or Diderot. He was an exile from France for the greater part of his long life; he died in 1778, at the age of eighty-four. For a time he lived at the court of Frederick the Great, and he spent three years in England, where he learned the English language exceptionally well. The freedom of the English people made a profound impression on him, and gave tone and color to his writings. For many years before his death he lived on an estate which he had acquired in Switzerland.

His *Lettres Philosophiques,* or *Letters Concerning the English Nation,* were first published in London. This book is a satire on France, her government and religion, concealed under cover of a survey of English institutions. An edition, secretly brought out in France, was promptly condemned by the Parlement of Paris and burned as "scandalous and contrary to religion and morals, and to the respect due to the powers that be."

Voltaire was as modern in his literary style, in the crispness of his phrases and in simplicity as the late Arthur Brisbane. And he frequently contradicted himself in important matters, just as Brisbane did, saying one thing at one time and precisely the contrary at another time.

He was not an original thinker, but a popularizer. As a satirist he has few equals in the whole range of literature; he is on the level of Dean Swift, but the mind of Voltaire was far more productive than that of the author of *Gulliver's Travels.* The essence of satire is to say one thing and mean another, and the satirists are the despair of censors. They scan the pages of the suspected book and nothing seems to be wrong. There is only praise for the subject of the biography, the hero, the king, the government, the prevailing institutions. Not a sentence of criticism or abuse. Yet the total effect is blistering and sarcastic.*

He was an inveterate hater of shams, superstitions, hereditary privileges, absurd legal procedures, suppression of free speech, pretensions of the nobility, torture in court trials, unjust methods of taxation, the pompous denial of self-evident facts, the luxury of

---

* The literary device in writing effective satire is, first, to treat the subject with great respect. Be reverent. Do not disparage, or fall into fits of literary rage. Second, treat the weaknesses of your subject as great, noble, or picturesque qualities; and be solemn about it.

Versailles, the exaltation of stupidity as a guiding principle in world affairs.

It is quite a catalogue—his aversions to this and that. He was a deist, which means that he believed in God but not in religion. He detested the Church; he was convinced that priests are the widely distributed instruments and willing tools of tyranny. Good and evil, he thought, were conceptions arising from the conditions of life, and without any fundamental basis. He says good actions are nothing else than actions from which we desire an advantage, and crimes are but actions that are against us. Virtue is the habit of doing the things which please mankind, and vice the habit of doing things which displease it.

To my mind this statement is unconvincing—nevertheless, it sounds well. I believe—and my belief is sustained by experience—that the good which people do is not always, by any means, motivated by a desire to gain an advantage; nor do I believe that virtue is the habit of doing things which please mankind. Certainly not in a great many cases. Everybody knows people of shining virtue who are detested by their neighbors.

Voltaire was a thoroughgoing materialist. He did not believe that God created the universe. Matter, according to him, was *self-existent and eternal;* and God was also *self-existing and everlasting.* These words mean nothing to me, nor do I believe, for a moment, that they meant anything definite to Voltaire. The human intellect has rigid limitations, unfortunately, and one is that the mind cannot conceive of anything coming from nothing, nor of anything that has no beginning or end. It may be that God and matter have existed forever—it may be true—but no man is able to form a mental concept of the pattern. It is just a lot of words and it would' have been more in line with Voltaire's character if he had said that he knew nothing about it, and had no opinion on the subject.

He had few constructive ideas. His mission, as he conceived it, was to destroy—not to create. That was left for others to do. In our day he would have been called, probably, "a debunker."

The Catholic Church in France was appalled by his popularity. He was witty; he wrote in phrases which people liked to quote. His literary production was prodigious. The French edition of his books, letters, correspondence and what not is in ninety volumes.

In 1785 the Church, in making its annual gift to the support

of the crown, gave eighteen million livres (or francs) to Louis XVI
on condition that the works of Voltaire be suppressed. (Voltaire
had then been dead for seven years.) The king agreed. Voltaire's
writings were suppressed, and then everybody began to read them.
The bootlegging of books had become a great industry in France in
the decade before the Revolution.

I am giving this much space to Voltaire—in a biography of
Lafayette—for the purpose of showing the unrest of the intellectuals in France during the prerevolutionary years. It is just as well
that Voltaire died before the Revolution. He would have been in
despair over its lawlessness and its cruelties.

In the eighteenth century, from the 1750's on to the outbreak
of the Revolution, all France was in a ceaseless turmoil about a set
of reference books.* Diderot, assisted by d'Alembert, Condorcet,
Voltaire, Helvetius and others, was engaged during that period for
many years in writing and publishing—volume by volume—the first
French *Encyclopedia*. To a twentieth century mind such an enormous fuss over a huge dictionary of arts and sciences seems bewildering until one remembers what is happening to books in Germany—and to authors—that are displeasing to the Nazi regime.

Condorcet wrote that the plan of the work was to

bring together in a dictionary all that had been discovered in the sciences,
what was known of the productions of the globe, the details of the arts
which men have invented, the principles of morals, those of legislation, the
laws which govern society . . . and even the history of our opinions.

The scheme, though comprehensive, appears to be innocuous;
but the ruling classes of France did not think so. To them it seemed
to be as full of explosives as a powder magazine. "Principles of legislation"—"laws which govern society"—"the history of opinions."
There was no legislation in France, so why get people to talking
about something they could not have, and comparing France with
other countries.

The Church was indignant. Such subjects as the history of
Christianity, the origin of the Bible, the lives of the popes and the
Protestant Reformation were to be discussed in the *Encyclopedia*.
The Clergy intended to suppress it if they could.

* The term "all France," as I use it here, means people who were able to read
and carried on some sort of intellectual life—such as the Nobility, the higher Clergy, the
more prosperous among the bourgeois, the women of the salons, the authors and teachers.

I may say here that the *Encyclopedia,* as finally completed after many vicissitudes, did not give a great deal of space to polemical articles, to history and government. It was not antireligious (or we would not consider it so today), but it showed small reverence for the Church. Most of its handsomely illustrated pages were devoted to descriptions of manufacturing processes, chemistry and the sciences in general. Nine pages were given to tennis and billiards. The art of dancing was treated in a long article.

Much attention, however, was given to the philosophers, to metaphysics, and to the philosophical systems from Plato to Locke. The articles on government favor a democracy as an ideal society, but at the same time there is exhibited a contempt for the populace, "which discerns nothing."

Lafayette was one of the subscribers to the *Encyclopedia,* but as he was usually bored by reading books there is some doubt as to whether he dipped deeply into the learned tomes. However, he must have felt their influence. Everybody he knew talked about the "new knowledge" and the intellectual renaissance. Democracy and republican institutions were openly discussed. The intellectual atmosphere was charged with a spirit of revolt against the existing order years before anything was done about it. Lafayette, in his role of professed republican, did not hesitate to set forth his views in conversations; and his views were those of Washington, flavored by Jefferson and Franklin.

Denis Diderot, editor and chief moving spirit of the *Encyclopedia,* is one of the most astonishing people that I have met in my journeys through the vivid eighteenth century. He was a son of a well-to-do hardware merchant. His father wanted him to be a physician or a lawyer, but he refused to be either, so his father opened the door and threw him out. He went to Paris and lived there for years in his early life by cadging money from people, or borrowing it from acquaintances and forgetting to pay it back. He was of a distinctly intellectual cast. Most of his time was spent in reading; his appetite for knowledge was voracious. But if the book he was reading happened to be dull in places he would fill in these arid sections with creations of his own imagination.

When he described a book that he admired to fascinated listeners his habit was to include the passages that he had invented himself, so upon reading the book they were bewildered at not finding in it what Diderot had said was there.

In arguing with people on controversial subjects, or in writing polemical articles, he frequently invented imaginary authorities to support his case. Authors who never lived; scientists who lived only in his fancy. He was a prodigious liar when it suited his purpose to lie.

Psychiatrists today know that, in many cases, lying is an expression of perverted idealism. The liar tells his lies because he lives in an ideal world, mentally, and he wishes that what he is saying were true.

In 1749 Diderot, who was then thirty-six, wrote a pamphlet (anonymous) about the feelings and perceptions of the blind. At Cambridge, in England, there had been early in the century a blind professor of mathematics named Saunderson—a remarkable fact, indeed, for one naturally thinks of blackboards and crayons and pencils and paper when it comes to mathematics, and how could a blind man manage all that?

Diderot described Saunderson as an atheist, and to sustain his opinions he quoted from "Dr. Inchlif's Life of Saunderson." But "Dr. Inchlif" never existed, and his life of Saunderson lived only in Diderot's imagination. The ruling powers and the Church called his bluff. The reputed atheism of Saunderson was not pleasing to them. Then Diderot denied that he had written the book; said he knew nothing about it. The authorities proved, however, that he was the author, and he was sent to prison for a few months.

Voltaire also lied cheerfully about some of his productions that appeared in print. Disclaimed authorship and declared that if he had written everything that was ascribed to him he would have to be four men.

Diderot was the energetic manager and editor of the *Encyclopedia*. The idea itself was not a new one: *Chambers's Encyclopaedia* had been published in England as early as 1727.

The first two volumes were suppressed in 1752. The Church and conservative people generally incited the suppression. But the volumes had, nevertheless, a considerable circulation. The work of writing and editing the forthcoming volumes went on just the same. Keep in mind, in considering this matter, that the *Encyclopedia* was not really a secret undertaking. It could not possibly be concealed. There had to be many contributors, specialists in one line or another. Those who wrote for it were called Encyclopedists.

Six years later, in 1758, after seven volumes of the work had been brought out, more or less under cover, the Council of State put a ban on the whole enterprise. The publication of the work was forbidden under heavy penalties; the sheets already printed were seized and destroyed. However, strange to relate, the preparation of the books continued and they were all printed (in the original edition) in Paris. It does seem that the governing powers might have stopped it effectively if they had really wanted to do so. The fact that they did not is illustrative of the slackness of all governmental methods near the end of the old regime. The *Encyclopedia* was finally completed in seventeen volumes.

The articles in the first edition are very uneven in quality and the production, as a whole, seems to be immature and poorly edited. No wonder, at that, when one considers the difficulties of its gestation.

4

Now here is Rousseau—named Jean Jacques by his father, a watchmaker of Geneva.

Rousseau was so unhappy, so miserably misplaced in all human affairs, that I cannot read his *Confessions* or his other books without a sense of pain.

Mankind degenerates under civilization, he believed. The primitive man, the American Indian, the savage without pretense or desire, was his ideal. At any rate, sometimes it was, according to his assertions, and at other times it was not. The foggy quality of his mental processes is one of his most striking characteristics. He had no practical experience in the shaping of human affairs, in commerce or in the professions. About half the time he did not know what he was talking about. He had no grasp upon the hard reality that lies under the surface of events.

The advance of civilization brings corruption, he asserted. In his *First Discourse* he says:

Astronomy is born of superstition; eloquence of ambition, hatred, flattery and lying; geometry of avarice; physics of a vain curiosity; all, and morals themselves, of a human pride. The arts and sciences, therefore, owe their birth in our vices; we should have less doubt of the advantage to be derived from them if they sprang from our virtues.

Preposterous, all of it. Do our vices give birth to the arts and sciences? According to Rousseau, the primitive man—the savage—has no vices because he lives in a state of nature, yet the facts are indubitably that savages live in filth; also that they burn and torture their captured enemies, and they die because of injuries or diseases which civilized people readily heal and cure.

What was the matter with that man? I am sure that I do not know, and I am describing him here simply for the reason that his writings had so much influence in France. He wrote, however, near the close of his life, that he never intended to advocate barbarism for civilized states. All that he intended, he said, was to encourage simplicity of manners and human relations.

His books were widely read, and he became a literary figure of great celebrity. Noble ladies made a pet of him, and he was supported by wealthy women for the greater part of his life. Why this happened is a mystery to me. In his enormously famous (and over-rated) *Confessions* he says that he was not much of a lover, and an awkward one. He was not a wit like Voltaire; his sense of humor was small. He was not a handsome person. It may have been that the friendly ladies liked his ideas and wanted to encourage him. France was so wearied of its splendors, its taxes, its art, and its poverty.

The most important of Rousseau's political writings is the *Contrat Social.* It is an essay on the relations of men to each other in civilized communities. The "social compact," as he describes it, is really a written or implied constitution, "a form of association which shall protect with all the common strength the person and property of each associate, and by which each one, uniting himself to all, may yet obey only himself and remain as free as before."

Obey only himself? What does that mean?

In all civilized societies every person must necessarily suppress some of his inclinations. No one can obey himself only; no one is wholly free. There are such impulses as Duty and a Social Conscience and they are often opposed to one's inclinations.*

* The suppression of desires—the sense of duty—is also strong in savage social systems. Among the American Indians members of the same clan could not intermarry. There were other inhibitions, and on the whole they were just about as inhibited as civilized people, but the inhibitions were not the same as ours.

Duty may be defined as the racial standard of behavior.

Farther on, Rousseau proposes as a feature of the social compact, "the total alienation of every associate [meaning every citizen] with all his rights, to the whole community." In that case no one could possess more than anyone else, or have more power than his neighbor, so nobody would have an incentive to infringe on the rights of others. He advocated the national ownership of all land; there should be no private ownership of anything that might be useful in promoting human welfare. That was an expression of Communism many years before the name of Communism was invented.

Why the monarchy did not put him in the Bastille and keep him there as a permanent boarder is a question that has never been answered. It is quite possible that the authorities thought he was just a harmless fool. Or perhaps he was saved by his statement that all large countries should be monarchies, and his preference for what he called *aristocracy*, meaning in his text a government directed by the ablest and wisest citizens. The American Indians, he asserted, are governed by an aristocracy of the wisest men, and look how free and happy they are. His conception of the Indians was erroneous. They were not governed by an aristocracy. The influence of the chiefs was moral only, and traditional. The Indian tribe was an anarchy, tempered by moral influence and custom.

But Rousseau was opposed to an hereditary aristocracy. He seemed to have in mind, as a governing body, a combination of the Academy of Political Science and the Authors League.

5

There was a man named François Quesnay, who was born in a village near Paris in 1694. He developed a system of political economy, called Physiocracy, which had many followers.

Quesnay taught two cardinal principles. First, that the land was the only source of riches, and that these were multiplied by agriculture; and, second, that agriculture and commerce should be carried on without any restrictions whatever.

Manufacturers, he maintained, do no more than pay the wages and expenses of the workmen engaged in them. But agriculture not only pays wages and expenses, but also produces a surplus, which is the revenue of the land.

There is not much sense in the conclusions of Quesnay; I am
setting them forth here only because of their enormous popularity
among the intellectuals of the eighteenth century. In the first place
the land is not the only source of riches—far from it. Agriculture
is the primary producer, but the greater part of its products are not
available for use until they have gone through a manufacturing
process. There is no real creation of a commodity until it is ready
for consumers and available to them.

Most of the profit of production goes to the manufacturer and
not to the primary producer, and also a great part of the profit goes
to distributors.

All taxes, Quesnay argued, should be levied directly on the
income derived from land, and indirect taxation in every shape
should be abolished. He seems to have been a forerunner of Henry
George with the single-tax theory.

His disciple Gournay, who was his chief spokesman, wrote:

In general every man knows his own interest better than any other man to
whom that interest is entirely different. . . . Hence, when the interest of
individuals is exactly the same as the general interest, the best thing to do
is to leave every man to do as he likes.

But the assertion that every man knows his own interest better
than any other man is not true. A great many people need guidance.
Gournay says further that "when the interest of individuals is exactly the same as the general interest, the best thing to do is to
leave every man to do as he likes."

But how does one know when the best interest of the individual
coincides with the general interest? We have given that theory a
good long tryout—here in America—and we learned that it is so-
cially unsound. It is the laissez-faire doctrine, the cornerstone of the
philosophy of individualism. The phrase *"laissez faire"* was originated by Gournay.

Society, to protect itself, must exercise some regulation over
business and industry. We cannot let everything go. We have found
that it does not work; that it leads to industrial and financial
catastrophes.

Quesnay's views on social economy made a great impression
on eighteenth century Europe. They were among the inspirations of
Adam Smith's *Wealth of Nations*, which is considered—even today
—one of the classic economic treatises of the modern world.

CHAPTER XV

BANKRUPTCY OF THE GOVERNMENT

I

OR LAFAYETTE the four years between the return from his American tour in 1785 until the outbreak of the Revolution in 1789 were pleasant; very likely the most pleasant period of his life. He was famous, rich, young and healthy. He dabbled in French politics, such as they were; agitated for reforms in the government and the methods of taxation; and made trips, with his gorgeous crowd of friends and retainers, to Potsdam and Vienna.

Besides, there was the beautiful Mme. Simiane and devoted Adrienne; and the growing children; and the superb house in Paris.

About six months was spent by him in organizing the French branch of the Order of the Cincinnati, composed of officers who had served in the American war.

Catherine the Great invited him to visit Russia as her guest. The invitation was accepted with enthusiasm, but he never made the trip, as the time for the visit grew near the riots and disorders in France were so menacing that he thought, in the circumstances, he had better remain at home.

In 1786 Lafayette took an active interest in the negotiation of a commercial treaty between the American states and the French government. He knew very little about commerce, but he was ably instructed by Thomas Jefferson, and he played an important part as an intermediary.

Practically all the tobacco consumed in France came from America, and the sale of tobacco and its products was a monopoly of the farmers-general. But the tobacco was not purchased directly from American planters; the French monopoly bought it in England from British importers. It was a costly, roundabout method which had the effect of raising the price in France and of giving an unearned profit to English merchants.

Jefferson and Lafayette succeeded in getting this practice abol ished, and in having the farmers-general purchase their tobacco i America. They, and the other American commercial agents, spen much time and effort to increase the overseas trade between Franc and the American states. Their work in this direction was not s successful as they hoped it would be, yet they did accomplish some thing. England was predominant in manufacturing, and the agri cultural Americans needed manufactured articles for which the could pay only by sending their own products across the sea.

The marquis succeeded in having the French importation ta on whale oil removed. The inhabitants of the island of Nantucket— the chief whaling center of the American continent—were so grate ful that they sent Lafayette a five-hundred pound cheese as an ex pression of their gratitude. By unanimous resolution of the Nan tucket population it was agreed that the milk given by every cov on the island for twenty-four hours should be used in the making o this overwhelming cheese.

At the conclusion of the commercial negotiations Jefferson wrote to Congress (October 22, 1786):

The assistance of M. de La Fayette in the whole of this business has been so earnest and efficacious that I am in duty bound to place it under the eye of Congress, as worthy of their notice on this occasion. Their thanks, o such notice as they think proper, would be grateful to him without doubt He has richly deserved and will continue to deserve it, whenever occasions shall arise of rendering service to the United States. These occasions wil continually arise.

The financial position of the French government was growing steadily worse, but France was not really a poor nation, although there were millions of poverty-stricken people among the French. The budget could have been balanced readily enough. The privi leged classes—the Nobility and the Clergy—did not pay much in the way of tax in proportion to their income, and they resisted any increase in taxation that would fall on them.

The taxes were paid chiefly by the rich bourgeois—the middle-class merchants, industrialists, shipowners—and the peasants. The court at Versailles cost the French people about thirty million livres (or francs) a year. That huge sum included pensions to favored courtiers, the support of the king, queen and the royal family; the upkeep of the royal palaces; the queen's losses at gambling; the pay

f thousands of servants; the building of new pavilions and play-
houses. It was nothing less than a monstrous fantasy, a nightmare
so mean and evil in all its aspects that today we contemplate it with
wonder.

2

In 1774 the young king, who knew nothing whatever about
finance, called in Turgot as a member of his Council and as con-
roller-general of the financial affairs of the kingdom.* The position
of controller-general corresponded generally to that of a modern
secretary of the treasury, but his field of activity and responsibility
extended beyond the treasury. He had some of the functions of a
prime minister of today.

Back in 1761 Turgot had been appointed intendant of the
province of Limoges (called Limousin), and he made an outstanding
success of the job. Limousin was one of the poorest districts in
France. Turgot could not change the fundamental laws, but he
made the nobles pay their taxes; he increased the product of the
soil by having the peasants taught better methods of farming; he
encouraged and developed the industry of making pottery, so that
today Limoges is one of the world's chief manufacturing centers for
fine tableware. Wheat was monopolized there, as in all France, by
restrictions on its movement and its sale. That was abolished by
Turgot. He was the intendant of Limousin for thirteen years and
became renowned throughout France because of his ability to get
results where other men had failed.

He was a Physiocrat, a disciple of Quesnay, which means that
he was an individualist, a wholehearted believer in the laissez-faire
theory of economics.

So he was summoned to Paris to put in order the financial
affairs of the nation. He was in trouble from the day he arrived until
he was dismissed. In hot water all the time. In the first place he was
just a businessman and not a courtier. Devoid of wit, awkward in
manner and brusque in speech, he made enemies on all sides. He
studied the expenditures of the treasury and tried to find out what
the Polignacs and other favorites of the queen did for the immense
sums paid to them. That alone was sufficient to make him unpopular with the little group of people who ruled France.

* Anne Robert Jacques Turgot was a Norman, a noble of an esteemed family.

He abolished the trade guilds which controlled workmen' wages, and which were—in effect—monopolies in the field of manu facturing. He declared that the right to work and set up a busines of one's own was the right of every man. This was, as we know, a fundamental doctrine of the Physiocrats. The dolorous outcries o the master craftsmen, the manufacturers, resounded all over the country. They declared that industry would be completely ruined that in a few years it would be flat on its back. The whole field o enterprise, they declared, was now thrown open to irresponsibl adventurers.

It did not seem possible for him to turn his hand to anything without appearing to harm a great many people. What those in power wanted him to do was not to reform the government bu simply to raise money.

Malesherbes, distinguished magistrate and a friend of Turgot urged him to advise the king to summon the States-General—a body representing the whole nation, including the Third Estate—and ope the financial problems of the government to general discussion Turgot did not like the idea. He had a horror of popular assemblies Although he was a just man himself and one who stood for freedom of the individual, he believed that a benevolent despot could d more for the benefit of mankind than any number of orators in a national assembly.

The Polignacs, the king's brothers, the Duc de Guise, the Princesse de Lamballe and her coterie—all these detested Turgo and his economies and attempts to balance the budget. Their hug subsidies were in danger. They, and hundreds of other attached t the court, did everything they could to mess up his plans and brin him into disfavor with the king. In the course of these proceeding they forged some letters, in imitation of Turgot's handwriting, i which the king was disparaged and the queen was mentioned in a disrespectful manner. Both king and queen were furious. Withou demanding of Turgot if he had really written the letters the kin sent him an order to give up his office and leave Paris at once This happened in May, 1776.

3

Turgot's successor was Jacques Necker, the Protestant banke of Swiss origin who had made a large fortune for himself. His repu

ation far outran his merits. Self-made millionaires are almost invariably, and in all countries, considered to be greater men than
hey really are.

A colossal vanity was one of the defects of his character. He
bragged of his own achievements and liked to be looked upon as a
magician of money—and so he was regarded, too, by the bankers,
he nobles, and by the court. He was his own press agent, and he
possessed a highly developed capacity for publicizing himself.

Notwithstanding his limitations Necker had an expert accountant's grasp of the situation. He realized that no institution—not even
a great national government—can go on continually paying out
more money than it takes in. He urged a reduction of governmental
expenses, and that services should be rendered by all recipients of
he royal bounty. Also, that the privileged classes—the Nobility and
he Clergy, who owned the greater part of the kingdom—should be
axed in proportion to their share of the nation's income. These were
ound proposals, but they got nowhere.

Lafayette was one of Necker's ardent admirers. He frequently
visited the controller-general and was a regular attendant at the
soirées of brilliant Mme. de Staël, who was Necker's daughter.
Necker believed in local self-government—the province, the commune, legislating for itself in all local affairs. That was one of the
pet ideas of Lafayette; he had seen it work in America. Eventually
Necker persuaded the king to try an experiment in provincial assemblies, and His Majesty agreed. Two assemblies were established, one
in Berry and the other in Haute-Guyenne. The assembly of Berry
alarmed the king and the courtiers by passing a resolution for equal-
ty in taxation, and for a national representative assembly, or congress, which would have a share in the government. That does not
appear to us today to be so dreadful, yet Versailles thought it was,
and the resolution was disapproved.

Necker met the wasteful extravagances of the court and the
government by borrowing on a large scale. His prestige as a financier
was so great that he was able to borrow immense sums, but he never
knew exactly how he was going to pay what he had borrowed. He
could float the most preposterous loans, borrowing from the wealthy
bankers, merchants, and speculators, paying even as high as ten
and twelve per cent interest.

His great reputation did not prevent him from carrying on

other unsound schemes for raising money. For instance, there wer
royal lotteries of a peculiar character. In order to promote a large sal
of lottery tickets it was arranged that nobody could lose. If a ticke
buyer did not win one of the prizes his ticket was still considered
permanent investment and entitled to four per cent interest annually

The treasury also sold annuities to raise funds, but no accoun
was taken of the age of those who purchased the annuities. The fixe
rate of payment was ten per cent on the amounts deposited. Ther
was no actuarial computation of the probable cost to the state. Th
beneficiary might be seven years old or seventy.

This device brought many millions of cash into the treasury
The beneficiaries, naturally enough, were in most cases young peo
ple, boys and girls.

These financial contortions were unworthy of Necker. He wa
no fool. In his own personal business dealings he would never hav
made such unprofitable and ruinous commitments. What were hi
reasons? We do not know, but we may guess, and the most reason
able conjecture is that he was trying to push the coming Disaste
further into the future, with the desperate hope that some unex
pected turn of affairs might develop in the meantime; a favorabl
situation which would put everything right.

In February, 1781, Necker presented a lengthy report o
finances to the king and immediately had it published under the titl
of *Compte rendu au Roi*. It was the first financial statement of th
French government that had ever been put in print for the perusa
of the people. Before that time all government doings in finance wer
secret. A hundred thousand copies were sold in a few weeks.

He would not have dared to publish this paper without th
king's permission, and the authorization to print would not hav
been given, we may be sure, if the report had not shown the finance
to be in a marvelous state of prosperity. Necker declared that, in
stead of a deficit, there was an annual surplus of ten millions—
statement that was wholly false, which the king, queen and thei
favorites all knew very well. So Necker's pamphlet on the finance
was really an advertisement for the regime. As a frontispiece o
this extraordinary literary production there was a steel engraving o
Necker himself, surrounded by the figures of Abundance and Jus
tice. The text of the report was feverishly rhetorical, and not a

all the calm, well-balanced statement that one expects from a secretary of the treasury.

The controllers-general, before Necker's time, had all been appointed members of the king's Council, by virtue of their high office. Necker was not so appointed. The reason: he was a Protesant, and there was an ironclad tradition, or rule, that only Catholics might have places in the Council. Necker's vanity was grievously wounded by this exclusion, from the start, but he kept on for years, hoping for the appointment. In 1781 he resigned in disgust from his position of controller-general.

4

After Necker the finances became fantastic in the hands of incompetent persons.* One of them was Calonne, and I am at a loss to describe him. He was certainly not a financial genius. He believed in extravagance as a system of governmental finance, thought that if one has to borrow money one must spend freely. The richer you look the more you can borrow, but just as soon as the government becomes economical people of wealth stop their lending. That was his idea—apparently; I am not sure about it, so I say "apparently." Certainly it accords with his actions.

The funds raised through loans might be distributed in a flood of pensions, gifts to courtiers and favorite ladies, salaries, perquisites and so on, and eventually it would go back to the people. Those who get the money also spend it. It was a policy of unlimited borrowing. At Versailles he was looked upon as God's finest gift to man. Yet I am not at all sure that this estimate of Calonne is entirely correct. Historians generally consider him featherheaded, trivial and foolish, but he seems to have had a wholly different side to his character. He had constructive ideas which were swamped by the hopeless entanglements of his situation.

In 1786 Calonne had reached the end of his rope. The public debt had increased by 653,000,000 livres in three years under Calonne's administration. In 1789 it amounted to 4,500,000,000 livres, and the annual interest to be paid on it took more than half

* I am discussing government money problems for the reason that they were among the direct causes of the Revolution.

the revenue of the government. The debt had increased threefold during the fifteen-year reign of Louis XVI, but please keep in mind that nearly half that increase had come into being on account of the French participation in the American War for Independence. Even as it was, the debt should not have been unmanageable. England, with a population one-third that of France, had a public debt of the same proportions and contrived to handle it.

Calonne did not know which way to turn. In August, 1786, he advised the king to summon an Assembly of Notables, and he said, in curious contradiction of his own practices:

It is impossible to increase taxation, and ruinous to be always borrowing; it is not enough to confine ourselves to economic reforms. The only thing to be done, the sole means by which the finances may at last be reduced to order, must consist in infusing life into the whole state by recasting all the vicious elements in its constitution.

Rather astonishing declaration, isn't it, coming from a controller-general who had thrown away money in such a whole-hearted way? The Assembly of Notables, which he urged the king to summon, was a hand-picked advisory body, without authority. On occasion—but at long intervals—the Assembly of Notables had been brought together by the French kings to consider the state of affairs. There was no case in history in which they had resisted the king's autocratic decisions. They had had their say and had gone home, after giving some friendly advice. Their chief function was to assure the nation that all was well.

5

At Calonne's suggestion the Notables were convened. One hundred and forty-four of them, all selected by Louis XVI or his ministers. There were no proletarians among the Notables, but there were seven princes of the royal family, thirty-six dukes and nobles, and the rest were important bourgeois, councilors of state, and so on.

Lafayette's name was on the first list of those chosen for the Assembly; then, on revision, it was struck off on account of his republican American ideas. The Versailles coterie had given him a nickname, mentioned only when he was not present. He was called "the American" because of his continual reference to the freedom of the American people, their representative government, their legislative assemblies, the moderate pay of their officials, the small burden of taxation, and the equity and honesty of American legal procedure.

The verbal picture he painted of America was not wholly true, but he thought it was. However, he was restored to the list through the influence of his friends, the Baron de Breteuil and the Marquis de Castries.

The Notables met on February 22, 1787. In his address at the opening session Calonne said:

One cannot take a step in this vast kingdom without coming upon different laws, contradictory customs, privileges, exemptions, immunities from taxation, and every variety of rights and claims; and this general lack of harmony complicates administration, disturbs its course, and increases expense and disorganization on all sides.*

Lafayette took a prominent part in the deliberations. He attacked the methods of the farmers-general, and the entire system of taxgathering. He declared that the members of the syndicate of taxgatherers enriched themselves by dishonest methods, and he made a detailed statement in which he gave names, places and dates.

When the king heard of Lafayette's attack on the existing order —the unjust and unequal taxation, the dissipation of the public money, the extravagance of the court—he flew into a rage and notified the Assembly, through the Comte d'Artois, that anyone who had the presumption to bring forth such grave charges must put them in writing and sign them.

The Bastille was staring the marquis in the face, but he kept his courage. He called for the minutes of the meeting at which he had made his speech, signed a copy of it and had it sent to the king.

As a postscript he added:

The millions that are being dissipated are raised by taxes, *and taxes can be justified only by the real needs of the state.* [*Italics are mine.*] All these millions abandoned to depredation or cupidity are the price of sweat, the tears, and it may be the blood of the people, and the reckoning of misery caused by the raising of these sums so lightly thrown away is a terrifying reflection on the justice and goodness which we know to be the natural sentiments of His Majesty.

Going further, Lafayette urged the king to appoint a commis-

* Mathiez, *The French Revolution*, p. 21.

siôn cônsisting ôf persons of absolute honesty and courage to investigate the accounts of the administration, the doings of the farmers-general and the pensions paid to courtiers.

Nothing was done; the marquis was not even sent to the Bastille, as would have happened to the author of such a communication to the king in any reign before that of Louis XVI. The king was an indolent monarch, stupid, slow of thought, but well-meaning. The whole problem was completely beyond his capacity.

Now another stew of trouble boils and bubbles. The Notables insisted on knowing the truth about the finances of the government. All of them had read Necker's "Account Rendered to the King," which was published in 1781, and that famous account showed that everything in the treasury department was flourishing, with more income than expense. Yet here was talk of financial disasters and proposals to increase taxes. What had happened in six years? Had Calonne thrown away all the money? Had he stolen it? To defend himself Calonne had to prove that Necker was a liar; that when his optimistic account was rendered to the king the treasury had an annual deficit instead of a surplus, and that his [Calonne's] extravagances were caused by the demands of the court, which were imperative and not to be resisted by anyone in his position.

So there we are; all the soiled linen is exposed to the public gaze. It was sensational. Today it would be called front-page news; not only all over the front page, but running back on other pages. For a little while the storm center of events was around Calonne. The Notables were shocked by his disclosures, and hated him on that account. They thought such revelations should be whispered —not shouted. The courtiers accused him of speculating in the funds of the state. They declared he had debts and mistresses. No doubt that was true, but almost everybody else in the controversy was well equipped in the possession of both these items.

The king dismissed Calonne in April, 1787, while the Notables were in session, and he left France as soon as he could get away. He never returned. The king is said to have declared (according to the gossip of the time) that he was sorry he had not had him hanged.

But who was going to take Calonne's place? Could any man be found who was willing to take over the management of this broken-down financial structure; who was willing to tinker with a budget so unbalanced that the hope of straightening it out could be only a pleasant dream; who was willing to obey with the alacrity of a docile servant every demand of Versailles?

Yes, indeed. Such a man could be found. Men want jobs, and they want distinction, and power. The Abbé de Vermond, the queen's reader,* had a friend who, in his judgment, was capable of managing the finances, and he suggested Loménie de Brienne, archbishop of Toulouse, to the queen. At that time Marie Antoinette was really the ruler of France; the king—dull and befuddled—accepted her opinion on many of the most important matters.

So Loménie de Brienne became controller-general of the finances. He was said to be an intelligent man, but exactly what does intelligence mean? It is a vague word for the reason that there are so many varieties of intelligence. There are intelligent housemaids, intelligent professors, intelligent swindlers.

The outstanding fact is that whatever variety of intelligence Brienne possessed, it was not in the financial category. It may have been that he was selected for that very reason. His knowledge and experience were negligible, and it might be possible to manipulate the finances before his eyes without arousing his suspicions.

However that may have been, there can be no doubt that he had an impossible task. No man in the world could have solved the intricate problems that faced him; not without recasting the system of government, abolishing thousands of privileges and exemptions, and cutting out all forms of useless expenditures. To these reforms the king would never have consented even though Brienne had proposed them—which he did not. He was simply a bewildered man bogged neck-deep in a morass of debts.

6

The Assembly of Notables wrangled, day after day, without making much progress. The powerful court party among them opposed vehemently every change or new venture that was contrary to the prevailing tradition, except in a few instances where the proposed reforms were of slight importance.

* The queen's reader's duty was to read books and the news of the day and to tell her about them.

Some of the members of the Assembly were of the opinion that, considering the condition of the kingdom, the States-General should be summoned by the king to meet within a reasonable time, and a resolution to that effect was introduced. It was opposed by the royal princes, and most of the higher nobles. Lafayette rose to speak, and after declaring that he was in favor of the resolution he made a proposal of his own. He said:

As the simplification of the manner of raising taxes should deliver the state from the financial companies, whose engagements end in five years, it seems to me that we should beg His Majesty to fix that period as one in which accounts of all these operations should be rendered to him, and to consolidate the happy result of them by the convocation of a National Assembly.

That proposal fell on the Notables like a bombshell. Two revolutionary measures were advocated by the marquis in one sentence. First, to wind up the operations of the farmers-general, and keep all taxation and financial operations under the control of the state. And, second, to establish a National Assembly.*

The existence of such an Assembly, with its consequent supervision of all affairs of state, could mean only a complete change in the character of the French government.

Lafayette had his say, but nothing came of his idea, except that it served only to deepen the king's distrust of him. The resolution, as passed, asked the king to summon the States-General within the next five years.

The Notables had recommended the creation of provincial assemblies, and these were established in 1787 by royal edict. The provincial assemblies were not elected by the people. The three estates—Nobility, Clergy and Commons—were all represented in them, but the members were selected by the king or his ministers. And every important act of the provincial assemblies had to be approved by the king before it became operative.

Loménie de Brienne advised the dissolution of the Assembly of Notables. He asserted that it put obstacles in his way, that its proposals were unsound, and that he would be better off without it. The Assembly was dissolved on May 25, 1787, and the confused Notables went home.

* Understand clearly the distinction between a States-General and a National Assembly. The States-General met only at the will of the king—the last one had been called in 1614—but a National Assembly (as the term was understood) would be a permanent congress, meeting at stated intervals, and representing all the people.

7

Brienne's first move to increase the revenue was to devise a stamp tax, a measure which was immediately approved by the king. It was closely similar to the stamp tax which made the British government so unpopular in the American colonies. Stamps were to be used on receipts, legal papers, drafts, bills, newspapers, posters.

The overtaxed people rebelled at this fresh imposition and the Parlement of Paris refused to register the edict. On August 6th the Parlement, having been summoned to a lit de justice, did register the obnoxious edict, but next day, in Paris, the members of the Parlement annulled the registration on the ground that it was not within their power to register edicts imposing new taxes. This argument was humorously naïve; the Parlements had registered tax edicts for several hundred years, but now, it appears, they had just discovered that they had no right to do it. They informed the king that only the States-General had the right.

Thereupon the Parlement was banished to Troyes, and there they resided in dingy exile. But these magistrates had suddenly become popular for the first time in history. They were regarded as heroes.

Behind the scenes Brienne negotiated with them. He would give up the stamp tax if they would agree to register a decree for prolonging and increasing the tax on incomes, to be levied "without any distinction or exception whatever." They agreed, and returned to Paris where there was a display of fireworks in their honor.

Yet, while all this dissension was going on, France was growing in prosperity, although there was much unemployment. The rich were getting richer. A flood of wealth flowed from the French West Indies; San Domingo alone produced half the world's supply of sugar. French fabrics were famous throughout Europe for the beauty of their patterns. Equally well known was the work of the silversmiths, the jewelers and watchmakers, the makers of luxurious furniture. Fine French wines and brandies had a world-wide market. The prosperous middle class inspired the Revolution—they and the lesser nobles and landowners—because of their dissatisfaction with their own status in the state, and their almost total lack of influence in governmental affairs.

They inspired the Revolution, and won it—and then lost it for a while to the common people, then got control of it again.

Lafayette, witnessing the coming storm, failed to see its direful progress. There were black clouds on the horizon and the wind was whistling through the trees when he wrote to Washington that events would bring France, by degrees—

Without a great convulsion to an independent representation and, consequently, to a diminution of the royal authority. But it is a matter of time, and will proceed the more slowly that the interests of powerful men will clog the wheels.

As a political weather prophet the marquis was a failure. But he was not the only one in France. There were millions of intelligent Frenchmen whose ability to foretell the future was on the same level as Lafayette's.

By the month of August, 1788, Brienne had become a washed-out failure. He could borrow no more money; every resource had failed. He made a formal declaration that the government was bankrupt. A pathetic little sum of 400,000 livres still remained in the treasury. The king dismissed Brienne, and sent him away from Paris. The last thing he did, just before leaving his office, was to take 200,000 livres—or one-half of the treasury's wealth—put it in his pocket and carry it away with him.

The king recalled Necker.

All France rejoiced, for Necker had a magic name. Paris rejoiced first, but when the news spread even to the little towns of Brittany, to the Pyrenees, to Alsace, to the Mediterranean, men acquired confidence, a feeling that as Necker had returned the worst was over.

Necker was asked to come back because it did not seem possible to carry on the financial system without him. There was no trouble at all in borrowing twenty-five million livres on Necker's word. So the civil servants were paid, the army and navy were paid, and Marie Antoinette's friends were given a few millions.

The recall of Necker was not the only important occurrence in the month of August, 1788. The king convoked the States-General, to meet on May 1, 1789.

CHAPTER XVI

THE STATES-GENERAL

I

THE PROVINCIAL assembly of Rennes, in Brittany, invited Lafayette to become a member of their body. He still possessed one estate in Brittany, and was therefore rightfully classed as a Breton noble as well as an Auvergnat. The Bretons were clamorous for reforms, smaller taxation and a reduction of expenditures by the court. In the latter part of 1788 the assembly at Rennes refused to register the new tax laws and protested against them. Among the signatories was the name of the Marquis de Lafayette.

The queen demanded of the marquis what he—a seigneur of Auvergne—had to do with the affairs of Brittany. He replied, "I am in the same situation as Your Majesty. You are the queen of France and also a member of the house of Austria."

Marie Antoinette considered that an insolent reply. Next day the king, through the minister of war, notified Lafayette that he was dismissed from the army, in which he held a commission as maréchal de camp, though not on active service. Incredibly foolish move. So long as Lafayette was an army officer the king could have called him to account for his activities, or Louis might have put him in command of some distant garrison where he would have been too far away to take much part, if any, in public affairs. But, by removing him from the army list, the king—inspired by the queen—gave him as much freedom of political action as any Frenchman could have at that time.

Thomas Jefferson, the American minister in Paris, who had once written to Madison that Lafayette's "weight with those in power is great" and "I think he will one day be of the ministry," now wrote in a different tone. In an official report he said:

The Marquis has drawn upon himself the enmity of the whole Court; on the other hand, his credit is growing among the nation. But for some time I have trembled for his liberty.

2

The Notables had been assembled a second time in November, 1788, to deliberate on the method of electing deputies to the States-General and other matters connected with the procedure of this unusual convocation of the three orders.

In 1614 every electoral area had sent only one delegate for each order, and no resolution was considered as carried unless it had the unanimous assent of the Nobles, Clergy and Third Estate. That may have been all right in 1614, when the States-General was expected to do nothing but approve the actions and ideas of the king, but there were so many elements of grave uncertainty in the minds of men in 1789 that such a simple club of sycophants would have seemed to the whole nation to be nothing more than a farce.

It was decided that the number of representatives should be greatly increased; that the three orders were to meet separately (as in 1614); and that no resolution could be carried without the affirmative vote of two orders.

Lafayette proposed that the Third Estate have double representation; that its deputies be equal in number to those of the Nobility and Clergy combined. Why not? The Third Estate, which means the common people and the middle class, included more than nine-tenths of the people in France. Some of the Notables took Lafayette's side, and there was a long dispute on this point. In the end his proposal was voted down.

But this particular question would not stay dead. In December (1788) the Parlement of Paris advised the king to double the representation of the Third Estate. Before the close of the year he agreed to do so.

In electing the delegates each order voted separately. The delegates of the Clergy all belonged to the priesthood, and every priest had a vote. Similarly the nobility selected its representatives. As for the Third Estate, every man in France (not a noble or a cleric) who had reached the age of twenty-five and paid any taxes at all was entitled to cast a vote. As practically everybody had to pay some tax this meant universal suffrage.

The machinery of election was rather elaborate in respect to the Clergy and the Third Estate. These orders elected local delegates who met in the chief town of the district, and this assembly decided on the deputies who were to represent the district at the States-General.

The king possessed an absolute veto power and thus would be able to nullify any resolution which came from the States-General even though it had the affirmative vote of all three orders.

There were 1,155 delegates in all; of these 266 represented the Nobility, 291 the Clergy, and 598 the Third Estate.

Early in 1789 Lafayette went to his native Auvergne to present himself as a candidate for the States-General before the nobles of the province. He found that the queen and her group of favorites at Versailles had sent agents to Auvergne to prevent his election. The leading members of the Third Estate, grasping the situation, and fearing the defeat of the marquis, offered to elect him as one of their representatives, if he would accept election at their hands. His family and his friends advised him not to allow himself to appear as a Third Estate representative. He wavered awhile, and then decided to stand for election before the Nobles. It was a mistake—though not a fatal one—which he bitterly regretted within the next few months.

Chinard says that "Lafayette hesitated and 'straddled,' as he often did in his later years." *

Jefferson wrote to Washington (May 10, 1789):

I am in great pain for the Marquis de Lafayette. His principles, you know, are clearly with the people; but having been elected by the Noblesse of Auvergne they have laid him under express instructions to vote for the decision by orders and not persons. . . . I have not hesitated to press upon him to burn his instructions and follow his conscience as the only sure clue, which will eternally guide a man clear of all doubts and inconsistencies.

He was elected by the Nobles, but it was a tight squeeze. Of the three hundred and ninety-three votes cast Lafayette had a majority of only three. Evidently his popularity with the Nobility of his native province could hardly be called overwhelming. But his popularity among the common people was immense. In all probability the Third Estate would have elected him unanimously.

Every delegate sent to the States-General was pledged to follow the instructions given him by his constituents. Imagine the discom-

* Chinard, *The Letters of Lafayette and Jefferson,* p. 77.

fiture of the marquis when he realized that, being elected by the Nobles, he was expected to cast his vote on the conservative side. But the prohibitions did not extend to speeches. Lafayette, and some other nobles with republican views, brought out their liberal ideas and advocated them—explaining diffidently that they could not vote for them without violating their instructions. The instructions of the constituencies which bound the deputies were tacitly laid aside in the course of time, and thereafter every man voted as he pleased.

In the interval of time between the elections—March, 1789, to the May of that year—the disorder among the people grew throughout France. This was due, in part, to a sudden increase in unemployment; and, in part, to the bad harvest of the previous year, with a consequent rise in the price of bread. A four-pound loaf in Paris cost fourteen sous, which was practically prohibitive to workingmen at the prevailing wages.

Then came the Révaillon riot on April 27th, a week before the meeting of the States-General. Révaillon, who may be described as a liberal, had been elected as a deputy from Paris to the States-General in opposition to a candidate proposed by the Duc d'Orléans. He was a manufacturer of wallpaper and employed many workmen. A story was circulated among the working people that Révaillon had said that a workman could live on fifteen sous a day. There is no evidence that he had really said any such thing; it was just a tale being passed around. A mob went to his house and factory and wrecked them. The riot spread throughout the factory district. Troops were sent for, and the mob attacked the soldiers. The troops fired on the rioters, and two hundred people were killed before order was restored.

Talleyrand wrote that he believed the riot was inspired by the Duc d'Orléans, and Lafayette was inclined to the same view of the matter.

3

But the *homme moyen*—whom we call the Average Man—hoped for the best. No, hope is not a strong enough word; he *knew* that all the troubles of the people would soon be over.

Is not the great and wise M. Necker sitting at the king's right hand? He will keep a level head.

The States-General is to meet. More than a thousand patriots from all parts of France. In their wisdom they will devise ways and means. The king himself, who loves his people, will put himself in their hands and follow their advice.

And the Marquis de Lafayette, courageous advocate of liberty, equality and justice, will be in the States-General, and what he says will be heeded by the whole nation.

Ah, poor little homme moyen! What is going to happen to you and your cheerful prophecies? The curtain is rising on a long drama of blood, misery and confusion. France is to be swept by a tornado of incalculable force.

On Monday, May 4th, the king received all the members of the States-General, which was to convene in formal session the next day. The deputies of the Third Estate were offended by their treatment at the reception. The Nobility and the Clergy were escorted up the wide staircase to the audience chamber, where they remained for a time in groups, chatting with the king and royal princes. The Third Estate deputies, on the other hand, were admitted through a side door and hustled quickly past the king. He did not speak a word to any of them.

Gouverneur Morris, who was at Versailles the day before, wrote that the beautiful lawn of the palace "was crowded with groups of gayly dressed officers and dignitaries of the church, each wearing the brilliant tokens of his rank. Ladies decked in the brightest colors and wearing the happiest smiles talked, sauntered about. . . .

"In striking contrast to these," he continued, "were the groups of the members of the Third Estate—shunned as if they bore the seeds of a pestilence among them. They talked in whispers, hurriedly and earnestly—they never smiled. Their costume of black hose and surtout and short black coat, to which they had been condemned by the old sumptuary laws and which denoted the plebeian, made the contrast even greater." *

The States-General began with a splendid ceremony—a proces-

* It may be worth while to state here that there were no peasants among the deputies of the Third Estate—nor any workmen. Few peasants could read. There was no labor party in France and no feeling—so it seems—that labor should be represented. Three hundred and seventy-four lawyers were members of the Third Estate. There were also many merchants, some writers and professional men.

sion through the streets from the Church of St. Louis to the Salle des Menus Plaisirs, where the sessions were to be held. The three orders marched separately: the Nobles in their gold-embroidered mantles with swords at their sides, wearing large hats with white plumes; the Clergy in the silken robes of the Church; the Third Estate in plain black. Among the Third Estate walked Mirabeau, a noble who had been rejected as a delegate by his own order. Promptly he offered himself to the Third Estate of his province and was promptly elected. He was the only noble on that side.

In this stately procession the six hundred commoners came first; then the Nobles and the Clergy. The king and royal princes walked behind all the others. Everyone carried a small lighted candle which glimmered faintly in the strong sunlight.

Brilliant tapestries, brought from the palace, hung from all the windows on the route. Banners waved overhead, and there was the rhythm and melody of music. Behold the gorgeous pomp and glory of old France marching in splendor, and with the throb of drums, to its grave.

The Duc d'Orléans, who was entitled by virtue of his ancestry to be in the king's party, but who was a deputy elected by the Nobles, walked alone—not with the Nobility, but just behind the Third Estate, and so close to the commoners that he seemed to belong to them.

4

The Duc d'Orléans is often referred to as a cousin of Louis XVI, but the cousinship is remote; he was really a distant relative. Both he and the king were descendants of Louis XIII. The richest peer in France, he was notorious for his vices and general unworthiness. He supported numerous mistresses, a racing stable which he had acquired in England, a gambling house, and a band of vicious retainers.

He was hated by the king and queen and he returned their hatred in good measure. During the Revolution—that is to say, during the early part of it, when it was believed that the system of royalty would continue—he conspired to supplant Louis XVI and get the throne for himself. As a member of the National Assembly he voted—in 1793—for the death of the king, regardless of the ties of blood. After the abolition of titles, he called himself Philippe Egalité and supported the cruel program of the infuriated revolutionists. They turned against him in the end, and he was sent to the guillotine in 1793.

But now we see him, morose and vindictive, dressed in glittering array, walking by himself and meditating upon schemes of ambition.

The great hall was packed and jammed. A lake of humanity on the floor. More than a thousand men; a thousand minds, including all varieties of temperament and mental capacity. Also all varieties of cupidity, kindness, sympathy, weakness, viciousness, hate, perception and vision.

Among the delegates is Robespierre, destined to become the heart and soul of the Reign of Terror. This ruthless destroyer—as he will be in time to come—is slight and timid in appearance. His complexion is bad, described as "greenish yellow." He wears heavy glasses, and peers with the fixed stare of an owl. He is only thirty, a lawyer of Arras, insignificant and unknown. He has left forever his dry legal documents and has gone forth to make for himself a resounding place in history which few will envy.

Gentle Bailly, distinguished astronomer and author, sits there, among the Third Estate, in a cloud of philosophic reflections and wishes for the human good. The hour is coming when he, too, pale and trembling, will meet Mme. Guillotine.

Another member, Pétion de Villeneuve—boorish, coarse and vulgar—is to make his mark in tragic history. He will be elected mayor of Paris, but will fall on evil times. Escaping the guillotine by a hasty flight, he will meet the brutal fate of being devoured by wolves in a forest.

Barnave, of Grenoble, wealthy, young and handsome—a deputy of the Third Estate—is destined to shine as a golden-voiced orator, a leader of men. All fine and glorious; but another and more malevolent destiny is waiting for him, farther along on the Road of Time. He will fall in love with the queen, not intimately, not to the point of kisses and embraces, but distantly. Smitten with her charm and fragile beauty, he will advise her and attempt to save her. Secretly, of course, but Marie Antoinette will keep his letters and hide them carefully. They will be found, read, exhibited, printed and circulated. Then the austere guillotine will extend its steely hand and beckon Barnave to the scaffold.

In the sea of faces one may discern Jacques Danton, who is to become one of the most renowned of the revolutionary leaders. An orator of burning eloquence, his favorite phrase was *"De l'audace, encore de l'audace, et toujours de l'audace."* Bold as he was, the guillotine was even bolder, and finally—under Robespierre's direction—Danton became one of its victims.

Seated among the black-clad deputies is fierce and brawny Mathieu Jourdan, who will be known later on as *Coupe-Tête* on account of his propensity to cut off people's heads in street-fighting and impale them on pikes. He has no brains, except perhaps those of a gorilla, and no plans. Why is he here? God knows. He is a deputy, duly elected. But the guillotine will have its little ironic joke. The day is coming when Mme. Guillotine will say to Coupe-Tête: "You are so used to cutting off heads that you really ought not to mind having your own removed." And that will be the end of Coupe-Tête.

Many of all three estates are to die, but they know it not; and many are to be saved, to run away to foreign lands; or to escape by reason of subtlety and ability.

There is Talleyrand among the Clergy. He is the bishop of Autun. A bishop without morality, religion or honesty; yet his mind is as keen as a razor, and he is the most accomplished political chess player in Europe. If not now—he will be that, and more, in the course of time. He can think faster than other men, and—having no convictions of his own—is able to adjust himself more quickly to circumstances. Talleyrand will live through it all. He will become the foreign minister in Napoleon's cabinet, and in that position he will enrich himself by taking bribes.* At the end of Napoleon's career, while France lies prostrate, Talleyrand will become a leading figure at the Congress of Vienna and will perform there an autopsy on the lifeless body of his own country. In the course of his long life he belonged to every party—revolutionary, Bonapartist, royalist— and on both sides of every controversy. He died peacefully in bed— in 1838—full of honors, venality and wickedness.

---

* Napoleon had a contempt for him, but that is nothing; frequently he kept men whom he despised in important places. He called Talleyrand *un bas de soie plein de merde*—a phrase that is unprintable in English translation.

The Abbé de Sieyès is a deputy among the Clergy. An able, far-seeing man—a man of probity, honor and wisdom. A revolutionist, and the author of a revolutionary pamphlet of enormous circulation called *"Qu'est-ce que le Tiers Etat?"* It is he who will write the constitution of the new France. He will go quietly through the Terror, and leave this earthly scene in 1836, at the age of eighty-eight, amid the hum and stir of a new age.

One of the deputies in the Third Estate is Pierre Dupont de Nemours. He, too, is destined to live through the violence of the Revolution and to found an American family that—at this time of writing—would make by comparison any wealthy family in France, in 1789, look like a nest of small shopkeepers.

The Duponts came from Rouen, where they were a family of prosperous watchmakers. It is interesting to reflect on the advantage of being a watchmaker. Rousseau's father was a watchmaker; so was the father of Beaumarchais—and Beaumarchais himself eventually acquired a sort of skill in the mystery of the trade. The Duponts had been watchmakers for generations. The original Pierre Samuel Dupont who became a member of the States-General was a liberal in his political views, or so he considered himself.

In the course of time, while living in our spacious land, in the midst of money-making ventures and war-profiteering, the Duponts abandoned their liberal views or misplaced them somewhere.

5

The king sat on a throne of purple and gold. On his plumed hat blazed the famous Regent diamond, the world's costliest jewel. At his left, and a little below him, sat the queen. Around them were the royal princes and the officers of the crown. All Paris was in the galleries, and by "all Paris" is meant those who by fortune, distinction or influence could contrive to get a ticket. Thomas Jefferson was among the spectators; Gouverneur Morris also.

The king made a speech in his loud, unmusical voice. It expressed undying love for the people. Necker read a long, tiresome paper on the finances. Unquenchable optimist, he declared that the financial situation was not as bad as it had been painted. There was a deficit, he admitted, but it was not unmanageable. The increased revenue under his administration would soon straighten it all out.

But in the meantime he wanted authorization to borrow eighty millions. Not only an optimist was Necker, but also a trickster. The amount of the deficit, as he gave it, was greatly understated.

Late in the afternoon the opening session of the States-General came to an end. The king and queen departed amid the handclapping and huzzas of the delegates and spectators.

Next day the three orders held their meetings separately. In the meeting of the Third Estate a resolution to invite the two higher orders to amalgamate with the commoners was adopted. The Nobility and the Clergy declined, but more than a hundred of the Clergy were in favor of joining the Third Estate. Among the Nobles only forty-seven were on that side. Lafayette was one of them.

For five weeks thereafter the Third Estate—or the "Commons," as they called themselves unofficially—went on a sit-down strike. They met daily, but there was no permanent organization, though they elected a presiding officer, and remained in the hall throughout the day, discussing this and that without taking any official action. The Nobility and the Clergy had organized promptly, but nothing was done toward the reform of national affairs, or anything else. The higher orders were paralyzed by the unexpected attitude of the Third Estate. Would a legislative act, although passed by the Clergy and Nobility be valid if it had been completely ignored by the third element of the States-General? That was a question without an answer. Nobody knew.*

When the deadlock had gone on for two weeks the king directed the three orders to get together at a conference, with the idea that they might reach a compromise. The committees met with a barren result. At this conference the Bishop of Langres proposed that the Nobility and the Clergy should unite in one body, so that there would be only two legislative chambers—a House of Lords and a House of Commons, on the British model. The king rejected this plan. If it had been adopted it is possible that the French nation would have become a constitutional monarchy by degrees, as Lafayette thought it would.

Looking at the state of affairs in 1789, down the long perspective of years, it does seem that Louis XVI could have saved himself

* There were really no "legislative acts," as we understand the term, within the power of the States-General. The conclusions of the assembly were expressed in the form of resolutions for consideration of the king. The States-General was a national advisory body. The phrase "legislative act" is used here as a convenient expression.

and his throne by becoming a constitutional monarch. He was really liked by the French people. Of course, they did not know him— few people know kings—but they thought they knew him. The whole nation detested Marie Antoinette, with the exception of her cronies and lickspittles at Versailles. But after all, the king was the king, and it did not matter so much about the queen, as she had no authority. (The fact is that she had a great deal of indirect authority.)

If Louis XVI had freely agreed to being a constitutional king he would appear in history today as the greatest of all Frenchmen, the father of his country, the George Washington of France. No doubt the city of Paris would have a towering statue of him in a conspicuous place, and in every provincial town there would be some kind of memorial. Versailles would be a shrine instead of a museum.

In taking his stand for the people he could not have avoided a minor civil war, for the Nobles never would have consented to such reforms as a constitutional government would require without force of arms. But the civil war would have been of small importance and soon ended. The Nobles and their retainers were too few in number to have made effective resistance; and some of them— Lafayette, for instance—would certainly have been on the other side.

It is entirely probable, considering this setup of circumstance, that Napoleon would not have been heard of, ever; there would have been no place for him and no need of him, and the authors of succeeding generations would have been spared the trouble of writing three thousand books about him. But we might have written just as many about Louis XVI—the great Liberator of the French People.

These speculations are interesting, perhaps, but unimportant. There are no *ifs* in history; it follows an inexorable pattern, and the design can be seldom foreseen. Louis XVI, in his surroundings, considering his training and inheritance, was completely unfitted to be the head of a constitutional monarchy.

On the tenth of June a final invitation was sent by the Third Estate to the two privileged orders, and they were notified that if the invitation was not accepted the Third Estate would organize immediately as the States-General of France.

A few days later some of the Clergy left their own order, and

joined the Commons. On June 17th Mirabeau proposed that the
name States-General be dropped, and that they should organize as a
National Assembly. The resolution was carried, and in that simple
fashion France acquired a Congress.

The government and the court viewed this move with consternation. The situation was getting desperately out of hand. The
Comte d'Artois—the king's brother—urged the suppression of the
Third Estate, and the king and the court officials agreed with him
that the best course would be to put an end to their meetings. Yes,
but how could that be done? Pondering heavily over that question,
they reached the childish conclusion that they would simply lock
the doors of the Salle des Menus Plaisirs, and the Third Estate, or
so-called National Assembly, having no meeting place, would disperse and go home. Don't laugh at that; when men lose their heads
they are likely to act very foolishly.

On the morning of June 20th the members of the National Assembly found that they could not get into their hall. The doors were
locked and soldiers were on guard. The indignant commoners thereupon went to the largest building near by. It was the Jeu de Paume
—or Tennis Court, in plain English. A roofed-over playground.
There they assembled and their first act was to take a solemn oath
"never to separate, and to meet whenever circumstances might
demand, until a constitution should be established and firmly based
upon solid foundations."

Then the privileged orders began to crack up. One hundred and
forty-nine of the Clergy came over and took their places in the
Assembly. Also two Nobles. Lafayette was not one of them. He
still continued to meet with his own order in idle, time-killing sessions. He declared to all that he knew he was in the wrong place,
but what could he do about it? He was still bound by the pledge
given to his noble constituency of Auvergne.

The blunders of the court party were tragic. The king summoned all three estates to a royal séance. He reprimanded the Third
Estate in a speech which was harsh and unmannerly. He gave them
a number of dictatorial commands. The three orders, he declared,
must continue to meet separately. He agreed to equality of taxation,
but all feudal dues and tithes, manorial rents and privileges, were

to be maintained. He declared that the resolutions of the Third Estate were without validity and were disapproved. In conclusion he ordered an adjournment of the session, with a command for all members to leave the hall.

Then the king arose and left, followed by the Nobility and most of the Clergy. The Third Estate remained and went on with their deliberations. In a short time the grand master of the king's household appeared and politely requested the commoners to get out. Mirabeau rose, and in his deep, thunderous voice, cried out: "Go tell those who sent you that the National Assembly will never leave here except at the point of the bayonet."

He was applauded by the Assembly. The court official retired and business went on. When this episode was reported to the king he ordered the Gardes du Corps to enter the hall and drive out the deputies by force. News of that move got around, and when the guards arrived they found that ten or twelve liberals among the Nobles, headed by Lafayette, stood in the doorway with drawn swords and refused to let the soldiers come in. When this was related to Louis XVI, he gave way, and said wearily, "Oh, well, if they want to stay, let them stay."

Next day forty-seven liberal Nobles went over to the Assembly and took their places. On June 27th the king commanded the remainder of the Nobility and Clergy to join them. This may have been a strategical move, though what thread of policy ran through it I cannot say; or it may have been a tacit acknowledgment of defeat. At any rate, whatever the final outcome might be, the Third Estate had won the first round of the struggle.

Both the Nobles and the Third Estate were advocates of reform. Both orders were dissatisfied with the state of the nation and wanted to make changes in the governmental structure. But the reforms contemplated by the Nobility—I mean here the nobles of the reactionary school—were diametrically opposite in pattern and purpose to those of the commoners. The Nobles thought the state would be much better off if it returned to feudalism. Away with all this foolishness of popular rights, of street-corner oratory, of arguments among ignorant waiters and hairdressers over taxation and treasury finances. Go back to the good old days and leave statecraft to the Nobility, who are trained in administrative methods, and whose business it is to govern. Let the feudal lords look after the welfare of their own dependents. Trust to their sense of fairness and justice.

That is what the reactionaries wanted, and the reactionaries made up a large majority of the noble deputies in the Assembly.

The Third Estate, on the contrary, demanded a republican form of government, with a written constitution; or a limited monarchy on the English model. There should be no taxation without the consent of the people, and all governmental expenditures should be made only with the approval of the National Assembly.

One of these conceptions had to go down in defeat. There could be no compromise, no possibility of getting together, for the opposing energies had no common plane of reference. In the end both of them lost and lay dying on the field of combat. It was like a prize fight where a giant leaps into the ring, flattens out both contestants and, shaking a hairy fist at the sky, shouts, "I am the winner."

CHAPTER XVII

FALL OF THE BASTILLE

I

Events were moving swiftly.

On June 26th the king secretly gave orders to have twenty thousand troops brought to Paris. Preference was given to the foreign regiments, of which there were many in the French army—German, Swiss and Flemish.

These regiments, on their arrival, were posted on the road from Paris to Versailles, and thousands of soldiers were within a short distance of the Salle des Menus Plaisirs. A swarm of alarming rumors were in the air. It was said that the only purpose in bringing the troops to Paris and Versailles was to disperse the National Assembly, and that Lafayette and Mirabeau were to be sent to the Bastille. Another rumor was that the foreign troops had orders to shoot down the inhabitants of Paris at the first sign of a demonstration against the king and the government.

It was a time of anxiety in the National Assembly. The palace gave out no information, and no one knew what was going to happen. On July 8th the Assembly passed a resolution in which it requested the king to send away the troops. His Majesty replied that the regiments had been brought to Paris for the sole purpose of protecting the National Assembly.

What nonsense! The Assembly was in no danger from the people, and everybody of intelligence knew it. Not at that time, by any means. But the time was coming when the Assembly would be frightened out of its wits by the fury of the Parisian mobs. The king said, further, that if they still considered themselves in peril they might transfer their sessions to some town farther away from Paris. This was a most transparent device to get rid of them. If threatened with dispersal while at Versailles they could always count on the formidable support of the Parisian populace, but if they were a hundred miles away that assistance could not be so readily given. The Assembly paid no attention to his suggestion.

By that time all the banks in Paris had closed their doors and were in a condition of quiescent bankruptcy. The treasury had taken most of their funds and had given them paper and securities which were selling far below their face value.

2

On July 11th Necker was dismissed by Louis XVI. As soon as the news came out the Stock Exchange suspended its operations, and the prices of securities fell precipitately. The hold that Necker had on the financial community is one of the most puzzling facts in that era of stupidity. He did not tell the truth; he concealed vitally important information; his financial measures were as unsafe as those of the trickiest of promoters. Nevertheless, people of money had faith in him.

He was dismissed from office not because of his acts as the national financier, but because he was continually urging the king to initiate reforms and make concessions to the liberal spirit. The court party was utterly opposed to this plan of action, and it was they who persuaded the king to drop Necker.

July 11th was a Saturday. On the evening of that day Lafayette rose in the National Assembly and read out his Declaration of the Rights of Man. It is an important document, perhaps the most important paper that Lafayette ever wrote in the course of his long life. Extremely interesting it is, too, in that it reveals clearly his point of view. Here it is in full:

Nature has made men free and equal; the distinctions between them are founded upon general utility.

Every man is born with inalienable rights; such are the right of property, the protection of his honor and his life, the entire disposition of his person, of his industry, of all his faculties, the pursuit of well-being, and the resistance to opposition.

The exercise of natural rights has no limits except those which assure the enjoyment of the same rights to the other members of society.

No man can be persecuted for his religious views, nor for his opinions, nor for communicating his ideas through speech, writing or printing, unless by calumny and libel he disturbs the peace of the citizens.

No man can be subjected to laws unless they have been accepted by him or his representatives, announced previously and legally enforced.

The principle of all sovereignty resides in the nation.

The sole object of any government is the common good; legislative, executive, and judiciary powers must be separated and distinctly defined; as no organization nor any individual can exercise an authority which does not expressly emanate from the nation.

The legislative power should be essentially exercised by deputies chosen in every district through the means of free, regular, and frequent elections.

The executive power is to be exercised by the King, whose person is sacred, and by all individual or collective agents who shall be accountable to the nation no matter what other authorization they may have received.

The judiciary power must be limited to the application of the laws; legal procedure must be public, and the administration of justice easy and impartial.

The laws must be clear, precise, and uniform for all citizens.

Subsidies must be freely agreed upon and distributed proportionally.

And as the growth of enlightenment, the introduction of abuses, and the rights of succeeding generations necessitate the revision of all human institutions, constitutional provisions must be made to assure in certain cases an extraordinary convocation of representatives of the people for the sole object of examining and modifying, if necessary, the form of the government.

The Declaration was discussed by Lafayette with Thomas Jefferson before it was read before the National Assembly. There were several immature drafts of the Declaration before the one I have set forth here. The original of the one I reproduce is written in French, and is in the Library of Congress. It has a few annotations by Jefferson. I am inclined to believe—without definite proof, however—that Jefferson wrote this paper, or inspired its wording. It is in the handwriting of neither Jefferson nor Lafayette, and the document in the Library of Congress was probably written by a copyist. It sounds, in its style and clarity, like Jefferson and not at all like Lafayette, who wrote in a muddy, turgid manner.

It reads well, but if one takes the trouble to dissect it, sentence by sentence, it loses much of its glamour.

He says, "distinctions [between men] are based on general utility." Maybe they are, and maybe not, but what is "general utility"? The feudal lord considered himself a useful person; and so did the king, undoubtedly. General utility is a vague term with many different meanings. Lots of people think that professional strikebreakers perform a useful service. Is an idle millionaire who loafs away his life more useful to the commonwealth that a coal miner?

In the next paragraph we come to the old, familiar phrase, "in alienable rights." What are inalienable rights? And suppose two inalienable rights run into a head-on collision, what happens then? Our venerable maxim, "the inalienable rights of life, liberty, and the pursuit of happiness" might get into a deadly fight with the inalienable right of property.

In all this we are dealing with high-sounding words, abstractions which serve to conceal thought—not to reveal it. In the second paragraph right of property is defined as an inalienable right, but it has never been so considered, except as a form of words, by any nation in the whole period of recorded history. The ownership of property is a privilege, not an inherent right. The privilege may be withdrawn by the exercise of national will; or by the king, emperor or dictator if the national will is suppressed. It has been done, over and over again, times without number.

People own property only by sufferance. Taxation may erase ownership, or the owners may be deprived by force, as they were in the French Revolution.

The phrase "right of property" seemed to guarantee—in the minds of million of Frenchmen—the possession of lands by the Nobility and the Church. Those two orders owned half of the soil of France. And what about feudal dues, tithes and restrictions of trade between the provinces? Not a word. These matters, and others of the same class, occupied the burning, passionate attention of the common people all over France. The famous Declaration was a bourgeois announcement—thoroughly middle class—and a dose of political soothing syrup, but I do not believe for a moment that Lafayette wrote it, or sanctioned it, with that thought in mind.

Lafayette was not insincere, nor was he a demagogue, but he was an aristocrat all his life, from beginning to end. He ardently desired the happiness of everyone; and men to be free, and to be paid fairly for their work, and to be protected in their rights and liberties by a national constitution. But he did not believe the common people knew enough to vote intelligently or to have much to

do with governmental affairs. He dreamed of a government of en-
lightened liberals.

The Declaration, put forth in the form of a resolution, was
referred to a committee. After much discussion and some changes in
wording, but not in principle, it was adopted by the Assembly.

3

Paris, in summer, can be as hot as New Orleans for a few days
at a time. Sunday, July 12, 1789, was a scorcher. The perspiring
people swarmed in the streets, along the banks of the Seine, and
in the parks. There were no wide, shady boulevards such as there
are now. The city was a confused jumble of narrow, twisting streets
like those one may see today on the Left Bank, around the Ecole
de Médecine.

Among these unhappy people agitators slipped about with the
bright suppleness of eels in water. There is hardly a doubt that
some of them were paid by the Duc d'Orléans, whose gnawing ambition was to take the place of Louis XVI as king of France. His
agents provocateurs went among the crowds. There were others who
had other motives. "Have you heard the latest news?" one person
says to another. Well, the news is that Versailles, the king and the
Austrian woman intend to starve the people of Paris. All the wagons
bringing grain and other food have been stopped on the roads. Soldiers are to surround the city.

Of the truth of this accusation no evidence exists. Anyone with
a grain of sense at Versailles—king, queen, prince, noble or what
not—would not have countenanced such a scheme. It would have
been the most certain way of starting an insurrection in Paris.

Through the streets rushed raucous newspaper vendors, selling
Marat's paper, *L'Ami du Peuple.* Jean Paul Marat is described in
many histories of the Revolution as a common horse doctor. Carlyle
called him a "horse-leech." This characterization is far from the
truth. Marat, son of a physician, received a first-class medical education. He went to London and built up a lucrative practice. His
interests were not confined, however, to medicine. He became a
scientist and an authority on optics.

The court at Versailles invited him to return to Paris. When
he came back he found a practice awaiting him among the court

nobles. The Comte d'Artois gave him an appointment as physician to his bodyguards. It is possible that he may have, now and then, looked over a sick horse in the stables of the Comte d'Artois, but he was not a veterinarian by profession.

What he saw of the dissolute and worthless Nobility had the effect of making him a radical revolutionist of the most intense type. He was a tremendous force in the revolutionary movement, as he was wholly devoid of the quality of compromise. When his influence began to be felt the court party invented the horse-doctor story to belittle him.

He was a man of great ability but he is known principally for the defects of his character, which were numerous. His bitterness of temperament developed into spite and malevolence, and he lost all regard for truth. He was permanently indignant; so irritated, indeed, that nothing could possibly happen that would make him more irritated than he was already. To defeat the enemies of the Revolution he would print lies with no basis in fact. In time he developed into a shrill, ill-tempered male virago. On that fateful July Sunday his newspaper declared that a plot against Paris was about to mature. On July 15th—that would be next Wednesday— there would be a *coup d'état*. Paris was to be seized by the king's troops and thousands of Parisians would be shot down or hanged.

Was there really such a plot? The story is quite improbable. Two days later—on July 14th—the Bastille was taken by the mob, and not one regiment of troops—of the many in and around Paris —came to the rescue of its garrison.

The vast courtyard, or *jardin,* of the Palais Royal was open to the public at all times. The palace was the private property of the Duc d'Orléans. It was an eighteenth century apartment house, with a vast number of rooms, and it had about the same appearance then as it has today—shops and cafés on the ground floor, and an arcade running all around the enclosure, which was shady and cool on a hot day.

On this noisy and fretful Sunday of July 12th thousands of people were strolling under the trees of the Palais Royal. In the afternoon, Camille Desmoulins, a lawyer who was also a journalist —a young man of twenty-nine—leaped on a table beneath one of he trees and harangued the crowd. Spontaneous; no premeditation; ιe just got up and talked.

His speech blazed with incendiary words. He was afflicted ·y a stammer which he lost in the passion and vehemence of public peaking. A rebel of the most pronounced type, he was opposed to .ll the ways and works of the existing regime.*

Desmoulins called upon the people of Paris to take arms and lefend themselves. "This evening all the Swiss and German battalons," he exclaimed, "will come forth from the Champ-de-Mars to ut our throats There is not a moment to lose." †

He was entirely mistaken. The government had no idea of ending soldiers that evening to cut the throats of the inhabitants ·f Paris.

Before the sweltering day came to an end, the mob was smashng the shutters of the stores that sold guns and was passing out the ιrms to the people in the streets. There was some piddling effort ɱade to keep any of them from getting into the hands of disreputa-ɔle characters, but without avail. The guns went to ragtag and ɔobtail, to patriots, to thieves, to fierce rebels and gentle-minded iberals. All Paris was arming.

Imagine the uproar on that Sunday night. The raids on the ɥhops, the impromptu processions, the yelling in the streets, the iring of guns. Yet there was a strong military force in Paris. On ɧe Champ-de-Mars—around the place where the slender frame of ɧe Eiffel Tower now stands—several thousand troops of the regu-ɩar army were encamped. They were under command of Baron de Besenval, a Swiss officer in the service of the French. When breath-ɩess runners came to him with the story of lawlessness he refused ɧo do anything; he said he had no order from Versailles and would ɩo nothing without orders. So that was that.

Early Tuesday morning, July 14th, the Invalides was invaded ɩnd twenty-eight thousand muskets were found there. The governor ɔf that refuge for aged soldiers made no effort to stop the mob from

---

* Desmoulins was guillotined in April, 1794, during Robespierre's Reign of Terror ɔn an accusation of what was called *modérantisme,* meaning moderation in his views. He was one of the early instigators of the Revolution, but in four years it had gone far beyond him. At the time of his execution his wife exhorted the people and endeavored to get them to save him. For this oratorical outburst she was promptly arrested, carried before the Revolutionary Tribunal, condemned to death and sent to the guillotine.

† Jules Claretie, *Camille Desmoulins,* p. 53.

seizing the arms; he could have done nothing in any event, as h‹
had no considerable body of troops; his institution was an ol‹
men's home and—only incidentally—a storehouse of arms.

But within ten minutes' walk to the westward of the Invalide
—ten minutes for even a slow pedestrian—were those thousand
of Besenval's soldiers. Why did not the governor of the Invalide
send a messenger and ask Besenval and his troops to come to hi
aid? Perhaps he did. As to that I do not know, but no strong-arn
protective force appeared, and the muskets were carried away.

While the armories were being despoiled, the well-to-do an‹
wealthy bourgeois, the professional men, the public officials—o‹
many of them—met in hurried conferences, here and there. Th‹
Revolution was already running away from its middle-class parents
With riot and disaster impending they formed an impromptu Na
tional Guard to protect lives and property. None of the proletaria
was permitted to join. It was to be a bourgeois militia, compose‹
of the substantial elements in the city of Paris. There was ‹
distressing dearth of muskets among them, but they intended t‹
demand arms from the War Ministry. The regular troops were un
dependable. The Gardes Françaises, a *corps d'élite* whose duty i
was to keep order in Paris, were at that moment locked up, impris
oned and impounded, in their barracks because the authoritie‹
thought they would join the mob.

4

The glowing copper-colored sun smote Paris with the whip‹
and lashes of torment on the morning of July 14th—a day tha‹
was to become memorable in French history. It is now the grea‹
national holiday of France, when thousands of couples dance i‹
the streets, and men with accordions and violins go around playin‹
dance tunes. Free food and free drinks in many places. At nigh‹
there are bonfires, and rockets sparkle in the sky. Anyone who ha‹
ever witnessed a French July 14th can never forget it. It is lik‹
our July 4th, except more so; very much more so.

On July 14, 1789, there was no dancing in the streets; only
wild rumor and alarm. The air was close and almost stifling in th‹
densely packed houses. The people poured out into the open air.

Everybody wanted to be armed, and there were not enoug‹

muskets, nor enough balls and gunpowder, even though the arsenal
of the Invalides had been plundered the day before.

Among these feverish, hot-tempered crowds a story went around
that there was a large store of arms in the Bastille, at the eastern
end of Paris. Long before noon thousands of men were making their
way toward that prison fortress. Some of them carried muskets,
but most of them had nothing in their hands. With them was a
detachment of the Gardes Françaises which had left its barracks
and was in full mutiny. The Gardes, under command of their sergeants, marched in military order. The mob straggled along in disorderly fashion. Mingled in the mob were many women.

The Bastille—of which not a stone now remains—was a formidable fortress with walls ten feet thick. It was surrounded by
a wide moat and could be entered only over drawbridges. No mob
could possibly capture it; heavy artillery and a long siege would be
needed.

The mob intended to demand the arms and ammunition stored
in the fortress. If refused, then what? They could only shake their
fists at the sullen walls and fire ineffectually at them. Nevertheless,
they did take the Bastille. Astonishing things happen, as we have
seen and shall see again.

The Bastille was a place of mystery. No word of information
ever came out of it. It was the king's prison for noblemen and
political prisoners. Peasants and workingmen were never sent there.
A trial, before judges with witnesses and legal evidence, was not
needed to consign a person to the Bastille for life. Nothing more
was necessary for one's incarceration than a *lettre de cachet* signed
by the king. He had the recognized right or power to send anyone
in France to the gaunt, towering fortress without trial.

In the time of Louis XV the king was in the habit of signing
lettres de cachet in blank, leaving the names to be filled in. These
were given to favorite courtiers and to his mistresses to use according to their inclinations. So if anyone tried to make love to your
wife, or annoyed you by loud talk at a dinner party, you might—
if you possessed one of these magic papers—just write in the offensive person's name, hand it to the authorities and that would be the
last of him.

Louis XVI—to the best of my knowledge and belief—never

handed out any of these blank commitments to jail. The prison was almost empty on July 14, 1789.

In the way of physical comfort life in the Bastille was not bad in comparison with other prisons. Every prisoner had a comfortable room, or cell, and abundant leisure, for there was nothing for him to do. He was given all the exercise he wanted. He had plenty of good food to eat, and the administration provided him with excellent clothes. But the prisoner was not permitted to write a letter, read a newspaper or a book, or receive callers, even if those who came to see him were his relatives. When inquiries were made the prison management replied, "We know nothing about him."

Underground, at the base of the towers, were a few dungeon like rooms, called *oubliettes*. They had no windows. After the fall of the Bastille a report was widely circulated that these dungeons had been used for the confinement of prisoners, and this assertion appears in some of the histories of the period. It has long since been disproved. The oubliettes were used for the storage of ice.

By noon on that fateful July 14th the shuffling, unorganized crowd stood before the Bastille. White flags of truce were waved and the terms of a parley were shouted back and forth. Two commissioners, sent by the Hôtel de Ville, went into the fortress to negotiate with de Launay, its commandant. Gracious and smiling he invited them to lunch with him. The outer drawbridge was let down and the mob swarmed into the exterior courtyard. But they were still outside the fortress. A wide moat filled with water ran around the prison, and the moat could be crossed only by letting down another drawbridge.

In all minds there was the story, the tragedy, of Henri de Latude. He was as conspicuous in the public eye as Tom Mooney the California convict, is in America today. The cases were different in some respects, however; after all, Mooney was tried before a jury and convicted. For Latude there was no trial, no court. He was an impoverished noble, a small landowner, and an army surgeon's apprentice. In 1749, Latude—then twenty-four years of age —attempted (apparently) to obtain some money from Mme. de Pompadour, the mistress of Louis XV, under false pretenses. The story of this proceeding is obscure, as the case was never heard in court. A package containing an explosive was sent to Pompadour— so runs the tale—and it was so ingeniously contrived that the fai

LAFAYETTE VISITING WASHINGTON AT MOUNT VERNON IN 1784

Painting by Rossiter.

lady would be blown to bits when she opened the box. It sounds extremely improbable, as Mme. Pompadour would not have deigned to open a package with her own hands. There is also much doubt as to whether the supposed "deadly" missive contained anything harmful.

The package was traced to Latude, or so they said. About the time it arrived Latude wrote Mme. de Pompadour an "indiscreet" letter, and the two events were supposed to be connected in some way.

Pompadour, scared breathless, had Latude sent forthwith to the Bastille. A little later he wrote a petition for release, and the administration of the prison—in an unusual moment of liberality—ventured to forward it to Pompadour. Her reply was an emphatic *"Jamais."*

For some reason he was transferred to the prison at Vincennes. He managed to get out of that jail and was free for a few weeks before they caught him. He was sent again to the Bastille. Secretly he made a rope ladder from threads pulled from the sheets of his bed, a few every day, so that when the bed linen was changed the loss of the threads was not noticed. It took him six years to do it. Imagine that! He did finally escape by means of his rope ladder, and fled to Holland. There he was discovered by Pompadour's agents. They seized him, regardless of the fact that he was in a foreign country, brought him to France, and clapped him in the Bastille again. After years of imprisonment he was adjudged a lunatic, and was sent to the insane asylum at Charenton. They let him go in 1777, but he was not free a month before he was sent to the insane asylum at Bicetre.

He bribed one of the attendants to procure some paper and ink, and he wrote a long and horrible account of his sufferings. The bribed attendant took the document and promised to deliver it to one of Latude's friends of long ago, if he was still living. But the attendant got drunk and lost the paper. This was in 1784.

A workingman's wife, Mme. Legros, found it on the floor of a market while she was shopping. She read it, and was so moved by its pitiful appeal that she took it to someone in authority in Paris. An investigation was made; Mme. Legros was informed that the man was insane, and medical certificates to that effect were shown to her.

But Mme. Legros was not convinced. Latude's story stirred her deepest emotions. She went to Versailles but, too poor to hire a carriage, she walked all the way. The poor woman was not welcome; by that time she had pestered many powerful people with her letters and petitions, and at Versailles they thought that she, too, ought to be in an insane asylum. Nevertheless, she contrived to get Latude's story to Louis XVI, and he—like the Pompadour of long ago—said "Never."

Then she walked back to Paris, and kept on. It was a one-woman movement of great vitality, for all France was in the right mood for it. The story spread all over the country; everybody knew of Latude and his miseries. He became—to some extent—a symbol of the discontent of the French people. Everybody talked of Latude. *"Du jour au lendemain,"* says Larousse, *"Latude fut la mode."* Eventually Mme. Legros and the people she had interested in the matter obtained the release of Latude.*

Mme. Legros was awarded a gold medal for virtuous deeds by the Academy of Sciences, but the king would not permit the Academy to state in public the reason for its award.

5

Probably every person who faced the Bastille on July 14th knew Latude's story; the grim fortress stood before them as a concrete, material representation of all that was hateful and vicious in the regime.

The garrison of the Bastille was small; it was composed of thirty soldiers from a Swiss regiment and eighty veterans—old soldiers, retired and on pensions. While the commandant and the people's commissioners were at lunch firing began. Nobody knows which side fired first. Before it was over about one hundred of the attacking force had been killed. The garrison lost only a few men. Then came the waving of white flags; a truce. De Launay agreed to surrender the place if the safety of the garrison was assured in a formal capitulation; otherwise—he declared—he would blow up the fortress.

But why did he surrender at all? No one knows to this day. It is true that he had only two days' supply of food, but what of

* After the Revolution he was given a pension on account of his sufferings. He died in Paris in 1805, at the age of eighty.

hat? There were thousands of the king's troops within a few miles; they could have dispersed the mob in half an hour. But no one knew if the regular troops were dependable. That may have been de Launay's reason for giving up the Bastille.

The articles of the capitulation were signed, and the people were admitted to the inner court. They released the seven prisoners (there were only seven, to the amazement of everyone, and one of them was an idiot, sent there for safekeeping) and would have massacred the garrison if the disciplined Gardes Françaises had permitted them to do it.

De Launay, despite his guarantee of safety, was dragged to the Hôtel de Ville and slaughtered in the square in front of it— the Place de Grève. It was a lynching, and wholly without justification, or the slightest excuse.

Then the swarming, yelling mob turned its attention to de Flesselles, the chief magistrate of Paris. His offense? Not much, it seems. He had tried, unsuccessfully, to divert the mob from its march against the Bastille. He was seized in his office in the Hôtel de Ville, brought into the open air, and his head was hacked off by the mob with the nonchalance of one who decapitates a chicken.

All night Paris roared like a madhouse.

But what of the newly formed National Guard—bourgeois to a man—with its twelve thousand members already enrolled and pledged to keep order in Paris? Nothing from them; no movement; all silent as mice. No wonder. They were not yet organized, but merely enrolled. And what of Marshal de Broglie—aged and stately —who commanded the troops in the region of Paris, and of the Baron de Besenval, with his five thousand trained soldiers encamped on the Champ-de-Mars? From them, nothing. Besenval had no orders; he would not move a step without a signed order, and for that obedience to rigid discipline he was dismissed from the army.

The king had spent the day, as usual, in hunting. He knew nothing of what had happened until two o'clock in the morning.

The National Assembly got the news of the Bastille late in the evening of the fourteenth. The Assembly had been in continuous session for days. Lafayette was in the chair; he had been elected vice-president. The aged president, worn out by fatigue, had gone home. The Assembly did not know what to do, and no action was taken.

CHAPTER XVIII

LAFAYETTE COMMANDS THE NATIONAL GUARD

I

THE FALL of the Bastille scared the National Assembly and the court of Versailles into a semipanic. It was all like lightning out of a blue sky; no one had dreamed of such an event. All in the way of disorder that had happened before might be called plain rioting, but the capture of a king's fortress was something different.

Yes, that was true—but what should one do? What should we all do? The king was urged to recall Necker, and he did. That was no solution of the problem, but those close to Louis XVI thought it was. So Necker was sent for; swift couriers riding whip and spur. He had been dismissed only four days before, and had not reached Belgium, where he had intended to go. Necker, immensely flattered by his apparent indispensability, came back and the Stock Exchange opened its closed doors.

The day after the affair of the Bastille the king came without his bodyguard to the National Assembly and made a confused, bewildered address. He agreed to sustain the Assembly, to co-operate, and he asked the deputies to help him. He said that he wanted their advice. In conclusion he declared that he had ordered all his troops to withdraw from Paris.

But why, in the name of common sense, should he send the troops away just at that time? They had been there for weeks—evidently for the purpose of keeping order—yet at the moment of insurrection they were sent elsewhere. The answer to this question is not clear, but the probability is that the troops could not be relied upon in a crisis. They might have gone over to the mob, as the disciplined Gardes Françaises did. So the troops are sent away and the king relies on the National Assembly. Relies, yes, but not sincerely. Already—and secretly—the king and queen are writing to their royal relatives in Austria and Spain for military aid.

Everything the king said before the Assembly was applauded, again and again. The era of good will had come at last, all for the king and the king for all mankind—for French mankind, at any rate. But it was merely pretense—the whole show—pretense on both sides. The king was simply playing for time in making his good-will gesture.

But the Assembly was not all of one mind. Some of the deputies remained silent during the storm of applause. Grim, determined men who were not impressed. Robespierre was one, Marat was another, and there were others. Amid the enthusiasm sinister motives were running around and entangling the threads of destiny, as usual.

After the royal séance the king departed, on foot, for the palace. Spontaneously the entire Assembly arose and accompanied him as an escort. In the streets were thousands of common people, the riffraff of the great city population, who had drifted to Versailles. When they heard that the troops were to be sent away they crowded around the king and burst through the encircling deputies to kiss his hands. The huzzas and yells roared and echoed in the peaceful streets. It was only half a mile from the Menus Plaisirs to the palace, but the procession was an hour and a half on the way. Grimy harridans put their hands on the king's shoulders and attempted to kiss his cheeks. The deputies had to pull them away forcibly.

A casual observer, a foreigner on a trip to France, let us say, upon witnessing this scene, would probably have written home that the worst was over; that the king and his people were reconciled.

On the same day the Assembly sent a delegation to Paris, to call on the Electors, and do what they could to pacify the people.* Lafayette was the leading member of the committee of eighty designated for this purpose.

The Electors received the deputation with honor. Lafayette made a speech and congratulated the people of Paris on "the liberty they had conquered by their courage." What did he mean by "lib-

* The Electors were, and had been for about two months, the municipal authority of Paris, a sort of board of aldermen with four hundred members. At first they had no official sanction. They simply assumed control and were tacitly recognized by the king and the National Assembly, as well as by the Parisian people. Let my readers remember that, even in American cities, committees of public safety have been organized at times, without official status, but nevertheless with great, almost dictatorial, powers.

erty"? They had acquired nothing by the capture of the Bastille. Pondering over it, and endeavoring to analyze its meaning, one must conclude that it is just a nice phrase which sounds well and means nothing.

There was much talk at this meeting of the National Guard, then being rapidly formed. Almost to a man the four hundred Electors were bourgeois—middle-class—though a few nobles must also be included. The National Guard was to be the sheet anchor of order in Paris. Who was to be its commander?

Moreau de Saint-Méry, president of the Electors, rose when all others had had their say and pointed, with a dramatic gesture, to a marble bust of Lafayette ensconced in a niche on the wall. The young marquis (he was not then thirty-two) was elected unanimously and by acclamation.

Now he is to be the most powerful man in Paris—master of thousands of soldiers; even more, the most powerful man in all France. For a while, but not long.

That being done, the Electors, with the advice of the deputation from the National Assembly, turned their attention to the selection of a head of the municipal government. Until then Paris had never had a mayor, in the American sense of the word. The chief magistrate of the city, called the *prévôt des marchands,* had acted as a sort of mayor, but his functions were closely limited. The last occupant of the office, M. de Flesselles, had had the misfortune to have his head cut off by a mob the day before this meeting. After that riotous event the mob disported itself by dragging his headless corpse through the streets. Finally tiring of the exhibition, they threw his body in a gutter. His head was in another part of town, being carried around on a pike.

So, one may see, with the office vacant, there was a splendid opportunity for a capable man to be his successor, but it was decided that he was to have the powers of a real mayor, and not merely those of a chief magistrate.

For this post of arduous duty and peril the Electors chose Jean Sylvain Bailly, author and astronomer, a man of books, telescopes, and midnight sessions with the distant stars. Upon his election Bailly was overcome by emotion. Bowing his head on the table, and covering his face with his hands, he said: "I am entirely unworthy of this honor, and incapable of bearing such a burden."

In both assertions he was quite right. But he accepted, and in so
doing he sealed his own doom. It would have been far better for
M. Bailly if he had declined the honor, had gone home and calculated eclipses of the moon.*

2

Lafayette had a more comprehensive plan for the National
Guard than its organizers in Paris had conceived. His idea was
that the National Guard ought to be national, and not merely
Parisian. Very sensible notion, and it took hold at once everywhere.
To get this straight one must understand that the National Guard
was a volunteer militia, carefully selected, however, as to personnel
and at first without pay.

Within a short time National Guard companies and regiments
were being organized all over the country.

The Gardes Françaises were discharged ignominiously from
the king's army because of the part they had taken in the capture
of the Bastille. Lafayette invited these disengaged soldiers to join
the National Guard. They were willing to come—most of them—
but as they were soldiers by trade without other means of livelihood, they had to be paid. That was arranged by the municipality
of Paris. That was satisfactory for the future, but their pay from
the king's government was grievously in arrears, and there seemed
to be no chance of ever getting what was due them. How about
that? Lafayette gave them their back pay from his personal fortune, with the hope of being reimbursed in the future. To get the
money he borrowed large sums from his bankers.

What was Versailles doing about all this? Is it possible that
the king and his counselors were willing to permit the existence of
two armies in the realm? One under their own direction, and the
other under the Marquis de Lafayette, the city of Paris and the
National Assembly? Well, the answer is that they did permit it,
and very likely they could not help themselves. The royal government was breaking up like a ship pounding on a rocky shore. All
was confusion; system and order existed only as figures of speech,
as shadows of a vanished reality.

* As he stood on the scaffold of the guillotine, the scene of his death in 1793, one
of the executioners said: "Bailly, you are trembling," and he replied: "It is not because
of fear; I am cold."

From now on we shall see Lafayette in the National Assembly only on rare occasions. He will be too busy with his new duties to have time to attend the meetings.

The very next day (July 16th) after his appointment as commander of the National Guard he was in his headquarters in the Hôtel de Ville when he heard a commotion in the Place de Grève. He went quickly to the entrance of the building and saw a mob dragging a priest to a street lamp to hang him. He was about to address the rioters when he caught sight of his son George, accompanied by M. Frestel, the lad's tutor, ascending the steps.

The marquis raised his hand for silence. All the clamor ceased. "People of Paris," Lafayette said calmly, "I have the honor to present to you my son," and he patted the boy's head. The crowd swarmed around with huzzas. *"Vive Lafayette," "Vive le fils de Lafayette."* In the excitement the priest escaped.

How volatile, how unstable, those people were! Lafayette was always calm, self-possessed, in the presence of physical danger. Instinctively he knew how to act, what to say. But, unfortunately, this confidence did not appear whenever he was confronted by an intricate political or intellectual problem. He hardly ever knew what to do and ran to people for advice.

3

During these weeks and months of uncertainty he wrote to his inamorata—Mme. de Simiane—once a day, at least; sometimes three or four times a day. In his letter on the evening of July 16th he said:

But this furious, drunken people will not listen to me always. At this moment, while I write, eighty thousand persons surround the Hôtel de Ville and say that they are being deceived, that the troops are not withdrawing, that the King must come. They will no longer recognize anything that I do not sign. . . . In this very moment they are raising terrible cries. If I appear they will calm down; but others will come.

Louis XVI did go to Paris on July 18th, four days after the fall of the Bastille, to show himself before the people, and to do what he could to pacify them. He could be of no use whatever unless he accepted the results of the Revolution, so he pretended to do so, but his acceptance was insincere.

It was a pageant, in its way—that visit of the king to Paris—but it was a sad and mournful one. Lafayette, on his white horse, met the royal carriage at the gates of the city. Slowly moving, the king and his entourage proceeded between double ranks of the National Guard to the Hôtel de Ville. Noisy crowds went here and there along the route. The windows and the roofs were alive with people. No one, however, shouted *"Vive le roi."*

When the procession arrived at the Hôtel de Ville, Mayor Bailly came out and presented a revolutionary cockade to the king. The monarch smiled, took the emblem, and stuck it in his hat. Now the Revolution is sanctioned, approved and certified, said the crowd packed in the Place de Grève; the king himself is a revolutionist. A roar went up from the streets of Paris and resounded in the skies, *"Vive le roi."*

Next day the British ambassador wrote to this government, "From this day we may regard France as a free country, the king as a monarch whose powers are limited, and the nobility as reduced to the level of the nation."*

The king went home—to the palace at Versailles—and Marie Antoinette received him as the wife of a stevedore would greet her husband after he had lost his week's wages in gambling. "Why are you wearing that cockade?" The king tore it angrily from his hat and trampled on it.

Stamp it underfoot; nobody but the queen sees you do that—and a few ladies in waiting. Things are not so bad. The mayor was obsequious, the people respectful, and Lafayette, detested and feared, was courteous. Necker had returned and even then, with the dust of travel on him, was hatching schemes to raise quantities of money.

An emigration of nobles—known as the First Emigration—began the day after the capture of the Bastille. They fled across the Rhine, to England, to Holland. Among the first to go was the Comte d'Artois, brother of the king. He departed without saying good-bye, secretly, and he never saw his brother and sister-in-law again. Yet he was destined to return in splendor, after many years, and be king of France. White-haired Marshal de Broglie—commander in chief of the army—fled also, not in uniform, not as a general,

* Mathiez, *The French Revolution*, p. 48. Mathiez adds, "The middle classes of all Europe realized that their hour had come, and thrilled with hope and joy."

not with his staff around him, but as a pleasant-mannered old gentleman in a hackney coach, and as one having business in foreign
countries. In the following weeks swarms of nobles left France.
No one tried to stop them; that came later. Eventually, on the other
side of the Rhine, there were masses of them, twenty thousand or
more, all planning schemes of vengeance.

Lafayette rode about Paris attended by two or three aides,
talking to the people and advising them to be calm. He was calm
enough himself, but others were not. Among them was Adrienne,
his wife. She was "half wild" with anxiety for him, and went about
the house clasping and unclasping her hands. It is not known if
Mme. de Simiane was also half-wild for his safety, but one may in-
fer that she was. What a pity it is that a man cannot risk his life,
or die, without bringing grief to some woman.

A few days after the taking of the Bastille Lafayette gave orders to have the fortress destroyed. Of course, he had no right to
order its destruction—no legal or technical right. The Bastille belonged to the king, or to the nation, as you please. Lafayette had
no authorization from either of them to tear down historic struc-
tures. A thousand workmen, paid by the city of Paris, were employed in its demolition, and that was a small, yet gratifying relief to
the prevailing misery of unemployment.

The only comment the king made when someone told him
Lafayette had ordered the destruction of the Bastille was, "What
insolence!" Lafayette sent the key of the fortress-prison to George
Washington as a gift. One may see it at Mount Vernon at any time;
a huge, heavy key in a glass case, not at all interesting to look at.

For months after the astonishing Bastille episode there was
no vigorous policy of any kind—or on any side—discernible in the
French nation. Unpredictable circumstances—both unpredictable
and uncontrollable—directed the current of events. Mathiez says,
"the old order was disappearing without an effort, like the sudden
collapse of a ruined, crumbling building."

Quite true; the old order was melting away, but what of a new
order? There was none; no man, or group of men, in France was
able to steer the ship.

The supineness of the Nobility in the face of disaster was
astonishing. They made little effort to stem the tide of revolt. In
some parts of France, the châteaux were wrecked, and the nobles

were driven off their lands. But in other parts of the country they were not molested at all, and the Revolution went on peacefully.

The Revolution at the beginning—and until it got completely out of hand—was a middle-class movement. The bourgeoisie had small sympathy with the workmen and the peasants, and they were bitterly active in repressing, or in trying to repress, the growing disorder among the laboring classes. Dupont de Nemours, a deputy of the Third Estate who called himself a liberal, was one of the most insistent in urging severe measures against the populace.

The National Guard of Paris—soon grown into a local army of sixty thousand men—accomplished very little in the way of putting down riots, and the same is true of the National Guard elsewhere, all over France.

Lafayette declined to accept the responsibility of being the head of the National Guard of the whole nation. That was an error which had disastrous consequences. He accepted the command of the Guard in Paris, and in the neighborhood. His relation to the local organizations in other parts of France was that of a friendly adviser. The result was a decentralization of military authority. The Guards, in many parts of France, soon lost its bourgeois quality. Almost anybody could join, and that was so even in Paris.

Before he had been in command of the National Guard for a week the mob was raging again through the streets. On July 22nd he went to his headquarters at the Hôtel de Ville and found the Place de Grève full of mad and drunken people who intended to kill M. Foullon, a man seventy-four years old who stood in their midst, covered with blood and shivering in fear. Foullon had been a minister of the crown and a farmer-general. He had amassed a large fortune, and it was said that his wealth had been gained by raising the price of food. That may have been true; or it may not have been. Anyway, there was the senile old man, begging for mercy, when Lafayette appeared. Among the crowd, it was said, and repeated from one to another, that Foullon had declared "if the people are hungry let them eat hay." Probably not true, that saying. Lafayette thought it had been invented by the Duc d'Orléans to incite the people.

The calm and brave young marquis speaks. Everyone listens, even the most savage, for they like Lafayette:

You have chosen me for your general; and this choice, which honors me, imposes on me the duty of speaking to you with liberty and frankness. You wish, without judgment, to cause this man to perish; it is an injustice that would dishonor you, and would brand me and all the efforts that I have made in favor of liberty, if I were feeble enough to permit it. . . . I want to see the law respected; the law without which there is no liberty, the law without which I should never have contributed to the revolution of the New World, and without which I would not contribute to the revolution that is in preparation.

The crowd stood there in silence; no huzzas of *"Vive Lafayette!"* Then the marquis, in a burst of inspiration, said—pointing to Foullon—"Take him to prison." This decision was applauded by Foullon; he clapped his hands. Yes, take me to prison. Tragic error on the part of the old man. The crowd yelled, "You see, they have an understanding. He will go to prison and they will let him out."

They took Foullon over to a lamppost and hanged him before Lafayette's eyes. Having hanged him, the mob hacked off his head, thrust a wisp of hay in his mouth and paraded the streets with his bloody head on a pike. Dragged along behind was his headless body.

Gouverneur Morris, waiting at the Palais Royal for his carriage, saw this gruesome procession, and that evening he wrote in his diary, "Gracious God, what a people!" The mob, with the head and corpse, politely parted its ranks and made way for his carriage to pass.

Foullon's son-in-law, Colonel Berthier de Sauvigny, a notorious grain speculator, was on his way to Paris. On his arrival at the city gates he was met by the mob. Through a window of his carriage they thrust the bloody head of his father-in-law with roars of laughter. Lafayette had been informed that Berthier was coming to Paris and he sent a detachment of the National Guard to meet him and act as an escort. The Guard rescued him in the nick of time and took him to the Hôtel de Ville. Along with the soldiers and Berthier's carriage went the yelling mob, Foullon's head bobbing about on a pike. His body, stripped and naked, was towed by ropes. Immediately after Berthier reached the Hôtel de Ville he was ordered to prison for his own safety. On his way to jail he was shot by somebody in the mob. Then they cut out his heart, stuck it on a pike and paraded through the streets with Foullon's head and his son-in-law's heart.

These people were savages in the heart of the most cultured nation in Europe. They, and millions of others, had been brutalized by tyranny, poverty, bad government, illiteracy, extortion, and unjust laws which they had no part in making and against which they had no opportunity to protest.

For generations—for centuries—men and women had been put to death by torture, frequently without even a pretense of a fair and impartial trial. They had been broken on the wheel in public, their shattered bones protruding through their flesh; victims living for days in agony before death put an end to their sufferings. Their little shops had been seized because they could not pay taxes that smote them as unexpectedly as a stroke of lightning. Thousands of them had been sent to the living death of the convict galleys on flimsy charges.

Louis XV, who was a voluptuary, obsessed by sex, had a virgin nearly every day for years. One of the duties of the king's chief valet was to procure these girls, and he had a number of assistants in Paris. Sometimes, indeed—strangely enough—this rascally valet had the co-operation of the king's official mistresses, Mme. de Pompadour, Mme. du Barry, and others. Anything to please the king. It is written that the great monarch, upon seeing a new girl, always said, "Take her away, clean her teeth, give her a bath, and bring her in again." In the end Louis XV caught smallpox from a gate-keeper's daughter. (I am taking this from gossip, and it may not be true, but people believed it at that time.) When he died of the disease the officials of the court dared not take his funeral cortege through the streets of Paris for fear it would be stoned.

A servant named Damiens tried to assassinate Louis XV. (He was not a servant in the royal household, but a stranger.) Damiens was a lunatic, a demented person, if the contemporary evidence means anything. He slashed at the king with a small knife, and made a slight flesh wound.*

The Archbishop of Paris ordered forty hours of prayer. They also closed the theaters. All domestic and foreign business was

* Damiens said that he did not intend to kill the king; he did not hate him. That is why he did not use a fatal dagger. All he wanted to do—according to his say-so —was to wound him and, in that way, to bring him back to God and the nation.

suspended. What they did to Damiens was something special, and plenty of that. This is what happened to him:

At a quarter to five in the afternoon the horror of his torture commenced. His right hand was burned; then he was tortured with red-hot pincers. Molten lead was poured into his wounds.

After that he was drawn and quartered. Being quartered means that horses are attached by ropes to one's arms and legs, and the victim is thus pulled to pieces. The account of the occurrence goes on:

The executioner had bought six horses, at a cost of three thousand six hundred livres, so that if one of the first four should fail it could be replaced without delay. Although these horses were very powerful and the two spare ones were used, they did not succeed in severing the limbs after many attempts, and the job had to be finished with an ax. The arms, legs and body were assembled, a fire was lit, and they were reduced to ashes which were scattered to the winds.*

Upon reading that authentic story can one wonder at the heads on pikes? Or the dragging of headless bodies through the streets?

Let us consider Gouverneur Morris for a moment. He was all for law and order. Seeing Foullon's body without a head dragged around he wrote, "Gracious God, what a people!" But would he have written that, or anything like it, if he had been in Paris at the time of Damiens's torture? No, indeed; I am quite sure he would have written in his diary, "Damiens, who tried to kill the king, was executed today."

4

The next day after the butchery of Foullon and Berthier, Lafayette resigned as general in chief of the National Guard. To Mayor Bailly he wrote: "The people have not listened to my advice, and the day in which the confidence that they promised is wanting, I must, as I said in advance, quit a post in which I can be no longer useful."

For two days the National Guard was without a head. Deputations from every section of Paris called on the marquis at his home and implored him to withdraw his resignation.† Bailly declared

* Moufle d'Angerville; *The Private Life of Louis XV*, p. 248.
† The "sections" of Paris were similar to the wards of American cities.

that he could not continue as mayor if Lafayette were not at his side. Even the fierce, unstable mob begged him to resume the command of the Guard. No wonder they did; he was not going to have anybody shot.

So Lafayette took back his resignation.

The municipal government was reorganized and made more compact. The chamber of four hundred Electors was replaced by an elective body of one hundred and twenty members.

The Viscomte de Noailles, a brother-in-law of Lafayette, and a member of the Assembly, on August 4th of that memorable year 1789 proposed the abolition of feudalism. The first sentence of his paper reads: "The National Assembly totally abolishes the feudal regime." Then it goes on to say that "taxes shall be paid by every individual in proportion to his income." This meant the suppression of all tax exemptions.

Further on: "All feudal dues [such as manorial rights, etc.] shall be redeemable by the communities for a money payment, or commuted at a fair valuation."

Still further: "Seignorial corvées, serfdom, and other forms of personal servitude shall be abolished without compensation."

It sounds splendid, but it was not as sweeping in its abolition of feudalism as it seems to be. There is that statement that feudal dues shall be "redeemable" in money. The dues—such as the champart, the tithes, the cens, a tenth of this produce, and a tenth of that—would still be in force unless the peasant communities could raise enough cash to pay the local marquis or count for his ancient rights. Not one commune in a hundred could possibly get together a sufficient fund to free itself.

Nevertheless, one may be sure that the Vicomte de Noailles meant well. He just simply did not understand the implications of his proposal. The act—or resolution—was passed with only a few dissenters and was sent to the king for his approval. He kept it for two months, dillydallying and saying that he had not got around to it yet, and so on.

Doniol, the well-known French historian who wrote of this period, said that he doubted the good faith of the National Assembly in this matter. He wrote: "The feudal forms disappeared, but the effects of feudalism would take a long time to die out, and would continue to exist owing to the difficulties of escaping from them;

and thus the interests of the landowners would be maintained without any apparent breach of the pledges of August 4th."

On August 14th the Assembly approved Lafayette's Declaration of Rights after having considered it for more than a month. But it was not passed without amendments, most of them rather trivial. Its essential character remained.

Then the National Assembly began to draft a constitution, with the Declaration of Rights as its preamble.

CHAPTER XIX

VERSAILLES MOVES TO PARIS

I

IN THE king's service there was a body of mercenary troops known as the Flanders regiment, so named because its enlisted men were recruited mainly in Belgium. The king, distrusting the National Guard, ordered the Flanders regiment to Versailles. On October 1st—the year is still 1789—the officers of the Gardes du Corps (the royal bodyguard) gave a banquet in the opera house of the palace in honor of the officers of the newly arrived Flemish regiment. As a matter of courtesy the officers of the National Guard stationed at Versailles were also invited.

It was an uproarious affair, marked by drunkenness and scenes of disorder. At the height of the confusion the king and queen appeared. In her arms the queen carried her son, the dauphin, and she held him up for the officers to see. The band began at once to play *"O Richard; o mon roi! l'univers t'abandonne!"* There can be no doubt that the dramatic appearance of the royal family was pre-arranged. The officers of the Gardes du Corps and those of the Flanders regiment were half wild with wine and loyalty. They snatched away the red, white and blue revolutionary cockades of the National Guard and trampled them underfoot. The white cockades of the king and the black ones of the queen were distributed hastily and everybody put them on, except the officers of the National Guard.

When the news of these doings, with the usual embroidery of exaggeration and alarm, reached the unquiet city of Paris the populace began to stir, and what a stir it was! The Palais Royal hummed like a hive of angry bees. Boisterous crowds collected in the streets and went here and there, plundering shops and cafés and throwing stones at everything that bore the king's name. It may seem strange that mobs of such size and ferocity could get together so quickly. The explanation is that about half the people of Paris were out of work. The laboring people were hungry; they wanted bread. Many of the bakers' shops were closed with the iron window blinds pulled down; they had no bread to sell, and even if there had been bread the poor could not have bought it; the price was too high.

The closing of the great houses of the noble *émigrés* had sent their many thousands of servants adrift. Owing to the uncertainty of the times large numbers of employers had discharged most of their people. There were tens of thousands of beggars. Many people were homeless, and prowled about the streets looking for little crumbs of work to pay for a bowl of soup and a night's lodging. The same state of affairs existed almost everywhere else in France, even in the country districts.

The French Revolution was purely economic in origin. An end could have been put to it at any time before 1791 by economic measures of intelligence and force. That is a dogmatic statement, necessarily, and may not be true. Yet it seems to be, and in accord with the historical evidence. What the Versailles government needed was not a lot of generals and Flanders regiments and cockades, but a New Deal of the most vigorous character. This would have required the spending of a vast amount of money for public relief, the construction of public works, the development of agriculture, the rehabilitation of industries. A lot of money would have been needed, but there was a lot of money in France.

After 1791 these measures would have been useless. By that time the Revolution had gone too far.

But just now we are considering the early days of October, 1789. Lafayette, responsible for the peace of Paris and for the safety of the king, sat uneasily in his headquarters or, astride his white horse, rode among the mobs advising the people to be calm.

In human affairs physical bravery has a special value of its own, and the young marquis was brave. Ragged, unwashed, nondescript men walked along with their hands on his saddle or on his horse's sides, proud of the honor of being so close to him.

Millions of Frenchmen—the common people, the illiterate— believed that Lafayette had inspired our American War for Independence; that he came over here, won our independence for us, and then went back to France to start a revolution in his own country and free the people. Such nonsense as this often has a great influence on men and women of low mental visibility. It is so easy to believe, as simple as a fairy tale, while real history is a complicated pattern of personalities and events.

The inciters of revolt, and they were many, asserted that the banquet at Versailles was an unexpected revelation of a royalist plot against the people. The orators of the Palais Royal declared that the failure of the king to approve the act of the Assembly for the abolition of feudalism was significant. It was, indeed, and the events at Versailles showed unmistakably the temper and inclination of the king and court. Marat called on the people to arm and march to Versailles; and so did Danton, Desmoulins, and many lesser men.

Paris was in a turmoil on October 5th, which was a Monday— a cold and cloudy day, with a gray sky, the kind of day that makes one want to stay at home and read before a cheerful fire.

But Paris was not reading before cheerful fires that day. There were fierce crowds in the streets and among them were as many women as men. They were there because they could not get food for their children. Into the Place de Grève the mob swarmed with the swirl and rush of an overflowing river. The people wanted to talk—or shout, if you please—to Mayor Bailly and General Lafayette, but neither of them had arrived. Lafayette came soon; messengers had been sent to tell him what was happening.

The National Guard also came in rigid military order. They made an imposing front before the Hôtel de Ville, but in a few minutes their ranks were broken by the women, who shoved them aside and thrust them out of the way. What decent man, soldier or no soldier, would shoot women?

The disorderly crowd wanted to go to Versailles, and demand this and that from the king and queen. But what? They had many confused desires; some wanted one thing and some wanted something else, but they were all—unanimously—sure that the king must be brought to Paris and kept in Paris, where he would be surrounded by his people. Would M. de Lafayette, commanding general, order the National Guard to accompany them, to lead the way? No, he would not, and he said so; and he advised the mob to keep away from Versailles, to disperse and go to their homes. He was talking against the wind. The fickle people, who had shouted themselves hoarse for Lafayette only the week before, now threatened to hang him. He quietly stood his ground, although he was for a time in great danger.

In the middle of the afternoon the news came that another section of the mob was already on its way to Versailles. This information was bellowed to the crowd by a messenger who had climbed a lamppost. Thereupon the great multitude in front of the Hôtel de Ville moved off in the same direction. What should Lafayette do? He did not know; was confused, perplexed. The Assembly of the City of Paris—called the Commune—was in an all-day session. He appeared before it and declared that he would follow its instructions. After a long palaver he was given orders to proceed to Versailles with a strong detachment of the National Guard for the purpose of protecting the king and queen and the National Assembly.

So, in martial array, the Guard took the road to Versailles, the marquis and his white horse among them. Officers were sent on ahead to announce the coming of the troops. The Guard arrived before the palace about midnight in a drenching rain. Lafayette was soaked to the skin, and so was everyone else.

The rabble was already there. Thousands and thousands of women, and other thousands who appeared to be women, but who were men in disguise. Dressed in their wives' discarded skirts, and in odds and ends picked from ragbags, they looked like scarecrows. The wearing of this fantastic apparel was inspired by the general conviction that the king would never order his Gardes du Corps to fire on women. They were quite right in their belief; the king gave orders when the mob appeared that the women were not to be fired on, no matter what they did.

The march of the mob on Versailles will always remain one of the outstanding events of French history. One may imagine the state of things when this disorderly and rain-drenched crowd arrived in the great square before the palace. They had no organization, no food, no place to sleep. Many of them were madly drunk, for plenty of wine and brandy bottles had been passed around on the twelve-mile pedestrian trip from Paris. Moving here and there among these bedraggled women was Théroigne de Méricourt, who was neither shabby nor bedraggled—only wet. She rode a splendid horse; her riding habit was scarlet and black, the racing colors of the Duc d'Orléans.

Théroigne de Méricourt was a black-eyed, good-looking Belgian. She had formerly been a mistress of the Prince of Wales, and was introduced by him to the Duc d'Orléans, or it may be more in line with truth to say that she was handed over to him.

The dissolute head of the Orléans clan set up a magnificent establishment for her in Paris. She was what the French today would call a *poule de luxe*. She was not only without morals, but also without a trace of honor or principle. All day long she had been seen stirring about, on her horse, among the Parisian mob, inciting a movement on Versailles.*

Before the dark palace the Flanders regiment of cavalry was drawn up, the riders sitting quietly on their horses.

When the National Guard of Paris reached the scene Lafayette was met by an officer of the king's household who said that he and his troops were welcome, and he added that the king had just sanctioned and signed Lafayette's Declaration of Rights.

The king had been hunting that day and, returning late, was astonished at the situation. The first thing he did was to give orders that all the bread in Versailles be distributed to the people.

The marquis, as wet as a fish, went immediately to the Salle des Menus Plaisirs to pay his respects to the Assembly and to report his arrival. The hall of the Assembly was a scene of pandemonium. The rain-drenched mob, to get into a dry place, had burst into the hall. There were too many of them for the spectators' galleries so they poured in on the floor, and took the seats of deputies. Some of them had raided the grocers' shops. Wine and food were brought into the Assembly hall. There was feasting among the rioters. Empty bottles rolled over the floor, and scraps of meat and bread were flung at the heads of the deputies. The noise was prodigious, though the Assembly made a pretense of remaining in session. The speeches could not be heard above the din. Some of the Parisian prostitutes had gone up on the dais of the president and were mocking the Bishop of Langres, the solemn gentleman who presided.

The Assembly finally adjourned amid a chorus of yells and catcalls from the mob. Lafayette had no control over the people. Almost out of his mind, he rode here and there amid the drunken crowd, and finally went to the palace to confer with the king, who seemed pleased to see him. It was arranged that Lafayette's troops

* Théroigne de Méricourt went mad eventually, and died in an insane asylum.

were to guard the exterior of the château. The Gardes du Corps and the Swiss guards were to protect the interior.

Lafayette's disposition of his men was quite inadequate. At the main entrance he posted only two men; these against a mob of many thousands. At another entrance—at the back of the building—there was no sentry at all; it had been completely overlooked. But one must say for him that there were extenuating circumstances. He was half dead with fatigue; he had not slept for twenty hours; he was hungry and his clothes were soppy with rain. The actual posting of the sentries was probably done by the officers of the National Guard, under Lafayette's orders. They had had little training, and were inefficient.

These arrangements made, he went to the near-by Hôtel de Noailles to change his clothes, eat some supper and sleep a few hours.

2

At six o'clock next morning he was awakened by an alarm. One of his aides hurried to tell him that the mob was attacking the palace. Lafayette dressed in haste and went at once to see what was happening. The rabble had broken through his flimsy defenses and had killed an officer of the Gardes du Corps. Jourdan Coupe-Tête, ferocious maniac, had cut off the officer's head and smeared the warm blood over his own beard and face. Seeing that exhibition of insane sadism, many of those in the mob had done the same thing. Picture that! Bloody people capering around a headless corpse! The Gardes du Corps could have protected themselves and the palace, but their officers had a most emphatic order—from the king— not to fire on the people.

When Lafayette arrived on the scene the wild and blood-smeared mob was running through the corridors of the palace, demanding the heart of the queen—the Austrian woman. She had fled, by a secret passageway, to the king's apartments. Another slaughtered officer was lying before the queen's door. Lafayette and his aides—with the National Guard—took charge of the situation. The Parisian horde was pushed back downstairs and outdoors, with repeated admonitions to put their trust in Lafayette. Outside they were at last, but not dispersed. They stood in a compact mass before the palace, howling that the king, the queen and the royal children must return with them to Paris, and remain there permanently.

From a balcony Lafayette addressed the crowd, or tried to, but little attention was paid to him. To put an end to the clamor the king decided to go to Paris, and from the balcony he made an announcement to that effect. Few could hear him, but the news passed around from mouth to ear through the turbulent mob.

Now the queen: the rabble must look on the face of Marie Antoinette; bring her out. Lafayette reflected a moment; then he went back in the palace and told the queen that she should appear before the people. "But, M. de Lafayette," she said, "have you heard what they have been saying of me? And the signs they made?"

What they had been shouting about her was unadulterated obscenity and the signs they made were gestures of cutting her throat.

"Yes, madame, I have heard and seen," Lafayette replied. "Come with me."

Marie Antoinette still wore the yellow-striped dressing gown that she had hastily thrown on as she ran to the king's apartments. She had not yet had time to make her toilette. When she appeared on the balcony the roar of sound smote her like a blow.

There stood the blond queen, her hair disheveled, in her flimsy *robe de chambre*. She was frightened, and with good reason.

France, look upon your queen. Marie Antoinette of Austria, look upon the French people who will one day destroy you.

Lafayette had an inspiration. He was by nature, instinctively, an actor of talent. Sweeping off his hat and bowing in the manner of a courtier, he kneeled, took the queen's hand and raised it to his lips. Marie Antoinette detested Lafayette, and he had a measureless contempt for her. Yet there they were, bowing and hand-kissing.

The crowd was silent for a moment; then it roared *"Vive la reine!" "Vive Lafayette!"* Gouverneur Morris was right. What a people!

3

The royal family left the château of Versailles at noon to go to Paris. The king and queen never saw the place again, nor did the dauphin, but Madame Royale—the little princess, then eleven years old—survived the terrors of the Revolution, became the Duchesse d'Angoulême, and frequently visited Versailles in her later years.*

Why did Louis XVI obey the mob with such placid resignation? Maybe not placid; maybe with inward rage; but anyway he did obey their roaring mandate. His grandfather, Louis XV, would never have dreamed of taking such a course. Nor would Napoleon. The answer to these questions is unknown because the motives of Louis XVI are obscure, relegated to darkness, or dissolved by the acids of secrecy.

But the vast pattern of conjecture is open to all. The best guess is that he left his palace, his home, and followed the rabble to Paris because there was nothing else to do. Suppose he had refused to go. In that case it is entirely probable that these rebellious people would have sacked Versailles, and its wealthy houses, as if it were a conquered city. He might have ordered the troops to fire on them, to drive them out with bullets and bayonets. The Gardes du Corps and the foreign troops would have obeyed him, but it is as certain as sunrise that Lafayette would not have obeyed him, nor the National Guard. So the ill-fated king went to Paris, to the palace called the Tuileries.

Lafayette sent the mob on ahead. Next in the procession came the National Guard, then the royal carriage. The marquis rode beside the coach of the king and queen.

The Tuileries palace was an immense building which stood just in front of the Louvre. It was burned in 1871 by the Communards. It was about a thousand feet in length, and reached from what is now the Rue de Rivoli to the Quai des Tuileries, the street that runs along the river.

On the morning of October 6th a galloping messenger was sent to Paris to notify the authorities that the royal family was coming and that the Tuileries must be prepared for their reception. It was a herculean job. No king of France had lived there for more than a hundred years. The hundreds of rooms were occupied by officers who lived on pensions, nice old ladies, retired officials and penniless nobles. None paid any rent. It was a vast nest of respectable nobodies. The messenger arrived and before nightfall all the tenants

---

* She died in 1851, at the age of seventy-three, when the French Revolution was remembered only by the elderly grayheads. She was a reactionary of a pronounced type and very aggressive. Napoleon said, "The Duchesse d'Angoulême is the only man in that family."

had been thrown out pell-mell. Puzzled architects walked through the wilderness of rooms and wondered what ought to be done to make them habitable by the royal family. There should be halls of reception, drawing rooms of spacious size, dining rooms, big and little, apartments for the king and queen. Besides, two thousand servants were coming eventually, as soon as adequate preparation could be made for them. The idea of bringing that many servants, ladies in waiting, cooks, butlers and idle followers to Paris was a stupid error. Most of the people in the city had no servants at all and at least a third of them were in a state of semistarvation.

That night the royal family slept on cots in two adjoining rooms. Months passed before the Tuileries was transformed into a royal palace, and even when the repairs were completed the great building possessed none of the splendors of Versailles. It was just a huge barrack.

It was evident to everyone, even to the slow-witted Louis XVI, that the king and queen had lost their pre-eminence in the social structure; that the rulership of France had passed out of the king's hands, and the assumption that he still possessed it was only a pretense.

Notwithstanding this obvious fact, the king had friends and supporters. Millions of Frenchmen could not conceive of France existing without a king, but they wanted him to be a constitutional monarch. These were the Moderates—the "Fayettists," as they were sometimes called—and in the early months of the Revolution they had a majority in the National Assembly.

There appear to have been four parties in the Assembly, but there was so much confusion in their motives and such an amazing diversity of opinions and objectives that it is difficult to define them clearly. Besides the Moderates, there were the members of the extreme right. Out and out royalists they were, committed to the policy of handing the government back to the king. On the other side of the chamber were the deputies of the extreme left—bold and implacable radicals—whose purpose it was to transform completely the existing government, to change the system of taxation, to give every man a vote, to seize the lands of the Church and the Nobility. But even they were monarchists—advocates of a limited monarchy—until the royal family endeavored to escape from France in 1791. After that episode the Left stood for an abolition of the royal

power and putting the chief executive power in the hands of a committee. They were led by such formidable revolutionists as Robespierre, Danton and Desmoulins. Mirabeau was also one of their
leaders, but we shall see further on that he was moved by ulterior
and secret motives, and that at heart he was a constitutional royalist.

Then there was, finally, the Orleanist group. Most of them were
venal and unscrupulous, and there is no doubt that some of their
leaders were in the pay of the Duc d'Orléans. They were never a
strong party, and their tactics were mainly obstructive.*

The strength of the extreme Left came mainly from the common people of Paris, the proletariat. The Leftist party was ably
directed. Their adherents were enrolled in political clubs of large
membership, such as the Jacobins and the Cordeliers. Emissaries
of these clubs were sent all over France for the purpose of spreading their ideas and forming local clubs. In these activities they were
assisted secretly by the Orleanists, who desired to cause infinite disorder throughout the nation, so that in the midst of the ensuing
chaos the Duc d'Orléans might seize the throne. Then he would
turn around and make the proletariat behave itself, or be shot down.

On October 16th the National Assembly left Versailles and
settled down in Paris, to be near the king—and the people. Versailles, with the court and the Assembly gone, had thereafter the
languor of a dead town. The Assembly resumed its deliberations in
the Manège, or royal riding school, which was close to the Tuileries.

The hatred of the king and queen for Lafayette had the burning quality of a red-hot iron. The drab Tuileries palace was to them
a jail, and they looked upon him as their jailer. The royalist party
spread a rumor that Lafayette was plotting to get rid of the king
and take his place. Not only the royalists took that piece of gossip
as truth—or pretended to believe it, at any rate—but some of the
leaders of the extreme Left also had it disseminated widely. They
were jealous of Lafayette's popularity and hoped to destroy it by
lies and well-planted suspicions.

Was it true? Evidently not. No one can say with certainty what

* My readers will understand, I hope, that this brief picture of the factions is
not intended to be comprehensive, nor complete in detail. The reason is that I am not
writing a history of the French Revolution but a life of the Marquis de Lafayette and
I am setting forth only enough of the revolutionary movement to furnish a background
for the subject of this biography.

notions are buzzing in people's heads, and we can judge them only
by their utterances, their actions and a knowledge of their character.
By all these standards we may say confidently that he had no intention of becoming a Cromwell. He was a royalist. From first to last
he advocated a constitutional monarchy with Louis XVI at the head
of it. Marie Antoinette in his opinion was *une femme damnée,* but
if a constitutional government were set up she could not have much,
if any, influence. He did not consider himself as a jailer of the king.
Far from it. On the contrary, he thought of himself as a protector
of the royal family.

To Mme. de Simiane he wrote:

I am in a great adventure, and I like to think that I shall come out of it,
without having had even an ambitious impulse to reproach myself for, and
after having put everybody in his proper place, I shall retire with a quarter
of the fortune that I had when I came into the world. . . . Bless us with your
angelic wishes, and reassure yourself about my situation. I believe that we
shall bring the kingdom through all right.

The glow of vanity shines through his phrases. "Put everybody
in his place . . . we shall bring the kingdom through all right." But
vanity does not necessarily mean a desire to seize national power.
Many actors are vain, and like to see their pictures in the newspapers and have admiring throngs around them, but there is no
record in history of an actor who aspired to be President of the
United States. Nor is there any screed in the historical documents
of a dictator or a kingdom-seizer anywhere who was impelled solely
by vanity. Of course, many of them were vain and delighted in self-
glorification, but their controlling impulse was—and is—a desire
for power. Lafayette's desire for personal power was impressively
small. He wanted to shine before the public, to be popular, to be
loved or admired by everyone as a patriot, an honest citizen and a
brave soldier.

After October 6th he was the strongest man in France. He
could have deposed the king and made himself the head of the state.
There is hardly a doubt that the people of France would have supported him. But in the seizure of power he could not have prevented
the shooting of his adversaries, and probably there would have been
mass murders in the streets. In their rise to power dictators must be
ferocious, cruel and unjust. They have to be.

In another letter to his lady friend Lafayette says that he is sorry for the sad plight of the king and queen, and continues in these words:

They would have been better served by a harder man. They are grown-up children who will not take their medicine unless they are frightened by stories of the werewolf. . . . Speak of me to all who recall the days that were so sweet and that I long to see come again.

That is a letter from a man who is sorely perplexed, and who longs for the sunlit past. If only Washington were there to tell him what to do. Majestic Washington, decisive, calm and resolute in the most desperate situations.

The king, steeped in duplicity, appeared graciously in the hall of the National Assembly and was received with profound respect. He had come to announce to the Assembly and to the nation that he was pleased to be in the midst of his beloved people in Paris, that he had come of his own free will, that he approved the Declaration of Rights, the abolition of feudal dues paid by the people, and the basic ideas of the constitution which the Assembly was then engaged in creating.

Very encouraging. The whole of France, except the inveterate revolutionists, was cheered up by the king's attitude. After all—said one homme moyen to another—he's our king; he means well; he loves his people.

But at that moment this lover of the people had secret agents in Vienna who were endeavoring to persuade the emperor—brother of Marie Antoinette—to invade France with an Austrian army. That was treason on the part of Louis XVI, of course, but he never thought it was. His mentality had been shaped in such fashion that he could not conceive of a reigning sovereign doing a treasonable act. Treason against whom? Against himself? Was he not an embodiment of the nation?

There were other secret doings. Gamain, the mechanic who had taught the king the delightful art of locksmithery, was called to the Tuileries, paid a handsome sum in gold, and he and the king constructed a secret cupboard, encased in a wall, for the royal correspondence. The receptacle was so ingeniously contrived that one might pass by it countless times, even stare at the wall or beat on it with hammers and never suspect that anything lay hidden there.

But a day was coming when loutish Gamain, whose moral fiber

was so base that it could not hold a secret, would run to the implacable revolutionists and king-haters and *tell all*. That will be a bad day for Louis XVI.

In the king there was nothing solid or sincere. Words and promises meant nothing to him. One might say that of Napoleon, too, and truthfully, but Napoleon possessed the smashing qualities of audacity and force, which were lacking in the husband of Marie Antoinette. Take Louis XVI apart, piece by piece; hold a psychological autopsy over him. What do we find? Nothing much. The inquisitive surgeons dissect brain and heart. There is a speck of this and a speck of that—generosity, capacity, knowledge—all so small that they can be discerned only under a microscope. Love of eating and drinking is large enough to be seen with the naked eye and very distinctly. But, going deeper, the psychological surgeons come upon a large slab of personality, bigger than everything else put together. In wonder they turn it over and over. Careful examination. It turns out to be a desire to kill animals, and the verdict of the autopsy is that this man should not have been a king but a huntsman or a game warden.

4

Gouverneur Morris considered Lafayette a misfit. He wrote in September, 1789:

I have known my friend Lafayette now for many years, and can estimate at the just value both his words and his actions. . . . He is very much below the business he has undertaken, and if the sea runs high he will be unable to hold the helm.*

I want to say here, as politely as possible, that I have small respect for the opinions of Gouverneur Morris. He was in France at that time as a promoter and pretentious commercial salesman. He carried prospectuses and contracts in every pocket. He was ready to sell one hundred thousand pounds of Virginia tobacco to the farmers-general on a moment's notice; to shave down the price, to give and take. Or, he could sell a vast tract of land west of the Alleghenies. Emigrate, go abroad, be a great lord in our Ohio wilderness; the country will grow up; here's the map, take a look at it; have you ever heard of such a bargain in your life? Well, if you

* *Diary and Letters of Gouverneur Morris*, Vol. I, p. 158.

feel that you would not like to live so far away from the cities, why
not buy an interest in one of our big commercial houses—mercantile, shipping, banking? Being in trade is considered a very honorable career over there; ask Rochambeau, Noailles, Lafayette.

He spoke French well, occupied a large house, and was a thoroughgoing snob. He tried to associate only with nobles, and he
records in his diary, with great satisfaction, that he has dined with
the Marquise de So-and-so, and the Duc de Quelque-chose. All the
women he met were, he thought, soon in love with him. That was
one of his most persistent delusions. Maybe one or two of them
were. Mme. de Flahaut, from his own account, seems to have been
his mistress. He wrote execrable verses to his lady friends, and included them in his diary. The diary has been long in print; one
may read it.

Far be it from me to detract in any way from the reputation
of Gouverneur Morris. I have no interest in him at all, except in
respect to his comments on Lafayette. A man of his type simply
would not understand the marquis, and was therefore prejudiced.
To him Lafayette was a deserter from his class in society—and
just think of the horror of a noble turning his back on the Nobility.
Certainly Morris would not have done it. Never. Moreover, Morris
considered himself a sort of American noble, in a way, with a coat
of arms, an ancestry, a fortune—and everything. But Morris did
not condemn Lafayette; his feeling was one of pity.

We have seen Lafayette's limitations. They were serious, but
he was not stupid, not a fool, and there was no evil intention
or meanness in his make-up. However, Gouverneur Morris was ready
and willing to straighten him out, and set him going on the right
road, for—you see—Mr. Morris knew more about the French than
they knew about themselves.

On November 25, 1790—I know I am running ahead of the
story—Morris called on the Lafayettes after dinner. "Madame," he
says, "receives me coolly enough. I stay some time, leaning on the
chimney piece." The marquis comes in after a while, and asks why
Morris does not come to see him. To that inquiry Morris replies,
"I do not like to mix with the crowd I find here." An insolent reply.
The men and women he found there were among those who were
trying to make a better government for France. Morris goes on:

He asks my opinion of his situation. I give it frankly, and while I speak he turns pale. I tell him that the time approaches when all good men must cling to the throne . . . that the thing called a constitution which the Assembly have framed is good for nothing . . . that his personal situation is very delicate; that he nominally, but not really, commands his troops. . . .

I reiterate to him the necessity of restoring the nobility, at which, of course, he flinches, and says he would like two chambers [he means legislative chambers, a Senate and a House] as in America. I tell him that an American constitution will not do for this country, and that two such chambers would not answer where there is an hereditary executive.*

Having told Lafayette what's what, Mr. Morris goes on his way. But before his departure he suggests that the marquis might seize on an occasion of disobedience of the troops and resign, "by which means he would preserve a reputation in France which would be precious, and hereafter useful."†

*How about England? It works there all right, and the English have an hereditary executive.

† *Diary and Letters of Gouverneur Morris,* Vol. I, p. 362.

CHAPTER XX

LAFAYETTE AND MIRABEAU

I

FROM THE beginning of the National Assembly, until his death
in April, 1791, Honoré Gabriel Riquetti de Mirabeau was the
most powerful and influential member of that body. He was a
man of great ability and driving force. No other person in the public
life of France at that time was his equal as a political realist.*

In 1789 Mirabeau was forty years old and his life had been a
stormy one. He came from a noble family of Provence, in the south
of France, and was the eldest son of a father who was neurotic—
or maybe only eccentric—to the edge of insanity.

Mirabeau *père* was a wealthy landowner who dabbled in political economy and occasionally wrote a book or a pamphlet. He
was on one hand an opponent of Rousseau and his childlike faith
in the simple life as a cure for all the ills of civilization; and, on
the other hand, he was a bitter critic of the monetary system
and its tendency toward the concentration of wealth in a few
hands. His literary style, like his speech, was fiery. Though his writings had a fairly large circulation, they were so erratic in temper
that most of their effectiveness was dissipated.

He called himself *L'Ami des Hommes*. Friend of men. Appealing title it was, but this lover of humanity was unbearably harsh
in his personal relations. He was a family despot; he treated his
daughter so cruelly that she killed herself. The Mirabeau ménage
was the scene of never-ending quarrels.

Young Mirabeau became an army officer at the age of seven-

* Honoré Gabriel Riquetti is universally referred to by historians of the period
as Mirabeau. He should not be confused with his brother, the Vicomte de Mirabeau,
who bore the nickname of "Mirabeau-Tonneau" ("Barrel-Mirabeau"), given him on
account of his barrel-like girth and his vast capacity for consuming wines and liquors.
Mirabeau-Tonneau was also a member of the National Assembly, but on the royalist
side, while his celebrated brother was a leader of the popular party. The vicomte did
not like his brother, and detested his activities as an advocate of the people. The vicomte
was not a man of notable ability; he played no conspicuous part in the Assembly.

LAFAYETTE IN 1792 AS COMMANDER
OF THE NATIONAL GUARD

From a painting by Court in the Musée de Versailles.

JEAN PAUL MARAT

teen, like Lafayette, but their respective careers were very different. Mirabeau got himself mixed up in a scandal with the wife of his colonel and was dismissed from the army while he was still a boy. Thereupon he adopted the profession of idleness for a while—until the breaking out of the Corsican War. He volunteered and was reinstated as an officer. During the campaign he gained some distinction.

Upon his return his arbitrary father ordered him to marry a rich young heiress—Emilie de Marignane—who had been selected for him. Mirabeau was willing enough to take her as his wife, but the girl's parents would not hear of it. They had learned of the young man's bad reputation by hearsay—in a highly exaggerated form, of course.

Reflecting on the matter, Mirabeau decided that the best way to get the girl would be to compromise her character, so early one morning he managed to climb, unknown to her, to the balcony of her room, and appear there after sunrise in a dressing gown. He was seen by the neighbors and passers-by, and gossip did the rest. The girl protested that she did not know he was on the balcony. The story does not say whether her parents believed her or not, but they consented to her marriage.*

It seems rather obvious that Mirabeau's great ability was pretty thoroughly balanced, if not overweighted, by his lack of moral principle.

At his wedding he went deeply in debt to give an enormously expensive party; then he learned, to his dismay, that his wife's family refused to turn over her dowry on the ground that it would be soon wasted if their son-in-law ever got his hands on it. He had no money of his own; his father would not give him a sou. Moreover, his wife was stupid. The young couple did not live together long. She went back soon to her father's house and the elder Mirabeau had his son sent to the Château d'If, a famous prison at Marseilles—a sort of Mediterranean Bastille. (In that era the heads of noble houses possessed extraordinary disciplinary powers over the members of their families.) It has been said that the father's motive in putting young Mirabeau in prison was to keep him out of

* There is another version of this episode. Etienne Dumont in his *Souvenirs sur Mirabeau,* says that Mirabeau actually had a rendezvous with a servant maid in the house, and that he let it be known where he was to spend the night, but did not say with whom. He was seen to enter the house and leave it.

the hands of his creditors. While in jail he had a love affair with a daughter of the governor of the prison and she helped him escape.

For a while he was a fugitive. Then he was caught and sent to prison at Pontarlier. There he made love to Sophie de Monnier, who was his jailer's wife. He seems to have had a great attraction for the daughters and wives of prisonkeepers. Mirabeau and Sophie de Monnier fled from France in destitution and for some time they lived in Holland and in England. They existed on the proceeds of his poorly paid writings, supplemented by borrowed money. It was a miserable life for both of them, reduced as they were to a poverty like that of stray dogs. Sophie was the mother of his child. Finally she committed suicide. While he was in exile he wrote many of the violent pamphlets which flooded France before the Revolution.

He developed a prodigious capacity for acquiring knowledge of all kinds—history, science, political economy, biography. In England he spent much time in the study of British institutions. He thought the English had the best government in the world.

Eventually he was brought back to France on a charge of "abduction and seduction." This accusation was based on his flight from France with Sophie de Monnier. He was sentenced to be beheaded "in effigy by the executioner"—a symbolic, but not physical execution; also a fine of five thousand livres was imposed. Besides, damages of forty thousand livres were awarded to M. de Monnier. Mirabeau had to pay the fine within five years, during which time he was to be imprisoned in the fortress of Vincennes. Having no money, he was unable to pay the fines. If the sum awarded to M. de Monnier was not paid, he would lose his civil rights. He was in a desperate situation. Through intermediaries he contrived to patch up his difficulties with de Monnier but he was not released from Vincennes until after his father's death.

Here we see a bitter foe of the existing order in the making. His pestered life was pictured in his mind as a crucifixion; unjust and inhumanly cruel. He was for liberty, freedom, equality, and a sweeping abolition of feudalism. But, at the same time, all this was entangled and interwoven with other patterns of thought. His bitter experiences had made a cynic of him, and he distrusted everybody and everything. A sensualist of the first rank, he cherished his vices and made of them not merely an amusement or an escape, but

Mirabeau—who was already called the "Tribune of the People"—
wanted the heads of both the royal houses to be in France together,
so that the Orleanist schemes would undermine those of the court.
There were doubtless other and more cryptic motives. Both the king
and his distant cousin had immense sums of ready money, and the
Tribune of the People had practically none. A poor man—however
shrewd and able he may be—must live, one way or another. As long
as Orléans, with his impulse to instigate disturbance, remained in
the country the king would be a better "prospect," to use a phrase
of the modern salesman.

But when the flashy Duc d'Orléans went back to the Marquis
de Lafayette and said he had decided not to accept the mission,
the marquis told him bluntly that he would have to go, and so he
went. Mirabeau was disgusted with the Duc d'Orleans. "They say
I belong to his party," he exclaimed. "I would not have him for
my valet."

3

During the fall and winter of 1789 Mirabeau endeavored stren-
uously to build up a friendship with Lafayette. They met frequently,
sometimes at the house of Thomas Jefferson, and had long discussions on the state of the country. Mirabeau argued that he and
Lafayette ought to form a two-man society for mutual support. Acting together, he maintained, they would be able to dominate the
situation, put down the riotous factions in the Assembly and among
the people, and set up—under royal authority—a constitutional government. Lafayette was to be the Richelieu of the new regime; and
Mirabeau was to stand beside him as friend and adviser.

"Be Richelieu over the court for the nation," he wrote to
Lafayette in one of his numerous letters, "and you will make over
the monarchy anew, while enlarging and consolidating the public
liberty. But Richelieu had his Frère Joseph; have then also your
Eminence Grise, or you will lose yourself and not save us. Your
great qualities have need of my driving power; my driving power
has need of your great qualities.

"You listen to mediocre men who wish to render us useless to
each other, and you do not see that in view of the fact that your
stupid partisans have more and more decried me, it is necessary

for you to unite with me and to believe in me. Ah, you forfeit you destiny!"

Lafayette distrusted these advances. He felt that a sinister purpose was concealed in them. He knew of Mirabeau's evil repu tation and reputed lack of moral and intellectual honesty.

The intuition of the marquis in this case was doubtless cor rect. The sinister motive was, in all probability, Mirabeau's plan for his own advancement with Lafayette tagging along behind him rather than in front. There was also, without doubt, a hankering for Lafayette money. But in politics, as in all public affairs, one has to deal at times with men who have not achieved haloes of virtue; indeed, it is often desirable to co-operate with them for special purposes.

If Lafayette had come to an understanding with Mirabeau, they would have been in an excellent position to direct the course of the Revolution. With all his faults, Mirabeau was a statesman, and the only man in public life at that time who had enough vision, personal force, and understanding to steer the ship. His insistence was not easily shaken off. On October 19th he wrote to Lafayette:

Whatever happens, I shall be yours unto the end, because your great qualities have strongly attracted me, and it is impossible for me not to take a very lively interest in a future such as yours, and one that is so strictly bound to the Revolution which leads the nation to liberty.*

Lafayette called frequently at the Tuileries and talked with the king and queen. He had no inkling, apparently, that they considered him their jailer, and certainly that was not his conception of the duties of his office. He had a garrison of his National Guard at the palace for the purpose of protecting the royal family. On one of his visits—in April, 1790—both the king and Marie Antoinette urged him to come to an agreement with Mirabeau. They had good reason for that suggestion; Mirabeau was then secretly in their pay. Lafayette refused, and said brusquely: "I do not like him. I do not esteem him. I do not fear him. I see no reason why I should seek an understanding with him." This remark was probably passed on to Mirabeau within twenty-four hours.

Mirabeau became an enemy of Lafayette. It may be accepted as an axiomatic truth that when A tries, humbly and ardently, to develop a friendship with B, and is repulsed with contempt, there-

* *Correspondence de Mirabeau*, Vol. I, p. 268.

after A—if he has any stamina and pride—will be an inveterate hater of B. Love and hate are twins, and exist side by side in the emotional structure of mankind.

4

In the spring of 1790 the queen, who evidently did all the thinking for the throne—such as it was—had an idea that it was absolutely necessary to win the support of some member of great influence on the popular side in the National Assembly. Well, who was the most powerful man there? Mirabeau, of course. Comte de La Marck, hovering around, was a friend of Mirabeau. He told the queen—and, no doubt, the king—of Mirabeau's financial troubles. The Tribune of the People was practically penniless, except so far as his long-extended credit might go, and that was near its end. The pay of deputies in the National Assembly was only eighteen francs a day. Should he see and converse with friend Mirabeau? By all means. The royal couple agreed in advance to furnish all the money required to bring Mirabeau over to their side.

The terms were stated by Mirabeau; he was to get two hundred thousand francs to clear himself of debt;· then six thousand francs a month right along as a regular salary. On the dissolution of the National Assembly he was to receive a further gratuity of one million francs. Mirabeau's fortune was made. But, from the royal point of view, there was a handful of sand in the gearing of this mechanism. The Tribune of the People, in these secret dealings, let his clients know that he would not be a puppet, a mere clerk who says only what he is told to say. That was emphatic. He would not advocate any measure which he did not approve. He stood for the monarchy, a constitution, and the freedom of the people, and he would advise the king to follow that direction. Also there was the Assembly to consider. He might possibly rise in the hall of legislation and declaim against the regime, the court, the king and queen. If so, his royal paymasters should understand that he did it to retain his popularity, for without popularity what have you? No influence at all.

With his debts all settled and six thousand francs rolling in every month Mirabeau began to live on a grand scale. He had almost as much income as Lafayette, if not more, for the wealth of our marquis was going down, owing to generosities, extravagances, and paying for this and that just because he liked people and wanted to make them happy.

Mirabeau kept constantly in touch with the court. Secret correspondence; comments on current affairs, and suggestions to be considered by the king. A bitter animosity toward Lafayette shows here and there in his notes.

He suggested that the king and queen "appear frequently before the people; to build up a reputation as popular rulers." Good idea, that was; but neither Louis XVI nor Marie Antoinette could develop it successfully. The basic elements of popularity did not exist in their personalities. When you look upon the whole mass of common people as slaves and human dogs, what can you do to make yourself popular? He advised the king to accept the constitution, but to keep the executive power in his own hands. There should be a ministry selected from the National Assembly by the king, and Lafayette should be watched carefully—for he intended to make himself mayor of the palace, Mirabeau declared. An ancient term —mayor of the palace—meaning a dominating war chief and executive who makes a puppet of the king and governs in the king's name. It was a malicious idea, and one without an atom of truth.

The sudden change in Mirabeau's style of living—from semipoverty to grandeur—aroused the suspicions of the fiery-eyed leaders of the Left, such as Robespierre, Danton, Marat and Desmoulins.

With an almost unerring judgment of men Mirabeau had already appraised these radicals. He belonged to their group himself. He considered Danton just a loud mouth, full of sound and fury, meaning little or nothing. Desmoulins was Danton's faithful follower and henchman. Marat possessed an oversupply of malevolence and vituperation, and nothing else.

But Robespierre!

Mirabeau listened to every word he said and stared intently at him. He divined that Danton could be bribed and, in fact, he was bribed. The king, through another person, had paid him ninety thousand francs for a law practice that was virtually nonexistent.

Robespierre was honest, unbribable, implacable. He was not a mere orator. His ideas were assembled, bolted tightly one to the other, and not flying around loose without cohesion or system. They formed the substance of an extremely revolutionary conception of society. "That man will go far," said Mirabeau. "He believes everything he says."

The leaders of the Left suspected the source of Mirabeau's income, and so did many other men who were not leaders of anything. But could they prove that he was in the pay of the king? No. His speeches still had their revolutionary quality. This technique of the paid advocate in legislation and politics is now well known; in those days of long-ago it was new to Frenchmen. The formula is simple. You must belong to the liberal party, and be a pronounced liberal in theory. You must make impassioned speeches defending the "rights of the people"—whatever those words mean—and standing firm against the invasion of "privilege"—whatever that may mean. Then say something adverse to "money barons." In this cloud of words you will shine. Then it is advisable for you to bring in a few unimportant measures of reform. Fight for them, stand by them, and say "to my dying breath." Your trifling reform measures will probably pass, as they amount to nothing anyway, but you will have created for yourself a reputation as a "defender of the people's rights."

Do not be the creator of any important proposals which involve sweeping and drastic reforms. Let someone else do that. Then you must take the other side and stand for a policy of caution. Also say, "Not one person within the range of my voice, or elsewhere, can assert with truth that I have ever failed the trust—the confidence—of the people."

Furthermore, say: "Shall we destroy the heritage of our civilization, the traditions of our race that have existed for centuries, just on a vote today in this legislative chamber? No, gentlemen, never; we shall not commit that infamy. Our social system is twisted and deformed by the power of wealth and privilege. Who knows that better than I? I point to my record. Look at it; read it; and dare not face me and say that I am not for the people. But should we, as sensible men, burn down the house because the roof leaks? Step by step we must go. Every day a rosier dawn. Let us not destroy before we can replace what we have torn down." *

* This formula is very effective and may be used by anyone, including newspaper editors and members of Congress. It is not copyrighted and is given away free with this book.

5

On July 3, 1790, Mirabeau met Marie Antoinette for the first and only time. He had seen her often in her public appearances, but had never spoken a word to her. Their meeting was arranged with all the intricate details of a mystery novel.

But why all the secrecy? Mirabeau was the head of the majority party in the National Assembly. It is difficult for a modern mind to comprehend the need of secrecy. Suppose the leader of the majority in our Congress wanted to say something to the president's wife. His secretary would telephone her secretary. He would go to the White House, have tea with the lady, unburden himself of his reverberating thoughts, and go away. No one would think anything of it, and the newspapers would not give it a line in their daily catalogue of robberies, murders, fears and alarms.

The difference is that the court—meaning the king, queen and their favorites—had evolved by degrees into a hostile force within the French nation. The court and the people stood face to face as enemies. The deputies of the Third Estate were never invited to social affairs at the Tuileries; they might as well have been non-existent, the ghastly distorted figures of a nightmare. Here we see duelists, weapons drawn, and mutual hatred in their eyes. How easy it would have been for the sovereigns to have had a garden party at the Tuileries with the whole National Assembly invited. "M. Robespierre," the queen might have said, "I am not as bad as you think I am, but I understand how you reached your conclusions; so many people tell lies about me. About you, too; I have heard stories about you which shocked me, but now that I see you I know they cannot be true. All of us are trying to create a new France. We must work together, and we shall succeed. You are a leader of men. I am only a woman; I can do nothing, but I feel deeply, and I know we must rely on forceful men like you."

"Yes, madame," Robespierre might have said, "we shall strive together toward that end, and you encourage me by your kind words."

But that is only a fantasy, without any relation to fact. Marie Antoinette would not have done that; nor Robespierre. Human destiny must move in its own way.

Comte de La Marck arranged the meeting of Mirabeau and

Marie Antoinette. The king and queen had gone to Saint-Cloud—across the Seine in the suburbs of Paris—for a few days, a week-end. Mirabeau was to present himself at a certain door in the wall of the garden at eight-thirty in the morning of July 3rd, rap on it and be admitted. He went to the rendezvous in a battered vehicle, with his young nephew, Comte de Saillant, disguised as a coachman.

The queen received Mirabeau in a summer pavilion. They talked about an hour. There is no record of their conversation. When Mirabeau returned to his carriage he said to his nephew, "She is very great, and very unfortunate, but I shall save her."

That shows what charming women can do to men. Marie Antoinette had no element of greatness in her. She was a fool, and a vicious one. She did not comprehend the nature of truth, or of fair dealing, and she had no conception of the real state of affairs in France. Nevertheless, she made a great impression on Mirabeau, who was as hard as a nail, and a cynic.

The favorable impression appears to have been wholly on his side; not on hers. Months later, when he asked for another interview, she refused to see him.

Mirabeau wrote again and again to the king giving his advice, but his counsel was disregarded, although most of it was sound and in line with the tendency of the times. Mirabeau complained to La Marck that his secret connection with the crown was useless; his client paid no attention to what he had to say.

That was true, but beneath the attitude of the crown was a deeper layer of purpose of which Mirabeau probably knew nothing. All that the king and queen and their intimates at court expected of Mirabeau was to keep the National Assembly in hand. They had no idea of adopting his suggestions. What they wanted to do was to gain time until they could induce Austria, Prussia, Spain and perhaps other royal kingdoms to invade France, put down the Revolution, hang the leaders of the republican horde, including Mirabeau —and also some nobles, jailer Lafayette, to mention one—then France could be itself again.

Their insistent emissaries were in every capital of Europe, urging the sovereigns to take action on the ground that the Revolution was a menace to royal authority everywhere.

Mirabeau, a tightrope walker in politics, had to shift nimbly from one side to the other to avoid a fall. Stories about him were

going around. Marat, in his incendiary *L'Ami du Peuple*, came out
in forthright fashion and declared that he should be hanged. Friend
La Marck, go-between and bearer of letters and cash, advised Mirabeau not to live so luxuriously, but the advice went unheeded. The
thunderous Tribune of the People had existed in destitution for so
many years that his mind was filled with shabby memories. Now
that was all over and he reveled among the fleshpots and disported
himself with wine and women. He lost much of his influence in the
Jacobin Club, which was the most powerful political organization
in France. Leadership of the Jacobins fell into the hands of Barnave, Duport and the brothers Lameth.

Miraculously Mirabeau contrived to keep his hold on the National Assembly. Among the people his popularity was immense and
continued to be so until his death despite the rumors about his
being in the pay of the court.

On one of his last days as a living man he said to his friend
Dumont:

I am dying, my friend. When I am gone they will know my value. The
miseries I have held back will burst from all sides on France.*

Some historians of that era say that he died from excesses, or
from drunkenness and pleasure, if you please to put it that way.
The facts, as reported, do not seem to sustain their assertions. The
descriptions of his illness indicate heart disease, which was not then
well known. Probably he died of myocarditis, or inflammation of the
heart.

Mirabeau's funeral was a day of mourning in Paris. It is written that a hundred thousand people walked in his funeral procession. It is also written that Marie Antoinette was glad to hear of
his death, and said so, but the king said, "Do not rejoice; we have
lost our best friend."

In the Pantheon—solemn sanctuary of great and distinguished
men—his bodily remains were laid. Mirabeau was alone in his vast
tomb. The Pantheon had been just recently decreed; he was its
first occupant. So there he lay in solitary and silent grandeur for a
time, for a cycle of months. But not forever. Two years later the
locksmith Gamain, with vivid gestures and excuses for himself as
an innocent party, told a committee of the Assembly of Louis's secret

* Dumont, *Souvenirs sur Mirabeau*, p. 267.

closet in the Tuileries. It was opened, and there was found Mirabeau correspondence with the king. Even more—there was a record
of his remuneration; his pay in the royal service.

The people took Mirabeau's body out of the Pantheon and
threw it in a nameless grave. His bust was taken from the hall of
the Jacobins and smashed.

CHAPTER XXI

THE FESTIVAL OF THE FEDERATION

I

THROUGHOUT the Revolution Paris was a gay city. The theaters and the expensive restaurants were crowded. The fashionable shops thrived and expanded. Vestris, a male dancer —an eighteenth century Nijinsky—was so popular that, to witness his exhibitions, one had to procure tickets weeks in advance. There were elegant dinners and balls. At night, standing before the theaters, were rows of torchbearers, awaiting their patrons, and in the street a long line of handsome carriages.

It was a curious social phenomenon. A new wealthy class was coming to the front—merchants, speculators, traders in money and traders in land. In October, 1790—the time being opportune— Talleyrand (himself a bishop) proposed in the National Assembly that the lands of the Church be taken over by the government— seized and appropriated without recompense. After some debate the motion was carried; the deed was done. But not with the consent of the Vatican. This act brought the pope squarely on the side of the foreign powers that were incensed and alarmed at the progress of the French Revolution. The village curés were urged by their superiors to incite the people to resist this act of the Assembly, to create disorder. Talleyrand was excommunicated. In many communities riots broke out and were suppressed by force of arms.

The next step of the Assembly was to abolish the authority of the Vatican in France, and to establish a national church. Priests who refused to take a solemn oath renouncing the pope were turned out of their parishes. Yet many of them—called "nonjuring" priests —were maintained secretly by the noble families, and by wealthy ladies. The personal chaplain of the king was a nonjuror. Those who took the oath, and a majority of them did, became servants of the state, and were so considered.

It is not known with accuracy how much of the soil of France

258

was possessed by the Clergy, but it seems to have been about one-fifth of the whole area, according to the most conservative estimates. The ecclesiastical lands were, therefore, an enormously valuable asset when the government took them over.

But how could the great prize be utilized by a treasury in dire need of cash? Some part of it might be sold at once—or soon—but there were not enough liquid funds in France to buy this entire great parcel of real estate.

It was decided to issue paper money against the seized estates. The bills were called *assignats* because the church lands were "assigned" and held as security for the currency. The treasury became speedily a factory for the production of paper money. Within the next six years—until 1796—forty-five billions of assignats were issued, and their purchasing power went down to only a small percentage of their nominal value. The assignats were paid out to all employees and creditors of the government. The money was a legal tender. Creditors were forced to accept it. Billions of governmental obligations were cleared off by payment of assignats. Gold disappeared from circulation; the assignats speedily became the only visible currency. The paper money fluctuated in value day by day, with a steady downward drift as more and more of it was issued.

History shows that in times of inflation sharp-witted and daring men often make fortunes. That is true in all countries and in all ages, but their fortunes are unstable. And it is equally true that many more people lose all they possess.

The French gamblers in Revolutionary values turned their assignats as quickly as they could into more substantial assets, such as the former church lands, houses, foreign securities and business enterprises.

This gigantic national adventure with paper money and ecclesiastical real estate accomplished more toward the establishment of the Revolution than anything else that had occurred from the beginning. Suppose the Revolution were overthrown by counterattacks within France, or by a foreign invasion. Would the new possessors of the lands of the Church be allowed to keep them? Assuredly not; the land would be restored to the Clergy.

The landless peasants had been able to acquire farms on easy terms, a small cash payment, followed by other payments extending over a term of years. The land was virtually given to them, for—

with the rapid decline in the value of the assignats—the future payments, as expressed in the contracts, went down to negligible sums. This vast transfer of farming lands marked the beginning of French yeomanry—the free peasant on free soil—unencumbered by feudal dues or tithes.

The newly rich as a class was then for the revolutionary movement, heart and soul. They were not so keen about it three years later. But even at the height of the Terror, and later—when the French were at war with half of Europe—large fortunes were amassed by profiteers, contractors, merchants and munition makers.

The submerged poor of the towns—laborers and craftsmen—benefited little by the flood of new money. It is true that there were more jobs to be had, but prices rose steadily while wages went up much more slowly. Food was so scarce that people actually starved to death in Paris.

Among the mythical sayings of that epoch is the one attributed to Marie Antoinette who, upon being told that the people did not have bread to eat, said, "Well, let them eat cake." According to the best evidence, she said nothing of the kind. The story was invented to discredit her, and was an unnecessary work of the imagination as she had already discredited herself quite sufficiently. She was a fool, but not so big a fool as this story implies.

2

The National Assembly tinkered away at the task of shaping the constitution. A first draft was written by the Abbé Sieyès but many changes were made by the Assembly before its adoption. Some of the controversies that arose in the course of the debates seem exceedingly strange to an American of the present time. The Assembly was almost evenly divided over the proposed right of the king to put an absolute veto on any measure that the Assembly might enact. The opponents of the veto fought bitterly on that point for, as the Abbé Sieyès exclaimed, "the absolute veto would give the king a lettre de cachet against the general will." It would, indeed. With a royal power of absolute veto there would have been no sense in having a constitution, and the National Assembly would have been nothing more than a debating society.

Lafayette was called in to arbitrate between the two factions.

He proposed a middle course; that the king be given the right of "suspensive veto," meaning that he should have the power to suspend any act of the Assembly for four years. At the end of that time if the legislators were still in the same frame of mind they might pass the bill again and the king would have no power to veto it.

It seems a worthless compromise, for legislation—a great deal of it, at any rate—cannot be held up four years if it is to be of any use. One wonders why it did not occur to him, or to somebody, that in case of a veto the Assembly might reconsider the bill and pass it, by a two-thirds vote, over the king's head.

The compromise was adopted, however, and the suspensive veto found its way into the constitution. The profound ignorance of the common people in respect to such matters is illustrated by their reaction to the suspensive veto. This term, in French, is "veto suspensif," and suspensif comes from the verb suspendre, meaning "to hang." The common people believed, at first, that the veto suspensif conferred upon the king the power to hang anybody at will. To set them right much laborious explanation was required, and many of them never did get it straight.

Lafayette advocated a Congress of two chambers, a Senate and a House. His plan had only a few supporters, and it was voted down by a huge majority. The Assembly feared that the upper chamber would soon become a nest of nobles, reactionaries and adherents of the king.

The constitution divided French citizens into two classes—active and passive. Active citizens were defined as those who paid a certain amount of taxes; passive citizens were those who paid a smaller amount, or none at all. The right of suffrage was given only to "active citizens" who had reached the age of twenty-five. Three million "passive" citizens were excluded from the franchise. There were about four million "active" citizens. Passive citizens were not permitted to possess firearms or to join the National Guard.

Here are some of the other provisions of the constitution, which is known in history as the "Constitution of 1791" for the reason that the king gave his approval to it in September of that year.

1. The king was subordinate to the constitution.
2. He could no longer draw freely on the national treasury, but

was to be supported by an annual appropriation of twenty-five million livres.

3. The king had the right to choose his own advisers, or cabinet, but members of the Assembly were not eligible as ministers. This foolish provision was included because the Assembly feared that the king might influence legislation by promising cabinet posts to deputies who would support his measures.

4. The king might be deposed for high treason or if he left the kingdom without permission.

5. The Assembly had the power to arraign the ministers before a High Court, and they were required to submit a monthly statement of the expenditures of their departments.

6. The king could not declare war or sign treaties without consent of the Assembly.

7. The country was divided into eighty-three departments. Each department controlled its own local affairs.

8. Trial by jury, in criminal cases, was established. Torture was abolished.

9. The division of the French people into three estates no longer existed. Any active citizen who had taken an oath to support the constitution was eligible as a member of the National Assembly, if he could get himself elected.

10. The constitution abolished privileges arising from birth but strengthened those based on wealth.

There one may behold a thoroughly bourgeois document; a constitution saturated by middle-class prejudices, and intended to protect the rights of the wealthy and not much else.

The life of the National Assembly was fixed at two years. The existing body would, therefore, be dissolved on October 1, 1791.

Later on an act was passed which forbade any member of the present Assembly from membership in the next one. This was an error of the first magnitude. In the Assembly were some of the ablest men in France, yet after October, 1791, they were to be retired. Then a large crowd of new members, wholly without legislative experience, were to take their places.

In February, 1790, there was an obscure plot that had as its objectives the escape of the king from France and the murder of

Lafayette and Mayor Bailly. The devious ins and outs of that conspiracy are not known to this day.

The prevailing belief was—and is—that it was conceived by
Monsieur, Comte de Provence, brother of the king. He hired the
Marquis de Favras, a poverty-stricken noble, to make the arrangements. But the plot was revealed to Lafayette by two of the agents
of Favras, who was thereupon arrested, tried, found guilty and
hanged. He went to the gallows without revealing his accomplices.
It was learned, however, that Favras, who had no credit of his own
at the banks, had nevertheless borrowed a large sum of money from
the banker of the Comte de Provence. While that news was being
spread, Monsieur appeared before the Commune of Paris and made
a speech in which he denounced Favras and disclaimed any knowledge of the plot. Perhaps there is some significance in the fact
that Marie Antoinette granted a pension to Favras's widow.

In June, 1790, Charles Lameth, a kinsman of Lafayette, proposed in the National Assembly to abolish all titles of nobility. The
resolution was passed. The king's impulse was to veto it, but his
advisers at court urged him to approve it on the ground that it
would be effective in arousing the animosity of the nobles throughout France against the Lameths, Lafayette and all who supported
the motion. The king followed their advice and approved the decree.

Thereafter, to the end of his life, Lafayette never used the title
of marquis. He preferred to be known as General Lafayette.

3

All over France "Federations" were being formed. These organizations were somewhat similar to the "Sons of Liberty," who had
so much to say in shaping the American Revolution. The Federations were patriotic associations sworn to uphold revolutionary ideas
and governmental reform. At the beginning they were local bodies,
without a central authority, and they differed widely in purposes and
methods. In some parts of France they seized the local government
and organized the communes according to their own ideas. In other
places they merely set up liberty poles and made speeches. And, in
still other places, they wrecked and pillaged the châteaux.

At first the National Assembly was alarmed by this movement

for the reason that it might lead to a disastrous decentralization and, ultimately, to the breaking up of the French nation into small independent states. Reflecting upon these possibilities, the Assembly wisely decided not to attempt to suppress the Federations, but to co-operate with them and direct their course.

With that objective in view the National Assembly, in concert with the Commune of Paris, planned a vast "get-together" meeting in which all the revolutionary elements of the nation would be represented. It was to take place in Paris on July 14, 1790—the first anniversary of the taking of the Bastille. It was to be called the Fete of the Federation.

The fete was not to be a convention, a debate, but a celebration. Nearly everyone in France believed that the Revolution was over, accomplished and done. Very few, if any, even dreamed that a cyclone was on its way.

To the fete came delegates from every part of the country. From the beginning of the kingdom of France there had never before been such a huge gathering of people in one place. The great field of the Champ-de-Mars was converted into an amphitheater that would hold a quarter of a million persons and still leave enough room in the center for the military maneuvers of the National Guard. The tiers of seats were placed on banks of earth which rose one above the other.

Although thousands of laborers had been at work on this project for weeks it was nowhere near completion on the first of July, and the city of Paris had no more funds to carry on the job. A general call for volunteers brought out a multitude of Parisians. As a spectacle of public enthusiasm it was astounding. Men and women who had worked in shops and factories all day came in the long summer evenings and spaded the earth, wheeled it in barrows and packed it down. Even small children ran here and there with their little spades. And it was not a task for the poor alone. All Paris joined in. Fine ladies with jeweled hands did whatever they could, which was not much—only a gesture of enthusiasm. The Parisian guild of actors came with their musicians. Many a well-dressed dandy of Paris spoiled his fine clothes and coarsened his hands in manipulating a shovel.

A week before the day of the fete the crowds began to flock in from the country. They came from far and near; some of them had traveled hundreds of miles. Thousands of them arrived on foot; the more prosperous in post chaises or in their own carriages. The National Guards, in their dusty uniforms, came in marching order.

These swarms of people were received by all Paris as a host receives a welcome guest. The city turned itself into a vast free hotel with guest rooms in every house. Tables with food were set out under trees and in the streets. Anyone was welcome to sit down at them and eat.

Lafayette was as busy as three men and as elated as five. He was having the time of his life. It was agreed that, in the scheme of ceremonies, he was to command the troops at the celebration and, besides, to have general charge of all the arrangements.

The king and queen, like disembodied spirits that have nothing more to do with the affairs of mankind, sat aloof in the palace of the Tuileries and contemplated these activities with resentment. In their minds were visions of the coarse country people in their ill-fitting clothes and heavy shoes, clomping along the streets or gazing for hours at the windows of the Tuileries; the blatant National Guards with their bands of music; the absurd orators bellowing of liberty and human rights; the detested Lafayette, renegade noble, posturing and bowing; the self-assertive National Assembly, as loud and worthless as a flock of crows, declaring that they express the national will. There can be no national will but that of the king; does not everyone know that? Maybe not; certainly not, or these people would not be so brazen in their insolence. One Austrian division of troops—when it arrives—will send these cowards into their holes and corners.

The king and Marie Antoinette had lost all sense of reality. They lived in a world of dreams.

Lafayette—and Mirabeau too—urged them to go to the Champ-de-Mars, look upon the toil of the people in preparing the scene; smile upon them and say pleasant words. No; they would not do that. It had been arranged that they shall be there on the 14th. Is not that enough?

Well, then, said Lafayette, ride out in the streets; let our people see Your Majesties. I shall be with you; you will be greeted with joy. The royal decision was a veto.

4

On the morning of the great day there was a drizzling rain that
continued for hours. More than two hundred thousand spectators,
with water trickling down their backs, remained in their places.
What difference does rain make? The French nation is turning into
a race of ducks, anyway, said the wits. Among this great multitude
there was a crackling fire of Gallic cheerfulness and laughter.

On the level ground of the arena the National Guards—thousands and thousands of them—were drawn up in serried ranks. At
one end of the amphitheater a dais had been erected, with a purple
canopy over it. That was for the royal party and the great dignitaries.

Officers in the handsome uniform of the Guards dashed about
on horseback. There was Lafayette on his famous white horse, which
carried the popular nickname of Jean Leblanc. Saluting, bowing,
pulling Jean Leblanc up so quickly that he reared on his hind legs,
went the marquis—but marquis no longer; just plain General
Lafayette, *citoyen de France*.

Qui est-ce qui cet homme-là?

*C'est le général Lafayette, madame. Vous avez entendu parler
de lui, n'est-ce pas?*

*Certainement, monsieur, mais je ne l'ai pas vu avant ce jour.
Qu'est-ce qu'il a fait?*

*Il a gagné l'indépendance pour les américains, et maintenant il
gagne la liberté pour nous français.*

After a long wait the king and queen arrived with their attendants. With them came the members of the National Assembly. Marie
Antoinette was annoyed because the king alone was placed on the
throne, while she was escorted to a box. That was the idea of Lafayette, and the queen knew or divined it. His reason was that under
the constitution the queen had no position of authority; she was
merely the king's wife. When Lafayette rode to her box and saluted
her with a bow her eyes spat fire at him.

The proceedings had to begin with a religious ceremony. Naturally. In the center of the plain was a high altar. Around it stood
several hundred priests who wore sashes of red, white and blue—

the colors of the Revolution. Talleyrand, bishop of Autun, mounted the steps to celebrate Mass. He turned back and said, in a low tone, to Lafayette, "Don't make me laugh."

In midafternoon, around three o'clock, the rain ceased, the warm July sun came out, and a rainbow, in delicate splendor, stood in the sky. Happy omen, said the people.

After the Mass, the colors of the Guards were blessed by the pious, but cynical, bishop who had the devil in his heart and eloquence on his tongue. Lafayette ascended the high flight of steps, laid his sword dramatically on the altar and repeated the oath of fidelity to the king and the constitution.

Then the king solemnly perjured himself and swore that he would maintain the constitution and the Declaration of Rights. Everybody took the oath—National Assembly, soldiers, civilians. The queen stood up in her box and held the dauphin in her arms. "Here is my son," she said. That vast swarm of people could not hear her words, but they saw her gesture. There were cheers for the king, the National Assembly, General Lafayette, the queen. A hundred guns roared and echoed in salute to the new order of things in France. Everybody had had a wonderful time.

Even the king was uplifted by the spectacle. The crowd had cheered him and the queen. When a quarter of a million people raise their voices all at once there is a stunning noise. To Mme. de Polignac he wrote, reviewing the events of the day, and said, "Believe me, madame, all is not lost."

The people swarmed around Lafayette. They kissed his hands, his coat, his cheeks. He could hardly disentangle himself from them. After he had mounted his horse they patted and kissed the flanks of Jean Leblanc.

Lafayette, not quite thirty-three years of age, was then at the summit of his career. He never got any further. When one stands on the top of a mountain, all roads lead downhill. Lafayette lacked the gift of turning popularity into power. From here on our story will be a clinical record of his decline in the fickle favor of the public. He made many errors of judgment because he did not understand the true nature of events. He was lacking in the clairvoyant quality of great men, nor did he possess the ability to nail down and clinch his political assets so that in case of disaster they would be strong enough to withstand the shock.

5

At Nancy there was stationed a Swiss regiment in the king's service—not in the National Guard. This Swiss regiment was held in high esteem by the revolutionists because its commander had refused to march against the people at the taking of the Bastille. Thereupon the War Ministry banished the regiment from Paris and sent it to Nancy, a quiet town on the eastern border of France.

A dispute arose between the soldiers and their officers over the regimental fund, which was contributed by everyone in the regiment, but was managed by the officers. The men declared that there was a shortage in the fund, and that the officers had taken the money. In reply to these accusations no accounting was made, but two members of the soldiers' committee were flogged and the whole regiment was held in barracks under a charge of mutiny.

The National Guard of Nancy took a hand in the dispute. The Guards, armed and in force, escorted through the streets the men who had been whipped and forced the officers of the Swiss regiment to pay each of them one hundred louis as an indemnity for their flogging. With the force of the National Guard to support them, the soldiers of the Swiss regiment investigated the regimental fund and discovered that most of it had disappeared. They declared they had been robbed and sent a delegation of eight soldiers to the National Assembly to make a complaint.

As soon as the eight men reached Paris Lafayette had them arrested, and on the same day (August 16, 1790) he induced the Assembly to pass a drastic act for suppressing mutinies.*

The garrison at Nancy was in the military district of Metz, which was under the command of the Marquis de Bouillé, who was Lafayette's cousin. Bouillé was a royalist and a reactionary of the most pronounced character, though Lafayette did not know it, apparently. In a letter to this cousin Lafayette urged that "the most vigorous measures" be taken against the mutineers. Bouillé and a strong force of troops marched to Nancy. Some twenty of the soldiers were hanged and more than forty were sent to penal servitude in the convict galleys.

* The demand of the soldiers for an accounting of the fund to which they had contributed was considered a mutiny.

Lafayette's excuse—or explanation—was that soldiers must not
estion the motives or honesty of their officers; that discipline must
maintained regardless of everything else.

His popularity dropped like a stone thrown in water. The Na-
nal Guard of Paris—Lafayette's own troops—held a memorial
ebration in honor of the soldiers who had been hanged at Nancy.
fayette was not present.

This was followed by a mass meeting where the citizens of
ris passed a resolution of protest against the "massacres at
ncy." After the meeting the crowd swarmed toward the National
sembly. Lafayette, at the head of a trustworthy regiment of the
tional Guard, met the mob and dispersed it. The people went to
ir homes, shouting *"A bas Lafayette!"*

Mirabeau, in one of his secret letters to the king, suggested
t everything should be done to "undermine Lafayette in public
inion, though it must be done as insensibly as possible." He sounds
e a modern publicity agent. Ruin your adversary, but ruin him
btly with praise which carries a dose of arsenic.

Louis XVI was not capable of such finesse. All he could do was
st to tell lies, and lying is the most pathetic, ineffectual way of
ndling human affairs. Every lie carries a boomerang concealed
its bosom. Subtle people seldom lie. They tell the truth, but not
e whole truth. They disseminate the truth, but in such a way that
has a double meaning and thus destroys itself by verbal suicide.

All of a sudden the popular hero of the Fete of the Federation
nd himself the subject of numerous diatribes in newspapers and
mphlets. Marat, in his venomous *L'Ami du Peuple,* called him a
edy courtier, and a servant of despotism. In some of the pamph-
s he was accused of being the queen's lover. Others held him up
shame as a traitor who had sold himself to the Tuileries.

The people no longer kissed the white flanks of Jean Leblanc.

The Duc d'Orléans was back in Paris, having returned from
"diplomatic mission." Poor, misguided fool; he should have re-
ined in England. But there he was again in Paris, in sumptuous
ury, surrounded by his strumpets, his paid pamphleteers and his
cret agents. It is entirely probable that most of the mud which was
own anonymously at Lafayette came from the Orleanist head-
arters.

6

I have said something already about the powerful political clubs, the Jacobins, the Cordeliers and others. These names arose from their meeting places, which were abandoned monasteries or convents. Of all the clubs the Jacobin was the most powerful. It was, at first, an association of middle-class revolutionists—merchants, bankers, men of letters, members of the Assembly. The annual subscription fee was only twenty-four livres. In time, by evolution, it became a center of violent activities. It possessed enormous energy; Jacobin clubs were organized all over France. Later —swiftly in time—the club was captured by the proletariat, and its bourgeois atmosphere disappeared. Lafayette was a member of the Jacobins, but he seldom attended its meetings. Its vast hall was a place of resounding, bawling oratory, and Lafayette was not an orator.

He was one of the founders of another club called "The Society of 1789." This club limited its membership to six hundred, and the public was not admitted to its sessions. The entrance fee was high. It was a gathering of distinguished men, and was more in the nature of a debating society and social assembly than a political club. Its meetings were sedate and courteous.

Among its members were Mirabeau; Brissot (the publicist); Thouret, a lawyer; Comte de Custine (a soldier); Dupont de Nemours; Lavoisier (distinguished scientist); André Chénier (poet); Marquis de Condorcet (mathematician and philosopher); Bailly mayor of Paris.*

As friends of the workingman the Society of 1789 did not shine. Chapelier, one of its organizers and a member of the National Assembly, brought up a proposal in June, 1791, for the repression of all combinations of labor for uniform wages, and a law was passed to that effect. It made labor unions illegal and was powerfully effective in debasing the status of the working people.

---

* Brissot was guillotined in 1793, at the age of thirty-seven. Thouret was guillotined in 1794. It was he who originated the plan to divide France into eighty-three departments. Comte de Custine was guillotined in 1793. Dupont de Nemours was not guillotined, but lived to be the ancestor of the family of American millionaires that bear his name. Lavoisier, one of the world's great scientists, was guillotined in 1794. (At that time many people pleaded for his release, and Robespierre replied, "the Revolution has no need of scientists.") André Chénier was guillotined in 1794, because he protested against the excesses of the Reign of Terror; Condorcet committed suicide by poison in 1794 to escape the guillotine; Bailly was guillotined in 1793.

7

It will be recalled that the National Assembly, after seizing the lands of the Church, abolished the authority of the Vatican in France and required the priests to take an oath of fidelity to the constitution. Catholicism was still the official religion of the state, but all other religions were tolerated.

Lafayette was opposed, in part, to these measures. If he had had his way, there would have been no state religion and all religious faiths would have been put on the same footing, as in America.

There was discord in the Lafayette household over this matter. Not a diminution of love between the marquis and Adrienne, but a conflict of opinion. Adrienne was a fervent believer in the Roman Church, and in the revered tradition that the pope was infallible, as he was the agent of God on this terrestrial globe. That France could be so lost in godless revolt that it would dare to make the priests mere servants of the National Assembly and put the churches in the same position as police stations and tax collectors' offices seemed to her to be abominable. But even worse, her beloved husband supported these laws. Almost needless to say, her mother and her sisters stood by her.

The curé of Saint-Sulpice, which was Adrienne's parish church, refused to take the oath. Rather ostentatiously, she attended the service at which he announced his determination, and it was then said, far and wide, by the papists that even Lafayette's wife would not countenance these unholy measures.

When Lafayette came home, worn out by the perplexities of his situation, he found—not occasionally, but usually—his house full of nonjuring priests and nuns who had come to Mme. la Marquise for comfort and protection.

But Adrienne was polite to the constitutional bishops and other ecclesiastical dignitaries who were invited to dinner by her husband. Courteous but cool. The kind of courtesy that leads the hostess to excuse herself soon, and retire to her room with a pleasant "bonsoir" to the guests. One time—and it seems to have been only once—the politeness was abandoned like a decayed fish. Lafayette gave a large dinner, with many guests, to the Archbishop of Paris, who was one of the most important ecclesiastics in France. The archbishop had

cheerfully taken the oath of allegiance. Adrienne refused to meet
him; she went to dinner at her mother's house. That caused a lot of
talk, naturally.

In all important affairs husband and wife—anywhere—usually
present a united front. If they differ, the husband may persuade the
wife to be on his side; or she may convince him that he is wrong;
or they may compromise on a middle course. Without this amalga-
mation of opinions and purposes the institution of marriage in a
civilized state, among intelligent people, would be impossible.

The rift between the marquis and Adrienne did not last long.
She followed her husband, and the story of her devotion and loyalty—as we shall see—would warm anyone's heart. But it is a grim
tale. When he was in exile and in an Austrian prison she defied his
enemies, defended his ideas, and was thrown into prison because
she refused to denounce him. For a time she was in imminent danger
of execution. Yet she escaped. Then she, too, went into exile and
voluntarily joined her husband in prison so that she might be near
him.

Her daughter Virginie, who became the Marquise de Lasteyrie,
wrote a life of her mother in which she says:

I do not think it possible to give an idea of my mother's way of loving. It
was peculiar to herself. Her affection for my father predominated over
every other feeling. . . . It might be said that she felt for him the most
passionate attachment, if that expression were in harmony with the ex-
quisite delicacy which kept her from any of the evil impulses generally
attendant upon that feeling.

Rather cryptic, that last statement. What does it mean—"any
of the evil impulses generally attendant upon that feeling"? I confess that I do not know. Are "passionate attachments" generally
accompanied by evil impulses?

Certainly Adrienne must have known of her husband's long-
drawn-out affair with Mme. de Simiane. Everybody else knew of it.
In eighteenth century France men were expected to have mistresses.
There was not a trace of puritanism in any class of French society,
from the highest to the lowest. If a man of wealth and distinction
did not have love affairs he was considered a queer fellow. Wives
too, might have lovers if they wanted them. No one cared much
about it. "Intrigues," wrote the Marquise de La Tour du Pin, "were

known as soon as formed. When they endured they acquired a sort of consideration if not éclat."

Adrienne de Lafayette had no lovers. She was dominated by her love for her husband. She was a woman of sober demeanor; a woman of serious temperament. Before the Revolution she seldom went to the court of Versailles—the center of gay life—and she had an active dislike for the lighthearted queen.

CHAPTER XXII

THE KING TRIES TO RUN AWAY

I

THE KING and queen had made up their minds to escape from France, with their children. On the other side of the Rhine they would be sheltered by their imperial relatives, and could plan in safety for an invasion of their country. But the escape, if done at all, would have to be done in deep-black, midnight secrecy. So, in the dark corners of the Tuileries royal spiders were spinning webs of intrigue.

What a spectacle! Under the new constitution Louis XVI had been granted all the rights of a constitutional monarch, with an enormous civil list of twenty-five million francs a year for the support of himself and his household. He was no longer to have the sole responsibility for the welfare of the nation; the National Assembly was to assume that burden, or the greater part of it. If the plan did not work out well, he could always blame the Assembly. His desire to escape seems incredible.

For this adventure there were months of preparation—from February to June of the year 1791. The king, through the Baroness de Korff—a Russian noblewoman in the service of Marie Antoinette —ordered the building of a large and handsomely furnished coach (said to have cost six thousand livres) for the transport of himself and his family.

Lafayette, as head of the National Guard, was responsible for the safety of the royal family, but they were not prisoners in the ordinary meaning of that term, though there were certain limitations on their movements. They might ride all over Paris and its suburbs, receive anyone, write letters; and, in fact, do anything they might care to do except leave France without permission of the National Assembly. Let us not forget that Louis XVI was still the head of the state, that he appointed his ministers according to his own

est judgment, and that he possessed the power of vetoing any act
f the Assembly.

It was rumored in Paris—and in time all over France—that
he king was preparing to run away. The royal preparations for
ight were too complicated, and there were spies in the Tuileries—
steners at keyholes and readers of letters. But, nevertheless, it was
onsidered by many as just a piece of gossip, a malicious story.

Lafayette asked the king point-blank if he was planning to
ave the country, and the king replied emphatically that he had no
uch intention. Nevertheless, the revolutionary newspapers kept on
aying that the royal family would soon escape, and with the con-
ivance of General Lafayette. After king and queen had gone, what
as to prevent Lafayette—backed by his National Guard—from
aking himself the ruler of France? That is what they said and
hey wanted a reply, but Lafayette made no answer because he con-
dered the question so foolish that it was not worthy of considera-
on.

On Easter Monday—this was in 1791—the king and queen set
orth in their carriage to drive to Saint-Cloud. Thousands of people
ood before the Tuileries and made an impassable human barrier.
'he royal coach, even with an escort of Lafayette's hussars around
, could go no further. Many times the king had gone to Saint-
loud without opposition. But not on this occasion; the swarming,
isorderly mob was bent on keeping him in Paris.

Lafayette rode up and into the crowd. Loudly and imperiously
e ordered the people to make way for the carriage. They did not
ove, and he called upon a National Guard regiment to drive them
ack. The soldiers stood stolidly in their ranks and refused to stir.
afayette was dumfounded; he did not know what to make of it.

He asked the king and queen to be patient; he would take care
f the situation. He was confident that he could depend on the
armelite battalion which was drawn up just around the corner.
o, he was not mistaken; the Carmelites would obey his orders.
'hile he was bringing them to the scene the king had the royal car-
age turned around and driven back to the Tuileries. Upon enter-
g the palace the queen said to those around her, "You must admit
ow, gentlemen, that we are prisoners."

Lafayette soon appeared and urged the king to resume his trip
 Saint-Cloud. The way was open; there would be no further trou-

ble; the Carmelite battalion would act as an escort. The king shook his head, saying that the trip was abandoned. His attitude put Lafayette in a bad position, for—as the people of Paris saw the incident—the commander of the National Guard had been flouted by his own troops and had no control over the mob. The only remedy for that unpleasant state of affairs was to take the king and queen triumphantly to Saint-Cloud under the escort of Lafayette's faithful Carmelites.

But Louis still persisted in his refusal and eventually the general gave up and went away in disgust. Always thereafter he believed that this episode was planned by the court to prove "that they were forcibly detained in Paris." He was sure that Danton was behind these doings, and that one purpose of the conspiracy was to reveal Lafayette as an incapable general, and another purpose was to prove that the king and queen were prisoners in reality, so that, later when they did flee toward the border they would have the perfectly human excuse—or justification—of any prisoner who attempts to get out of jail.

It was Danton—Lafayette thought—who hired the mob with the king's money. His view of the matter was probably correct though he had no concrete evidence to support it. We know now however, that Danton had received money from the king, and Lafayette knew it at the time.

Lafayette went immediately to the Hôtel de Ville, wrote out his resignation as commanding general, and handed it to the Commune, which was then in session. Then, worn out by vexation and fatigue, he fainted. Upon being revived he went home and related the events of the day to Adrienne. When he told her of his resignation she was overjoyed. Fine. Splendid. Now her beloved husband was out of the Revolution and its dangerous predicaments. Henceforth he would be only an observer of events.

She rejoiced too soon. Next day the house in the Rue de Bourbon was besieged and invaded by delegations that begged him to withdraw his resignation. Delegations from every one of the sixty battalions of the National Guards, from the Commune, from the citizens of Paris. Was there a delegation from the Guards who had refused to obey his orders? Evidently there was, for the record says that "every battalion" sent its pleading representatives.

Within four days he was again at the head of the National Guard.

2

The closed-in, whispering court circle of Louis and Marie Antoinette was as busy as a colony of ants. The long-planned escape of the royal family was to be made in June. Comte de Fersen, the Swedish nobleman who was the reputed lover of the queen, was called from Belgium to assist in the preparations. He was devoted to the king as well as to Marie Antoinette. An intensely secretive person was this tall and handsome young man; he would never betray a confidence.

Mme. de Korff's luxurious coach had been built and paid for. Baroness de Korff was a friend of Fersen. Applying for passports she declared that she was going to Russia and intended to take eight persons along; her two children, their governess, three men (domestic servants), a valet and a maid.

The queen's diamonds were entrusted to Léonard, her hairdresser; he was not to accompany the royal party, but to leave the same day. A large amount of feminine apparel was sent in trunks to Brussels. Mme. Campan, who aided in these preparations, says she advised the queen not to bother about clothes, as they might be bought anywhere. Marie Antoinette was not moved by that argument, but somebody had to take the trunks, and so they were put in the care of one of the queen's women, who was to go on ahead.

An exotic air of the theater pervaded the whole project. In this atmosphere of absurd make-believe the king was to be dressed in the clothes of a valet, and to play the part. Marie Antoinette was cast as a governess, taking care of the two children of a lady who appeared in the role of the Baroness de Korff, but who was in real life Mme. de Tourzel. The last-named person was actually the governess of the royal children. The maid in the list of players was Madame Elisabeth, the king's sister. The three male domestics were members of the king's bodyguard; one of them was to play the role of coachman.

The direction of the flight, as planned, was to be almost straight eastward from Paris, through Châlons. A few miles beyond Châlons is the village of Clermont-en-Argonne. At that point the fugitives would turn northward. Their destination was Montmédy, a small town within a mile or so of the frontier. It was within the military jurisdiction of the Marquis de Bouillé, whose headquarters were at Metz. He commanded all the royal troops in that part of France, but not the National Guard. The greater part of the royal troops in that sector were German mercenaries.

At Montmédy, under the protection of Bouillé, the royal party would be safe, and close enough to the frontier to cross it at any time without hindrance. Bouillé was a royalist, a dyed-in-the-wool enemy of the Revolution—not in public, but in secret—and he had the confidence of the king. Messengers with letters went back and forth between him and the Tuileries.

Finally it was all arranged in detail. The king insisted that at every stopping place—that is, at the relay stations where horses were changed—a detachment of cavalry be posted to meet the royal carriage and escort it to the next station. Bouillé wrote that the presence of so many soldiers along the road might arouse suspicion, but eventually he agreed to do as the king desired. To create a plausible pretext for the presence of the troops an announcement was made in the villages that a "treasure" would soon come through from Paris; hence the military escorts.

If there had been no troops waiting for the coach it would have gone straight through, in all probability, without hindrance. On that main highway carriages were going back and forth all the time. There was no novelty, even, in the appearance of a luxurious equipage attended by footmen and outriders.

That the royal family was planning to escape seemed to be a matter of common knowledge in Paris during the first two weeks in June, 1791. How could it have been otherwise with so many people involved, more or less? Hundreds of servants, ladies in waiting, valets and officers of the royal household suspected that something was afoot, and they—or some of them—imparted these suspicions to their friends. The revolutionary newspapers printed all the flying rumors.

The Assembly was disturbed, and questioned Lafayette. He had recently talked with the king and he assured the Assembly that no flight was planned—taking the king's word at its face value. He went even further. He told the Assembly that he would stake hi

own life on the sincerity of the king. It was an unfortunate assertion and one that was to haunt him for many a day thereafter.

3

On the evening of Monday, June 20th, Mayor Bailly—who was
at home, sick in bed—sent for Lafayette. Information had just been
received, the mayor said, from a woman employed in the palace, to
the effect that the royal family intended to escape that very night.

Considerably perturbed, Lafayette went to the Tuileries, saw
the king, who was getting ready to go to bed, and remained there
until he was tucked away under the covers. That seemed conclusive.
Lafayette left the royal bedchamber around eleven o'clock but he
did not leave the palace immediately. Before going home he summoned Gouvion, who was in command of the guard at the Tuileries,
and together they made the rounds of the sentinels' posts.*

As soon as Lafayette was driven home in his carriage Louis and
Marie Antoinette arose and dressed—Louis as a valet and the queen
in the soberly sedate garments of a governess. Then, in their dis-
guises, they and Madame Elisabeth and the two children left the
Tuileries by an unused passageway that led to the bank of the Seine.
There was no sentinel at that exit. The queen left after the others,
had to go back for something, but she knew where the rendezvous
was.

Before leaving the Tuileries, the king wrote out and signed a
formal statement, which he left in a conspicuous place in his room.
In this document he disavowed his acceptance of the Declaration of
Rights and said, further, that all his oaths in support of the Revolution had been forced on him, and he withdrew them. It was, in
effect, a letter of abdication and defiance.

At a little distance from the palace Comte de Fersen, dressed as
a cabdriver, was waiting with an inconspicuous coach to take them
to the Porte Saint-Martin, where the new royal carriage was stationed. Fersen did not accompany them in their flight. He wanted
to go but the king would not permit him to put himself in danger.
From the start of the adventure there were delays. The queen was
half an hour late, and they had not gone far before an accident

* Gouvion had served under Lafayette in America and was known to be an able
and trustworthy officer.

happened to the new vehicle. That had to be repaired, and it took some time.

The itinerary had been carefully worked out, but the numerous delays spoiled the arrangements. The royal party was to be met by the first cavalry detachment at two o'clock in the afternoon. The Duc de Choiseul and forty horsemen reached the meeting place at eleven. Two o'clock came and went, then three, four and five, while the men sat glumly on their champing horses. A crowd of peasants, with unfriendly looks, gathered around. They thought the soldiers were bent on doing them harm.

Choiseul lost his head. He might have ridden along the road toward Paris to meet the carriage, but evidently that did not occur to him. Instead, he sent a messenger eastward to tell the other cavalry detachments that the treasure was not coming that day. That done, he and his horsemen rode away.*

The king was astonished when he arrived and learned that the troopers had left without explanation. After eight that evening the royal carriage reached Sainte-Menehould, where the relay station was run by a man named Drouet. It was a long summer evening, and the sky was still light. While the horses were being changed, Drouet studied the features of the valet who paced up and down before the carriage. He thought he had seen that man before but could not place him in memory. And he caught a glimpse of the governess in the carriage. She looked like Marie Antoinette.

The valet produced a fifty-franc bill to pay the charges. Drouet glanced at the engraving of the profile of Louis XVI on the treasury note. Ah, it was the profile of the valet. Drouet had served in the dragoons and had seen the king and queen several times. He made no comment and the carriage went on its way.

On his bar lay the last issue of Marat's newspaper. There was an article in it predicting the flight of the king. The postmaster picked up the paper and read:

He is to be smuggled out of the country, on the pretext that his cause is the common cause of all the rulers of Europe! Parisians, you idiots,

* The Comte de Provence, the king's brother, who had been living at the Luxembourg, evaded his guards and fled from France on the same night that the king and queen departed. He went in an ordinary carriage, without ostentation, and was not stopped at any place on the way. He reached Belgium without mishap. Twenty-three years later he returned to France, after the fall of Napoleon, and reigned for ten years as Louis XVIII.

am tired of repeating to you, watch the king and the dauphin, and put the
Austrian woman under lock and key. The loss of a single day may cost the
lives of three million Frenchmen!

Drouet—who was an ardent revolutionist—knew that, on his
best horse, he could overtake the carriage, but what could he do
against several men? He decided to take a short cut to the little
town of Varennes and be there ahead of the royal party. Once there,
he would inform the municipal authorities of his suspicions.

At eleven o'clock that night—Tuesday, June 21st—the lumber-
ing, six-horse coach was stopped at Varennes. Its occupants were
forced to get out and appear before the chief official of the place,
who was a small grocer. For hours the royal family sat in a shabby
little room above the grocer's shop. There, by the light of guttering
candles, they were questioned by the *procureur* and other people. A
crowd of yokels hung about the doorway and peered in at the scene.
Meanwhile, horsemen had been sent galloping over the dark countryside to rouse the National Guard.

For a long time Louis denied that he was the king, though he
admitted that he looked like him. He stuck by the tale of his passports. Then, all of a sudden, he gave up and cheerfully admitted his
identity. Not only that; he was so good-natured about it all that he
presented the town officials to the queen.

There was a wide streak of fatalism in the make-up of this
foolish, unfortunate monarch.

The wise men of the town did not know what to do. Had anyone the power to stop the king and hold him against his will? Some
said No; some said Yes. Eventually it was decided to hold him until
they heard from Paris, and late at night the royal party huddled
down to sleep in such poor quarters as Varennes could afford.

The next day a dusty rider, on a foam-flecked horse, arrived
from Paris with an order from Lafayette and a resolution of the
National Assembly. It said the king had been "abducted" by the
enemies of the Revolution. The people of Varennes heard that statement with goggle-eyed wonder. The king had said nothing about
abduction, or kidnaping. However, they could puzzle that out in
Paris. Varennes could not make head or tail of it.

The decree of the National Assembly—hastily passed—was
that the king was temporarily deprived of all authority, and must
be brought back. National Guards were ordered to form a strong

escort. Somewhere on the way the royal party would be met by three commissioners of the Assembly.

The Marquis de Bouillé, upon hearing that the king had been overtaken, abandoned his army and fled forthwith across the border. He went to England and lived there to a ripe old age.

The return to Paris began on Wednesday. Carriages, horsemen; and on foot the plodding National Guard detachments. The weather was beastly hot. Progress was slow; they did not reach the Tuileries until Saturday, June 25th.

About halfway they were met by Barnave, Pétion and Latour-Maubourg, the commissioners sent by the Assembly. The purpose in sending the three commissioners was to assure the safety of the royal family when it reached the turbulent streets of Paris. Barnave and Pétion crowded into the royal carriage. There was not enough room for them, and the queen had to hold the dauphin in her lap. Latour-Maubourg refused to ride in the second carriage; he would not sit with lackeys and valets, so a horse was provided for him. Everyone was hot, dusty, perspiring and sticky.

Barnave was so charmed by Marie Antoinette that he forgot his revolutionary ideas, and all the past. Her smile was a sun that warmed his soul. The queen was, after all, a delicate, gracious woman in distress, and Barnave was *un galant homme*. At every stopping place he ran out to get something for the queen, a cool drink, perhaps; and he took the little boy on his knees to relieve her of her burden. Never before, in her life of vanity and foolishness, had she met a man, not a noble, who possessed so much innate courtesy. She was astonished and wondered if many of the common people were like Barnave, who was a gentleman in deportment, speech and consideration for others.

Pétion was quite different. He was indeed a man of common breed. He sweated like a horse and he tried to flirt with Madame Elisabeth in a coarse, jesting manner. He ate a chicken, tearing it to pieces with his hands and throwing the bones out the window past the queen's nose. (Oh, Marie Antoinette; forget Pétion. The dark curtain of fate stands between all of you and the future. A day will come when wolves will tear Pétion to pieces just as he has torn that chicken.)

The forlorn party arrived in Paris in the late afternoon of Saturday. Through silent thousands of people the carriages moved slowly. The roofs of the houses cut sharply across tne gray sky, and in the air there was the dusk of a Parisian day. The National Guards were everywhere, holding back the crowds—and there was Lafayette, on his prancing white horse. The queen stared in amazement; both she and the king had thought that the first thing the mob would do—after the news of their flight—would be to kill Lafayette. But there he was, alive and in command.

As soon as the royal family reached the Tuileries the king ordered a huge dinner; he had been half starved on provincial food. Then he changed his clothes. On every hand there were servants, lackeys, maids—all of them obsequious and attentive. Life had resumed its ancient course.

While he was dining, Lafayette appeared and said, "What are your orders, sire?"

The king replied, "It seems that you are not at my orders, but I am at yours."

CHAPTER XXIII

TIME MOVES ON

I

THAT HECTIC week in June (1791) was a time of great anxiety for Lafayette. He had bet against fate and lost the wager. Voluntarily he had staked his head on the king's sincerity. Would he have to pay? For a time it looked as though he would; he was in extreme danger.

2

At eight o'clock in the morning of Tuesday, June 21st, Lafayette had been awakened by a frightened, white-faced bearer of bad news. The king had gone; he could not be found; there was no trace of the king, the queen, or any member of the royal family. But are you sure? said the marquis, pulling on his clothes. He had left the king in bed at eleven o'clock the night before. Are you sure?

Oui, M. le Marquis, nous sommes bien certain qu'ils ont partis.

Within a few minutes, without waiting for his horse, Lafayette was on his way to the Tuileries. He was joined by Mayor Bailly and Vicomte Alexandre de Beauharnais, who was president of the National Assembly.* The tocsin was ringing—the solemn tones of the bells quivering in the air—and crowds were already gathering in the street. The three men, on foot, hurriedly pushed their way through the masses of people.

At the Tuileries they found Gouvion, commander of the palace guard. Red-faced, embarrassed, he stammered out his story. The escape was inexplicable, he said. His guards were posted at every exit (he did not know at that time of the unused door) and he himself had been up all night. "The flight must be stopped," said Lafayette. "The king, queen, the royal family must be brought back to Paris."

* Vicomte de Beauharnais was guillotined in 1794, during the Terror. His widow married Napoleon Bonaparte and became the Empress Josephine.

"But who has the power to arrest the king?" Beauharnais asked. "Who will take the responsibility?"

"I will," Lafayette replied, and immediately he dictated this order:

The enemies of the Revolution having carried off the king, the bearer is charged to inform all good citizens that they are enjoined in the name of the nation in danger to seize him from their hands and to bring him back to the bosom of the National Assembly. It is about to meet, but meanwhile I take upon myself all the responsibility for the present order.

Lafayette does not say that the king has run away, but that "the enemies of the Revolution have carried off the king." This fiction was adopted by the National Assembly that same day, even after the king's farewell letter was found and read.

Copies of Lafayette's order were quickly prepared. Riders on fleet horses were dispatched on every road from Paris to the frontier.

The Assembly convened, and Lafayette was summoned to make a statement or report. The radical Left tried to howl him down, but he managed to state that he had had no idea the king was preparing to leave; that the palace was securely guarded; and he told what he had done to overtake the fugitives and bring them back.

In a decree of the Assembly suspending the authority of the king the word *enlèvement* ("abduction") was used to describe the circumstance of his flight. The distressing fact—as we look at it down the corridor of years—is that the National Assembly wanted to keep the king on any terms, notwithstanding the indisputable evidence that he was a proved liar, perjurer and traitor to the French nation.*

To a modern mind it seems that the best way of disposing of Louis XVI would have been to expel him from France. Certainly he could have done less harm outside of France than in it. At the Tuileries he and Marie Antoinette were really spies for Austria and for the émigré nobles; and their vast host of servants and retainers cost the French nation twenty-five million livres a year.

But there were millions of Frenchmen who did not believe the nation could be held together without a king; that it would fly into

* I am referring only to the National Assembly of 1789-1791. Its successor, that convened in October, 1791, gradually adopted a different point of view.

fragments and sail off into the realm of chaos; the king, they thought, was the cement which held it all in one piece. Other millions were convinced that the royal family kept the powers of Europe from pouncing on France from all sides; and as long as they were held as hostages the country was safe from attack. That idea was far from true, as we shall see.

If the king had succeeded in escaping across the border, what then? In the first place, he would have been deposed by the National Assembly—no doubt of that. But who was to take his place? The Orleanists had a ready answer. There is your future king, they certainly would have said, pointing to the Duc d'Orléans, known in the swirl of revolutionary delirium as Philippe Egalité—Mr. Philip Equality, to put it in plain English. A member of the Assembly is Mr. Equality; he has given up his titles; he is a man of the people. Yes; maybe so, but the Assembly as a whole does not believe it; he is a hypocrite—everyone knows that—and a rascal of almost astronomical proportions.

No, he did not have a chance to be king of France. Too much opposition.

But why not set up a republic on the American model, with a president, a congress and a constitution? The idea received little support. Even Lafayette was opposed to it. The French people, he said, needed a king. They were too ignorant and wholly unaccustomed to self-government. When Dupont de Nemours and La Rochefoucauld argued for the abolition of royalty altogether, Lafayette rose and said, "If you dethrone the king, I and the National Guard will declare his son king the next day."

A fact of outstanding importance is that there was not even one man in the revolutionary movement—with the possible exception of Mirabeau, and he had died in the April of 1791—who possessed the astuteness to direct its course. The National Assembly was a cage of fluttering birds.

Many people at the center of French affairs, including the king and queen, believed that Lafayette, supported by his formidable National Guard, was planning a coup d'état which would make him a dictator. Very probably such a stroke, if sudden and decisive, would have been successful. But he had no such idea, or plan.

As a dictator he would have been a hopeless misfit. He did not care so much for power as he cared for celebrity. He was always

nning to people for advice, which is a fatal habit for a dictator to
ve. Dictators do not need advice; all they need is information—
d obedience. They make the decisions themselves.

3

For the first time in months Lafayette attended a meeting of
e Jacobin club—on Tuesday, June 21st—while the whereabouts of
e king was still unknown. He heard himself furiously denounced
y Danton. "You, M. Lafayette," shouted Danton, "who only re-
ntly agreed to answer for the person of the king with your own
ead, you dare to appear in this assembly without having paid your
ebt! You swore that the king would not go away. What have you
say for yourself?"

Lafayette stared, in wide-eyed astonishment, at the speaker.
e knew that Danton was in the king's pay, and his information was
ot founded on hearsay; Danton himself had told him so—but in
onfidence. Lafayette did not reply to him directly, nor even look
t him, but made a mild and meaningless speech about the blessings
f liberty. Then he left the hall amid the imprecations of the au-
ience. It was not a shining occasion for him.

What should be done with Louis XVI? What was to be his
tatus in the future? His functions as a sovereign were suspended
or the time being. Should he be permanently deprived of authority?
n the Assembly Robespierre urged that a national convention be
alled to decide on his fate. Condorcet, friend of Lafayette, proposed
e deposition of the king and the establishment of a republic. How
an we, he declaimed, keep a perjurer on the throne of France? This
ttitude on the part of Condorcet severed his relations with the con-
itutional party and his friendship with Lafayette, who never spoke
him again.

Gallant young Barnave—he was only thirty years of age—
ith the queen's starry eyes and vibrant voice still lingering in his
emory—rose to explain elaborately that Their Majesties never in-
nded to leave France and were going only to Montmédy, where
e king could meditate on the affairs of state without being harassed
y the Parisian mob. In conclusion Barnave said:

ou have made all men equal before the law; you have achieved civil and
olitical equality; you have given to the state everything that the sovereignty

of the people demands; one step further and you will commit a deplorable and criminal act; one step more in the extension of liberty will lead to the destruction of royalty and, in the extension of equality, will mean the destruction of property. . . . Today, everyone knows that all interests demand that the Revolution be closed.

Note the reference to property in Barnave's speech. That was the central idea of his oration; all the rest consisted merely of high-sounding words. Let these common people come into power, gentlemen of the Assembly, and you will regret it. You will see what will happen to you, your families and your property.

Already the "passive citizens" were restless. They could not vote, and it was illegal for them to possess arms, but just the same the ultra revolutionists were giving them guns and ammunition.

Lafayette warmly supported Barnave, and his personal influence had more to do with carrying the Assembly than Barnave's eloquence. On July 15, 1791, it was decreed by the National Assembly that the person of the king was inviolable and that he should be restored to regal authority when he gave his formal approval to the constitution, but not until then.

Thereupon the entire contingent of royalist members—two hundred and sixty of them—resigned from the Assembly and went home. Such incredible stupidity! As a minority party, acting as a compact group, they might have had a definite influence on legislation, but they threw that chance away and departed in "high dudgeon," as a certain state of mind is now sometimes called. Their dudgeon must have been rather high, indeed, or they would not have left their beloved king without any party at all in the National Assembly.

One of the most extraordinary features of the French Revolution is that the royalists—the nobles—the princes—the king—appear to have had no ability to defend themselves. At the beginning of the Revolution the existing regime had control of the whole of France—army, navy, treasury, taxes, resources. There were thirty thousand noble families, but these did not represent the whole strength of the royal party by any means. Millions of Frenchmen, even those of low degree, were for the king. Why? Because of the power of tradition combined with lack of imagination.

Would it have been possible to mobilize these vast forces to uphold the monarchy? I cannot say; no one knows. But there are certainties here and there which any historian may observe. There was very little drive and smash among the Nobility. Nor any capacity for large-scale organization. Versailles, center of administration, was merely a museum, or show place, or theater, of elegantly dressed human dolls.

The prevailing desire of the noblemen was to run away, to get across the Rhine, to Coblentz, and spend there days and months in futile plots.

4

The people of Paris—meaning the multitude of the poor and the revolutionists—were opposed to the decree of the Assembly which upheld the king after his attempted escape. The leaders of the Assembly feared an insurrection. They urged Lafayette to take all possible precautions, and to disperse any disorderly demonstration.

The Jacobins and the Cordeliers—the two most prominent radical clubs—summoned the people to a mass meeting to protest against the action of the Assembly. On Sunday, July 17th, a petition for the dethronement of the king was to lie all day long on the "Altar of the Country" in the Champ-de-Mars. Everyone was invited to come and sign it.

Early that morning an unemployed wigmaker and a friend—who had a wooden leg—crept under the platform of the dais. They carried a small cask of wine and a gimlet. The wine was brought to drink, and the gimlet was brought to bore a few holes through which they might peep vertically up under the skirts of the women who came to sign the petition. Unfortunately for them their gimlet pierced the sole of a woman's shoe. She made a loud outcry. The lascivious wigmaker and his wooden-legged companion were dragged out, also the cask of wine. It was immediately called a keg of gunpowder, with which they had intended to blow up the sacred Altar of the Nation. In the uproar all explanations were useless and unheard. Their heads were hacked off and carried around Paris on pikes.

As soon as Lafayette was informed of these doings he rode, at the head of a detachment of National Guards, to the Champ-de-Mars and found a furious mob in possession of the field. While he was ordering them to disperse a man fired at him point-blank and the bullet whizzed by within an inch of his head. The man was seized and the Guards were about to kill him when Lafayette told them to take him to prison. Thereupon the leaders of the crowd came up and told Lafayette that there would be no more disorder. He took them at their word, posted a company of the Guards near by, and went home.

Late in the afternoon he was informed by the National Assembly that the mob collected on the Champ-de-Mars was about to attack the Assembly and the Tuileries. Mayor Bailly had already proclaimed martial law, and its symbol—a red flag—floated from the Hôtel de Ville. Lafayette joined the mayor and, accompanied by a strong force of the National Guard, proceeded to the scene of disorder. Upon being commanded to disperse the rioters threw stones. To frighten them the Guards fired a volley in the air. The mob merely jeered and kept on bombarding them with missiles. Lafayette ordered the soldiers to fire into the mob. Twelve of the rioters were killed and about twenty wounded. The crowd melted before the gunfire and soon the vast field was deserted. But a swarm of rioters besieged Lafayette's house in the Rue de Bourbon and demanded the head of Mme. Lafayette. Her husband had not yet reached home, and knew nothing of this occurrence until it was over.

Adrienne prepared bravely to resist, with the aid of her household servants and a squad of National Guards. The mob was climbing over the garden wall when a troop of cavalry came by on the way to its barracks. The cavalry drove off the rioters and posted a guard around the house.

The disorders of that July 17th had been instigated chiefly by the Jacobins. When the news of the "massacre at the Champ-de-Mars" was brought to the club—which was then in session—it caused the utmost consternation. The members expected the National Guard to appear any moment and the leaders saw visions of themselves dangling from the gallows. They thought the counter-revolution, backed by Lafayette and his troops, had already begun. There was no formal adjournment of the session. Most of those present fought to gain the exits, and many leaped from the windows. Danton left in a hurry and did not stop until he had got to London. Robespierre took secret lodgings in Paris, and was not seen again for some time. Marat found refuge in a cellar. Desmoulins, Fréron and Brissot hid themselves away somewhere.*

The disorder was suppressed, peace was restored, the red flag came down from the flagstaff of the Hôtel de Ville. But Lafayette's popularity was gone. Henceforth his name was a word of execration among the common people. He was looked upon as a military representative of the bourgeois and a sycophant of royalty.

Lafayette was no longer a member of the Jacobins. The club had become too radical for him. With Charles and Théodore Lameth, the Vicomte de Noailles, Adrien Duport and others he founded a new club called the Feuillants, named after the vacant monastery in which it met. The Feuillants stood for the king and the constitution and for the cessation of all revolutionary activities. It is a noteworthy fact that every one of the new club's organizers—mentioned above—had been among the original leaders of the Revolution. Lafayette was the author of the Declaration of Rights, his brother-in-law Noailles had proposed the abolition of feudalism; the Lameths, his distant relatives, were the authors of the legislative decree which swept away all titles of nobility. Duport, during the first eighteen months of the National Assembly, had been one of the leaders of the Left.

One may observe—and without a telescope—the drift of events. The out-and-out monarchists were gone; they had no longer any influence; their cause was dead and could be resuscitated only by foreign intervention. The field was left clear for the revolutionists and they were breaking up into two mutually hostile groups. On one side were the constitutionalists, whose creed was the king, the constitution and a bourgeois state. They were burdened with enough dead weight to sink their ship. There was the perjured king; they had him on their hands. And the "passive" citizens—three million men deprived of suffrage; the ridiculous "suspensive veto," which gave the king the power to suspend any legislative act for four years—a four-year veto granted to a king who could not be de-

* Brissot was an impecunious journalist who had been for a long time, around the beginning of the Revolution, a pensioner of Lafayette. He ate three meals a day at the Lafayette table and borrowed money from the marquis which he never repaid. He turned against his benefactor in 1790, and was thereafter an inveterate enemy. His full name was Brissot de Warville. In the 1780's he spent some time in America and wrote a book about his travels, called *Nouveau Voyage dans les Etats-Unis*. This book has always seemed to me to be light and inconsequential. Brissot was guillotined in 1793, during Robespierre's Reign of Terror.

pended upon to keep his word for even an hour. There were also the assignats, rapidly depreciating paper money that poured in a flood from the printing presses, thus raising prices without a corresponding increase in wages. The feudal dues, abolished by Noailles's famous resolution, still existed. The communes could not raise the money to buy exemptions.

The reputed "abduction of the king," as descriptive of his flight to Varennes, had become a facetious phrase all over France. But the constitutionalists—tongue in cheek—still spoke of it in solemn tones.

Their opponents, among whom the Jacobin leaders were outstanding figures, stood for democracy, rule by the people, abolition of royalty, no distinction between citizens (such as "active" and "passive"), seizure of the lands of all the nobles, distribution of wealth on more equal terms. Also, they were insistent on a revision of the constitution.

5

The ancient despotisms of Europe were beginning to stir in the summer of 1791 after the king, queen and the royal children had been brought back from Varennes. The revolution in France was a menace to all monarchies.

On August 25th Emperor Leopold of Austria—brother of Marie Antoinette—and the king of Prussia met in conference at Pillnitz. Neither of these sovereigns was ready for a war with France at that time, yet they wanted to register their disapproval of the Revolution. That was done in a document known as the Declaration of Pillnitz, which is one of the most ineffectual proclamations that one is likely to encounter in history.

The Declaration was an invitation to all European powers to join Austria and Prussia for intervention in France; but there was a proviso which nullified completely the effectiveness of the proposal. Nothing was to be done in the way of intervention, the Declaration stated, unless the monarchs of Austria and Prussia were supported actively, in a military sense, by all the nations of Europe. Such a condition took intervention out of the sphere of realities. The two monarchs could hope for no assistance at all, except possibly from Spain, and even that was doubtful. Nevertheless, the Declaration sounded like something important.

But it had one practical result: it enraged the French people. The nation was threatened and got ready to defend itself.

Defend ourselves, exclaimed the revolutionary leaders. *Of course we shall, but let us do even more; let us carry the Revolution into Austria and Prussia. Carry it to every corner of Europe. Hit them hard and strike first.*

On September 14th of that year—1791—the king appeared before the National Assembly and gave his formal approval to the constitution.*

The king said, in signing the constitution, "To extinguish all hatreds let us all consent to forget the past." The king was at once restored to authority as executive head of the nation. The long, arduous two-year session of the Assembly came to an end on September 30th, and a few days later the newly elected Assembly convened. It was far more radical and revolutionary than its predecessor.

The émigrés, concentrated mainly at Coblentz, reviled the king and queen for their acceptance of the constitution, and continued to urge the European powers to invade France. They called Louis a *soliveau,* which means a nonentity, a blockhead.

To the great joy of Adrienne de Lafayette her husband definitely resigned as commander of the National Guard on October 8th. Henceforth he was to belong to his family, and be out of danger. So thought devoted Adrienne. In his farewell address to the National Guard he mentioned the loyal acceptance of the constitution by the king, and said further:

Thus, the day of the Revolution has given place to an organized government, and to liberty and prosperity which it guarantees; and since everything leads to the pacification of the country, in view of the public happiness, the menace from its enemies should seem more absurd whatever combinations they have formed against the rights of the people, as there is no free soul who can conceive the thought of compromising any of its rights; and liberty and equality, once established in two hemispheres, will never retrograde.†

There you have a speech composed entirely of woolly words. They remind one of a Fourth of July oration in an American town.

* The constitution had been in force for more than a year, but only with the tacit consent of the king.

† *Mémoires de ma Main,* Vol. III, p. 121.

Were "liberty and prosperity" guaranteed? No, indeed. At that moment millions of people in France did not have enough to eat, or decent homes. "Public happiness"? The public happiness was not very noticeable, one must say. The "menace" of the enemies of the Revolution was not absurd; it was formidable, or would soon become so. "Liberty and equality." What about the active and passive citizens? Was there any equality there?

Lafayette believed truly that the Revolution was over, and he was not alone in that opinion. It is entirely probable that his conviction was shared by most of the intelligent, respectable people in France. They were mistaken. All that had occurred so far was merely a curtain raiser to the great drama—the little comedy that is played as a cheerful relief to the tragedy that is to come.

Next day, after his resignation, Lafayette, Adrienne, and the family—in a procession of carriages—proceeded to their distant estate of Chavaniac, in the hills of Auvergne. He intended to be, so he said, for the remainder of his life a country gentleman. The long journey was a triumphal progress. At every stopping place there were cheering crowds, bands of music and rippling flags. Everybody wore the tricolor cockade; little girls timidly presented bouquets. The Parisian unpopularity of Lafayette had not yet affected the provinces.

In November the National Assembly issued three decrees of paramount importance:

1. Monsieur, Comte de Provence, was summoned back to France. The nobles across the Rhine had designated him as the regent of France, with all regal authority, upon the theory that his brother the king was held as a prisoner in Paris. The Assembly demanded that the Comte de Provence return and give an account of his activities.

2. The émigré nobles must all return to France before January 1, 1792. In case of their failure to do so their lands would be taken by the state and considered national property.

3. All priests who refused to take the oath to uphold the constitution were to be treated as "suspects"—or, in other words, as enemies of the nation.

The king approved the decree which summoned his brother to

return. The two other decrees were rendered null and void by his
suspensive veto.

6

Country gentleman Lafayette was quite unfitted for his role.
He hardly knew one plant from another, but he thought of Washington and his knowledge of farming, so why not be a George Washington?

That was all very well, but he was soon bored. There were the
sleepy little villages; even the revolutionists in them were mild and
tame; and the accounts of the estate—who could make head or tail
of them? All that should be left to lawyers and clerks.

In faraway Paris the mayor resigned. Bailly could not stand
the strain any longer; he was sick and tired and ardently desired to
go back to his telescopes and distant stars. Pétion was proposed as a
candidate to succeed Bailly, and the opposition nominated Lafayette. Pétion had the support of the Jacobins. Couriers came four
hundred miles on fast horses to tell the marquis—now called general—of his nomination. There were eighty thousand registered
voters in Paris—meaning "active" citizens—but they knew so little
about voting and what it meant that less than ten thousand went to
the polls. Pétion was elected by 6,728 votes; Lafayette got 3,126.
(The election was held in November, 1791.)

All France, greatly alarmed by the Declaration of Pillnitz,
believed that war was impending. The National Assembly decided
to create three armies for defense of the eastern frontier—each to
consist of fifty thousand men. The veteran Rochambeau, who had
been the French general at Yorktown, was designated to command
one army; Marshal Luckner was the head of another one; and
Lafayette was appointed to command the third army, much against
the inclination of Louis XVI, who suspected his motives. He was
firmly convinced that Lafayette was plotting to overthrow the monarchy and put himself at the head of the nation.

Lafayette accepted the command and returned at once to Paris,
where he arrived on December 22nd. He had spent a little more
than two months on his ancestral estate; he was not to see it again
for many years.

CHAPTER XXIV

ATTACK ON THE TUILERIES

I

IN THE FALL of 1791 the political situation was complicated. The revolutionists had drifted into two major parties which were intensely hostile to each other. The Jacobins—party of the extreme Left—were ultrademocratic. Their leader was Robespierre, who was not a member of the new National Assembly, as he had belonged to its predecessor and was, therefore, ineligible for reelection under the law. His unofficial position did not lessen his influence in the least degree.

All the political clubs met every evening and discussed pending legislation with fervor and vehemence. In their relation to the National Assembly the clubs were lobbyists in riotous masses; not the kind of sleek, courteous and subtle lobbyists to which the American Congress is accustomed. By shouting in the galleries of the Assembly they often created an uproar which made it impossible to hear the speakers to whom they were opposed.

The Jacobins were a minority in the new Assembly—only one hundred and sixty members in a total membership of seven hundred and forty-five—but by fiery insistence they made up for their lack of numbers. They were not Communists—nor Socialists. The state ownership of industries was not in their creed. They stood for individual freedom and ownership of property, but they also advocated a more equal distribution of wealth, universal suffrage with all citizens on a plane of equality, abolition of royalty, and a general betterment of the conditions of the working classes.

At the other side of the Assembly, on the extreme Right, were the Girondins. They were so called because most of their leaders came from the department of the Gironde, of which the wealthy city of Bordeaux was the chief community. The deputies of the Gironde stood for the privileges of wealth, the rights of property, the constitution, and a government by "the better people." It should be understood, of course, that only a few members of that large legislative body actually came from the Gironde. It was simply a name devised to label a type of conservative opinion. The Girondist deputies came from all parts of France.

In the Center, between the Jacobins and the Girondins, was a large, multicolored party of independents, who voted one way or another according to their inclinations.*

The Girondins were closely allied to the Feuillants Club—the political organization created by Lafayette, Barnave, the Lameths, Noailles and Adrien Duport. Speaking in general terms, it may be said that the Feuillants and the Girondins were on the same side of the fence. They were anxious to bring the Revolution to a close. Their argument was: What else can be done? The Revolution has been accomplished; everybody has liberty and equality; the king has accepted the constitution; so why keep on stirring up trouble?

The hard-boiled Jacobins had little faith in such assertions. They declared that the nation had exchanged the rule of the Nobility for the rule of wealth. They hated the treacherous king and queen, the speculators in food, land and money, the constitution and its defenders.

Lafayette favored the Girondins, the Feuillants, the king, the monarchy. In other words, he was all for "law and order." This phrase has a pleasing sound and it appeals to all who desire to live in peace and comfort. But it is rather cloudy with a variety of meanings. Every king of France, from the beginning, had been wholeheartedly for law and order. Even the atrocious Louis XV; but he wanted the law to be of his own devising, and the order to be abject submission.

In the modern power picture, the millionaire takes the place of the king. He also believes in law and order, and for the same reason. Every millionaire in the world today is for law and order; the law will enable him to get his profits and a peaceful state of public order will enable him to spend them or invest them.

The poor people in the slums of Paris in the year 1792 were not so sure about the benefits of law and order as they should have been. That was due, undoubtedly, to their ignorance. They did not know

* The complexity of opinions and objectives is extremely confusing, so I am making this statement as short and clear as I can, for a comprehensive account would be bewildering. It appears that few of the party members on any side agreed wholly with the party program, so there was a great deal of shifting about and general uncertainty.

how to appreciate the advantages of law and order. The moral is—
there is a moral to everything—that they had not been brought up
properly. If their tutors and governesses had taught them the benefits
of law and order, they would not have run around Paris trying to
get hold of muskets, bullets and pikes while their underfed children
sat at home eating stale and moldy bread in stinking, crowded little
rooms. If they had known what law and order really meant in the
scheme of general welfare, they might have stayed at home and
perished quietly.

2

All parties in France anticipated a war with Austria and Prussia,
and nearly all the party leaders were pleased at the prospect. The
spirit of pacifism was dying of anemia. But, though the impulse
toward war was almost universal, every political group had a different
reason for desiring it.

The Tuileries—the coterie of the king and queen—wanted to
bring on a war because they were firmly convinced that France would
be conquered, the Revolution suppressed, and the absolute monarchy
restored. They never comprehended—until too late—the dynamic
vitality of the revolutionary movement.

The Girondins—meaning the higher bourgeois, the wealthy
middle class—desired a conflict with Austria and Prussia for the
reason that a war with foreign powers would reunite all factions in
a common purpose. They were well aware of the strength of the
French nation; the French would hold their own, but in the end
the bourgeois would come out as the winners and the Revolution
would be stamped flat—as a war measure. Even under the mere
threat of war armies might be created that could be relied upon to
check the excesses of the revolutionaries.

Pétion wrote in February, 1792, that the middle classes, the rich
bourgeois, were becoming a new aristocracy: "They consider themselves on an equality with the nobility who despise them and are
only waiting for a favorable moment to humiliate them." Continuing,
he said:

The masses, on their side, are angry with the middle classes and indignant
at their ingratitude; they remember what services they have done them.
. . . The privileged classes are secretly trying to bring a war that will lead
us to our ruin. The middle classes and the masses together made the Revolution; nothing but union between them can preserve it.

The Jacobins were divided in opinion, though the emotional weight of desire was on the side of war. They were confident that in the stress and tumult of national self-defense the entire government, from top to bottom, could be seized by the masses. In that case the royal family might be destroyed or banished, the bourgeois subdued, and a truly democratic government established.

In his bitter opposition to war Robespierre was almost alone among the leaders of public opinion. He thought and said that the nation should avoid war, if possible, for these reasons: If France lost the war—was conquered and subdued—then all the benefits of the Revolution would be lost; if France won, the victory would be followed by a military dictatorship, with the army upholding the dictator. He had Lafayette in mind, evidently, as a possible war lord.

At the Jacobins on December 12th he said, "To whom would you entrust the conduct of this war? To the agents of the executive power? If so, you will be abandoning the safety of the empire to those who want to ruin you." He added, "They want to drag you into a compromise by which the court will gain a wider extension of its power. They want to embark upon a sham war, which may lead to a capitulation."

A mind reader of exceptional clairvoyance could not have expressed more clearly the motives of Louis XVI and Marie Antoinette.

Following the counsel of the Lameths, who—by a curious twist of fate—had become welcome advisers of the court, the king came before the National Assembly on December 14, 1791, and announced that he had sent an ultimatum to the Elector of Trèves to the effect that all émigré nobles must be banished from his territory—which meant Coblentz, a center of antirevolutionary activity—before January 15, 1792, or France would take military action.* His speech was applauded by the Assembly. As soon as he returned to the palace he sent a secret message, in his habitual role of duplicity, to his brother-in-law, the Austrian emperor, in which he suggested that the elector be urged to resist the French ultimatum with the support of Austria.

On the same day he wrote to the friendly sovereigns with whom he kept up a continual correspondence:

The physical and moral state of France is such that it is impossible for her to carry on for half a campaign, but it is necessary that I should appear to enter upon it wholeheartedly. . . . It is necessary that my course of action

* Trèves was a small semi-independent German state on the Rhine. It could make no effective resistance to a French army without the aid of Austria or Prussia.

should be such that the nation may find its only resource in its troubles in throwing itself in my arms.

To render the "physical and moral state of France" even more deplorable he stopped the manufacture of arms and munitions and began systematically, and secretly, to weaken the defenses of the frontier.

About the same time—in December, 1791—the king wrote to his brother sovereigns and suggested "a congress of the chief European powers, supported by an armed force, as the best means of putting a check on factious persons here."

Frederick William of Prussia replied that he was willing to attend a congress, or intervene in military fashion, or do anything else to help, but he wanted to be paid for his trouble. Louis XVI assured the Prussian king that he would be compensated by the French treasury.

Marie Antoinette wrote to her brother, rather succinctly: "It is armed force that has destroyed everything; armed force alone can make everything good."

3

Defeatist elements were strong and active in the three armies on the eastern frontier. Lafayette, upon taking command of his army, soon learned that he was at the head of a badly trained, undisciplined mob. He was aghast at the lack of supplies of all kinds—arms, munitions, clothing and means of transport. The plot to cripple the armies that had been hatched in the Tuileries was being secretly carried out.

From precisely the opposite direction came another defeatist program. The Jacobin leaders caused many of their followers to enroll as volunteers. As soon as they became soldiers they began to undermine the morale of the army by spreading distrust of the officers. The Jacobins, as a whole, desired a war, but they wanted it to be carried on under Jacobin leadership. Consequently, for the purpose of forcing the noble officers out of the armies—and most of the officers were nobles—their emissaries in the ranks endeavored to develop a half-mutinous lack of discipline. They disseminated the idea among the men that their generals intended to lead the army into a trap and would have an excuse, therefore, to capitulate to the enemy.

So there, on the border of France, stood the armies of Rochambeau, Lafayette and Luckner; before them only a quiescent but potential enemy while behind them there were many lively enemies.

The Emperor Leopold was averse to war; he thought the difficulties of France, and of Europe, might be solved peaceably by the exercise of patience and diplomacy. Even if he had desired to fight, he was fully aware that the fighting would have to be done by Austria and Prussia alone, as the Declaration of Pillnitz, sent up as a trial balloon, had received no response that could be relied upon. With these thoughts in mind he advised the Elector of Trèves to obey the French ultimatum and disperse the émigrés at Coblentz. Accordingly that was done and the diverse militant parties in France suddenly found themselves without a tangible reason for war.

But there were still plenty of intangible reasons, so the war parties—royalists, Jacobins, Girondins—persisted in their warlike intentions. A pretext for war could be found. Revolutionary France, under the impulse of its pent-up pressure, was exploding like a comet that, sweeping through the universe, bursts from excessive speed and force before the startled eyes of mankind.

Among the observers of these mad events was a lean and shabby army lieutenant on the roll of reserve officers. His name was Napoleon Bonaparte; he came from an ancient noble family of Corsica; he was almost as poor as a genteel beggar, and he lived on his tiny pay as an officer in reserve. Few persons of importance had ever heard of him.

But he was destined, in the end, to pick up the fragments of the French Revolution after it had burned itself out in flame and fury and to lead the French people into a dynamic career of conquest.

But let us note, with emphasis, that revolutionary France was already a strong military power before Napoleon arose as its leader. It had held its own territory, had invaded other countries, and was feared by every despotic state in Europe before Napoleon began his famous career by a rain of shells on the English and Spanish war vessels in the harbor of Toulon.

His existence, dramatic as it sounds, was wholly unnecessary. France was safe, even if Napoleon had never risen above the rank of a minor officer of artillery. Under him the French became a pack of hunting dogs and their hunting ground was the whole of continental Europe. They planted the French flag in every capital; they swarmed over the ancient kingdoms; they knocked down the royal dynasties as if they were houses of cards set up by children. He led obedient France to defeat and destruction in the end, but he established a romantic ideal of military glory which persisted among the French people until it was destroyed by the horrors of the World War.

But Napoleon has little to do with this narrative. We are now in the year 1792, when revolutionary France is uncertain of herself, but full of fire and courage. She is a new nation—new in ideals and outlook—facing the world.

Europe—beware of this flaming France! Be cautious, move slowly, be patient. You have a delusion that you are dealing only with a disorderly mob; that after you have shot down a few of them the rest will run away.

No; that is all wrong. Miracles are to happen, and the miracles will not be welcome to many of you.

So it is written in the stars, but God forgot to teach us how to read the stars. If He had done so it would have saved us from an enormous amount of trouble and waste of energy.

4

Emperor Leopold of Austria was found dead, March 1, 1792, lying on the floor of his room. He had died from an overdose of an aphrodisiac. The empty bottle was still clutched in his lifeless hand. He was only forty-five years old at the time of his death. Before his dead body was a secret closet with the door open. It was filled with women's undergarments of lace and silk.

His successor was Francis II, an impetuous young man of twenty-four whose judgment was poor and whose temperament was extremely combative. From the moment of his accession there was hardly any doubt in either France or Austria that the two countries would soon be at war. Though the Elector of Trèves had expelled the émigrés from his small territory they continued to live in Austria. The Prince de Condé had organized, on Austrian soil, an army of twenty thousand men for the declared purpose of invading France.

The replies of Francis II to the French diplomatic notes were peremptory and angry refusals to do anything whatever in accord with the views of revolutionary France. But, on the advice of his counselors, he did not declare war. Let France do that, said the ministers. In that case the French will be the aggressors and after we have won the war we shall be in a position to claim indemnities.

Early in March the French war minister, Comte de Narbonne, summoned Lafayette, Rochambeau and Luckner to Paris for the purpose of planning a campaign. The king attended this conference of generals. It was decided that Lafayette's army should invade Flanders; that Rochambeau should hold his army in readiness to support him; and that Luckner should take his stand on the Rhine and be ready to repel an invasion.

The plan, as conceived, was excellent as a strategic conception. Upon his return to the palace the king revealed the plan to Marie Antoinette and she sent it, by a swift courier, to the Emperor of Austria.

Lafayette was in Paris several weeks on this occasion. He was the subject of violent abuse at the Jacobin Club. Robespierre demanded his dismissal from the army, and said in the course of a lengthy diatribe:

It is the genius of Lafayette which deceives so many good citizens in the capital and the departments, and if this hypocrite had not existed they would have been friends of liberty with us.

Lafayette returned to his army, but the Jacobin leaders declared that he had only pretended to return, and was still in Paris, hidden at the Tuileries, where he was advising the king and queen in a conspiracy to destroy the Revolution.

Louis XVI, on the twentieth day of April, 1792, appeared before the National Assembly and proposed a declaration of war against Austria. His speech was enthusiastically applauded. One deputy alone spoke against the proposal, and his speech was received in cold silence. When the matter was put to a vote, only ten deputies voted in the negative.

So the war began, and during the spring and summer of that year the French armies met with disaster. France had gone into the war blindly, without sufficient preparation and the enemies behind the armies were quite as strong as those in front. Austria was promptly joined by Prussia as an ally.

Lafayette was ordered, late in April, to advance into Belgium. He did, and if his army had been even moderately well supported there is little doubt that his campaign would have been successful. On May 1st he was within a short distance of Namur. The Austrians that opposed him had been driven back, but the French armies that were supposed to protect his flanks had retired in defeat. General Dillon's troops had run away at the first sight of the enemy; his soldiers had mutinied and murdered their general. Then they cut up his body and burned the pieces. General Biron—better known as the Duc de Lauzun—had met the Austrians and had been ingloriously defeated. In the midst of these defeats Rochambeau resigned from his command and wrote to Lafayette that he was through with the whole affair.

Lafayette, discouraged and uncertain, withdrew his army from Belgium. At any time in the summer of 1792 the Austrians and Prussians might have gone straight to Paris. But they were in no hurry and were elated by their easy successes.

On June 16th Lafayette sent an astounding letter to the National Assembly. As a general in active service he had no right to address the Assembly except through the minister of war and, even in that case, he could only make a report of his military operations. He wrote to the Assembly about the unruly populace, which was none of his business, and said, in part:

Can you deny that a faction . . . the Jacobin faction, has caused all these disorders? It is this faction that I openly accuse. Organized as an empire apart . . . blindly directed by a few ambitious leaders, this sect forms a distinct corporation in the midst of the French people, whose powers it is usurping, by subjugating its representatives and its agents. It is that, in its public sessions, attachment to law is called aristocracy and its infraction is called patriotism.

In profound astonishment the National Assembly heard the letter read. The Assembly in 1792 was an immature Congress, uncertain of itself, and did not know what to do. In the end it did nothing but acknowledge the receipt of the general's communication.

The Jacobins were not obsessed by uncertainties. Right or wrong, they knew what they wanted. Lafayette, long under suspicion, was put at the head of their black list. Desmoulins shouted, "I knew it all along. For two years I have said that Lafayette is a great scoundrel." Danton declared that Lafayette was hand in glove—partner and associate—with the tyrants who had set out to conquer France.

On June 20th a mob from the factory districts of Paris appeared before the Tuileries, broke open the gates and invaded the palace. (The iron gates of stout iron grillwork may have been opened for the people to enter by the king's command; about this there is some doubt, but it has no significance.) These rough people demanded that the king withdraw his suspensive veto of the decrees of the Assembly respecting the émigré nobles and the refractory priests. Of course their raid on the Tuileries was inspired by able Jacobin leaders; otherwise they would never have dreamed of coming on such a mission. They ran all over the palace, into the rooms, insulted the queen and put the red cap of the Revolution on the king's head. He wore it cheerfully and drank a glass of wine with them.

But he refused to lift his veto from the decrees, saying that it was not the time nor the place to make such a demand.

Finally, after several hours of clamor, the mob departed in good humor. Where was the National Guard? Who knows? Where was Pétion, mayor of Paris? He arrived after it was over and said he had just been informed. The king, in anger, ordered Pétion out of his presence.

As soon as the news of this uprising reached the army, Lafayette, in indignation, left his command and went to Paris. On June 28th he went to the Assembly and denounced the Jacobins in a vehement speech. They were responsible for the disorder, he declared; the Jacobin Club should be closed, and the leaders ought to be tried for inciting riots. His speech was applauded by the Right and the Center. The Left was strangely quiet. A report was circulating to the effect that Lafayette's army was on its way to Paris; and, in the circumstances, the Jacobins thought they had better keep their mouths shut.

It would have been better—probably—for Lafayette in the long run if the rumor had been true. Here we see some of his failings. He was not a dictator by temperament or inclination, yet he did not hesitate to put himself into positions in which he could succeed only by exercising the brutal methods of a dictator. He was not a great statesman because he was a theorist lacking the sense of reality, which is the first quality of statesmanship. No statesman of the first rank is ever a theorist *au fond*, though it is true that statesmen of great ability do display theories flamboyantly for the same reason that a county fair displays flags and colored ribbons—just to attract attention. Statesmanship may be defined as a capacity to utilize social facts to attain definite objectives of social value.

Lafayette was not a great soldier, though he was a courageous one. Had he been a great general he would not have let his army remain inactive so long on the Belgian border while France was being invaded. He was not even a shrewd politician. If he had been one he would not have got himself involved in a life-and-death controversy with the powerful Jacobins without an aggressive political party behind him ready to back up all his moves. Although he was an upholder of constitutional monarchy he was never able to get the king and queen on his side. However, that may not be a reflection on his lack of diplomacy. Louis XVI and Marie Antoinette were such fools that the task of helping them might have been an impossible one for anybody. They looked upon him as a designing rascal. "It would be better to perish," said the queen, "than to be saved by M. de Lafayette."

Having accomplished nothing in Paris, Lafayette, in disgust, went back to his army. Early in July he submitted to the king a secret plan for the escape of the royal family from Paris. He proposed that the capital of the nation be transferred to Compiègne, where it would be fifty miles away from the Parisian mobs. The departure of the king was fixed for July 15th, but Louis finally refused to co-operate in the adventure. He was afraid of being held as a hostage by Lafayette.

Despite the effort at secrecy this abortive plan of escape somehow reached the Jacobins and the people. Gouverneur Morris wrote—on August 1st—to Thomas Jefferson: "I verily believe that if M. de Lafayette were to appear just now in Paris unattended by his army he would be torn to pieces."

In the meantime the armies of the Allied powers were in French territory, advancing slowly under command of the Duke of Brunswick. On July 25th the duke issued a proclamation addressed to the French people. It is a famous document, but quite too long to quote in full. Here are some extracts from it:

The town of Paris and all its inhabitants without distinction shall be bound to submit on the spot, and without any delay, to the King; to give that Prince full and entire liberty, and to insure to him and all the royal family that inviolability and respect to which the laws of nature and of nations entitle sovereigns from their subjects.

He went on to say that "their imperial and royal majesties"— meaning the Emperor of Austria and the King of Prussia—would hold personally responsible for anything that may happen—

under peril of their heads, and of military execution without hope of pardon, all members of the National Assembly, the municipality, the National Guards, the justices of the peace, and all others whom it may concern.

Furthermore, he declared, that in case "the least violence, the least assault, be perpetrated against the royal family," the city of Paris would be given up to military execution and "the guilty rebels to the death they have deserved."

The duke's proclamation must be classified as one of the great inspirational papers of the French Revolution. People may be inspired by anger as well as by ideals, religion or other emotions. The revolutionists realized the stirring qualities of the proclamation; they had it printed and circulated all over France, with appropriate comments.

The Duke of Brunswick was a hopeless fool, but such fools do appear in history and sometimes they have great influence in human affairs. The silly proclamation of the Duke of Brunswick unified all the revolutionary parties in France. He was one of the important revolutionists of that time, but it was certainly not what he intended to be.

5

It was now definitely decided by the republican leaders to overthrow the monarchy. A ferocious assault was made upon the Tuileries on August 10th by the Parisian sections.

One of the noteworthy features of this memorable attack is that it was well advertised in advance. There was no secrecy about it. For a week or more everyone in Paris, including the city officials, the National Assembly and Their Majesties, knew that an uprising was imminent. The conservative element in the Assembly had been so thoroughly cowed that no effective plan to forestall the attack was prepared. Doom was approaching; what could one do?

Only Mandat, the local commander of the National Guard, took active measures to defend the palace and the Hôtel de Ville. But, even before the armed mob reached the Tuileries, the National Guard had mutinied and declared they would not shoot down their brethren. Only the Swiss guards of the king could be counted on to make a vigorous resistance.

Before the firing began, and while the rioters were battering at the gates, the king—upon urgent advice—decided to leave the palace and take refuge in the midst of the National Assembly. The royal party walked across the Tuileries gardens in a sad procession and arrived at the Manège at eight-thirty in the morning. There they remained all day.

In midforenoon came through the sultry summer air the rattle of musketry, like the beating of a thousand drums. The pale-faced Assembly sat in frightened silence. Members rose occasionally to make a pretense of carrying on the business of legislation. The king said he was hungry and a roast chicken was ordered for him. He ate the whole chicken, every scrap of it. His self-possession was superb, and so was his appetite.

Now and then runners came to tell what was happening. The mob had attacked the Swiss guards and a furious battle had taken place. While the battle was going on the king wrote a hasty order to the commanding officer of the Swiss guards. He was to cease firing and retire. Instantly he and his soldiers obeyed the king's command. Thereupon they were pounced upon and massacred by the infuriated people. Of the nine hundred guards present for duty six hundred were killed. Their fate was shared by about two hundred servants of the palace and friends of the king who had volunteered for the defense. The populace lost about four hundred men.

Around midday the battle was over. The mob was in possession of the palace. The courtyard was as bloody as a butcher's slaughtering pen.

That night the royal family was lodged at the near-by convent of the Feuillants. Louis and Marie Antoinette and the two royal children occupied four small rooms in which there was no furniture. They slept on mattresses placed on the floor.

For the next three days the king and queen were brought to the sessions of the National Assembly for protection. On the third day Louis was suspended—but not deposed—as the head of the French nation. The royal family was then sent, as prisoners, to the Temple.*

The constitutional monarchy had come to an end.

The place of the king was taken by an Executive Council, consisting of six members elected by vote of the Assembly. This was merely a temporary measure. It was decided that the Constitution of 1791 was unworkable; and it was decided also that a convention should be called to form a new constitution. The delegates to the Convention were to be elected by universal manhood suffrage with-

* The Temple had been the headquarters of the Knights Templar until they were overthrown and disbanded. It consisted of a number of buildings surrounded by a high wall. Not a trace of it now remains. The Square du Temple—a public park and playground—occupies the site.

out any distinction between active and passive citizens. Until the Convention met the National Assembly was to continue to be the legislative authority.

Two days after the attack on the Tuileries the Assembly suppressed all royalist newspapers.

Danton, inveterate enemy of Lafayette, was the first chairman of the Executive Council. The Council decided to send three commissioners to Lafayette's army. He was to be subordinate to them and make no move without their approval. The commissioners were Jacobins. Upon their arrival Lafayette had them arrested and put in prison at Sedan, where he had his headquarters.

His intention was to march on Paris and set things right by force of arms. By that he meant a restoration of the constitutional monarchy. To do so he had to depend, necessarily, on the loyalty and obedience of his army. The troops were paraded, in solemn and formal fashion, and each battalion was asked by Lafayette to swear devotion to the king and the constitution. Two battalions flatly refused to take the oath, and a number of other battalions did not seem very enthusiastic. That was disquieting and it made Lafayette think as profoundly as he could.

But even more disquieting news came the next day. The Executive Council, with the approval of the Assembly, relieved him of his command. General Dumouriez was coming to take his place. Lafayette was summoned to return to Paris and to account—with excuse, apology or justification—for his misdeeds.

There was a glint of cold steel in those summons.

To go back to Paris, in the circumstances, meant simply a journey to death and extinction. Lafayette held the sensible opinion that, "He who fights and runs away may live to fight another day." On August 19, 1792, he rode across the border into Belgium, which was Austrian territory. He was accompanied by twenty-two officers and a number of servants.

His intention was to go first to Holland, then to England. There he hoped his family would join him. His ultimate destination was the United States. He wrote to Adrienne, who was at Chavaniac with her children:

As for me, my destruction has long been decreed. With more ambition than moral sense, I could have had a very different existence; but there will never be anything in common between me and crime. I have maintained to the last the constitution to which I swore. You know, my dear heart, that my feelings would have been in favor of the Republic if my reason had not spoken in favor of monarchy and the will of the community had not made the defense of the constitutional king a duty. And so I have become the target for universal attack from both sides. . . .

I make no apology either to my children or to you for having ruined my family; not one among you would have desired to owe his fortune to conduct contrary to my conscience. Come and join me in England; let us settle in America; there we shall find the freedom that no longer exists in France; and my affection will try to compensate you for all the joys you have lost. Adieu, my dear heart.

To his great astonishment he was seized at once by the Austrian authorities and held as a prisoner. He spent the next five years in Prussian and Austrian prisons.

CHAPTER XXV

LAFAYETTE GOES TO PRISON

I

IN THE SUMMER of 1792 it was generally believed throughout Europe, outside of France, that the Duke of Brunswick's army would be in possession of Paris by October. Swiftly thereafter the revolutionary movement would be suppressed, its leaders sent to jail, or to the gallows, and the monarchy restored.

Gouverneur Morris, writing in his *Diary*, says that the Revolution is lost. That was an impression gathered in the Parisian salons where he drank tea and chatted with the ladies and their elegant gentlemen friends. He records a conversation with a M. Bertrand, who was a cavalry officer. Bertrand told him that "Paris waits but the moment to surrender," and he intimated that the cavalry would join the invaders.

On September 10th Morris wrote that "The number of troops to be opposed to the combined armies seems now to be as inferior as the discipline and appointments. Lord Wycombe [an Englishman] dines with me; he says that he hopes the end of the French affair will cure other nations of the rage for revolutions."

The Allied armies advanced slowly; the Duke of Brunswick was convinced that the French would not be able to make an effective resistance, so there was no necessity for haste.

The fortress of Longwy was besieged by the Prussians on August 16th. Within a week that strong strategical point was surrendered. Soon thereafter Verdun, the most important fortified place in eastern France, was taken.

The Austrians had surrounded the city of Lille and were trying to bring about its surrender by starvation and bombardment. The citizens of Lille faced their troubles with admirable fortitude. From the batteries of the besiegers incendiary shells rained on the town and there were numerous fires, day and night. The people organized impromptu fire brigades, women as well as men working at the pumps, and the fires were soon extinguished. A shell fell and burst within a few feet of a barber who was walking along a street, and he was knocked down by the explosion, but no fragment of the bomb had touched him. He picked up half of the shell, which was lying near by and declared that he would use it as a shaving bowl. For the rest of the day he shaved his compatriots free of charge, making his lather in the shell. This story spread over France, and long thereafter "Austrian" shaving bowls were in fashion among the revolutionists. They were made of iron and shaped to resemble the hemisphere of a bomb.

France was facing a desperate crisis. Every day came news of fresh disaster. The King of Spain moved an army near the French border and prepared to invade France. The King of Sardinia, whose territories included the province of Savoy, joined the Allied sovereigns. Though he did not know it at the time, he was saying farewell to his beloved Savoy. In August the French minister of foreign affairs announced that every European power, except Denmark and Sweden, had broken off diplomatic relations with the French government.

Lafayette's flight, the incompetence of generals, the threats of the Duke of Brunswick, and flying rumors of treason and conspiracy led to a general frenzy. The prisons of Paris were crowded with thousands of "suspects"—meaning those who were accused of treason against the revolutionary state. They were awaiting trial. Among them were nobles, nonjuring priests, journalists, former officials, and nondescripts—such as king's messengers, counterfeiters and foreign spies.

The Committee of Surveillance of the Commune of Paris was alarmed by the presence of such a large number of prisoners in the city when the soldiers were leaving for the front. If they should break out of their prisons, or be released through the treachery of officials, they might seize Paris and take over the government. So the Commune reasoned, but the reasoning was without sense, and was simply an excuse for a massacre. Paris was in no danger from those who were held in jails.

The Commune decided to put to death all persons in prison who were classed as suspects. Marat, a member of the committee, was said to be the leading instigator of the movement. Probably he was; it was in accord with his savage, uncompromising character.

For four days—September 2nd to 5th—the prisons were invaded by the assassins of the Commune and eleven hundred persons were massacred. At first there was a pretense of trying the suspects before revolutionary committees, but that was soon given up and the prisoners were turned over to the mob in the streets, regardless of evidence or justification.

The Princesse de Lamballe, one of Marie Antoinette's cherished devotees, was one of the victims. She had been held in the prison of La Force on a charge of espionage, royalist sympathies and treason. The charges were undoubtedly well founded. After a brief mock trial she was thrown to the yelling crowd.

Her head was hacked off, stuck on a pike and the mob paraded back and forth under the windows of the Temple so that the queen might see it. The king, standing at a window, saw the bloody head of his wife's friend and told Marie Antoinette not to look. But she did look—and fainted. That is the way the story goes, but I doubt the last part of it. I may be wrong, but my own estimate of Marie Antoinette does not include fainting. She could look on hell and damnation without losing her nerve. A woman of courage and composure, her chief defect was not fear, but a total lack of understanding of social movements; and she looked with contempt upon anyone who was not a noble of high degree. In her personality there was no sense of adjustment or capacity to adapt herself to circumstances.

The Princesse de Lamballe was the first woman to be a victim of revolutionary fury.

2

The September massacres were over, and revolutionary France had then to win or die. The French expected no mercy nor did they intend to show any to their enemies.

The tortoiselike slowness of the Allied armies during the summer gave time for the French nation to pull itself together, to get its second wind. Gouverneur Morris wrote early in September: "The Duke of Brunswick seems to be waiting awhile for the operation of others. . . . The inactivity of the enemy is so extraordinary that it must have an unknown cause."

Within two months the map of military operations was completely changed.

Twenty miles west of Verdun, on the road to Paris, is the village of Valmy. There on September 20th (1792) the Duke of Brunswick's Prussians encountered the French under Dumouriez and

Kellermann. The King of Prussia accompanied Brunswick's army. The émigrés had assured him that the progress of the Allies through France would be a jolly parade; that they would be welcomed by the people; that the miserable revolutionists—the scum of the earth—would run like rabbits.

They did nothing of the kind. The French stood their ground, and the French artillery proved to be much superior to that of the Prussians. Valmy was not a great battle in a military or strategical sense, but it stands out in history as the turning of the tide of invasion. The revolutionary ragamuffins had beaten the best troops in Europe. Goethe was there, as an observer. He saw the battle from the Prussian side, and when it was over he said, "From this place and this day dates a new era in the world's history."

Before the end of September the Allies began their retreat toward the Rhine. Longwy and Verdun were again occupied by the French. On October 5th the Austrians abandoned the siege of Lille.

The day after the battle of Valmy—on September 21st—the Convention met for the first time, displacing the National Assembly as the supreme legislative power. On that same day, by unanimous vote, the Convention abolished royalty in France, and a republic was proclaimed.* Thereafter Louis XVI was only an ordinary citizen who bore the name of Louis Capet—a Frenchman in prison awaiting trial for treason against the nation. Also in prison was his wife, Marie Antoinette Capet. She, too, was held for treason.

During that memorable September French troops entered Savoy. They took Nice on the twenty-ninth of the month, and within a few weeks the province of Savoy was overrun. It has remained French to this day.

The Comte de Custine's army, invading Germany, took Spires with three thousand prisoners, on September 25th. The French had reached the Rhine. On October 19th the powerful fortress of Mainz surrendered to Custine, and two days later he occupied Frankfort.

Dumouriez—successor of Lafayette and in command of Lafayette's former army—entered Belgium during the last week of October. On November 6th he fought the great battle of Jemappes. There the Austrians were decisively defeated; they left four thousand dead men on the field. By December 1st the French possessed the whole of Belgium.

* The chief executive power was entrusted to a committtee of the Convention, the membership of which was frequently changed.

To the statesmen of Europe these events were as startling as an earthquake. The royal families looked on in amazement. What had happened to their trained and disciplined armies? Did these revolutionary hordes have a savage magic of their own?

Yes, they did. They possessed the magic of courage, fervor and propaganda.

All over Europe the agents of French propaganda were at work. Common men in the ranks of the imperial armies, and behind the ranks—peddlers, waiters, clerks, valets—distributed secretly the pamphlets which explained the meaning of the French Revolution and the Rights of Man. To the soldiers of the enemy men whispered, "Would you shoot down your brethren who are trying to make you free?"

3

When Lafayette deserted his army he was a man without a country. He had abandoned the French Revolution, which was France; and the Revolution had disowned Lafayette. His name was a word of execration among the émigré nobles. They looked upon him as a traitor who had conspired against his own class. But the hatred was not universal. A man detested by everybody would be a monster, and monsters seldom exist. Lafayette had friends among the nobility and among the revolutionists—many of them—but the weight of prejudice, or opinion if one may so call it, was against him.

Across the sea was the young American nation, and there everyone loved him.

He applied for permission to pass through German territory on his way to Holland. To the chief authority of the region he wrote that he and his officers could not be considered enemies "since they have renounced their places in the French army."

The party was detained until the matter could be referred to Vienna. It was a long delay; the capital of Austria was five hundred miles from the Belgian frontier. Much of his time in waiting was spent in writing letters. To William Short, American minister at The Hague, whom he had known very well in Paris, he wrote:

You will greatly oblige, my dear friend, by leaving for Brussels as soon as this letter reaches you, and insisting on seeing me. I am an American citizen and an American officer. I am no longer in the service of France. In demanding my release you will be acting within your rights, and I have no doubt of your immediate arrival. God bless you.

Mr. Short never came and there was no reply to the letter. It was referred to Gouverneur Morris, the American minister to France, who sent Short a long-winded, pharisaical reply commenting on the fate of Lafayette. He wrote, in part:

Truly his circle is complete. He has spent all his fortune on a revolution, and is now crushed by the wheel which he had put in motion. He lasted longer than I expected. I have long lamented his situation, and feel more than ever a desire to alleviate his distress. His imprisonment was among the events which appeared to me not improbable. . . . I do not exactly see how the United States could claim him. If claimed and delivered up, would they [the United States] not want to put him to death for having attacked a neutral power; or else, by the very act of acquitting him, declare war against those who had taken him?

Such perfect—and evil—nonsense, put in diplomatic phrases! It is true that the United States had no right to *demand* the release of Lafayette, but a courteous request that the Allied powers should let him go, on condition that he come to America, would not have constituted a breach of international etiquette, and it is possible that —if sent just at that time—it might have brought about his release. Neither Austria nor Prussia knew what to do with him.

Morris's supposition that the American nation might put him to death for having attacked a neutral power was too foolish to deserve attention. It was not a crime for an American citizen, as an individual, to serve in a war against a neutral power—but he would have to take his chances and not rely on the support of this nation.

The United States was a weak nation, but not as weak and ineffective as Mr. Morris made it appear to be. We were the largest oversea buyers of European goods, and the world's greatest exporters of wheat, tobacco and other agricultural products. All Europe wanted to be on friendly terms with us.

Mr. Morris advised Mr. Short to confine himself to "prayer and solicitation." He said, further, "My opinion is, that the less we meddle in the great quarrel which agitates Europe the better it will be for us, and although the private feelings of friendship or humanity might properly sway us as private men, we have in our public character higher duties to fulfill than those which may be dictated by sentiments of affection toward an individual."

At the time this advice was passed out Gouverneur Morris was up to his ears in meddling. To Louis XVI he was sending memoranda which contained plans for circumventing the Revolution and defeating it, and the king had been so impressed by his royalist sympathies that he turned over to him a large sum of money which he was to hold in trust, so that it would not appear in the royal assets. After the royal family got out of France, if ever, or in case of the restoration of the king to power, Morris was to return the money. He deposited these funds in London and did return them to the king's daughter several years later.

He meddled so competently in the interest of royalty that after the king was executed the revolutionary government requested the United States to recall him. That was done and James Monroe was sent to France as his successor.

In course of time word came from Vienna. The prisoners were separated into three groups. The line officers and common soldiers were released and expelled from the country, but they could not go back to France. Another group of officers was sent to Antwerp as prisoners of war.

Lafayette, Latour-Maubourg, Bureaux de Pusy and Alexandre Lameth were to be held as hostages for Louis XVI, on the ground that all four of them had been members of the National Assembly. These reasons for the imprisonment of Lafayette and his fellow officers were not sensible, nor were they founded on any sort of sound policy. The outstanding fact is that all of them were deserters from the French armies. It would seem that in the interest of the Allied cause desertions should have been encouraged, and one does not encourage deserters by putting them in prison.

Nor is it true that Lafayette, or any of the others, was held as a hostage for the French king and queen, though that was the import of a solemn assertion made at the time of their captivity. Louis and Marie Antoinette were executed by the revolutionists but Lafayette and his companions were not beheaded, hanged or shot.

The order from Vienna said that they were to be turned over to the Prussians as prisoners. The Prussians sent them to Wesel in Westphalia, where they were put in cells in the fortress.

Then came a letter from the Duke of Saxe-Teschen to Lafayette. The duke was an uncle of Emperor Francis. The letter said:

As it is you who are responsible for the Revolution that has overturned France. as it is you who have put your king in irons, despoiled him of all

his rights and legitimate powers, and kept him in captivity, as it is you
who were the principal instrument of all the disgraces that overwhelm this
unhappy monarch, it is only just that those who are working to re-establish
his dignity should hold you until the moment when your master, after having recovered his liberty and his sovereignty, can, in his justice or his
clemency, decide on your fate.

There is hardly a word of truth in that statement. Lafayette was
not responsible for the French Revolution; all he had advocated were
some measures of reform. He did not put the king in irons (as a
matter of fact, nobody put him in irons), nor did he put the king in
captivity. On the contrary, he endeavored to save the monarchy.

Lafayette left France simply to escape being killed. He was no
longer in sympathy with the aims of the Revolution; he wanted to
be done with the whole affair. The Revolution had got too big for
him, too fierce and dynamic, and he knew it.

                                4

Late in December of that year—1792—Lafayette and his fellow
prisoners were transferred to the fortress of Magdeburg in Saxony.
They were taken in open carts like common criminals. The weather
was cold; it was midwinter; but the sun shone, and the air was brac-
ing. After four months of confinement in gloomy cells the trip of more
than two hundred miles was stimulating.

On their way, at the town of Hamm, Lafayette and his companions alighted from their cart at the moment when the king's
brothers then in exile—the Comte de Provence and the Comte
d'Artois—stepped out of a carriage that had stopped just in front of
the prison vehicle. The royal princes stared at Lafayette for a brief
instant, and he stared at them. No one spoke. Mutual contempt was
too great to sustain the frail bridge of conversation.

Both these princes eventually became kings of France. Lafayette
did not see either of them again for many years.

At Magdeburg the prisoners were confined in semisubterranean
dungeons. Lafayette's health was impaired by inaction, worry, lack
of exercise and sunlight. But his valet was permitted to attend him.
Through this servant he got news of his fellow prisoners. They were
all in the same plight.

He says in his *Mémoires* (Vol. IV, p. 218) that his cell was only

three feet wide by five and a half feet long. Later on—years later—
the Prussian authorities asserted that his account of his imprisonment was not true; and that he had a much larger cell than the one
he describes. One is inclined to believe that he exaggerated his privations. It may be recalled that he was five feet, nine inches in height,
and it would have been impossible for him to stretch out at all, when
lying down, in a cell five feet, six inches in length.

He says further that he was deprived of pen, ink, paper and
pencils; nevertheless, he did contrive to write letters and send them
out. That was accomplished by bribing one of his guards. Occasionally
newspapers were smuggled in.

He learned, by means of the newspapers, that Louis XVI had
been executed on January 21, 1793, after a long trial before the Convention. Malesherbes, a venerable lawyer of great distinction—a
patriot and citizen of probity—volunteered to defend the king. The
charge against him was "conspiracy against the safety of the state,"
which may be expressed in one word as treason. The defense was
skillful, but the evidence against Louis Capet was overwhelming.
He made a good impression on the Convention at first by his self-
possession and good humor. But he lost that advantage as the trial
proceeded, when it became obvious to everyone that he was lying.
He denied every charge flatly, or took refuge behind a lack of
memory. He said he knew nothing of the iron safe, notwithstanding
the fact that the key to it was found in possession of his valet. He
refused to recognize his own signature and declared that he had
never seen the incriminating documents.

The voting on the question of his guilt began on January 14th,
and as every member was allowed to state at length the reason for
his attitude the balloting went on for six days. The Convention decided unanimously that the king was guilty (a few members did not
vote at all). In the decisive vote on the penalty three hundred and
sixty-one deputies voted unconditionally for death; twenty-six others
voted for the death penalty but recommended a reprieve. Three
hundred and thirty-four were in favor of imprisonment.

The balloting was concluded on January 20, 1793, and on the
next day Louis XVI was sent to the scaffold and guillotined. His
demeanor was courageous, and it was obvious to all who witnessed
his execution that he met death without fear. On the scaffold he

attempted to address the crowd, but his voice was drowned out by the roll of drums.*

One may imagine the emotions of Lafayette upon reading the news of the king's trial and execution. Was the civilization of the world turning into chaos? Did not the French people have any respect for their own sacred constitution? He had respected it, had stood by it valiantly, and for that reason he had to flee from France. The plain fact is that the bourgeois constitution did not express the will of the people of France. They detested it and all those who stood by it. Into the world it came as a pitiable waif, and it was not long before even its parents disowned it.

On February 1st the French Convention declared war against England and Holland, and on March 7th against Spain. These declarations of war were not so militant and uncalled-for as they may seem to be. They served only to clarify the situation. A state of war already existed, under the guise of neutrality, with England, Holland and Spain. The acts of the Convention were simply gestures designed to give the war a formal status.

Pitt, the English prime minister, had his secret agents all over France. At his disposal were five million pounds, appropriated by Parliament for "a secret purpose." The purpose—suspected at once by the leaders of French opinion—was not long in doubt. In July a secret service agent of the English, then at Lille, laid aside his portfolio of papers for a moment. It was picked up, carried away, and examined. The documents therein proved conclusively that many persons in the service of the French government were receiving money from the British. Plots to set fire to arsenals and munition factories were revealed. These memoranda also disclosed the purchase from departmental clerks of the plans of the French. After reading the documents Robespierre wrote in his notebook: "Have two plans; the real one, and another to be revealed by the clerks."

Some of this large fund was to be used in depreciating French exchange in foreign countries by purchasing assignats in France and selling them abroad at a loss. That was a blow aimed at the French export trade.

* The guillotine had been in use in France for only a few months. The invention of this deadly machine is usually ascribed to Dr. Guillotin, a member of the Convention. The historical fact is that he did not invent it, but only proposed its adoption as a less cruel method of execution. Under various names the guillotine had been in use in other countries before it was adopted by the French.

Lafayette read that on March 10th a Revolutionary Tribunal with extraordinary powers had been created in France; and later that a Committee of Public Safety had come into being. This committee was dominated by Robespierre, though he did not become one of its members until July. Its organization marked the beginning of the Reign of Terror.

The Committee of Public Safety—with its almost unlimited and autocratic powers—soon superseded the Convention as the chief authority in national affairs, although the Convention still met and transacted its legislative business. To put the situation in plainer terms, one may say that the whole of France was placed under martial law in the face of the imminent danger of foreign invasion and the menace of internal enemies.

Those who look upon the Terror as nothing but an exhibition of sadistic cruelty are either ignorant of the situation or choose to disregard the underlying motives. Robespierre and his Committee of Public Safety constituted a dictatorship, but it was a dictatorship inspired by national distress.

Here are some of the outstanding facts:

In the spring and summer of 1793 the French armies—that had been so gallantly victorious in the fall of 1792—were falling back on all fronts. Many of their officers were suspected of treachery. Dumouriez, who had conquered Belgium in 1792, sold himself to the Allies and deserted.

There was a startling deficiency in arms and munitions.

Tens of thousands of people in France were conspiring against the Republic. Of this there was abundant evidence. An intense opposition to the Revolution had developed among the bourgeoisie.

Two French admirals—of noble birth—surrendered the entire Mediterranean fleet to the English without firing a shot.

The government was being victimized by army contractors and swindlers. One contractor had been paid more than five million livres for services worth not more than one-third of that amount. Flimsy shoes with paper soles had been sold to the army. Samples of this footwear were exhibited to the Committee of Public Safety.

The precipitous rise in the cost of living was breeding riots in Paris and all the large towns. France produced enough food to feed her population, but the depreciation of the value of the assignats was so great that the poor could not afford to buy the necessities of life.

In various parts of France there were insurrections. The uprising in the Vendée, on the west coast, amounted to a civil war and was subdued only after the insurgents had been defeated in several battles.

5

The Girondins were expelled from the Convention on June 2nd. This was done by a vote of the Convention, which was terrorized by the Jacobin mobs. The expulsion of the Girondins was an unconstitutional act, but by that time the constitution had become merely a scrap of paper, without binding force. Thereafter the legislative body was almost wholly Jacobin in character. The government had evolved into a dictatorship of a party exercised for the benefit of consumers, workingmen, peasants and small property owners. This party was led by men of the middle class who had joined their fate to that of the revolutionary movement.

These movements have a striking parallel in the progress of the Russian Revolution, which was led at the beginning by liberals of the Kerensky type, who were soon overthrown by the radicals.

Lafayette was an eighteenth century Kerensky, and others of the same temperament were Barnave, Vergniaud, Danton, Noailles, Desmoulins, Abbé Sieyès, Bailly and Roland—the husband of the famous Mme. Roland.

Robespierre and his associates may be compared to Lenin, Trotsky and Stalin. Under Robespierre the proletariat, for a brief period, became the chief political power in France.

On September 17, 1793, the Convention—at the demand of the Committee of Public Safety—passed the "law of suspects," a drastic decree which gave legality to all the operations of the committee during the Reign of Terror.

Suspects were: (1) Those who by their conduct, speech or writings, have shown themselves to be opposed to the Revolution; (2) those who cannot satisfactorily explain the sources of their incomes; (3) those who have been refused certificates of good citizenship; (4) public officials who have been dismissed for cause; (5) all former nobles, together with their husbands, wives, fathers, mothers, sons, daughters and other relatives who have not shown a proper attachment to the revolutionary cause; (6) all émigrés who had not returned to France before March 30, 1792; (7) those who, though not opposing the Revolution, have done nothing for it.

That was indeed a sweeping measure, and an unjust one; but dictatorships are always unjust, either in peace or in war, as they subordinate the national will to the arbitrary decrees of a minority. The excuse—or we may say justification—of the Robespierre dictatorship was the urgent necessity of defending the Revolution against foreign and domestic enemies.

The list of suspects might be made to include millions of people. Of course it did include, obviously, Adrienne Lafayette, her children, all the relatives of the Lafayette family and the family of Noailles. The Duc d'Ayen—Lafayette's father-in-law—had already escaped to Switzerland, but his wife and daughters were still in France.

6

In January, 1794, Lafayette was transferred to the fortress of Neisse, in Silesia, on the Polish border. He was kept there until the middle of May.

The Prussians were anxious to get rid of him. He was really a prisoner of the Austrians who had seized him in the first place, and had then induced the Prussian government, their ally, to take charge of him and his associates. Lafayette had not been captured in battle, nor had he surrendered. Technically, he was not a prisoner of war. He had left France voluntarily, had entered the enemy's lines, and had announced that he was through with the Revolution.

Finally, after much dillydallying, he was turned over to the Austrians on May 17, 1794, and sent as a prisoner to Olmütz. This town is about one hundred and ten miles north of Vienna; it is now in the territory of Czechoslovakia.

The conditions of life at Olmütz were quite as bad as those at Magdeburg, and—in some ways—much worse. Beneath Lafayette's window ran an open sewer and his room, at all times, stank with its odors. The discipline of the prison was harsh and precise. He was not allowed to send or receive letters, or to read newspapers, though he could get books from a lending library if the books had been approved by the prison officials. At certain hours he was permitted to walk in the courtyard, attended by a guard.

The food furnished by the prison administration was barely enough to keep a man alive, though prisoners might buy food if they had money. Lafayette did have money; funds were deposited on his account, from time to time, with the government at Vienna. But the American consul was unable to learn where he was imprisoned. The Austrian government, answering inquiries, always replied that he was alive and well, and that was the extent of the information anyone could obtain.

In respect to his money, and the cost of food, he was cheated outrageously by the prison officials. There was little or no check on their rapacity and he had to accept whatever lying statements they made.

In this tomb for the living Lafayette was kept for three years and four months.

CHAPTER XXVI

THE ATTEMPT TO ESCAPE

I

DWELLING in London was Justus Erich Bollman, a young Hanoverian physician. He was tall, blond and blue-eyed. Adventurous in spirit, he had small liking for sickrooms, pills and soothing mixtures. As a doctor of medicine he was a misfit. Here and there his fancy ran, depicting perils on land and sea. Had he lived today he might have been a daring aviator, or an explorer, or a soldier of fortune.

Through the generosity of an uncle he had acquired a good education, not only in medicine, but also in languages, literature, history, and the classic wisdom of the ancients. After he had his degree of doctor he went to Paris to take a postgraduate course. While he was there he practiced medicine in a small way. In the salons of wealthy liberals and well-wishers of humanity he met many people of distinction. His manners were good and the ladies liked him.

In the chaotic month of August, of the year 1792, Mme. de Staël, daughter of the fabulously wealthy Necker, came to Dr. Bollman and implored his aid. What she wanted on this occasion was not a prescription but a passport. Her lover, the Comte de Narbonne, was on the proscribed list and would be soon immured in prison as a suspect. She had asked her husband, who was the Swedish ambassador, to give him a diplomatic passport, but M. de Staël thought the relations of France and Sweden might be impaired by such an action on his part, so he refused.

Dr. Bollman was ready and willing to oblige the charming lady. He got a passport for himself and then, in some underhand way, got one for Narbonne under another name. After that the count and the doctor set out for London, where they arrived safely. The news of their trip soon reached France, and Dr. Bollman's name was added to the list of suspects with a black circle drawn around it. To go back to Paris would be foolish and fatal, so Bollman remained in England. Mme. de Staël appeared a little later, and she and Narbonne lived openly together. With his Parisian practice gone and his income dried up Bollman was a derelict.

The French émigrés kept him alive. Most of them, but not all, were as poor as mice and unable to help anybody. Mme. de Staël had piles of money. Comte de Lally-Tollendal was wealthy, and so was the Princesse d'Hénin—friend and confidante of Lafayette.

There was much talk among them of Lafayette and his fate. The émigrés on the Rhine, in Prussia and Austria detested him and were glad that he was in prison. But the Princesse d'Hénin and her little circle in London had a deep personal affection for him, and made plans for his escape. They thought of bribing his jailers. Before trying that, however, they decided to appeal to the King of Prussia. (Lafayette was then at Magdeburg.) They thought if the king could be made to understand that there were French nobles in exile who desired Lafayette's release it would be an effective argument.

Lally-Tollendal wrote to the Prussian king and told him that His Majesty had a wrong conception of Lafayette. He said further:

It was due to his desire to save Louis XVI that he destroyed himself. He was neither the cause nor one of the causes of the Revolution. It is true that he played a great part, but he was always on the side of the good, and not the evil, of the Revolution.

He also informed the Prussian monarch that in June, 1792, Lafayette planned to suppress the Revolution by marching his army on Paris. "The day after his arrival in Paris," wrote Lally-Tollendal, "I spent part of the night with him; we were discussing whether war should be declared against the Jacobins . . . war in the full meaning of the word."

That was all true, but it had no effect. Frederick of Prussia had already taken the stand that he alone was not responsible for Lafayette's imprisonment. In his capacity as jailer he represented the Allied sovereigns, and he could not—or would not—release Lafayette until all the powers arrayed against France had consented to his liberation.

So there was no hope in that quarter. The London coterie, aided and advised by Thomas Pinckney, the American minister in London, began to think of ways and means to take him out of the hands of his jailers.*

* Thomas Pinckney was a native of Charleston, South Carolina, and a member of a distinguished family. He had been educated in England and France, had served as an officer in the American Revolution, and after the war was governor of South Carolina. He was appointed American minister to Great Britain by President Washington in 1792.

Certainly very little planning could be done in London. That was a job for somebody who would undertake the mission and who could be trusted. The name of Dr. Bollman came up at once, and it was the unanimous opinion of the group that he was the right man for the adventure. Being a German by birth, he spoke the language, and was intimately familiar with the ways of the people. Furthermore, he was adroit, clever and cool in peril. A large fund for the venture was quietly raised in London. Bollman was to play the role of a wealthy physician and scientist who was on a visit to Germany partly for pleasure and partly for the purpose of visiting hospitals and attending the meetings of scientific societies.

So Bollman departed in the late spring of 1794, with a pocketful of money. Besides, he carried authority to draw on Dutch bankers for a great deal more. The blond Hanoverian was precisely in his element, and was as joyous as a desert-parched duck turned loose in a pond. He was to play a dramatic part; he had lots of money; and he was looking squarely at the glowing face of Danger. Can anyone imagine a more happy combination of circumstances?

Almost as soon as he reached Neisse he found out that Lafayette was no longer in that prison. All trace of him had been lost; nobody knew where he had been taken. Bollman wandered around Germany for weeks. He could make his inquiries only in a most casual, indifferent manner, lest he should attract attention and have the all-pervading Prussian secret police at his heels. Someone who seemed to know what he was talking about told him that Lafayette had been taken to Austria. He made up his mind to go to Austria, and started at once.

On his way to Vienna he stopped for a few days at the town of Olmütz, where there was a fortress in which prisoners were confined. From the talk of the innkeeper he learned that several French political prisoners—very important men—were confined in the fortress, but they were known to the guards only by numbers. The commandant and a few of the higher executive staff knew their names, and they refused to tell, the innkeeper said. It was the talk of the sleepy little town.

Bollman went into a conference with himself on the receipt of this information, and he came to the conclusion that Lafayette was probably one of the prisoners. But even so, Bollman could not remain much longer in Olmütz. The baleful eye of the local police was already turned upon him. In despotic countries the authorities suspect everybody, quite naturally, especially strangers. But he was saved from police inquisition by the commandant of the fortress who, upon hearing that a distinguished scientist was in town, acted in his capacity as local host, and invited Bollman to dinner. The police could not go any further. If the commandant thought so highly of the stranger he must be all right.

On this occasion Bollman displayed the arts and sciences; was serious, witty, humorous, profound. He did not fail to tell his host that he had got away from France just in time to escape the guillotine. He had stopped in Olmütz to rest a few days, but had to leave the next morning for Vienna. The commandant invited him to come again. Bollman made no inquiries about political prisoners in the fortress; to have done so would have been a fatal mistake.

He was in Vienna only a few weeks before he departed ostensibly for England. When he reached Olmütz again he pretended to be overcome by a sudden illness and went to bed at the inn.

In the medical profession it is a tradition, almost as old as God, that a doctor should never prescribe for himself in a case of illness. Why that is so is an esoteric question beyond the scope of the present inquiry. It would seem, as a matter of ordinary common sense, that a physician ought to know himself better than he knows anybody else. If he is not acquainted with his own ills and frailties, then how can he expect to know those of other people?

The famous Dr. Bollman, lying in bed at Olmütz, summoned Dr. Haberlein, the medical man of the fortress, to attend him. The poor little military doctor, who had the title of major, was tremendously impressed by the great scientist of medicine. He assured Dr. Bollman that he would be up in a few days; it was nothing serious. Dr. Bollman was of the same opinion, but he distrusted his own judgment and wanted a brother medico to decide. The honorarium which he passed out to the military doctor was large; it was more than Major Haberlein's pay for a month.

When the doctor was getting ready to leave Bollman said—in substance, "By the way, how's Lafayette?"

Dr. Haberlein was surprised. He said, "Why, how did you know that Lafayette is in prison here?"

Glib-tongued Bollman replied at once. "Is it a secret? Everybody in London knows it. I don't know how I learned—somebody told me. I don't recall who it was."

The prison doctor said that Lafayette was well, but of course nobody wanted to be in prison, deprived of liberty, yet perhaps after all that kept him out of trouble. Similar platitudes were uttered by Dr. Bollman.

Then Bollman wanted Dr. Haberlein to take a card of greeting to Lafayette. The doctor was doubtful about that, though of course he would like to oblige. The prison regulations said emphatically that no communication—oral or written—should be brought to prisoners from people outside the prison.

Bollman took one of his own visiting cards and wrote on the back of it the names of three or four of Lafayette's friends in London. "This isn't a communication," he said, as he handed it to the prison physician. "It is merely a greeting. I wouldn't know Lafayette if I met him in the road, but I am acquainted with some people who know him. Just hand him the card and say that I've passed through Olmütz. I want to be polite, you know."

Dr. Haberlein wanted to be polite too, so he took the card to the imprisoned marquis and told him what he knew of Bollman, his wealth and scientific attainments. Lafayette pondered over the information and felt sure that his friends were stirring in his behalf.

It appears from the scrappy, incoherent records that Bollman pretended to be called back to Vienna. At any rate, he went there and remained several weeks, attending lectures and making friends among the physicians. Evidently he was endeavoring to throw off suspicion, if any existed, of his purpose in coming to Austria.

2

Again Dr. Bollman started to leave Austria. He traveled in a fine coach of his own, in great state. Again he fell ill at Olmütz and had to go to bed. It seems that Olmütz was a hotbed of infection— or something—for Bollman. The nature of his illness is not stated, but the husky young physician was familiar, of course, with the symptoms of any disease one might name.

On this occasion he was ill for some time, but the learned Dr. Haberlein brought him around all right. Bollman said he felt too weak to continue his journey, and that he intended to go back to Vienna to recuperate. Dr. Haberlein thought he was wise in doing that. While he was ill Bollman persuaded the doctor to take an unsealed letter to Lafayette. Haberlein accepted the mission reluctantly. Bollman pointed out to him that not even the prison authorities could object to such a harmless missive. The letter contained nothing apparently but some news of Lafayette's friends in London. But there was one sentence of great importance, wherein Bollman expressed the hope that the recipient would read the letter with the *same warmth* that he had given to letters sent to him by his friends when he was at Magdeburg and Neisse. The innocuous letters delivered to him at those prisons had secret communications written in lemon juice between the lines and on the backs of the sheets. To bring out the invisible writing one simply holds the letter close to a flame; that of a candle will do.

In the secret writing Bollman had set forth a plan for the prisoner's escape. The plan was elaborate and would have failed, in all probability. Bollman wrote that, by bribing the prison guards, he hoped to smuggle in some small saws that would cut through the bars of the cell; also some rope. At an appointed time he would be waiting outside the prison and would be prepared to get Lafayette out of the country.

Lafayette did not believe that Bollman's scheme would succeed. One fatal objection to it was the presence of a guard at the door of his cell, day and night. Even if he had a saw how could he use it without being observed? But he had a plan of his own which he laboriously wrote in lemon juice on the blank margins of an English book. He informed Bollman that, on the doctor's recommendation, he was taken for a drive in the country every other afternoon. With him there were always two guards, besides the coachman. One of the guards, a corporal, sat at his side; the other, an ordinary soldier, rode with the coachman usually. He wrote that he was always accompanied by the same men.

At a certain point at some considerable distance from the prison he was allowed to alight from the carriage and take a walk across a field with the corporal at his side. At the other end of the field there was a grove of trees. He suggested that Bollman procure two saddle horses and have them waiting and hidden in the grove. Upon reaching the end of the field he intended to overpower the corporal; then he and Bollman would mount the horses and ride away swiftly toward the Prussian border, which was not many miles to the northward. He thought they might easily slip through Prussia in disguise.

On the next visit of Dr. Haberlein to his cell Lafayette asked him to thank the young man for his note; and would the kind doctor give him an English book? Lafayette had found the book very interesting, and he wanted to show his gratitude to Dr. Bollman for his thoughtful attention by sending him a little present. The doctor agreed to deliver the book; no harm in doing that. There is no doubt that the poor and obscure army surgeon was awed and pleased by his acquaintance with two such eminent men—the noble marquis and the wealthy scientist. That would be something to talk about to his grandchildren.

Yes, Major Haberlein, it will be indeed something to talk about, but not with pride. The day is coming when you will wish you had never laid eyes on Lafayette and Bollman.

The young man, now recovering from his illness and preparing to go back to Vienna for a rest, spent hours in his locked room at night, scorching the pages of the English book with a lighted candle and watching the yellowish brown writing appear.

Then, on the day of his departure, with his carriage at the door, he gave Dr. Haberlein a large fee with the careless gesture of those who are so rich that they no longer know the value of money. After saying good-bye it occurred to him that he had forgotten something. "Oh, I remember now. Will you please give this little note to the marquis. It's unsealed. Read it; I thank him for sending me the book." How wonderfully courteous these people are! Notes of thanks on every occasion. Thank you for this: thank you for that. Gift of a book; more thanks. To Dr. Haberlein, with money bulging his pocket, it seemed that the politeness of these great people should be adopted by everyone. The world would be a much more pleasant place to live in.

Dr. Bollman departs; the carriage rolls away toward Vienna after a chorus of good-byes, God-bless-you, and come-again-soon from the innkeeper, all his servants and the worthy doctor.

That night the marquis, in the drab dinginess of his cell, held a candle to Bollman's letter. He read that Bollman had accepted his plan; that he was going to Vienna and would get the horses there; that he would return in about a month; if he returned at once he might be suspected.

He wrote further than on his return he would stand by the roadside on one of the days when Lafayette rode to the country. On the approach of the carriage he would pass his handkerchief across his forehead. That would serve to identify him. Would the marquis please make the same gesture with his handkerchief? Then, he went on, he planned to be waiting with the horses the next time the marquis had an airing.

3

In a Viennese restaurant frequented by medical students Bollman sat, by chance, next to a young man of twenty-one. They talked about one thing and another—the state of Europe, the medical schools in Vienna, the excellence of Viennese wines, the frightful excesses of the French Revolution. Bollman's companion spoke of Lafayette and wondered where he was. He was in Austria, surely; that much was known; in prison somewhere. Bollman said he knew nothing about the marquis. He had never seen this young man before; maybe he was an agent of the secret police.

There was a special reason, said the young man, why he would like to get news of Lafayette. He produced his card; his name was Francis Kinloch Huger. He came from South Carolina, in the United States. When he was a three-year-old child Lafayette arrived in America to take part in the American Revolution. The marquis had spent his first night after he landed at his father's house. Francis Huger said that he did not remember Lafayette—he was too young at the time—but Lafayette's coming was a memorable episode in the Huger family history. Now that young Francis Huger had come to Vienna to study medicine the thought of Lafayette was always in his mind. "I would like to do something for him if I could."

Bollman reflected, in silence, on Huger's statement, wondering if it were true. When they parted that evening they had agreed to meet again in a few days. At their next meeting Bollman told Huger of his plan to rescue Lafayette. Would Huger help carry it out? Useless question; of course he would.

Early in November, 1794, they were on their way to Olmütz in Bollman's coach. In Vienna they had bought two saddle horses. One was a pillion horse—which means that it had a pillion saddle and was trained to carry two riders on its back. Bollman and Huger expected to ride away from the scene of rescue on the pillion horse; the other horse, with a single saddle, was for Lafayette.

Soon after their arrival in Olmütz, Bollman, standing on the roadside, exchanged handkerchief signals with Lafayette. A note fluttered from the carriage. Bollman picked it up. It said that Lafayette was prepared for the adventure and that they should make the attempt on his next ride in the country, which would be November 8th.

On the morning of that day Bollman sent his carriage to Hof, a village on the border of Prussia. It was to wait there until he arrived. After the rescue of Lafayette, Bollman and Huger were to ride lickety-split to Hof and go on in the carriage.

At the stopping place for exercise in walking Lafayette and the corporal got out and strolled across the field, while the carriage waited. Beyond the field Lafayette saw two young men. They drew their handkerchiefs across their foreheads. Lafayette engaged the corporal in conversation about the way to handle a sword, and to demonstrate his remarks, he seized the hilt of the corporal's sword. At that moment Bollman and Huger appeared, running toward them.

The corporal did not give up without a desperate struggle. With a fierce grip he held on to his prisoner. Bollman, Lafayette and the corporal rolled on the ground. In attempting to stuff a handkerchief in the soldier's mouth as a gag Lafayette's hand was badly bitten. Finally, Huger put an end to the corporal's resistance by knocking him out in pugilist fashion.

Peasants, at work near by in the field, stared at the fight in stolid bovine amazement for a moment, then they went on working.

While this was going on, with its smash, bang and uproar, one of the skittish horses took fright and dashed away. The pillion horse remained, and Lafayette was persuaded to mount it. Bollman and Huger told him that they would look out for themselves. To get a mental picture of these occurrences one must keep in mind that they all happened in less than sixty seconds, amid great haste and confusion. The corporal's outcries had been heard by the coachman and the soldier and they were hurrying toward the scene.

At Hof, on the border, Bollman's coach was waiting. Bollman and Huger would rejoin Lafayette there. Huger shouted to him, "Get to Hof," in English. Lafayette thought Huger said, "Get off," so he rode away without any particular destination. Evidently he knew nothing about Hof and Bollman's carriage that was waiting for him.

Bollman had brought a considerable sum of money for Lafayette's use. These funds had been supplied by the group in London. Before the marquis rode away Bollman thrust the money into his hands.

Some peasants caught the runaway horse and brought it back. Both Huger and Bollman attempted to get on its back, and the horse—unaccustomed to two riders—threw them. Bollman was hurt so badly that he could not walk. Huger insisted that Bollman take the horse. He did, and Huger went away on foot; his desination was the Austrian frontier. He did not get there.

Lafayette rode about the countryside for hours, looking for a road that would lead him across the border. The evening twilight came on; he was completely bewildered. His clothes were torn, dusty and bloody. His bitten hand was painful; his horse was in a lather of fatigue.

At nightfall he came to a village and offered two thousand crowns for a fresh horse. It was foolish, indeed, that offer of two thousand crowns for a relay. There he was, disheveled and bloody, willing to pay enormously for the use of a fresh horse. Soon there was a crowd around him, and the mayor came hurrying up. Everyone knew that there was something wrong.*

I wonder why he did not say that his horse had thrown him and so accounted for his torn clothes and the blood on his face and hands. It would have been a reasonable explanation. As it was, the mayor of the village was about to let him go when a man spoke up and said, "That is General Lafayette; I saw him when he was brought here from Prussia."

Huger was captured within an hour after the ineffectual attempt to rescue the prisoner. Bollman could have got away readily enough, but he rode around northern Austria for a week looking for Lafayette.

By November 17th all three of them were in the prison of Olmütz.

4

Lafayette was put in close confinement. No more carriage drives; no more books; no more conversation. New regulations were devised with special application to Lafayette. Even the officials of the fortress were forbidden to talk with him unless a witness was present.

* While Lafayette was in America during our Revolution he served as a member of the court-martial which sentenced Major John André to death as a British spy Major André, riding to New York City—then held by the British—had concealed in his shoes the plans of the fortress of West Point. On the way he was stopped by three villainous-looking men, thieves and camp followers of the American army. Young Major André offered them a thousand pounds if they would let him go. If he had given them two pounds and his watch they might have released him. The offer of such a huge bribe led to André's seizure and his tragic fate. Certainly Lafayette should have learned something from that.

Bollman and Huger were kept in irons for three months before being brought to trial. Then they came before a military court which endeavored to trace "the conspiracy" to its source. There was an assumption on the part of the authorities that half the world was involved; that the Austrian Empire was about to be blown sky-high. But nothing came of it; there was no evidence.

Young Huger said, before his judges:

I had decided to go back peacefully to my distant homeland, when an unexpected opportunity came to me of doing a service to the man who had done so much for the liberation of my country, who had helped it to win the independence I enjoy at home. I had no desire to do any injury to anyone; my desire was to restore an unhappy man to liberty and to his friends. My conscience is clear and I cannot regret my intention. At twenty-one years of age one is influenced more strongly by passion than by reason. If among the gentlemen who are to pronounce judgment on me there are fathers, I ask them to think of their sons, and to reflect that I had to decide entirely for myself and had no one to advise me.

Bollman was as defiant as Huger. Each of the young men took the whole blame upon himself, and neither could be made to say a word that would implicate anyone else. "If Lafayette is a criminal," said Bollman, "then I am one too, for I accept his principles as mine." They both declared that Dr. Haberlein was an innocent messenger—going back and forth—and that he knew nothing of the plot.

After a few months imprisonment Bollman and Huger were set free and ordered to leave Austria. The government at Vienna did not want to create any more sympathy for Lafayette by keeping his friends in jail.

But what they did to Dr. Haberlein was plenty. He said, at the trial, that he did not know how it happened and that—even then—he had no sense of guilt. There were a few harmless messages. That he would admit, but there was nothing in them worth mentioning. Poor doctor! They threw him out of the army, and he lived thereafter in sordid poverty.

The corporal who had allowed his prisoner to escape was reduced to the ranks.

Huger returned to the United States and lived for many years in serenity on his South Carolina plantation. On Lafayette's visit to America in 1824 Huger went to see him. He was then fifty-one and

Lafayette was sixty-seven. They had never met before, except for one minute of excitement while they were struggling with the prison guard, and thirty years had passed since that day.

Dr. Bollman was an adventurer by instinct and career. After the Olmütz exploit it does not appear that he ever practiced medicine. His life is full of shadows. He came to America and engaged in fantastic financial enterprises. Lafayette, on his release from Olmütz, gave Bollman a pension for life. It was seized, attached, impounded by his creditors.

In 1806 he was involved as an associate of Aaron Burr in the latter's scheme to separate Louisiana and the southwestern territory from the United States and set up a republic or empire with Burr at its head. (This accusation was not proved in court; Burr and his friends were set free after a trial for treason.)

Lafayette wrote to Jefferson a letter (April 29, 1807) in which he interceded for Bollman. He referred to Bollman's part in the attempted rescue from Olmütz and said further:

I shall only say of the accused that while the enemies of liberty in Europe . . . are far from sympathising in the misfortune of a man who had done so much for the noted friend of freedom [meaning Lafayette himself], it behooves me, the object of his noble Olmütz enterprise, to be intrusted [interested] in his fate by every attachment of sentiment and gratitude.

Jefferson, who was president at that time, did not share Lafayette's opinion. He wrote in reply (July 14, 1807) that "Bollman was Burr's right hand man in all his guilty schemes. On being brought to prison here he communicated to Mr. Madison and myself the whole of the plans, always, however, apologetically for Burr, as far as they could bear. But his subsequent tergiversations have proved him conspicuously base. I gave him a pardon, however, which covers him from everything but infamy. . . . Be assured he is unworthy of ever occupying again the care of any honest man."

CHAPTER XXVII

THE REVOLUTION DIES

I

WHILE Lafayette was lying in his silent and gloomy dungeon the French Revolution was moving with accelerated speed. The Girondins—the middle class—had lost control, and the ultrarevolutionary Jacobins had become the rulers of France. The Girondins declared that the Jacobins were anarchists. That was erroneous; they were really a working-class party with many shades of opinion. They were called the Montagnards—or "Mountaineers"—a nickname which came from the location of the seats of their deputies in the Convention. They sat on the highest tier of benches. The Montagnards did not have an actual majority in the Assembly, but their voices were decisive. The Moderates were in deadly fear of the Paris Commune, the fierce mobs, and the yelling galleries. But within a year that was changed. The Revolution had then run its course.

After the summer of 1793 the royalists and the nobles—as a class —had no longer any influence in French affairs. The lands and other possessions of the émigrés were seized by the nation and sold at auction. The newly rich acquired these estates for a small fraction of their real value. The nobles on the list of "suspects" considered themselves lucky if they could escape from the country with nothing but the clothes on their backs and the family jewels.

There are exceptions to this general statement; there are always exceptions to any generalization of historical facts or movements. Some of the nobles lived placidly in France throughout the Revolution, and even managed to retain their possessions. The Abbé Sieyès who had been one of the prime movers of the Revolution, but who opposed Robespierre and the Montagnards, went through all the perils and alarms without being molested. He died in 1836, at the age of eighty-eight. Upon being asked what he had done during the Reign of Terror he replied, *"J'ai vécu."*

337

If the violence and excesses of the Revolution were plotted on a map of France, the result would be a spotty exhibition ranging in color from deep red to pure white. For instance, in the district of Calvados not one person was sentenced to death during the Reign of Terror, while in Lyons there were 1,667 death sentences between December 4, 1793, and February 10, 1794. Lyons was then, as now, an industrial city controlled by wealthy manufacturers. The silk industry, which was the mainstay of Lyons, went all to pieces during the Revolution. Many thousands of people were thrown out of employment. They did not have enough to eat. These starving workmen rose against the reactionary city government, and their insurrection was suppressed with great cruelty. The Girondists—the middle class —took charge, and Lyons, as the Revolution progressed, was in a state of civil war against the rest of France. Eventually the city was taken by the revolutionists after a siege. Then the Jacobins went in for wholesale executions of the bourgeoisie. The guillotine was too slow; the condemned were shot in batches.

During the insurrection in the Vendée more than four thousand opponents of the Revolution were shot. But Central France—the region of the great plateau—saw little of the Terror; there were only a few death sentences.

In the fall of 1793 the army was democratized. It was an astonishing overturn of traditional military authority. Young men who had been soldiers in the ranks were made officers, sergeants became generals. The Nobility was displaced.

Among the newly made officers was Charles Pichegru, the son of a common laborer. He was so unusually intelligent that he attracted attention as a youth and was given a free education at a provincial college. In 1783 he went into an artillery regiment as an enlisted man, and rose to the highest rank possible for a noncommissioned officer, that of sergeant major. When the Revolution began a regiment of volunteers elected him as their lieutenant colonel. In October, 1793, he was made a general of division. Pichegru and his army overran Holland.*

The most promising of these democratic officers was Lazare

---

* In that campaign the entire Dutch fleet was captured by a division of Pichegru's cavalry. It is probably the only time in history that a fleet of war vessels surrendered to horsemen. The fleet was frozen immovably in the thick ice.

In 1804 Pichegru plotted against Napoleon and was sent to prison to await trial. One morning he was found dead, strangled.

Hoche. He had been in the army all his life—that is to say, since the age of seventeen. The Revolution made him a general, the youngest of all the general officers in the French service. His career was brilliant but brief. He died in 1797, at the age of twenty-nine. Said by his contemporaries to be equal to Napoleon as a strategist, Hoche would have played, undoubtedly, a great part in French history if he had lived.

The whole aspect of the war was transformed in a few months. The republican armies—there were fourteen of them—took on a new vigor. They began to win on all fronts. Revolutionary France was at war with five nations. The invaders were driven out of the country; the French armies carried the war into enemy territory.

On August 23, 1793, the Convention decreed a general conscription of men and resources. Every able-bodied man was registered as a soldier on reserve and large numbers of them were called to the colors. Resources of all kinds—food, materials, animals—were made subject to military requisition.

This decree was soon followed by laws regulating the wages of workingmen and the prices of basic necessities. The maximum of commodity prices was fixed at one-third advance over the price of 1790, computed statistically. Wages were raised fifty per cent. There were severe penalties for violations of these laws, but a government cannot force a shopkeeper to go on doing business against his will. In Paris, and in all the large towns, the food stores were soon empty of merchandise. Tradesmen had nothing left to sell, and many of them closed their shops. On the regulated scale of prices there was no longer a profit to be made. For months the townspeople lived from hand to mouth. The government was forced to seize food supplies in the agricultural districts and distribute them through a rationing system.

The Convention was an unwieldy body of nine hundred members. For the sake of efficiency many of its important functions were delegated to committees. One of them—the Committee of Public Safety—evolved by degrees into a dictatorship. Robespierre became a member of that committee on July 27, 1793—exactly one year and one day before he himself was sent to the scaffold.

On July 13th Jean Paul Marat, sanguinary and implacable, was assassinated by Charlotte Corday. Maximilien Robespierre was thereafter, until his own downfall, the leading figure of the Revolution.

2

Even today, after all the historical research and documentation, Robespierre remains an enigma. He is usually depicted as a blood-thirsty sadist during the Reign of Terror, and that characterization seems to be supported by ample evidence. But he was certainly not a monster of cruelty in his earlier years. Before the Revolution he was a judge in a provincial town. He resigned from the judiciary because, in the course of his duties, he had to sentence a criminal to death. "Yes, I know he is guilty," Robespierre explained, "but the thought of putting anyone to death is intolerable."

The key to his strange personality may be found—perhaps and probably—by considering it in the light of mental pathology. During the last two or three years of his life he exhibited most of the symp-toms of paranoia. The paranoiac traits are now well known, but in the 1790's there was very little comprehension of such things.

He imagined nonexistent plots against the Republic and against himself; he was in constant fear of assassination and went to and fro surrounded by a tough-looking guard of three or four men. Death and destruction hovered, and he felt that it was his duty to strike first. He accused men sometimes because they looked at him in a peculiar way; or because they used, in speaking, certain queer com-binations of innocent words; or because of mere idle gossip.

Side by side with the development of these paranoiac impulses his vanity grew prodigiously. In his adolescence he had been a shy shadowy youth who preferred to live in solitude. The vanity that he acquired in his later days can only be defined as the pride of virtue. He seemed to consider himself an incarnation of Virtue, or the idea turned into a person. The adoption of a personal myth is not at all uncommon among paranoiacs. Their delusions of persecu-tion have an urgent tendency to embody themselves in definite mental patterns—and they live the part.

Robespierre was known as the "incorruptible." No one could bribe him. He had been brought up in bitter poverty, with noble and wealthy people all around and in daily view. In the course of time he began to hate not only the rich but also everything that can be acquired by money. He was poor and lived in shabby little rooms over a stationer's shop in Paris, ate the simplest food, was never drunk, and his clothing was cheap. Imagine a clean-looking, neat, slender

COMTE DE MIRABEAU

FRANCIS

KINLOCH

HUGER

From a painting by
Charles Fraser in 1825.
Now in Metropolitan
Museum of Art.

ERICH

JUSTUS

BOLLMAN

Date about
1796.

man with a timid countenance and you will have a mental portrait of the great terrorist.

He was an idealist. A person may be a paranoiac, with a fixed notion and an objective of monstrous proportions, out of all relation with reality, and yet at the same time be very competent, intelligent and generous. Such people may have logic and foresight—but not in relation to the *idée fixe*. As soon as they enter that realm they live in clouds and dreams and fierce, deadly resolves.

The mild Robespierre became the fierce Robespierre. He would save humanity regardless of the means. There was to be a beautiful, splendid civilization and, in his commanding position, he would do his best to create it. Let us not think of Robespierre as a butcher of the human race but as one who dreams of a better world and who is ready and willing to destroy every human insect that opposes his idea. Then, by the side of these motives, stood the towering shadows of vanity and fear. He wanted to live in the memory of men as a liberator of humanity, a glowing figure in history; and, at the same time, he was afraid that he would be murdered before he had succeeded in his designs.

The fatal error in his vivid plan of the future may be summed up in the plain fact that people love to be slaves and will fight to the death to keep on being slaves.

Robespierre was no soldier; no leader of desperate assaults. He preferred to inspire rather than to act; to have others carry out his ideas. Perhaps this was partly because of his ineffectiveness as an orator and writer. He lacked the thunder of Mirabeau, the wheedling subtlety of Danton, the yelling ferocity of Marat, but he was superior to all of them in his conception of the future.

He was not a Communist, though he has been described as one by historians. The essence of communism is collective ownership of production and distribution. It implies a suppression of individualism unless the individualistic tendency leads to human welfare. Under communism the worker is supposed to be no longer just a machine, or a stray dog wandering around hoping to pick up scraps. He is one of the owners of the nation, of its industries and resources. That is the basic theory of communism, and it is a lofty conception, but difficult to carry out.

Robespierre's views—as quoted by the historian Aulard—state very definitely his position as it was in April, 1793. In a speech before the Convention he said:

We should declare that the right of property is limited, as all others, by the obligation of respecting the rights of other people; that the right of property must not be injurious either to the security or to the liberty or to the existence, or to the property of other men; and that every trade which violates this principle is essentially illicit and immoral.

These ideal principles of life and social relations have never been put in better form. They possess the direct succinctness of the Ten Commandments.

Robespierre said, at the same time, that, "Society is bound to provide for the subsistence of all its members, either in procuring work for them, or in guaranteeing the means of existence to those who are unable to work."*

At another time Robespierre said:

The food necessary for the people is as sacred as life itself. All that is necessary to preserve life is property common to the whole of society. It is only what is in excess of this that may become private property, and may be given up to the industrial activities of the traders.

He hated wars of conquest, though he believed in adopting a strong policy of military defense. When the revolutionary armies were winning everywhere Robespierre tried to have them recalled and the war brought to an end. He argued that it was only one step from military victory to imperialism. And so it turned out to be, in the end. France built up an army of 800,000 men—the most powerful armed force that had ever been created in Europe up to that time. This vast army was not all at the front, nor in ranks, but it consisted of trained men, ready and eager to go.

In a few years it was taken over by Napoleon when he seized control of the government, and it became a weapon for the conquest of Europe.

While Robespierre was slowly rising to power he realized that the Revolution was a failure so far as the common people were concerned. It had been a rich man's revolution and a poor man's fight. The workers and peasants had obtained little or nothing of value. Nearly half of them were "passive citizens," without votes. The factory workers were forbidden to form labor unions. Strikes of laborers were prohibited by law. Feudalism had been abolished on paper, but not in fact.

All around—everywhere—one might see the cheerful, smiling

* Aulard, *Histoire Politique de la Révolution Française,* p. 291.

faces of the *parvenus* and witness the insolent manners of those who had made fortunes, such as speculators in food and assignats; purchasers of lands, rights and privileges; army contractors and gamblers in foreign exchange.

As in America, during the 1920's, the community was speckled with people who had "cleaned up" on this or that. Large, hastily acquired fortunes were numerous. The old regime of the nobility had disappeared; in its place there had arrived a regime of raw and strident capitalism. In the confused new allocation of wealth the brazen, the greedy and the vulgar were climbing to the top. To men and women of that type the Revolution—which once they had so eagerly welcomed—had become a festering sore, a stench in the nostrils. It was high time to put an end to it on the ground that it was a public nuisance.

But how could that be done? The Montagnards were in control of the government. Visionaries like Robespierre, who argued that human rights came before property rights, were at the head of affairs. Men of substance could not make themselves heard. They had built up their fortunes through the exercise of shrewdness, industry, ability, and were these fortunes to be at the mercy of a rabble sitting in the Convention? No, a thousand times no, said the profiteers. But one had to express such opinions in whispers for the reason that Robespierre and his Revolutionary Tribunal might cut your head off if they knew what your ideas were—and also take away your fortune, and that would be just too bad.

Well, what shall we do? Consider it as sensible men. The invasion and subjection of the country by foreign powers would not be a solution. It is true that the conquering powers would suppress the Revolution; but, alas, it was equally certain that they would also restore the lands and chattels to their former owners, and all classes of the French, rich and poor, would become victims of the returned émigrés's fury.

In this conclusion they were entirely correct. Lombard, secretary to Frederick of Prussia, accompanied the émigrés attached to the army of the Duke of Brunswick. He wrote, on July 23, 1792: "their language is horrible. If we were prepared to abandon their fellow citizens to their vengeance, France would soon be no more than one vast cemetery." The Duc de Castries wrote in April, 1793: "No more gentleness; no more half-measures. The brigands who have ravaged

France, the monsters who have assassinated the king, must disappear
from the face of the earth."

The men of property decided—against their will—that the war
should be carried on and have their support. But, in taking that stand,
they placed themselves on the horns of a dilemma. If the French
were victorious, if they won the war and made a peace favorable to
France, the radical leaders would get all the credit for it and be,
therefore, encouraged to put more of their leveling ideas into practice. On the other hand, if France were conquered these men of
substance would lose all. The obvious thing to do, in the circumstances,
was to overthrow the revolutionary party by militant forces inside
France; or, in other words, to promote a counterrevolution.

That is what they proceeded to do, organizing quietly.

The queen was brought to trial in October and sentenced to
death. She went to the guillotine on October 16, 1793—about ten
months after Louis XVI had met his fate on the scaffold. There were
good reasons, in the formal legal sense, for the execution of Louis
XVI; and even better reasons in the relationship of men to one another
in a civilized state. He was a traitor to the nation which he had solemnly sworn to lead and defend.

But Marie Antoinette was only the king's wife, with the title of
queen. She had never possessed any legal authority. Certainly she
had advised the king, and in the wrong way, but he did not have to
accept her advice. Her death sentence was inhuman and unnecessary.
She might have been sent to her brother in Austria, with her servants,
properly escorted, and a courteous note from the French revolutionary government to the effect that as there is now no place in
France for queens we return this queen to you. Of course she would
have plotted to the best of her ability against the French, but that
was being done already on a large scale and she could have contributed nothing worth while.

Then why did they kill her?

One motive was to impress the French people with the idea that
the Robespierre dictatorship would hesitate at nothing.

There was also another motive: A gesture of defiance to all
monarchies. Through the murder of Marie Antoinette it announced
to the world that the French people would fight to the bitter end. It
was in the nature of an ultimatum and the cancellation of all possible
peace negotiations unless the terms were dictated by the French.

The Robespierre dictatorship succeeded wonderfully in creating a state of dread. Its category of crimes punishable by death included not only actions and misdeeds, but also thought and speech. There could be no free expression of the opinions of dissenters. Many persons were sent to the scaffold on mere suspicion. In October a formal accusation against the entire Girondin party was made in the Convention. Twenty-one of its leaders were selected for immediate trial. They were all tried in one batch. The trial lasted six days. There is no verbatim report of the proceedings in existence, but the available descriptions of the demeanor of the judges, prisoners, witnesses and spectators that have come down to us through the dimming years remind one of the trials in Moscow of the Trotskyites before the Stalinist tribunal. The Girondins were really condemned beforehand, just as the Russians were in 1937. They were all sentenced to death and went to execution the next day, which was October 31, 1793.

What is known in history as the "Reign of Terror" did not begin until January, 1794, but from the summer of 1793 on to the downfall of Robespierre the guillotine was busy in Paris. One hundred and seventy-seven persons were executed in the Place de la Révolution, now known as the Place de la Concorde, during the last three months of the year 1793. As the days and weeks went by the daily number of executions increased, until—toward the last—the condemned were brought to the scaffold in swarms.

In forty-nine days in June and part of July, 1794, the number of persons sent to their death on the scaffold was 1,376—in Paris alone. It was a wholesale slaughter. The bodies of the victims were not turned over to their relatives. Bodies and dissevered heads were thrown pell-mell into carts. At the end of the day the carts, with blood dripping from them, were driven to the little Picpus Cemetery and thrown into pits, which were hastily covered with earth.

A persistent belief—held by most people even today—is that only nobles, royalists and traitors to the Revolution were guillotined. It is not true. The nobles and the wealthy formed only a small portion of the victims. Louis Blanc, who had the time and patience to look up the records of 2,750 persons sent to the scaffold, found that only 650 of them belonged to the well-to-do classes. Among the others were many food speculators, poor but indignant writers of antirevolutionary pamphlets, street orators, people without visible sources of income, members of the Convention who consistently voted with the opposition, priests, and persons under general suspicion. Even seam-stresses and tailors.

A member of the Convention whose name was Jean Baptiste Carrier was delegated to proceed to Nantes with full authority to put down an insurrection which was instigated and nourished by the Catholic clergy. Carrier was a person of incredible ferocity. The prisons were jammed with so-called "suspects." To empty the jails he caused about two thousand prisoners to be drowned. These unfortunates were thrown from lighters and rafts, with their feet and hands tied, into the river Loire. They were sent to their death without trial. Among the victims were many women; also some boys under fourteen. The river was full of floating corpses, drifting back and forth with the tide.

Carrier's doings were too atrocious for even the revolutionary committees to approve, and he was recalled before he had managed to kill the whole population of Nantes. He was criticized on the floor of the Convention and in the Committee of Public Safety, but nothing was done. One reads with great satisfaction that, after the fall of Robespierre, the head of this bloodthirsty person was neatly snipped off. He was still young at the time of his death, with a long life of murder and cruelty before him, but the Fates ordained that he should perish at the beginning of his brilliant career.

An effort was made to dechristianize the nation. The churches were to be secularized and turned into temples for the "worship of Reason." Robespierre opposed this act, but his opposition was not strong enough to prevent it. Although he was a deist himself and did not believe in Christ and the Bible, he thought it would be unwise to adopt any measure which would deprive the people of their religion.

What was the motive behind the movement to abolish Christianity? That is certainly a pertinent question, but it cannot be answered in a sentence. There were several motives. One came from the action of the pope in urging the clergy to incite insurrections in France after their lands were taken over as national property, and the priests had been compelled to take an oath as servants of the state, or else be excluded from their religious functions. The Church had been, for centuries, a foreign sovereignty within the borders of France. That was intolerable to the mind and tempo of the Revolution.

Unquestionably another motive was that of defiance, like that which led to the execution of the queen. A policy of defiance in a weak nation is fatal, for the reason that it may provoke the enmities and reprisals of stronger powers, and ultimate defeat. But France was a strong nation, and in no danger of conquest.

In these circumstances the underlying purpose of a defiant attitude toward other peoples is to divert attention from domestic issues. At this time of writing, in the year 1938, one may observe this defiant motive plainly at work in Germany and Italy.

In carrying out the policy of abolishing the Church, a new calendar of months and days was adopted on October 5, 1793, but the arrangement dated back and was regarded as beginning on September 22, 1792, the day on which the Republic was proclaimed. That is to say, the Year I began on that date.

In the revolutionary calendar the year was divided into twelve months of thirty days each. The seven-day week was abolished. In the month there were three periods of ten days, called *decades*. The tenth day of each decade was a day of rest. Besides the twelve months there were five days—in leap years six days—set aside for national holidays. These days were not included in any month. They came at the end of the year—that is, from September 17th to the 21st. Christmas, Easter, and all saints' days were taken out of the calendar.

This scheme of months was not abolished until 1806, when— under Napoleon—it was replaced by the Christian calendar. It was conceived by Fabre d'Eglantine, and the rather poetic but logical names of the months were his invention. Robespierre sent him to the scaffold in 1794 for móderantisme, or moderation, but kept his calendar.

Below is given a table of months and dates. The first column is the name of the month in the revolutionary calendar; the second column states the first day of that month in the Christian calendar:

Vendémiaire	beginning	September 22.
Brumaire	"	October 22.
Frimaire	"	November 21.
Nivôse	"	December 21.
Pluviôse	"	January 20.
Ventôse	"	February 19.
Germinal	"	March 21.
Floréal	"	April 20.
Prairial	"	May 20.
Messidor	"	June 19.
Thermidor	"	July 19.
Fructidor	"	August 18.

The month of Fructidor ended on September 16th. Then came the five national holidays.

The movement to dechristianize the nation was not successful. The popular opposition to it was so great that the churches were permitted to continue their services, though some of them were taken over and turned into "Temples of Reason." These temples were really ethical culture centers. Above the doors of the temples this sentence was inscribed: "The French people recognizes the Supreme Being and the immortality of the soul."

The Temples of Reason were open to all, but their services were poorly attended. The Festival of the Supreme Being, on 20th Prairial (June 9, 1794), was a ceremony of great beauty. A young woman appeared as the Goddess of Reason. Impressive as it was, it left the spectators untouched. It was really a theatrical performance, but not more theatrical than many of the ceremonies of the Church.

3

When the guillotine was first introduced it was a novelty of such fearful and fascinating import that vast crowds surrounded it. As a public spectacle the executions were as popular in Paris as gladiatorial contests had been in ancient Rome.

It was not long, however, before the public interest waned and was succeeded by disgust. Mingled with this sense of repulsion was a general feeling of amused or arrogant contempt—if one may believe the chronicles and memoirs of that era. The guillotine had become the universal standing joke of Paris, but it was certainly no joke for those who were condemned. If we had the time it would be interesting to trace the evolution of these attitudes. The bearing of the victims of the guillotine no doubt had something to do with it. Almost invariably they met their fate with bright-eyed fortitude. There was no weeping and wailing. Sometimes they made amusing talks to the executioners and spectators. Meeting their friends in the streets, men said, "Well, I see you still have your head on." And the usual reply was, "Yes, but maybe not next week." Like soldiers in the trenches, danger had become a part of one's daily life. But when terror is no longer feared, then terror itself is in danger.

At dinner parties tiny guillotines, made of cardboard, were placed beside the guests' plates. Impromptu dramas, with the guillo-

tine as a feature, were got up and played in the salons of the great
houses. In one of these plays, as described by a writer of reminiscences, the accused, made up as a comedy character, was brought
before a ridiculous revolutionary tribunal and charged with stealing
a cat's milk. His defense was that the prosecutor had got the occurrence exactly backward. The cat, he said, had stolen his milk; the
cat ought to be put on trial. Thereupon the judges and the jury had
a fist fight among themselves; some wanted to let the man go, while
others demanded death. When peace was restored it was decided to
compromise the matter. The accused was sent to the scaffold and the
court ordered the cat to be found and put to death. It was a comprehensive verdict; the guilty party could not escape.*

The location of the guillotine in the Place de la Révolution
caused outspoken criticism. There it stood, an *abattoir* for human
beings, in one of the most beautiful squares in Paris. It was called a
"disgusting spectacle" and a "public disgrace." In deference to public
opinion the guillotine was moved in June, 1794, to the Barrière du
Trône-Renversé (now called the Place de la Nation), which at that
time was on the outskirts of the city.

It is interesting to learn that the sale of luxuries increased during the Reign of Terror. Everybody seemed to be having a rather
good time, except those in prison, and the poor unfortunates who
were having their heads cut off. The theaters were crowded; the
magasins de luxe were full of customers. It is also worthy of note
that hundreds of thousands of people in Paris went about their daily
work and were never troubled at all.

The position of Robespierre was greatly weakened by the fact
that France was no longer in danger of invasion. The French armies
were winning everywhere. The agricultural harvest of 1794 promised to be one of the largest in French annals. (And so it turned out
to be.) Business was getting better day by day; fortunes were being
made; the city of Paris was expanding, with new streets, new buildings, in the suburbs. There were many poor people who could not
live on their wages, but what of it—said the profiteers—the poor we
always have with us. The tide of the Revolution was ebbing away;
so many people of substance were sick and tired of it.

In the midst of all this civilized activity sat the grim Revolutionary Tribunal; and there was the guillotine, and there were the
hordes of informers, spies, paid ruffians; and there was Robespierre.

* Roverier, *Anecdotes de la Révolution Française*, p. 82.

The Committee of Public Safety had evolved into a Committee of Public Menace. Some of its members realized that, and resigned or—retaining their seats—were quietly conspiring against the Robespierre regime.

The Reign of Terror had ceased to terrorize; it had degenerated into a vicious annoyance. Under the leadership of Fouché, Tallien and Barras, the foes of the Robespierre regime had been secretly organizing for some time. In this movement there were many men of ability and energetic courage.

Robespierre knew of the plot to destroy him; certainly not all the details, but he knew the names of the leaders, and he awaited the issue, biding his time, with a silent resolution to strike first. There they stood, the two opponents, with daggers drawn. It was to be a fight to the death and both parties were fully aware of it. The grim guillotine stood ready to finish the mortal existence of the losers. Robespierre depended absolutely on the support of the Communes, which meant the Jacobin Clubs. His enemies relied on the middle class, the businessmen, the so-called respectable citizens who believed that the Reign of Terror—and the Revolution—had gone far enough and must be suppressed. The duelists circled warily about each other in the arena of French politics.

All of a sudden the issue came to a head with dramatic intensity through a small incident. Tallien had a mistress—she was afterward his wife—whose name was Thérésa Cabarrus, a Spanish woman by birth. Her father was a banker and had been, at one time, the finance minister of Spain. She must have been a wonder as a good-looker. In all the descriptions I have read of her the writer never fails to depict her as a raving beauty and usually falls into a sort of literary swoon over her charms. Listen to Mme. de La Tour du Pin, who was a cynic and did not admire many people. Of Thérésa Cabarrus she says:

A more beautiful human being had never issued from the hands of the Creator. . . . Her hair, black as ebony, seemed to be made of the finest silk, and her brilliant complexion was as clear as ivory. . . . The least movement revealed an incomparable grace, while her voice, which was harmonious and slightly marked by a foreign accent, exercised a charm which no words can express.

I have gazed at Isabey's portrait of Thérésa, and I must say—in all frankness—that her picture is somewhat disappointing, though she was evidently good-looking enough, in a luscious way. A plump person, with fine eyes, a delicately formed mouth, and a mass of ringlets tumbling about her ears. She had an air of coarseness—in the portrait. But her charm may have been chiefly in vivacity and grace of movement.

Robespierre, or the Committee of Public Safety, or somebody representing them, had the beautiful lady arrested and sent to prison as a suspect. It would have been better for Robespierre to have committed suicide at once.

Apparently there was no evidence of treason or what-have-you against the girl. She seems to have passed all her time in just being beautiful, which is, as we all know, an honorable occupation. Then why was she thrown in prison? The answer is clear enough, but let us not be more Freudian than we have to be. Robespierre could not endure the situation, and something had to be done. There was the most beautiful woman in the world, living with Tallien and running around with him, while Robespierre spent his time pondering on social problems. Robespierre was an ascetic without piety, but he controlled the prisons and the guillotine. Tallien was his inveterate adversary; he might make him come to terms by imprisoning the Cabarrus lady; and if that were not enough he would send her to the guillotine.

The scheme had one serious defect: Tallien would not hesitate at killing Robespierre. He was a fearless and aggressive man, and he had a large following. From his imprisoned inamorata he got a letter in which she wrote that she was doomed to die in a few days— they had told her. "What a coward you must be," she said, "to let them kill me."* Tallien made up his mind that he would assassinate Robespierre with his own hands unless he could overturn the Robespierre regime immediately. He planned a coup d'état for the next day.

Robespierre was also planning a sort of coup d'état for the next day. He intended to get rid of the opposition once and for all. Tallien was to be given a one-way ticket to the guillotine.

When two coups d'état, with opposing motives, run into each other headlong, the spectacle must be worth seeing.

---

* This letter may be apocryphal, an invention after the event. Its existence rests only on hearsay.

4

On 8th Thermidor—July 26, 1794—Robespierre rose in the Convention and spoke for two hours. His long harangue was an attack on the management of public affairs in which he mentioned frequently "the league of scoundrels." When the members of the Convention yelled at him to give the names of the "scoundrels" he shuffled about and changed the subject. He had lost the support of the Convention, though he did not know it at the time. His speech was interrupted frequently; once by Cambon who declared that, "One man alone paralyzed the will of the Convention; that man is Robespierre." His address was full of cloudy phrases. Levasseur, a member of the Convention, wrote: "The vagueness of his language, the threats which it concealed, the indirect accusations which it left hanging over some of the deputies, finally his personal justification itself . . . were not of a nature to reunite opinions."

At the close of his speech there was some faint applause. A resolution to print and distribute the speech was proposed and defeated. He must have seen that he was surrounded by an atmosphere that had suddenly become chill and forbidding.

Both sides realized that the next day would be decisive, and the leaders spent the night in exhorting their followers, and in making their plans.

It was a day of pitiless, blazing heat—the ninth day of Thermidor. When the perspiring Convention met excitement was in the air. The galleries were packed. Saint-Just, friend of Robespierre, ascended the rostrum to speak, but he had not said twenty words before Tallien ran to him and rudely pushed him from the stand. Robespierre then made an attempt to say something, but was driven back to his seat. By that time the Convention was in utter confusion. Collot d'Herbois, who presided, attempted to restore order—but with no success. The enemies of Robespierre kept yelling "Down with the tyrant." In vain he looked for support to his friends, the Montagnards. Many of them had turned against him; the rest sat in cowed silence. Tallien produced a dagger in a melodramatic manner and announced that he intended to kill Robespierre then and there unless the Convention decreed an accusation against him. No doubt he meant what he said.

With such a fierce uproar going on the Convention was perplexed. Decree an accusation against Robespierre! Very well, but on what grounds? Everything that Robespierre had done in the past was done with the Convention's approval. How could it spit in the face of its previous actions without an excuse? In that moment of bewilderment Robespierre himself furnished an excuse—a rather slender one, but it would do. He rose and managed to make himself heard. To the presiding officer—the president of the Convention—he shouted: "For the last time, will you give me leave to speak, *president of assassins!*"

Ah! That was an insult to the Convention. President of assassins! His arrest was decreed in a few minutes, and a little later he was taken away by gendarmes together with his brother, Augustin Robespierre, Saint-Just, and a number of his followers. They were to be put in prison.

But there was a hitch in the proceedings. Fleuriot, mayor of Paris, was a Robespierrist, and he sent orders at once to all the prisons that they were not to receive Robespierre. He directed that Robespierre and his associates be brought to the Hôtel de Ville for "protection."

Then, if Robespierre had been a man of action, he might have saved himself and his friends. He could have summoned the Commune—the sections of Paris—to protect him. He puttered indecisively with that notion for hours, and finally did sign a call to arms, but it was too late.

The Hôtel de Ville was invaded by his enemies. Someone fired at Robespierre and broke his jaw.* His brother, in trying to escape, leaped from a window and was fearfully mangled—but not killed—by the fall. Robespierre's friend Le Bas blew out his brains and Couthon, another associate, was dragged from under a table. Saint-Just alone coolly submitted to arrest.

Next day Robespierre and twenty-one of his adherents were brought before the Revolutionary Tribunal for sentence. The proceedings did not last ten minutes. All were sentenced to immediate death—and the sentence came from Robespierre's own tribunal.

Late in the afternoon they were carted to the scaffold. That evening all Paris was a scene of gaiety. There was no regret over the passing of Robespierre. He had lost his friends. At the news of his death there was feasting and dancing.

* There is a lot of uncertainty about this incident. He may have attempted suicide, and those who were on the scene at the time thought he did. A gendarme, whose name was Méda, boasted after it was all over that he had shot Robespierre.

CHAPTER XXVIII

OPENING OF PRISON DOORS

I

Wнат was happening to Adrienne and the Lafayette children during those days and months of peril?
They were at Chavaniac when the news came late in
August, 1792, that Lafayette had left his army with a party of officers. Soon thereafter Adrienne learned that the revolutionary authorities considered her husband a traitor and had decreed his death when
—and if—he could be brought back to France. She passed the next
few days going through his papers, hiding some and burning others.
His swords of honor and other military trophies were buried. Valuable
paintings were taken from the walls and secreted in a safe place.
Chavaniac was preparing for a raid.

Then came a letter to Adrienne from her husband, written in
Germany and sent to her through a third person. He told her to go
to England and join him there. In excitement and joy she was getting ready to leave when a squad of soldiers appeared at the château.
They produced an order from Roland, minister of the interior, to
arrest Mme. de Lafayette and bring her to Paris. Of course, she had
to obey the summons, but she persuaded the officer in charge to let
her go first to Le Puy, the administrative headquarters of that department, and lay the matter before the local officials.

She was accompanied to Le Puy by her daughter Anastasie, her
aunt Louise Charlotte and five servants. Why five servants were
needed, in the circumstances, is difficult to understand. Probably it
was just the habit of a lifetime; she was a great lady and had always
been surrounded by maids and lackeys.

There was no order for the arrest of Aunt Louise Charlotte (she
was seventy-three years old), nor for Anastasie, but they insisted on
going along.

The other daughter—Virginie—was in Langeac, which belonged
to the family. The boy, George Washington Lafayette, a lad of
twelve, had been sent by Adrienne to the home of a friendly curé in

354

the mountains of Auvergne. His tutor, M. Frestel, had gone with him. Frestel was the kind of man who devotes his life, year after year, to the fortunes and welfare of a wealthy or noble family. There are many such people. Patient, quiet, gentle, intelligent—he was at the same time a born inferior, an educated lackey who had somehow lost, if he had ever possessed, *le pouvoir de volonté*. His career was one of wholehearted loyalty and devotion to the family of Lafayette.

Upon listening to Mme. de Lafayette's protest the commissioners at Le Puy decided to keep her there, temporarily a prisoner, until they could communicate with Paris. They wrote to Roland and urged that she be allowed to remain at Chavaniac. In reply Roland agreed on condition that she give her word of honor not to leave her estate without permission. So they all went back home—Adrienne, Anastasie, Aunt Louise Charlotte and the five servants.

At the suggestion of Gouverneur Morris she wrote a letter to the King of Prussia. It was by no means a cringing, begging epistle, but rather haughty in tone. She asked him to release her husband as a matter of justice and fair play.

Also she wrote to George Washington, then President of the United States, begging him to intercede. The Father of Our Country did not reply directly to her letter at that time, but he instructed the American diplomatic representatives in Europe to do whatever might be possible to effect the release of the marquis.

Letters sent by post to and from Chavaniac were sure to be opened and read, for Adrienne—her husband a fugitive accused of treason—was suspected of dastardly plots by the revolutionary committees. She did not use the mails. A faithful man named Beauchet, husband of one of her former maids, acted as a postman. He went back and forth between Chavaniac and Paris. Adrienne's letters to her family in Paris were delivered in person by Beauchet; the others were turned over to the American minister to be forwarded. In 1793 she had some news of her husband—several letters that had been sent by him surreptitiously from his Magdeburg prison to the Princesse d'Hénin in London and forwarded by her in a roundabout way to Adrienne. After he had been transferred to Olmütz no message came from him. She did not know where he was, alive or dead, until his attempted escape in November, 1794, became an item in the news of the world.

With Frestel, the tutor, she planned to get her son George out of France. George and M. Frestel were to go to Bordeaux and sail from there to England. Arriving in London they were to get in touch with Thomas Pinckney. Then, following Pinckney's directions, they were to go to America, where George would be under the protection of his great and powerful godfather.

Frestel procured a license as a peddler and he and George peddled their way to Bordeaux. When they got there Frestel discovered that they could not depart from France without passports, which were not issued unless precise documents were presented with the application. The tutor was undecided as to his next move, so he took young George to Normandy, where Frestel's parents lived. He hoped to escape to England through a northern port. That effort came to nothing. In a few weeks they returned to Chavaniac.

So the winter of 1792 passed, in doubt and anxiety. Lafayette's estates, and those of the Noailles family, were taken by the government and treated as national property. Under the law émigrés lost all claim to their belongings in France; later, this decree was broadened to includes the estates of all nobles who were condemned to the guillotine.

Adrienne laid her case before the local commissioners and the authorities at Paris. Her husband, she argued, was not an émigré, but a French officer who was held in prison by the enemies of France. Her contention was rather thin, and was, of course, ineffective. If Lafayette was not an émigré, then what was he? He had deserted his army and had fled to an enemy country. It was true that he did not intend to take up arms against France, but he had announced that he was opposed to the course of the Revolution.

With the sequestration of the estates there was no more income; the family at Chavaniac was on the borderline of abject poverty. Adrienne sent Beauchet to Paris with a letter to Gouverneur Morris. She described the state of her affairs, and her desperate need of money. Would the United States government officially guarantee a loan of 100,000 livres—that is, become an endorser of her note for that amount—which she planned to borrow?

In his reply Morris said, quite properly, that he had no authority to pledge the credit of the United States. But, he said, he himself would advance 100,000 livres to Mme. de Lafayette as a personal loan. He added that he was running no risk, as he was sure that the American government would reimburse him if madame, unfortunately, found it not possible to settle the obligation. Very pleasant correspondence.

It was far from pleasant later on. The Lafayettes, after years of financial distress, were ready eventually to repay the loan. By that time the livre (or franc) had greatly increased in value. The depreciated currency (assignats) had been replaced under the Directory by new money, and the financial system had been reorganized. Lafayette and his advisers calculated that the 100,000 livres which Madame de Lafayette had borrowed from Morris was about equal in value to 38,000 livres of the new currency. Interest added, the total obligation, they argued, amounted to 53,500 livres. Morris refused to accept that sum as payment in full, and a bitter correspondence went on and on. He demanded 100,000 livres.

Morris—then in America—wrote to Mme. de Lafayette that "with the one hundred thousand francs I lent you I might have bought real estate in the center of Paris which would bring me now ten thousand livres yearly rent."

The debt was finally settled in 1804, by the payment on the part of Lafayette of 53,500 livres.* It was angrily accepted by Morris. The debt was wiped out, but there was also wiped out all amicable relations between Gouverneur Morris and the Marquis de Lafayette. Thereafter Mr. Morris looked upon the marquis with the contempt that a solid citizen has for a debt evader; and the marquis contemplated Mr. Morris with the feelings that one usually has for extortioners.

Far away, across the Atlantic, President George Washington read Adrienne's letters. She did not ask him for money but only for the influence of the United States in getting her husband released from prison, so that he would be free to come to America with his family. He could do little or nothing about it, but he divined that Mme. de Lafayette was in financial distress, and he deposited to her credit 200 guineas of his own with Amsterdam bankers, and she was informed that she could draw on this fund. Later on, the American Congress voted $24,000 for the relief of Lafayette, his wife and children. (It may be remembered that he had never drawn any pay as an officer in the American army. This money was not a gift, but merely his deferred salary.)

* I do not know how this amount was calculated. Lafayette himself, in a letter to Thomas Jefferson, says that the sum advanced by Morris in depreciated currency (equivalent to 38,000 livres in new currency) had grown to 68,000 livres by the addition of interest at five per cent. Compound interest from 1793 to 1804, added to the principal, brings the total up to 68,243 livres, according to my own calculation. Then why was 53,500 livres offered in payment?

2

The order which sent Adrienne to prison came to Chavaniac early in November, 1793. She had been expecting it for some time; the wives of the émigrés all over France were being sent to jail. They took her to Brioude, a near-by town where there was a prison for aristocratic women.

The noble ladies who were confined there did not like her at first because of the general belief then prevailing among the nobility that Lafaytte was the source of most of their troubles. In a short time, however, her fellow prisoners dropped their attitude of animosity. Adrienne had an appealing personality. She was generous, forgiving and thoughtful of others. She was nunlike in her self-abnegation. In her make-up there was a strong tendency toward seclusion, to martyrdom and religious mysticism. .

As in all French prisons at that time, the food was insufficient, but she had some money and could buy whatever she needed. She lived in a room with four other women, all of whom were poor and undernourished. Adrienne paid most of their living expenses and also did the cooking.

For six months she was held at Brioude, uncertain of her impending fate. Frestel, the tutor, came to see her occasionally and he brought the children with him on these visits. Mme. de Chavaniac (Aunt Louise Charlotte) was not allowed to come, as she was also under arrest but the authorities permitted her to remain at home on account of her advanced age.

The Lafayette estates were put up for sale. Mme. de Chavaniac —assisted by the Marquise de Grammont—managed to purchase them. The marquise was Adrienne's sister Rosalie. She sold her jewels and contributed the proceeds. In the financial statement referred to above Lafayette includes a debt of 40,000 livres to his brother-in-law, the Marquis de Grammont, to cover this and other loans.

In May, 1794, an order came to send Mme. de Lafayette to Paris for trial before the Revolutionary Tribunal. She considered it virtually a sentence of death. Few of those who were brought before that grim array of judges escaped with their lives, and it was not likely that the wife of the "infamous" Lafayette would be set free. Prisoners were transported in carts, but Adrienne was allowed to go in a carriage which, of course, she paid for out of her own funds.

Though she did not know it, her husband—in that month of May—was also on the road to a new prison, to the fortress of Olmütz. The three children remained at Chavaniac. In prison at Paris, awaiting trial, were her aged grandmother, the Maréchale de Noailles; her mother, the Duchesse d'Ayen; and her sister Louise, wife of the Vicomte de Noailles, who had fled to London. Her father, the Duc d'Ayen, had fled to Switzerland. It seems to have been a habit of the nobles of that revolutionary era to run away and leave their women-folk at home. They may have thought—it was a reasonable supposition—that the women would not be molested.

The long journey from Brioude came to an end on 19th Prairial, of the Year II of the Republic, which means June 8, 1794. It was the day before the Festival of the Supreme Being.

For two weeks Adrienne was confined in the prison of La Force; then, for some reason now unknown, she was sent to the Plessis prison in the Rue Saint-Jacques. The building had formerly been a college for young nobles; as a youth Lafayette had lived there. Daily Adrienne saw batches of prisoners leave for execution. She had no doubt that the same fate was awaiting her. On June 10th Robespierre had an act passed which deprived accused persons of all right of defense before the Revolutionary Tribunal. Thereafter until the rule of Robespierre and his Terrorists was overthrown on the 9th Thermidor—or July 27th—the arraignment and trial of prisoners was nothing but a tragic farce.

The proceedings of the Tribunal were carried on amid great confusion and haste. The spectators frequently made so much noise that even the prosecutor's accusations could not be heard. Stupid mistakes were perpetrated; innocent persons were mistaken for the guilty because of a similarity of names; prisoners charged with minor offenses, not punishable by death, were sometimes sent to the guillotine because of some misunderstanding.

On one occasion a summons was prepared for François Simon Loizerolles, a young man of twenty-two. By mistake the fatal paper was served on his father. Without correcting the error the father—who was a gray-haired man in his fifties—accepted the summons and was taken forthwith before the Tribunal. So little attention was paid by the judges and the jury to the prisoner's name and description, as set forth in the indictment, that the elder Loizerolles succeeded in having himself condemned in place of his son.

Five days before the Reign of Terror came to an end Adrienne's grandmother, mother and sister were executed. It was a revolting deed, so hideously cruel that I am reluctant to write about it. In contemplating this sordid murder one should keep in mind Carl Sandburg's remark about the brotherhood of man. He said "the brotherhood of man is sometimes not so much a beautiful dream as a humiliating reality."

The three women did not know what the charge against them was until they were brought before the Tribunal. Then they were informed that they were accused of having conspired with two women named Levis to have Robespierre and other members of the Committee of Public Safety assassinated.

The Duchesse d'Ayen asked the prosecutor to speak louder, as she was partly deaf. This request brought a roar of laughter from the bench of judges, the jury and the spectators.

"So, *citoyenne*," the president of the Tribunal remarked, "you conspired *deafly!*" More laughter.

When the merriment had subsided Adrienne's mother declared that they knew nothing whatever of the plot. "But you knew the Levis women?" asked the prosecutor.

"No, I never *knew* them," she replied, "and I *saw* them only *once* in prison." (The Levis women had already been executed.)

Thereupon the court commanded her to be silent. No evidence whatever was presented by the prosecution, and the women were not permitted to produce any evidence or even to make a defense.

Although the Duchesse d'Ayen had just declared that she did not know the women conspirators, the judge said to the jury: "You have heard the accused, of her own will, admit that she knew the Levis women."

That is all there was to the trial. All three of them were found guilty and sentenced to death within a few minutes after they had entered the courtroom.

That same afternoon, in a crackling thunderstorm and a torrential downpour, they were carted to the guillotine. The Maréchale de Noailles was eighty years old and feeble. In the tumbril, as it proceeded toward the place of execution, she sat with her hands tied behind her back. The rain and wind made bedraggled ringlets of her white hair which blew about her face. Very likely the poor old woman did not know what it was all about.

3

Mme. de Lafayette did not learn of the execution of her relatives until about a week after it had occurred. Then the Terror was over, or—to be more explicit—the French Revolution, as we moderns understand that term, had come to an end.

Thousands of "suspects" were released from prisons, but not everyone. The guillotine was still at work, but the victims were the Jacobins, the Montagnards, the Terrorists. There were not so many executions; the trials were more sedate and legal.

They kept Adrienne for months; they did not let her go until January 22, 1795—or 2nd Pluviôse of the Year III, by the revolutionary calendar—yet she might have won her release long before that time if she had not been so haughty and insolent when called before the commissioners who were examining suspects. She refused to answer questions and showed a rather sharp contempt for the commission and all its doings. Her attitude revealed an uncompromising aristocratic spirit. At the time of her eventual release she was one of the few remaining inhabitants of her prison; it had become a place of silent, deserted rooms and echoing corridors.

Her freedom was obtained partly—and perhaps wholly—by the perseverance of James Monroe, the American minister at Paris.

As soon as she was out of prison she called on Mr. Monroe to thank him for his endeavors in her behalf. That duty done, she departed for Chavaniac. She had learned of her husband's attempt to escape from Olmütz—all Europe and America had the news—also of its failure and his subsequent imprisonment.

At Chavaniac she found Aunt Louise Charlotte and her two daughters. She had not seen any of them for eighteen months and they welcomed her as one returned from the dead.

At that time Adrienne was not thirty-six years old. (She was born on November 21, 1759.) But she had gone through more trouble than most women of sixty.

Before leaving Paris she had sent her son George to America with M. Frestel. Following are extracts from her letter to President Washington:

Monsieur: I send to you my son. While I have not had the consolation to be heard by you or to obtain the kind of service that I believed proper to deliver his father from the hands of our enemies, because your views were different from mine, I still have confidence in you and it is with this very sincere feeling that I place my son under the protection of the United States. . . . My desire is that my son lead a very obscure life in America; that he resume the studies that three years of misfortune have interrupted . . . and that he may work to make himself capable of discharging the duties of a citizen of the United States, the sentiments and principles of which will always be in accord with those of a French citizen.

This letter was probably composed by M. Frestel, though written by Mme. de Lafayette. Her education was quite imperfect; she had difficulty in spelling even ordinary, everyday words. Her reading, such as it was, consisted almost entirely of religious books.

Adrienne stayed at Chavaniac only one week. She had planned to enter Austria, with her two daughters, on an American passport, and join her husband in prison, if the Austrian authorities could be induced to give their permission. Commendable spirit of self-sacrifice. No doubt she would comfort her imprisoned husband, but why drag in the young girls? Anastasie was then eighteen and Virginie was nearly thirteen. What effect would life in a foul-smelling, dismal jail have on them?

With the Austrian venture in mind, she returned to Paris to make the arrangements. The two girls accompanied her. At Brioude they met unexpectedly Adrienne's sister Rosalie and her husband, the Marquis de Grammont, who were on their way to Chavaniac to bid good-bye to Adrienne before she left France. The Grammonts were so poor that they could not travel by post chaise, so they walked all the way from Franche-Comté, a distance of about two hundred miles. They led a horse with baskets slung over its back. Their three little children were carried in the baskets.*

Adrienne did not get away from France until September of that year—which was 1795. After the fall of Robespierre the new government decided to return to their heirs the property of those who had been guillotined. But this decision applied only to property still held by the nation. Estates that had been purchased by individuals could not be returned. The profiteers who had acquired them for trifling sums, and who now were among the rulers of France, would have raised such a prodigious row that the idea of returning the properties had to be dropped.

* The reader may recall that Rosalie sold her jewels to contribute to the fund to save Chavaniac.

(Among the profiteers—pardon this digression, which has as its excuse the topsy-turvy life of the period—was Gabriel Julien Ouvrard. He was as amazing in his way as Beaumarchais, though without the latter's brilliant wit. In 1789, about the time of the beginning of the Revolution, Ouvrard cornered the entire paper supply of France by contracting to buy the product of every paper mill in the kingdom. He was then a youth of nineteen, and so badly educated that he could hardly read and had to spell out the words. During the Revolution, when France was at war with five countries at the same time, he turned his talents to profiteering in guns and munitions. He piled up a large fortune, and throughout all the troubled years he sailed along in great fashion, untouched by disaster. He was one of the founders of the Bank of France. He lived until 1846.)

Some of the Noailles property—most of it, indeed—was not yet sold and was recovered, eventually, in great part. For months Adrienne went around seeing officials, getting papers signed, and doing this and that to straighten out the tangle of red tape that seems inevitable in everything connected with legal procedure, not only in France but everywhere. The quiet little nunlike person showed that she had a better head for business than her husband.

Lafayette, all his life, looked upon money, upon mercantile and financial devices, with contempt. Upon his return to France, after the War for American Independence, he could have organized successfully an enormous enterprise for the acquisition and sale of American lands and securities, and the development of commerce with the United States. It might have been appropriately called *La Compagnie Lafayette pour le Commerce Français et Américain* —a grand, high-sounding title. What a "clean-up" could have been made in selling the stock! Or, if he had not cared to do that, there were financial houses in America that would have given him a partnership without the investment of a dollar on condition that his name might be used. But none of this was in his circle of thought or action.

4

Adrienne's American passport described her as Mme. Motier of Hartford, Connecticut. On September 5, 1795, she and the girls sailed in an American vessel for Hamburg, in Germany. In near-by Altona lived the Comtesse de Tessé, an aunt of Adrienne de Lafayette. In the early days, before the Revolution, Mme. de Tessé had been considered a sort of fool and nuisance by the Noailles family. But in the end she showed more foresight than any of them. Not long after the first crack of the Revolution's thunder and lightning she sold everything she owned—or for which she could find a purchaser—and left for Germany. She had a small estate at Altona and an income from securities that amounted to something.

The mother and her daughters were welcomed by generous and hospitable Mme. de Tessé, but they did not stay long. Adrienne was eager to go, to hurry away to Austria. Mme. de Tessé wanted to keep the girls with her. No, that would not do; Adrienne knew their father would like to have them with him. How cold and unmotherly such an attitude appears to be! But it was not really cold and unmotherly; it was an expression of masochism—her love of martyrdom. She conceived the world as a place of suffering. All must suffer. Did not Christ and his apostles endure torments? The soul is purified, cleansed and strengthened by bodily privations.

That was pure nonsense, of course, but let us not be harsh in our opinion of Adrienne. Nine-tenths—at least—of the human race at that time, and before that time, and now, pass their lives in careers and attitudes which have no sound reason in them. Important and powerful civilizations have been founded on nonsensical theories.

The Lafayette family found that it was rather difficult to get into jail. Austrian officials to whom Adrienne spoke of the matter replied in a tone of *why-my-dear-madam*. They had never before heard of anybody wanting to go voluntarily to prison, but they had heard much of people trying to get out of prison—and among those was the Marquis de Lafayette.

Eventually, in her efforts to get into jail, she managed to obtain an interview with the emperor. He listened, and said that she and her daughters might stay in the prison of Olmütz, but she would not be permitted to come and go. Once there, she had to remain, or if she left—which she was free to do—she could not return.

Count Ferrari, the minister of war, said, in signing the permit
for her to live in the fortress:

I regard it as my duty to ask you once more to reflect upon your
decision. I must warn you that you will be accommodated in very bad
conditions, and that the regulations to which you will have to submit will
have very grave inconveniences for you and your daughters.

5

A chill October day in the year 1795. Lafayette sits in his cell.
For nearly a year he has not spoken to anyone except his jailers,
and they always come in pairs so that they may be witnesses against
each other. He has no books, nothing to read, and is never allowed
to take even a walk, under guard, in the courtyard of the prison.
He lives on repulsive food, served in filthy dishes.

He hears the guards shuffling along the corridor; it is a familiar
sound, and he pays no attention. There is a pause before his door,
a key grates in the lock, the door is thrown open and into his dim
cell come Adrienne and the girls.

It was the most dramatic and bewildering moment of his life.
The first thought that entered his head was that he had become
suddenly insane and was seeing visions. He had believed—in his
ignorance of what was happening in the world—that his family
was safe in England.

The Lafayettes occupied three cells, between which there was
no communication except through the prison corridor. They all met
three times a day at meals in Adrienne's cell; these meetings usually lasted several hours. At eight in the evening the girls were conducted to their cell, where they slept together in a single bed. At
nine o'clock all lights were extinguished.

The rigidity of Lafayette's confinement was relaxed to some
extent after his wife and daughters came. They were permitted to
have writing materials and to correspond with friends and relatives
on condition that the letters, both going and coming, should be in-
spected by the authorities of the prison.

As voluntary prisoners they had to buy their own food and also
pay for the prison service, whatever that may mean. The bills were
outrageous; they could have lived at the best hotel in Vienna at less

expense. At meals knives and forks were prohibited, and they picked up the food with their fingers. Lafayette had only two shirts and no shoes. Anastasie snipped bits of cloth from an old corset and made a pair of slippers for her father. Adrienne spent most of her time writing a biography of her mother—the Duchesse d'Ayen—on the wide margins of Buffon's *Natural History*.

The incarceration of the Lafayette women was soon known everywhere, and it was a public sensation. The French Reign of Terror was over; the hot fervor of the Revolution had subsided into a mild philosophic debate. Even in France the imprisonment of harmless women had begun to take on some of the aspects of moral leprosy. In vain the representatives of the Austrian government explained that Mme. de Lafayette and her daughters were voluntary prisoners; there was no charge against them; they could leave at any time. That was true, but nevertheless the publicity served powerfully to call attention to the plight of Lafayette. "After all, what are you holding him for? What is he accused of, and what are you going to do with him?" said many influential people in Europe and America.

An anonymous writer, who signed his articles with the pseudonym of "Eleuthère," wrote a series of articles for the London *Morning Chronicle* in which the prison life of the Lafayette family was described with great accuracy of detail. These articles were reproduced in Continental newspapers, and in the United States.

Who was "Eleuthère"? His identity was unknown to the public until after Lafayette's release; then it was disclosed that the articles had been written by a Frenchman named Masclet, who had fled to London. At that time he had never seen Lafayette, but later—after Lafayette's release—they became friends. But from whom did he obtain his information? That was a mystery for a long time. Emperor Francis was incensed by the articles when they were brought to his attention. The officials at Olmütz assured him emphatically that the stories did not—and could not—emanate from the imprisoned Lafayettes. At great expense the Austrian secret police endeavored to discover the source of the information, but without success.

It is now known that the facts were furnished by Adrienne de Lafayette. Mme. de Lasteyrie, in her biographical account of her mother's life, wrote that a system of secret correspondence with friends in France was arranged by the rector of the University of Olmütz, "which allowed my mother to write letters that a friend carried across the Austrian frontier, and to get answers that were not subject to the inspection of the keepers."

President Washington was moved to write "a private letter" to the Emperor of Austria on May 15, 1796. He begged the emperor to release Lafayette. The sentiment was sound but the argument was weak. He wrote, in part:

In common with the people of this country I retain a strong and cordial sense of the services rendered to them by the Marquis de Lafayette; and my friendship for him has been constant and sincere. It is natural, therefore, that I should sympathize with him and his family in their misfortunes, and endeavor to mitigate the calamities which they experience; among which his confinement is not the least distressing. . . . Permit me only to submit to your Majesty's consideration, whether his long imprisonment and the confiscation of his estate—and the indigence and dispersion of his family —and the painful anxieties incident to all these circumstances, do not form an assemblage of sufferings which recommend him to the mediation of humanity? Allow me, Sir, on this occasion to be its organ, and to entreat that he may be permitted to come to this country on such conditions and under such restrictions as your Majesty may think it expedient to prescribe.

What the Emperor Francis thought of Lafayette's services in helping the American colonies win their independence would hardly be printable in a book for general circulation. No reply—no acknowledgment—was made to Washington's courteous letter. Probably the emperor was offended by it. Suppose the governor of a state got a letter, written in impeccably courteous terms, saying, "Honorable Governor, will you please let Tommie Jones out of jail? He assisted us in our burglaries and we love him."

Be not so haughty, Emperor Francis; other offensive letters are coming, but not from George Washington. They will be delivered by messengers of steel and in them there will be not even a pretense of courtesy. They will not beg but demand, and with them will come the thunder of guns. You will look upon the frightened rabble of your Austrian troops and the huddled conferences of despairing generals who can hardly move because of the weight of medals pinned on their chests. Napoleon Bonaparte is on his way.

6

By midsummer of 1797 Bonaparte and the French army were within three days' march of Vienna. They had come through northern Italy and were in possession of the Italian provinces of Austria. The emperor asked for a truce, a parley. The truce dragged on wearily, while Napoleon fumed. The Austrians suggested a congress of European powers to decide who was right or wrong. In reply Napoleon said, in substance, "There will be no congress. I'll make all the decisions, and if that doesn't suit you suppose you drive us out of Austria. Just go ahead and drive us out and then you will have it all your own way."

That was, of course, the speech of a bully. Napoleon was a bully, but the Emperor Francis was also one. Austria had to submit.

During the suspension of hostilities "Citizen-General" Bonaparte received a letter from the Directory in Paris, signed by Lazare Carnot, executive president. It said succinctly:

With reference to the new demands addressed to the Directory, Citizen General, concerning the Olmütz prisoners, the Directory reminds you of the desire it has expressed to you of seeing an end of their captivity. It does not doubt that you will share its interest in their misfortune.

Napoleon did not greet this communication with enthusiastic applause. At the bottom of his nature there was only one aim; and that was, to push himself ahead. It was entirely possible—even probable—that Lafayette, once again in France, might become the national hero. Napoleon had reserved that role for himself.

Yet, on the other hand, it would surely be a feather in his cap if he could point with pride to a stern demand which set Lafayette free. The problem was therefore to get Lafayette out of prison and also to keep him out of France.

After he had made it known that he would not consent to peace between the two countries without the release of Lafayette he sent General Clarke to Vienna with secret instructions. The import of them was that Napoleon would be pleased if the emperor freed Lafayette on condition that he was not to return to France.

The Austrian government had lost all interest in Lafayette; it had other troubles. The emperor would have been glad enough to free him—just to get rid of him—without any proviso except his perpetual exclusion from Austria.

The difficulty concerning the disposition of Lafayette was met rather neatly, though all concerned were quite aware that they were actors in a comedy. Louis Romeuf—a former aide-de-camp of Lafayette, but then in the service of Bonaparte—was sent, with the approval of the Austrian authorities, to Hamburg with instructions to arrange with the American consul for Lafayette's passage to America.

Romeuf departed for Hamburg and returned with what purported to be a deportation order, approved by the American consul. But the name signed to the papers was that of John Parish, who was a *former* consul, not then in office and without any authority. Mr. Parish agreed to take charge of Lafayette and expedite his departure.*

At that time Lafayette had no intention of emigrating to America. It is true that our land of freedom was always in the back of his mind as a place of permanent residence eventually; but he had little money and no substantial income; he was in debt; and Adrienne was too ill to stand an ocean voyage. Besides these obstacles, he was convinced that he still had a career in Europe.

Nevertheless, both the Citizen-General Bonaparte and the Emperor Francis had saved their faces excellently. Bonaparte had demanded freedom for Lafayette—a phrase which would sound well in France. The emperor made it clear that he had not agreed to the demand—but had freed the prisoners of Olmütz as a gracious gesture to mark the restoration of peace between the two great nations; and in Austria that would appear as an exhibition of generosity. Moreover, Europe was to be rid of the disturbing marquis. To give color to that pretense, a man who had once been an American consul agreed to assume responsibility for the prisoner and send him on his way.

The prison doors opened on September 19, 1797. The Lafayette family was to be escorted to Hamburg—as prisoners of Austria. Lafayette had been in prison for more than five years, and his wife and daughters for nearly two years.

* In all accounts of these events which I have seen in books John Parish is set down unequivocally as the consul at Hamburg. Replying to an inquiry, the State Department informs me that John Parish was dismissed from office in 1796.

CHAPTER XXIX

LAFAYETTE AND NAPOLEON

I

THE DISTANCE from Olmütz to Hamburg is about four hundred miles. The Lafayette family took fifteen days to make the trip. Adrienne was seriously ill, and they had to travel slowly. Her arms and legs were swollen and there were open sores on her body. The prison physician at Olmütz called it scurvy, but the record goes on to say that he "was baffled."

If it was nothing but a case of scurvy, why was he baffled? Of all the serious diseases that afflict mankind scurvy is the most readily curable. It responds quickly to a diet of fresh vegetables and lemon juice—or to lemon juice alone—and this remedy was well known at that time. From the vague description of her symptoms it appears that the scurvy was complicated by some other ailment, which may have been rheumatism or gout.

Virginie says in the biography of her mother that the prison doctor could not speak French, "but he expressed his anxiety to my father in Latin. She had a violent eruption, first on her arms that swelled so much that she could not use them nor even lift them; then on her legs; and fever all the time. This condition lasted for eleven months, from October, 1796, to September, 1797."

Adrienne never wholly recovered. After her experience at Olmütz she was an invalid for life, though she was able to get about and attend to her duties. Now and then there were recurring spells of the prison illness. One of them was the cause of her death in 1807.

Lafayette had suffered in health too, and had lost some of his buoyant illusions. But he would soon recover. Chinard, in an admirable and concise summing up of his character, says: "There was in him a naïveté, a child-like resiliency, a faith and unconquerable hope which always enabled him to bear and even forget the worst miseries."*

*Chinard, *Letters of Lafayette and Jefferson*, p. 195.

The health of the two young girls does not seem to have been affected by their confinement in prison. They possessed the freshness, the resiliency, of youth. To them Olmütz was just another experience; something to remember and talk about. Life was a series of incidents—some pleasant, some unpleasant—but what of it? It was like going to a county fair; one does not expect to be pleased all the time, but everything one sees is a new discovery. They had not yet learned of the brooding meanness and evil which move beneath the surface of life.

So, traveling with slow pace through Prussia, were those four people. Lafayette, bitter in thought but hopeful of another day when he would appear on a white horse amid the applauding crowds of Paris; Adrienne, sick and pious; and their two daughters, young, healthy and eager, looking forward to new experience.

In 1795 Prussia had made peace with France, and there was no great love among the Prussians for the Austrian Empire. Friendly crowds greeted Lafayette everywhere, to his great surprise—and encouragement. He was still a prisoner of the Austrians. An escort, responsible for him and his family, rode beside the carriage from Olmütz to Hamburg, where he was turned over to the American consul. The fiction that he was to depart for America at once was duly observed, but by that time all those concerned knew that he did not intend to leave Europe.

Now more trouble.

A reception had been arranged at Hamburg for Lafayette by Mr. Parish and the ubiquitous Gouverneur Morris, who was there at the time. Not only that; they had provided lodgings for the Lafayette family. But Lafayette, instead of coming across the ferry at once, went aboard an American ship in the harbor on the captain's invitation. He had dinner on the ship. Late in the afternoon he and his fellow prisoners—Alexandre de Lameth, La Tour-Maubourg and Bureaux de Pusy—who had also been confined at Olmütz, came ashore in one of the ship's boats. The irascible Morris writes:

The prisoners, instead of coming to town on the ferryboat, in which case they could have arrived between nine and ten o'clock in the morning, embarked on board an American ship, dined on the ship, and so wasted their time and everybody else's.

Furthermore, Lafayette disregarded the lodgings provided for his family and went to an inn where, as Morris says, he spent fifty

guineas in two days. In that comment one hears the voice of a creditor. Fifty guineas—about two hundred and sixty dollars—does
seem to be a prodigious sum for the expenses of a family of four
in a two-day stay at an eighteenth century inn. But let us not forget that Lafayette was an extravagant spender who cared nothing
for money and never appeared to understand its value. Numbers of
people came to welcome him and—no doubt—he entertained them
in sumptuous fashion.

The Austrian minister made a formal transfer of the custody
of Lafayette to the American consul, who was probably the real
official on this occasion, with Mr. Parish hovering around. During
these proceedings he took occasion to remind the consul that Lafayette had been released on the understanding that he was to leave
Germany within twelve days. However, to keep the record straight,
it may be worth while to say here that Lafayette himself had made
no such agreement. The Austrian minister also declared that the
prisoner had not been released on the demand of France, but because of the friendship of the Austrian Empire for the United States.
That statement was wholly untrue, yet one may perceive its moti-
vation. The Austrian Empire was so thoroughly saturated with pride
that, to preserve its self-respect, it could not admit that it had
yielded to any kind of demand.

Lafayette went to pay his respects to the French minister. His
name was Reinhardt, or in formal fashion, Citizen Reinhardt. There
was in France a legal inhibition against the use of the terms *monsieur*
and *madame*. All men, of whatever rank, were called *citoyen* and the
women were known as *citoyenne*. Citizen Reinhardt, very pleasant
and courteous, kept Lafayette in conversation for a long time. What
did Citizen Lafayette think of the state of affairs in France? What
did Citizen Lafayette think of the Directory—the committee of five
who possessed dictatorial powers? Citizen Lafayette's opinion was
decidedly adverse. If he had flattered the Directory he would, in all
probability, have been invited to return to France.

Lafayette's views were reported to the Directory by Citizen
Reinhardt. The all-powerful Directors were so offended that they
determined definitely to keep Lafayette out of France; moreover,
they sold his estates in Brittany at auction, and put the procee
in the national treasury, or—at any rate—as much of the proceed

CHATEAU OF LA GRANGE, NEAR PARIS

The home of Lafayette from 1799 until his death in 1834.

FACSIMILE OF LETTER FROM LAFAYETTE
TO FRANCIS KINLOCH HUGER, SEPTEMBER 7, 1824

Written during Lafayette's last visit to America.

as remained after the Directors had taken out their pickings. After that had been done Lafayette did not own a foot of ground.

Adrienne had some possessions. Under the law, passed after the fall of Robespierre, which returned the property of guillotined nobles to their heirs, Adrienne had managed to regain her share of the Noailles belongings. The property was fairly extensive, but little income came from it.

The hovering Austrian and German officials did not know exactly what to do when Lafayette refused to leave for America. He agreed eventually to go to Wittmold, the country estate of Adrienne's aunt, the Comtesse de Tessé, which was then in Danish territory. That was satisfactory to all of them.

2

The home of the eccentric countess was full of people, of émigré nobles. Many of them lived in the neighborhood and came to the house every day. Others lived in the house. Some in the house, others in other houses. But all were at home, in a way of speaking, in the house of the Comtesse de Tessé. There they talked all day and evening. French speech ran in swirls and eddies through the rooms. Discussions of all kinds, but chiefly discussions about the state of the world, of France in particular, and even more in particular of those persons who resided in, at or near Wittmold. The conversations were philosophic, though the men and women of that place were not philosophers and had no intention of becoming philosophers. They talked in philosophic terms because the French mind, like that of the ancient Greeks, flows in philosophic patterns. That is what makes the French such deadly realists. If you carry any kind of sweeping argument concerning the social structure to its final, pinpoint conclusion—and have the power to enforce it— you are bound to do an immense amount of harm to a lot of people.

But Mme. la Comtesse de Tessé did no harm to anyone nor did she wish to harm anyone. She spent her time on her farms, planting and growing. She had more than a hundred cows, and she sold the milk, the butter, the cheese. There were many fruit trees, and many acres planted in wheat, flax and vegetables. Early and late she was up and doing among her plow hands, her milkers, her butter churners, her sewing maids.

But she, too, had much to say in terms of philosophy. She was a libertarian, an atheist (or a deist), a scorner of Biblical stories, a believer in the great rationalists, a disbeliever in the ancient French traditions. She disagreed with nearly everyone. It did not matter; most of the people who came to her house did not take her seriously and let her rattle along.

Lafayette liked her and took her seriously, and she liked him. They talked by the hour about freedom, equality and the rights of man.

Among the guests was Mme. de Montagu, who was one of Adrienne's sisters. She could not endure her brother-in-law's ideas. She would often leave the room when he came in. To Mme. de Grammont, another sister, she wrote:

Gilbert is every bit as good, every bit as simple in his manners, every bit as affectionate in his caresses, every bit as gentle in dispute as you knew him. . . . I avoid, as much as possible, discussing directly with him anything that touches the Revolution, the things that he defends as well as those he condemns. I am afraid of exploding. . . . I see with pleasure that those about me approve my reserve. . . . Poor Gilbert! God preserve him from ever being again on the scene!

In November—this was about a month after their arrival at Wittmold—the Lafayettes rented a small château in the neighborhood. The Latour-Maubourgs went to live with them.

Lafayette spent much time in writing letters, in catching up with the delayed correspondence of five years. To Citizen-General Bonaparte he wrote that the "prisoners of Olmütz" thanked him for their liberation, and added that they had "the most lively interest in the illustrious general to whom we are still more attached for the services that he has rendered to the cause of liberty and to our country than for the personal obligations that we glorify ourselves in owing him, and that the most intense gratitude has engraved on our hearts."

At that moment he appears to have been a Bonapartist. The attraction did not last long.

There were letters to Francis Huger, to Talleyrand, to Masclet, to Washington, to Jefferson, to Charles James Fox, and to many others.

To Mme. de Simiane he wrote that his political career was

over. "I shall be full of life for my friends, and for the public a sort of portrait in a museum or a book in a library." Sad farewell to the world, but he really did not mean it. He was expressing a mood. Continuing, he wrote: "But, as nearly all hearts are too narrow, too fearsome, too apathetic, for the complete development of truth, of liberty and justice, my reason tells me that there will be nothing for me to do, and that even my reputation is interested in terminating my political life. . . ."

During the winter—in February, 1798—his son George returned from America in company with his faithful tutor. George was a good-looking youth of nineteen with American speech on his tongue. He had had a wonderful time, had stayed awhile at Mount Vernon with his renowned godfather, had seen something of America, and had picked up a few scraps of learning in Boston. Like the sons of most men of great celebrity, he was destined to be overshadowed, all his life, by his father's distinction. This law of Fate— if it really is a law of Fate—is hard on the sons, but it is better for the human race. Otherwise we might develop a special breed of demigods, which would lead to a rather unpleasant state of affairs all around. Those who met George Washington Lafayette soon realized that he was not likely to create an unpleasant state of affairs for the human race.

George landed at Havre on his return from America and went to Paris before going home to his parents. While in Paris he had called on General Bonaparte to pay his respects. The rising military genius was not at home, but Josephine was. She received young Lafayette cordially, and said, "Your father and my husband must make common cause."

Lafayette began to write his *Mémoires* during that winter of 1797-98. He was not a good writer—he had never been trained to write, and his literary instinct was weak—so his *Mémoires* cannot be classed as a great autobiography. He worked on his notes for years and years, neglecting the job for long periods at a stretch, then coming back to it. Finally the work was published in six volumes. The books are tiresome, full of redundancies and repetitions —also startling inaccuracies—and are characterized generally by poverty of style.

Before this prodigious literary effort was begun he wrote three or four documents or pamphlets which were published. One of them

—Souvenirs en Sortant de Prison—is a general survey of the French
Revolution. It is an argument for a constitutional monarchy, in part.
He pays warm tribute to Louis XVI and condemns his execution.
Another one—*La Démocratie Royale*—is a brief for his own con-
duct during the revolutionary period.

Lafayette was only forty, an early age for the writing of
memoirs. Did he really believe that his career was over? Hardly.
His purpose in writing seems to have been financial; he wanted
desperately to make some money.

3

The young Comte de Latour-Maubourg fell in love with Anastasie de Lafayette, and she with him. No wonder. They were both
attractive young people, were living in the same house, and Anastasie—then nearly twenty-one—had not met an eligible young man
in several years. There was nothing whatever to be said against
Charles de Latour-Maubourg except that he was practically penniless. Anastasie was no better off. Lafayette gave his consent and so
did Adrienne. The wedding took place on May 9, 1798. Adrienne
had to be carried to the chapel on a sofa. There had been a return
of the Olmütz malady and she was unable to walk. Anastasie's
trousseau was supplied by generous Mme. de Tessé.*

In the summer of that year Adrienne, partly recovered from
her illness, went to Paris with the idea of trying to induce the Directory to permit the return of her husband to France, and also to
look after the confused family finances. Accompanying her were
Charles (her son-in-law), Anastasie and Virginie. George remained
at Wittmold with his father. On the journey some doubt arose as
to the status of Charles. He was an émigré and they concluded
that he would probably be refused permission to enter France. So
Charles and Anastasie stopped at Utrecht in Holland while Mme.
de Lafayette and her youngest daughter proceeded to Paris. There
she hoped to obtain permission for the entire family to return to
France.

During the preceding months Lafayette had worked fitfully on

* The Lafayette family tree, for which I am under obligations to René de Chambrun, shows that the Comte and Comtesse de Latour-Maubourg had one child—a
daughter—who married M. de Perron de Saint-Martin. They have only a few descendants now living.

his *Mémoires*. It was in that period that the conception of a grand literary, political, historical production came into his mind. This was to be nothing less than a description of the political and legal structure of every country of Europe. These various systems were to be compared, each with all the others. But that is not all. The work was to have a vertical as well as a horizontal dimension. In the light of history he intended to show how these various social systems had evolved in the course of centuries.

The accomplishment of such a project would have required the services of a historian of the capacity and vision of Gibbon, and it would have taken his time for fifteen years at least.

Adrienne was too poor to live in comfort in Paris, so she took lodgings with Mme. Beauchet, her former maid, in a mean quarter of the town. She went about on foot—dragging herself wearily along the street and up innumerable stairs.

She called on Barras, then at the head of the Directory, and many other officials. Lafayette's petition to be allowed to return to France was courteously but firmly disapproved. The Directory informed madame—the Citoyenne Lafayette—that "the time had not yet come for consideration of the case." She was also informed that she might come and go on her passport, as she pleased. And the Noailles property was there, intact.

Lafayette wrote to her frequently. Letters of love and tenderness—and advice. In the meantime he had given up the Danish house and had moved to the village of Vianen, near Utrecht in Holland. Mme. de Tessé and Mme. de Montagu visited him there to see how he was getting on. They were astounded at his poverty. No one in the house had enough to eat, and Mme. de Montagu wrote that they all went to bed hungry every night.

To Adrienne in her poor lodgings in Paris came a bulky letter from her husband. He had enclosed a plan, or synopsis, of the vast literary undertaking that he had in mind. Would she please go around to publishers and show it to them? Also would she find "a good writer and patriot" and send him to Utrecht? He needed a writer to do the actual work. In short, he wanted a publisher engaged to bring out a book of which not a word was yet written and, also, he wanted a ghost writer.

Adrienne, slow in resentment and capable of quiet and suffering endurance, became momentarily a spitfire. She wrote him a scorching letter that told him plainly what was what. He was astonished, and quite taken aback. The next post to Paris carried his humble apologies. Then he laid aside his plan for the greatest book of the century, and it remains to this day in the blissful realm of unborn children.

Mme. de Lafayette left Paris and went to Utrecht to rejoin her husband and children in February, 1799. He was then planning to go to America, and take his family with him. He wrote Alexander Hamilton and George Washington of his intention. Their replies were not reassuring.

France and the United States were in the midst of a hot-tempered quarrel. Lafayette's friends in America believed that if he and his family arrived before the dispute was settled the event would be misinterpreted by both the French and the Americans. Washington wrote that he would welcome Lafayette "with open arms . . . when harmony is re-established between this country and France." Hamilton's letter was in the same tone. Lafayette's idea of establishing a new home in the United States was promptly abandoned.

The estate of Adrienne's mother was awaiting a fair and amicable division among the heirs. Adrienne's two sisters, Pauline de Montagu and Rosalie de Grammont, journeyed to Holland, and there—in the small house of the Lafayettes at Vianen—there was a family conference. But it was more than that; it was a joyous family reunion which ran on for days despite the cold house and the skimpy meals.

Adrienne's portion of the inheritance was the château of La Grange, its fields and woods. La Grange is about forty miles east of Paris in the department of Seine-et-Marne. Around the château were eight hundred acres of good farming land. The property was valued at more than half a million livres. If properly cultivated the estate could be made to yield a good income; that is to say, it would be an excellent income for most people, but not so much for anyone with Lafayette's highly developed habit of spending.

But he was still excluded from France. To manage the estate intelligently he would have to be on the ground. Yet, even if he were permitted to return, neither he nor his wife had the capital needed to purchase farming equipment or even to put the place in order. That, however, might be managed by borrowing.

Adrienne returned to Paris with a renewed hope of persuading the government to lift the ban of exclusion. The weary year dragged on. At Vianen Lafayette played interminable games of chess with a retired Dutch general, studied the war maps, wrote letters by the hundred, made notes for his *Mémoires,* and read many books on the art and mystery of agriculture. He hoped to be a gentleman farmer; yet, in the back of his mind, thoughts of a new political career simmered and bubbled.

Napoleon—still known as Citizen-General Bonaparte—had returned from his campaign in Egypt and was an acknowledged and greatly admired national hero. Everyone of intelligence knew that he was the coming man, that the supreme power would either drift into his hands or be seized by him.

Lafayette was advised, in an urgent letter from Adrienne, to write to the Citizen-General and give the ladder-climber his best wishes. To Bonaparte he wrote at once. He said, in part, "I rejoice in all my obligations to you, Citizen-General, and in the happy conviction that to cherish your glory and to wish for your success, is a civic duty as well as an act of attachment and gratitude."

It was a gracious letter. Napoleon never acknowledged it. He considered Lafayette a back number, a has-been hero who had missed his great opportunity in that he had not seized the uncertain revolutionary government when he had the power to do it. To the Napoleonic mind such a failure was nothing less than stupid. In exile at St. Helena Napoleon characterized Lafayette as a "simpleton"—which he certainly was not. It would have been more in line with truth for him to have said that Lafayette was an idealist. But Napoleon could not understand idealists; to him they were incomprehensible. Nevertheless, he did not want Lafayette to return to France. Simpleton as he was, he might cause a lot of trouble.*

On the 18th Brumaire (November 9, 1799) he had himself made First Consul and virtual dictator of the French nation. He took over the supreme power from the weak and venal Directory

---

* According to Las Cases, Napoleon said (*Mémorial de Sainte-Hélène.* Paris, 1823. 8 vols. Vol. IV, p. 203):

"Lafayette était encore un autre niais; il n'était nullement taillé pour le haut rôle qu'il avait voulu jouer. Sa bonhomie politique devait le rendre constamment dupe des hommes et des choses."

He said further: "Je n'ai point attaqué les sentiments ni les intentions de M. de Lafayette; je ne me suis plaint que de ses funestes resultats."

with the ease of an adult taking a toy out of the hands of a baby. The government he set up was called a republic, but it was a mere farce. The Legislative assembly had no more to say in essential matters than the Italian parliament under Mussolini.

Meantime, Lafayette had been considering the idea of returning to France without permission. He was encouraged in this course by his French correspondents and by Adrienne. Within a week after he had learned of Napoleon's coup d'état he entered France with a false passport, and went straight to Paris. As soon as he got there he wrote a letter to the First Consul in which he said:

I have thought that the continuance of my proscription would be convenient neither to the government nor to myself; today I arrive at Paris.

Before departing for the country where I shall go to join my family, before even seeing my friends, I cannot delay, for an instant, this opportunity to address myself to you; not that I doubted that I should be in my place whenever the republic will be founded on a worthy foundation, but because my duties and my feelings urged me to express to you my gratitude.*

Bonaparte was furious; he declared that he would expel Lafayette, that he would throw him into prison; that he would confiscate his property. Talleyrand was at that time employed, in high official position, as Bonaparte's chief rascal. He summoned Lafayette and urged him to return at once to Holland.

Never, said Lafayette; let them put me in prison; I am used to prisons. Let them expel me. What will the French people say? I am a Frenchman, and here I intend to remain in my own country.

Then he read to Talleyrand a paragraph from the speech Napoleon made on assuming power. On that occasion—quite recent—the First Consul had said:

We desire a republic founded upon true liberty; upon civil liberty and upon national representation; we shall have it, I swear it. I swear also in my own name and in those of my companions in arms.

That is precisely what Lafayette had advocated for fifteen years. Napoleon gave in. He was not, in those early days, very sure of himself. Like an elephant crossing a bridge, he tested every plank before he put his weight on it. As a matter of public policy it would not be subtle or wise to send to prison one of the foremost re-

* *Mémoires de ma Main,* Vol. V, p. 154.

publicans of the French Revolution, in view of Napoleon's own speech about republics, civil liberty, and national representation. Distressed and visibly agitated, Adrienne called on Napoleon. He wore the courteous manner which he could put on just as an actor dons a wig and a mustache. The spasm of red anger, and stuttering, and smashing vases on the floor, had passed. The tantrums were over and a smooth sagacity wove in and out through his words. He told Adrienne that many of his doings were dictated as a matter of statesmanship which she might not understand, but her husband would grasp his meaning. It was all right; they could stay in France, but please "avoid all demonstrations. I rely on his patriotism."

The Lafayettes were on their way to La Grange in a few days. They were to remain there for years; until the end of their lives.

4

The great house stood cold and stark against the wintry sky. It was seven hundred years old. Generations of men and women had lived within its thick stone walls. The old house, still and quiet, had watched them come and go.

When the Lafayette family arrived in 1799 the château was appalling in its lonesome, weed-grown desolation. But Lafayette's energy soon changed all that. On borrowed money and long-term credit he cleaned up the place and began to develop the farms according to the best methods set forth in the agricultural treatises. He turned out to be a better farmer than anyone expected him to be.

In a few years he possessed a large flock of merino sheep. Their wool became famous throughout France on account of its superior quality. Only five hundred acres were farmed; the rest of the estate was devoted to wood and meadow land. He planted apple and pear trees. They grew wondrously. He did not sell the fruit but made cider from it, and his cider was in great demand in that part of the country. Wheat and potatoes were also profitable crops. He put up a model dairy farm on the estate and sold its products.

But La Grange, as an agricultural industry, was never very profitable. Lafayette had borrowed so much money to improve the estate that the interest on the loans absorbed most of the income. In 1802 his net income from the property was only 7,500 francs.

The expenses of the château were large. All his family resided there, and there were many visitors who enjoyed his hospitality.

The news of Washington's death reached France early in the year 1800. A memorial ceremony, under the auspices of the French government, was held at the Invalides in Paris. All the great dignitaries were there, from Napoleon down. Lafayette did not go; he had not received an invitation. The fact that he was Washington's dearest friend and "adopted son" was simply ignored, no doubt at Napoleon's suggestion. He might have captured the occasion—so the First Consul thought—and that would have been embarrassing.

The ceremony was a solemn farce. Lafayette's name was not mentioned by the orator of the day, nor by anyone else. George Washington Lafayette, who was in the audience, told his father that even Washington was mentioned only casually and briefly. The ceremony was a glorification of Napoleon. Many battleflags, taken from the Turks in Egypt, were unfurled. The audience was made to understand that although Washington was all right in his way, a small man—of limited mind—doing his best, Napoleon Bonaparte was the real savior of humanity—a great lawgiver, a lover of liberty, a man of kindly heart, a general of superexcellence, another Julius Caesar (but better than Caesar), a statesman of vision, a born leader of men and nations.

After the foot-kissing of Napoleon was over, the memorial ceremony in honor of Washington was adjourned with a benediction.

In traits of character Lafayette and Napoleon were not so remote from one another as they appear to have been. Both of them made a god of Popularity, which is a changeable and capricious god. Napoleon knew how to organize popularity, to step on its head and rise into the higher levels. Lafayette was not an organizer. Both Napoleon and Lafayette had vast ambitions, but Lafayette was limited in his ambitious aspirations by ideals and principles. Napoleon was not burdened with such delicate social conceptions. All he wanted to do was to make a place of great power for himself. Lafayette also desired to be a conspicuous and powerful man—but only with consent of the people, and only in a position which would aid in developing the happiness of mankind. Napoleon eventually lifted himself so high in the air, on the heads and bodies of other men, that he got into the stratosphere and exploded like a rubber ball in a vacuum.

Lafayette had never seen Napoleon until the latter returned to Paris, in 1801, from his victory of Marengo. He called on the great soldier and they chatted pleasantly for half an hour without saying anything worth while. It was merely a visit of courtesy. Later on, Lafayette met Napoleon's brother Joseph accidentally. Talleyrand came out of his cabinet—a French word for office—with Joseph Bonaparte. Lafayette was in the waitingroom. Talleyrand introduced them. Lafayette liked Joseph, and Joseph liked him. They became friends.

Not long afterward Lafayette was invited by Joseph to a weekend at his country place. He found there Napoleon and all the Bonaparte family, and he had several long talks with the Man of Destiny. The invitation to Lafayette may have been arranged for the express purpose of enlisting his support, but of this there is no evidence. It sounds like one of Napoleon's subtleties. The ideas of Napoleon and Lafayette did not coincide, though these conflicting opinions were expressed without rancor. Naturally, Napoleon thought Lafayette wanted something; he could not conceive of a person who did not want a favor of some kind. It happened that Lafayette did want a small favor. Would the First Consul have stricken from the list of proscribed émigrés the names of the Comte and Comtesse de Tessé, so they could return to France? Granted. Why, of course; anything else? No, nothing else, thank you.

5

Thereafter, for some time, Lafayette was besieged by Napoleon's kindly attentions. He proposed to send Lafayette to the United States as minister representing the French government. This post was declined, although it would seem, on first consideration, to have been an ideal position for Lafayette. He turned down the offer without giving any reason, but the true reason may be readily divined. In such a diplomatic post he would have been expected to accept Napoleon's policy, and he was not prepared to do that. He distrusted Napoleon and all his works.

French senators, under the Consulate, were appointed by the chief executive. Talleyrand was instructed by the First Consul to offer a seat in the Senate to Lafayette. That peace offering was also politely refused.

Joseph Bonaparte tried to arrange a marriage between his brother Lucien and Virginie de Lafayette. Nothing came of that.

Mathieu Dumas, one of Lafayette's old friends—then in Napoleon's service—was sent to La Grange to find out the cause of Lafayette's attitude. He told Dumas that he did not care for any appointment whatever; that he wanted to be considered as living in retirement. "If Bonaparte had been willing to serve the cause of liberty, I should have been devoted to him," he said. "But I can neither approve an arbitrary government, nor associate myself with it." These comments were duly reported to the First Consul.

Nevertheless, they were on friendly terms for some time thereafter. At Lafayette's request Napoleon placed him on the retired list of the army with a pension of six thousand francs a year. Josephine was holding a sort of court at the Tuileries in an effort to attract the old Nobility and turn them into Bonapartists. It was a rather pathetic affair; the surviving aristocrats of the Faubourg Saint-Germain paid no attention to it. But Lafayette attended her *soirées*, had a very good time, and was much admired by the generals and their wives. George Lafayette was given a commission in the army.

The conversations with Napoleon came to an end in 1803. For the next twelve years Lafayette played the part of country gentleman. He seldom went to Paris. At La Grange he read of the Napoleonic victories, the great battles, the conquest of nations. His soldierly instinct must have been stirred, but he made no public comment on national affairs.

His son George resigned from the army in disgust. Despite his heroism in Italy, he was never promoted. Lafayette suspected then —and we know now—that orders had come from Napoleon that Lafayette's son was not to be advanced in rank.

A new generation had grown up since the days of Robespierre and the Terror. They were dazzled by Napoleon—a conqueror who was taking Europe to pieces and putting it together again. To millions of them Lafayette was a dim point in consciousness, recollected with the difficulty that one has in trying to recall a date in history. And there were other millions who had never heard of him.

CHAPTER XXX

DEATH OF ADRIENNE

I

LAFAYETTE was in retirement, but he was not a hermit. There were house guests at La Grange every week, a profusion of food and wine, and long discussions of the state of the nation. Some of the guests were Americans; Englishmen, too, after the treaty of Amiens in 1803, when Great Britain was for a while in a sort of cat-and-dog peace with France. Then there was the correspondence. It took hours of Lafayette's time every day, writing to people with whom he was on terms of confidence.

The management of his farms occupied his forenoons. Wearing a wide-brimmed hat, he rode around his fields and orchards, giving directions here and there. The estate was earning money, but Lafayette was also spending money, and the money-spending amounted to a good deal more every year than the money-earning. For fifteen years he lived in a fever of anxiety over his financial affairs.

The whole family lived at La Grange; the house was large, and there was plenty of room. In June, 1802, George Washington Lafayette—then twenty-three years of age—married Emilie de Tracy, who was a daughter of one of Lafayette's old friends. After the wedding the Lafayettes and Tracys journeyed to faraway Chavaniac. Aunt Louise Charlotte, a vivacious lady of more than eighty, was still living there. For days the ancient château was noisy with laughter, music and dancing. Mme. de Montagu appeared, coming from afar. With her, among others, came the Marquis de Lasteyrie, a prepossessing young man. He and Virginie fell in love instantly, and they were married the next year—on April 20, 1803.*

The marriage was delayed for some time on account of a serious accident that happened to Virginie's father on February 23,

* The Marquis de Lasteyrie and his wife—Virginie de Lafayette—have numerous descendants now living in France. René de Chambrun, whom I have already mentioned, is one of them. M. de Chambrun's mother is Clara Longworth, of Cincinnati, a sister of Nicholas Longworth, who died a few years ago after having served for many years in Congress. Mme. de Chambrun is the author of a scholarly book on Shakespeare.

385

1803. On that day Lafayette slipped on the steps as he was leaving the Ministry of Marine and broke the bone of his left thigh. He was forty days in bed. The surgeons attempted to hold the broken femur in place by means of a newly invented brace. The device was a failure, and when Lafayette finally got on his feet he was a lame man. For the rest of his life he limped about on a cane.

In 1803 the United States acquired the vast Louisiana Territory by purchase from Napoleon. Thomas Jefferson was then the American president. Soon after the United States took possession of the Territory Jefferson wrote to Lafayette: "I sincerely wish you were here, that we might avail ourselves of your service as governor of Louisiana, where the seat of the government, New Orleans, is among the most interesting spots of our country, and constitutes the most important charge we can confer. I believe too you would have found it a pleasant residence, but the circumstances of the country require that officer to be on the spot, and to enter instantly in his charge."

What you have just read is the sole basis for the legend that Lafayette was offered the governorship of the newly acquired territory and declined it. Jefferson did not make an offer; he merely expressed a wish.

At the close of the American Revolution the Continental Congress made a provision for gifts of public lands to officers and soldiers. Lafayette was then a man of wealth, and he did not make an application for land. The time limit expired, and the subject was closed. Jefferson, upon learning of Lafayette's financial troubles after his release from the Austrian captivity, had a bill passed by Congress which conferred upon the marquis 11,520 acres—or eighteen square miles of land—in the public domain north of the Ohio. This was in March, 1803.

Shortly afterward Jefferson had the grant transferred to Louisiana, where land was more valuable. He directed the agents of the government to locate Lafayette's tract close to the city of New Orleans.

Lafayette was very grateful, and so expressed himself in a letter to President Jefferson. But the land which had been selected was the controversial subject of so many counterclaims, conflicting titles and general confusion that he did not obtain possession of it for seven years. I shall return to this topic farther on.

2

The years spent at La Grange were the most peaceful, and the happiest, in Adrienne's life, since her childhood, despite her slowly declining health.

Among the numerous guests at the château was Fanny Burney, who stayed there for a while in 1803 with her husband, Comte d'Arblay, at one time an officer on Lafayette's staff. The lady was —as everyone knows—as garrulous in print as a modern newspaper columnist. She had an observing eye and a quick perception of personality and characteristic incidents.

Of Adrienne's manners Miss Burney wrote that they were "pleasing and amiable"; that her eyes were "singularly expressive"; and that her mind was "religiously humble." She said that General Lafayette "displayed on every occasion the tenderest gratitude to his wife, who had followed him to captivity, and to whom, *from that period*, he became by universal account far more warmly and *exclusively* attached than he had *ever been formerly;* though her virtues and conduct had always been objects to him of respect and esteem."

The italicized words are enlightening. The impetuous young man had grown up into what we Americans call a "home body." He had acquired sedateness. No longer did he remain away for days at a time without giving any account of where he had been. Through suffering and disillusionment he had learned to esteem the ordinary virtues which, in his earlier years, he had accepted as a matter of course.

At La Grange Lafayette rose early and went to bed early. He spent hours every day and evening in his study, making notes, writing letters and reading. Without plan or system was his reading, and it did him very little good. In his library one wall of the room was covered by books on the American Revolution and those who had taken part in it.

Adrienne de Lafayette died on Christmas Eve, 1807. It was the twenty-eighth birthday of her son George. Adrienne was forty-eight.

I do not know, except in a general way, the nature of her fatal illness. It has been described as "malignant blood poisoning" and also as a return of "her old illness contracted at Olmütz." She had scurvy at Olmütz, according to the medical authorities, but scurvy does not last long among patients who have vegetable and fruit juices in their diet. It is not a farmer's disease, and Mme. de Lafayette had lived on a farm for years. Why malignant blood poisoning? That, too, is a mystery. Physicians to whom I have submitted all the reported facts say that the symptoms, as outlined, are too sketchy for a diagnosis. We know, however, that Adrienne had a fever, that she could not walk, and that open sores appeared all over her body. During the last days she was delirious most of the time, with lucid intervals.

The disease, whatever it was, moved slowly. She was desperately ill long before the end. Lafayette and his son George had gone to Chavaniac in the summer of 1807. Mme. de Tessé, upon learning that her niece was ill, went to La Grange. She looked upon the invalid, saw the shadow of death on her face, and had her removed at once to Paris, where she could get better medical attention. Mme. la Comtesse sent a letter at once to Adrienne's husband; he was urged to return, posthaste. Lafayette reached Paris weeks before his wife died. It was a dreary illness with death as a certainty in the end.

Lafayette was not a Christian; he cared nothing for religion; he was neither for it nor opposed to it. He believed that religion did no harm to anyone and might even help those who believed in it. In his mental pattern there was a blank compartment which, in many other people, is occupied by religious fervor. He did not go to Mass, or to other sacred ceremonies, except on rare occasions when he was moved by a sense of politeness to those around him.

Adrienne, on the other hand, was intensely pious. For years she had carried on her devotions in secret, for fear of annoying her husband. Much of her time was spent in prayer in the quiet of her own room, in fingering the holy beads, in humility before the image of a crucified Christ. But she had two gods. One of them was Général le Marquis de Lafayette, and the other was the God who lived in heaven. Gladly she would have died for either of them.

Lafayette and his stricken wife had many talks in the gray afternoons, when he sat by her bedside and held her pale hands in his. Some of these intimate conversations have been recorded by those who were present.

Saying good night, he bent over and kissed her. She clung to him.

"I love you dearly," he said.

"How good you are!" she murmured. "It is true—true! You do love me, and I love you so much. If you do not find yourself loved enough, blame it on God. He did not give me any more faculty for it than that. I love you in a Christian way, in a worldly way, in a passionate way."

Not long before her death she looked at him intently, and said, "*Chéri,* you are not a Christian." He made no reply.

"Ah," she said, "You are a Fayettist."

He smiled faintly and asked, "Aren't you also a Fayettist?"

"Yes, with all my heart and soul," she exclaimed. "I could give my life for that sect."

Mme. de Tessé, with outspoken frankness on her tongue, declared that Adrienne's religion was "a mixture of the catechism and the Declaration of the Rights of Man."

Just before Adrienne died she embraced her husband, bade him farewell, and said, "When you see Mme. de Simiane give her a thousand caresses for me."

Well, that was something to think about as a piece of advice from a dying wife. I do not know whether Lafayette ever gave Mme. de Simiane any more caresses, but—from my knowledge of men—I am willing to hazard a guess that he never made another affectionate gesture toward her as long as he lived. Adrienne had settled that affair.

In a long letter to Comte Caesar de Latour-Maubourg, elder brother of the Charles who had married Lafayette's daughter Anastasie, the bereaved husband wrote: "I have never seen her so deceived as during a few moments of delirium when she convinced herself that I had become a devout Christian. The self-deception did not last long and was accompanied by doubts which showed me that it was a wish rather than an illusion."

Adrienne was buried in Picpus Cemetery, that forlorn little graveyard far out in eastern Paris. There lay thirteen hundred victims of the guillotine, among them the women of her own family, in nameless graves.

Lafayette was profoundly affected by his wife's death. He walled up the door of her room, leaving only a small hidden entrance for which he alone possessed a key. When he was at La Grange he would go into the room every day and remain there for a long time. No one else ever entered it, and it remained just as Adrienne had left it; his personal shrine.

It may be seen now at La Grange—a large, circular room in one of the towers of the château.

To Mme. de Montagu, who was Lafayette's sister-in-law, he wrote this touching letter the day after Adrienne's death:

This, my dear sister, is a word for your poor father to whom, as well as to your mother, I owe that wonderful treasury of tenderness, kindness, perfection and happiness of the past thirty-four years. It was not until she was gone that I could appreciate her quite, so closely was she bound to my very existence. I embrace you and your husband with my whole soul, dear Pauline. I shall always see you seated on her bed with her holding your hand.

3

Napoleon was forced to abdicate in March, 1814, following his crushing defeats. He had been on the defensive since the destruction of his armies in the Russian campaign. His dramatic career had culminated in military suicide. All Europe was opposed to him; he made bitter enemies everywhere and had created for himself an unenviable place as the world's greatest nuisance. Even in France his support was lukewarm. The French people wanted peace. Napoleon's own marshals turned against him.

The Allied powers, invaders and conquerors of France, gave Napoleon the sovereignty of the island of Elba, in the Mediterranean. Elba was an empire of pocket-handkerchief size—eighty-five square miles in area, with less than twenty thousand inhabitants. The insult to Napoleon's pride and dignity was unendurable to him; and it was also intentional on the part of the Allies. They would have saved themselves much trouble in the year to come if they had sent him as a prisoner at once to the desolate rock of St. Helena. As soon as he had arrived at Elba he began to make plans to escape and return to France.

Then came the Bourbon restoration. The Comte de Provence, brother of Louis XVI, ascended the throne as Louis XVIII. He signed with the Allies the Treaty of Paris in which France gave up all the territories acquired since 1792.

The new Bourbon king was as fat and wheezy as an overstuffed poodle. He had a Gargantuan capacity for food and wine. During all his idle years as a royalist émigré he had gorged himself. He had triple chins and was a Falstaff in girth. Even when he reviewed his troops he sat in an armchair while they marched past. Although he was not lacking in intelligence he had very little knowledge of the new generation that had grown up since he fled in 1791. Moreover, he was ridiculous in appearance and manner, and to be ridiculous in France is a sort of social crime.

At the time of his accession he was laid up in England with the gout, and his brother—the Comte d'Artois—came to France to act in his place as lieutenant-general, for a few weeks, until the ponderous king was able to appear.

Lafayette had not seen the Comte de Provence and the Comte d'Artois since that day in January, 1794, when as a prisoner he was being transferred from Wesel to the Prussian fortress of Neisse. They stared at him a moment on that occasion, and he stared at them, without speaking. They detested the sight of him.

Nevertheless, upon seeing the Comte d'Artois arrive in Paris in 1814, he went home and wrote his fatuous note to M. le Comte:

Monseigneur: There is no period or sentiment of my life that does not contribute to make me happy to see your return become the signal and pledge of public liberty and happiness. Profoundly joining you in that national satisfaction, I feel the need of offering to Monsieur the homage of my personal attachment and respect. . . .

These vague phrases are characteristic of Lafayette's epistolary style. Despite their cloudiness the idea emerges that he approved of the Bourbon restoration and believed it would lead to "public liberty and happiness." Also that he tendered his personal attachment to the Comte d'Artois.

Was he sincere in penning this tribute, or did he write with his tongue in his cheek? Who can say with certainty? I can only express my own conviction that Lafayette was never a hypocrite; that he

He was willing to suffer for his opinions and make no compromise for the sake of renown or success. If he had come out wholeheartedly for Napoleon in 1797 there can be hardly a doubt that he would have become one of the resplendent marshals of the Napoleonic empire. But he had no faith in Napoleon after he had seen and talked with him and he preferred to remain in obscurity.

His chief defect was not a lack of honesty or sincerity, but an inability to perceive the full implications of social movements and events. Louis Madelin says of Lafayette, in his *Figures of the Revolution:* "He outlived by more than forty-five years the events in which he was so eminently embroiled . . . he was never able to get a clear insight into his own attitude to the movement nor could he perceive the real meaning of the Revolution itself." That is a truthful and penetrating observation.

If contemporaneous accounts be accepted as a picture of the time we must conclude that there was no great "national satisfaction" over the return of the Bourbons. When the new king came to Paris some of the people in the streets cheered feebly, but on the whole his reception was one of stony silence.

Lafayette was soon disillusioned. Swarms of royalist émigrés poured back into France. They had insolent manners; they spoke of the French people as "the French," with a sneer, as if they were referring to an inferior and alien race. The tricolor flag, that had floated in triumph on so many battlefields, was thrown into the dust heap, and the white banner of the *ancien régime* was raised again as the national emblem. Lettres de cachet were fluttering about as in the time of Louis XV. Men were imprisoned without an opportunity to be heard in their own defense, and without being informed as to the charges against them.

Among the returned émigrés there was a movement to revive feudalism, to restore the "good old times"; also a movement to give their estates back to the nobles who had been deprived of them. Lafayette thought it was his duty to appear at court, so he attended one of the king's receptions at the Tuileries. The king received him graciously and conversed with him at length. But the insolent nobles treated him with disrespect. They stared at him through their lorgnettes and turned their backs on him. Although few, or none, of them had ever accomplished anything in their lives worthy of even a paragraph in history, their manner toward world-famous Lafayette was marked by the vulgar disdain which is always a quality of the snobbish soul.

That was the first and last time he ever attended a reception at the court of Louis XVIII.

The king was pleased, as a mark of royal good will, to *grant* a new charter, or constitution, to the people of his realm. The French did not like to have a constitution *granted* to them; they thought themselves entirely capable of deciding the shape and structure of the government. However, they made the best of the situation. The troops of the Allies were still in the country, even in Paris.

The people were astonished when they observed the date at the head of the first royal decree. It was asserted in the document that it was given out in the twentieth year of the reign of Louis XVIII. He had been on the throne for twenty years and they had failed to notice it. Could it have been possible that Napoleon was just a dream, a delusion? He had certainly made a tremendous stir to have been nothing but a phantom.

Yes, yes, there had been a man named Bonaparte who claimed to have some authority; a disturber of the peace, and a disgrace in the eyes of all respectable men and nations. His fate had been settled and the French people would never be troubled by him any more. But the point is that while that vicious Bonaparte person was raging up and down the land Louis XVIII had been the king of France right along, all the time. So that is why the royal decrees say, "In the twentieth year of our reign."

The city of New Orleans claimed that part of the Lafayette land grant was on ground held as a military reservation because of its proximity to the forts. It was municipal land which the city had no intention of turning over to General Lafayette. That was one of the complications that soon appeared.

The law in respect to the disposition of public lands provided specifically that no parcel should consist of less than six hundred acres—almost a square mile. But where, in the vicinity of the growing city of New Orleans, could be found unclaimed tracts of this size? Jefferson suggested to the surveyors that, in cases where the tract was too small—and bordered on the lake—a part of the lake might be included to make up the legal number of acres. In the end, after a vast amount of haggling and confusion, some of the tracts had to be located on the west side of the river.

Lafayette was, of course, in France and the time required to send a letter from Paris to New Orleans was two to three months, and six months had usually elapsed before a reply got back to France. To overcome these delays Lafayette gave a power of attorney to Jefferson, Madison and Gallatin, and it was they who were supposed to make the decisions. But even so, they usually referred the important questions to Lafayette with their own recommendations.

A man named John Gravier claimed prior ownership of some of the tracts, and that held up matters for a long time. In 1806 Gravier offered to pay $94,000 for part of the land claimed on behalf of Lafayette, and the latter—overburdened by debts—might have accepted the offer if he had not been dissuaded by some of his American friends. Among them was Victor Dupont, who declared that the whole grant was worth $300,000 or soon would be by reason of the natural rise in real estate values.

Years went by. The marquis was troubled greatly by his inability to obtain title deeds. If he had them, he wrote, it would be possible to borrow money on them. On April 8, 1808, he wrote to Jefferson:

I am on the brink of ruin, and would have been, by this time, past every possibility of redemption had not the benevolent patience of creditors enabled me, hitherto, to wait the expectations formed several years ago.

On July 28th of the same year he wrote that he had managed to borrow 200,000 francs to meet his pressing obligations.

Again—on November 16, 1810—he wrote to Jefferson that his debts, with accumulated interest, had risen to 600,000 francs and he doubted that the land, if all sold, would more than pay his debts. But he says, also, that at last he had received "patents"—or titles— for eight of the tracts.

It came out satisfactorily in the end. All the disputes were settled; he sold the land—or most of it—at good prices. To Jefferson he wrote on August 14, 1814: "Thanks to the munificence of Congress and the kindness of my friends, I now am perfectly clear of debts and pecuniary embarrassments. I feel a grateful satisfaction in giving you the pleasure to hear it."

His "pecuniary embarrassments" soon rose again to vex him. Within ten years he was once more heavily in debt.

CHAPTER XXXI

RETURN TO PUBLIC LIFE

I

NAPOLEON escaped from Elba in February, 1815, and reached
France—near Cannes—on March 1st.
    His journey to Paris was a triumphal march. Troops
sent to oppose him went over to his side without firing a shot. There
was much dissatisfaction in the army. The military personnel as a
whole, including both officers and men, had been taken over bodily
by the new government and was being reorganized. Officers who had
served for years in Napoleon's campaigns, and who knew no trade or
profession except that of soldiering, were being dropped in wholesale
fashion. Their places were taken by royalists, most of whom were
wholly without military experience. The same weeding-out process
was also being applied to the men in ranks.
    Outside the army the Napoleonic party was in a definite minority.
The people of France certainly had no great affection for Louis
XVIII. How could they have had? He had done nothing to deserve
it; and the multitude of nobles returned from exile were like the
plague of locusts that once descended upon Egypt. But the people
wanted peace more than all else. It was hardly probable that the
obese king in the Tuileries would go in for world conquest—but who
could predict what Napoleon might do?
    There was consternation in royalist circles as the imperial ad-
venturer advanced toward Paris. Noble fugitives—and others with
heavy consciences—were on the roads to the frontier, taking with
them whatever possessions they could get together hurriedly. One
is amazed at their panic fear, at their lack of organization, at their
failure to resist. They went pell-mell to the Allied powers, like little
children who run screaming to mother when a large, shaggy dog appears on the lawn.
    The Comte d'Artois, despite his boasting courage and his fire-
and-brimstone threats, was somewhere near the head of the race to

the frontier. But he should not be excessively criticized on that account. He had early information of Napoleon's landing, and also better horses than most of those on the road.

King Louis XVIII was late in starting. He did not leave Paris until the day before Napoleon arrived. His progress was slow as he had taken with him all the national treasure that he could lay his hands on. Toiling along the road, behind his carriage in the flight to Belgium, were sixty carts laden with silver coin and bullion. Napoleon sent a force of cavalry after him with orders to retrieve the silver. It was brought back, and Louis might have been taken also, but he was allowed to depart in peace. Napoleon did not want him as a prisoner.

2

From the day he gained control Napoleon was beset by extraordinary difficulties, most of them entirely hopeless of solution. The plenipotentiaries of the Allies—meaning England, Russia, Austria, Prussia, and some smaller states in session at the Congress of Vienna declared that "Napoleon Bonaparte has placed himself outside civil and social relations and that, as an enemy and disturber of the world's peace, he has given himself over to public vengeance." They resolved not to receive any communications—either direct or indirect—from the French government as long as the usurper was at the head of affairs. Letters sent by Napoleon to the foreign sovereigns were returned with their seals unbroken.

It was to be a war to the bitter end. What were the chances of France's holding her own in a fight to the finish with the Allies? One may say without reservation that the chances were excellent, provided that France remained on the defensive, and if—a big IF—Napoleon were supported with vigor and enthusiasm by the French people.

Waterloo, where Napoleon was confronted by the troops of all the Allied powers, was won by them on the narrowest of margins. The Duke of Wellington; in command of the Allied armies, showed about as much comprehension of battle tactics as a junior lieutenant. The Allies were saved from defeat, and won that historic battle, by a stroke of luck.

If France had been solidly behind Napoleon, the defeat of

Waterloo would have had no more effect on the fortunes of the French nation, or upon the fate of Napoleon, than the smashing victory of the Confederate army at Bull Run, in 1861, had upon Abraham Lincoln and the Union cause.

As soon as Napoleon had arrived in Paris from Elba, in March, 1815, and had taken over the government, he announced that he intended to promote a constitutional monarchy, with the democratic principle as its foundation. A legislative assembly, national representation, a vote for every man, a policy of peace, happiness and comfort for all—with himself, of course, at the head of the government, not as a dictator or war lord, but as a constitutional monarch.

Some believed him, had faith in him, and spoke well of him. Others did not believe a word he said, and these disbelievers were greatly in the majority.

Lafayette had no faith in him, and announced publicly that Napoleon had been and always would be an enemy of the people.

The Legislative Assembly consisted of two chambers—the Peers and the Deputies. The peers were appointed for life; the deputies were elected by the voters. In the hurried reorganization of the government both chambers were dissolved. The House of Peers was to be re-created with Bonapartists—appointed by Napoleon—in the majority; naturally, of course. There was to be a new election of deputies for the lower chamber.

Lafayette had announced to the voters of Seine-et-Marne that he was a candidate for deputy from that department. Meantime, Joseph Bonaparte called on Lafayette and informed him that his brother Napoleon had already drawn up a list of those whom he intended to appoint as members of the House of Peers, and that Lafayette's name stood at the head of the list.

Rather brusquely Lafayette said he would not accept the appointment. Continuing, he said:

It does not suit me to re-enter political life by the peerage, or by any other favor of the Emperor. I am a man of the people; it is by the choice of the people alone that I must come out of my retreat. If I am elected I shall join with you, as a representative of the nation, to repulse foreign invasion and foreign influence, reserving nevertheless all my independence.

Every effort was made by the Bonapartists to win him over to their side. He was invited by Joseph to meet Napoleon's generals and counselors. All without success; his mind was made up on the subject of Napoleon.

In May he was elected to the Chamber of Deputies, as a representative of Seine-et-Marne. His son George was elected deputy from the department of Haute-Loire. It was the first political office that Lafayette had held in twenty-four years. When the Chamber assembled early in June he was elected a vice-president of that body.

Napoleon was much disappointed by the results of the election. The out-and-out Bonapartists constituted only a small minority in the Chamber of Deputies. Most of the members called themselves "Liberals," a vague term then, as now.

On the first day of the new session Lafayette had a brief conversation with Napoleon. They had not seen one another in twelve years. Lafayette was startled by Napoleon's change in appearance. He saw before him a haggard, careworn man who looked much older than his age. (In 1815 Napoleon was forty-six and Lafayette was fifty-eight.)

Within a week Napoleon left for the front, for Belgium, to take personal command of the army that was facing the motley, multitongued army of the Allies under the command of the Duke of Wellington.

On June 21st he was back again in Paris, returning from the great disaster of Waterloo, half dead with fatigue, worry and illness. His army was defeated, dispersed, destroyed. But all the soldiers of France were not in the army at Waterloo. Within call there were hundreds of thousands of men already trained as soldiers; men who had served in the historic campaigns. France was a nation of young veterans. Napoleon understood that clearly. He knew that Waterloo was only an incident, but the Chamber of Deputies wanted to get rid of Napoleon, and the deputies made the most of the defeat at Waterloo.

In the Chamber—in closed executive session—Lafayette proposed that the nation demand the abdication of the emperor. Lucien Bonaparte defended his brother and accused the French of fickleness.

Lafayette replied, saying:

By what right do you assert that the French people are fickle, of having failed in regard to the Emperor Napoleon? The nation has followed him in the sands of Egypt, and in the steppes of Russia, on fifty fields of battle, in his defeats as in his successes. And for having followed him we have shed the blood of two million Frenchmen.

Long after midnight a motion to demand Napoleon's abdication was carried. He knew that it was final; that there could be no further reliance on popularity or renown. Applause was dead; the people on the streets stared at him coldly when he appeared in public. Many of his former friends urged him to quit; to leave the country. With a spluttering, erratic pen he signed his abdication, and recommended his son to the French nation.

Lafayette wanted Napoleon to go to America and he spent a week arranging passage for him to the United States in an American vessel. But Napoleon did not want to go to America. That is a pity. He might have lived among our sturdy lovers of freedom for years, as his brother Joseph did, having a very good time.

Instead of coming to our genial shores, he surrendered to the British, trusting to their sense of fair play and generosity. These qualities seem to have been somewhat overrated in this case; they sent Napoleon to St. Helena, and there he died in 1821.

3

The Bourbons, burning with hatred and vengeance, returned to France. They were supported by the armies of the Allies. Paris and other strategic points were occupied by foreign soldiers—by the English, the Prussians, the Austrians and the Russians. An indemnity of eight hundred million francs was imposed on the nation, and the foreign troops were to remain on French soil until it was paid.

These aliens had small sympathy with the French people but, except in a few instances, they were not actively hostile. Their role was that of detached lookers-on in a land stewing in a brew of fratricidal passions—a land where they did not understand the language nor the habits nor the mutual antagonisms of those around them.

The ferocities of the White Terror—which is the name given by historians to the era of persecution that followed the Bourbon restoration—were inspired by the royalists who, after crushing the party of Napoleon, had everything their own way. Their leader was not Louis XVIII, but his brother, the Comte d'Artois. The king was mild in manner and peaceful in disposition. He was certainly not a great statesman, yet he had one excellent quality of statesmanship; he believed it was good policy to bury animosities. In this course he was encouraged by the Duke of Wellington, commander in chief of the

Allied forces in France. But Louis XVIII was not strong enough in moral backbone to control the course of events.

The Legislative Assembly was dismissed and a national election was held to select deputies for a new Chamber. Lafayette, of course, lost his seat. The election was manipulated in a way that would make even the most brazen and corrupt political machine in America green with envy. Practically all the new deputies were royalists. The opposition was trifling. The Bonapartist peers were thrown out of the upper chamber.

One of the first acts of the new Assembly was to suspend freedom of speech and freedom of the press.

Individual rights were also suspended. Note that they were not abolished, according to the letter of the law, but only *suspended*. The suspension was drastic, however, and so far as certain unfortunate persons were concerned they might as well have been abolished. Anyone, under this act, might be seized, imprisoned and held without trial or explanation. Houses were searched without warrant, property taken and men thrown out of employment.

Then there were the "prevotal courts"—*les cours prévôtales.* These courts were "black chambers" where the accused person was tried in secrecy, and in which one might be convicted and sentenced to death merely on suspicion, without any definite charge.

The former generals of Bonaparte were hunted down, driven from the country or brought to trial and shot. Some were dexterous enough to change their political complexion with the swiftness of a chameleon and appear on the royalist side, with proof that they had been royalists from first to last.

There were massacres of Bonapartists in Marseilles, Toulouse, Avignon; also in Brittany, and La Vendée. Among those tried by court-martial were Joachim Murat, Napoleon's brother-in-law and former king of Naples; and Marshal Michel Ney, who had been called by Napoleon, "the bravest of the brave." Ney was a rough soldier of violent passions and incredible physical endurance—the kind of man who seems to have been born on a battlefield. Ney and his corps, acting as a rear guard, saved Napoleon's Grand Army from total destruction in the retreat from Russia in 1812. After the exile of Napoleon to Elba in 1814 Ney swore allegiance to Louis XVIII and entered his service. By royal decree he was made a peer of France.

Upon Napoleon's unexpected return from Elba, Ney was put in

command of troops and sent to meet the advancing usurper and disturber of the king's peace and dignity. Upon departing on this mission he declared that he would "bring Napoleon back in a cage." But as he approached Napoleon he forgot all about cages and ran, with apologies, to join his former chief. At the battle of Waterloo he distinguished himself. After Napoleon's downfall he attempted to escape from France, and failed. He was brought to trial on a charge of treason and shot by a file of soldiers.*

* A myth to the effect that he survived is still going strong. The legend is that the soldiers were persuaded, or bribed, not to fire at him, but as the volley sounded he fell on his face as if shot. Later, another man recently executed was buried instead of him. Ney was subsequently spirited out of the country. He came to the United States and was for many years thereafter a quiet, aging schoolteacher in a placid North Carolina community.

My grandfather, who was a student of history, heard of this Peter Ney, the schoolteacher who claimed to be Marshal Ney, and traveled two hundred miles to have a talk with him. When he was ninety years old he told me that after spending two days with the schoolteacher, he was convinced of the truth of the story.

Nevertheless, it is all moonshine. After Ney's execution his body was exposed for twenty-four hours in public view. Hundreds of people who knew Marshal Ney well looked upon him without any doubt as to his identity.

The myth is beset by vast improbabilities. At the time of his "execution" he was forty-six, could not speak English and had absolutely no fitness for teaching children. His education was limited. He had been a lifelong soldier, by instinct and training.

The spurious Ney of the North Carolina country school was probably a crackpot who had read and dreamed and mooned over Ney and his fate so long that he had identified himself with the subject of his dreams.

CHAPTER XXXII

TROUBLED YEARS

I

AGAIN LAFAYETTE was just a country gentleman after his brief plunge in the troubled waters of politics. The White Terror, with its *cours prévôtales*, its spies and letter openers, its committees of search and its volleys of gunfire, had passed by him, but not without glares of anger in his direction. In the Faubourg Saint-Germain he was detested. The stately old nobles had long memories. The Revolution was far behind them, but they could still hear its surf booming against the cliffs of history. To them Lafayette was, and always would be, "that republican"—a traitor to his class. Something should be done about him; but what? The aristocratic women were more bitter than the men, perhaps because they knew less of the stern realities of things as they are.

By the *jeunesse dorée*, the hangers-on and imitators of the Comte d'Artois, Lafayette was despised, feared, admired and condemned in streams of thought that became entangled in varicolored snarls. Despised as a revolutionary, admired as a patriot and a man of courage, condemned as a republican and feared because of his potent influence. His past was historic, and not devoid of glory. They were willing to let him have his past if he would expect nothing of the future.

Nothing could be done to Lafayette. Persecution would have roused a most unpleasant resentment all over France. The people of substance had not forgotten that it was he who had forced the final abdication of Napoleon by convincing the Chamber of Deputies that it was the only wise thing to do. It was not possible—or practicable, at any rate—to pin anything on him. For him there was to be no inquisition behind closed doors, no blank cell of imprisonment, no proscription of human rights, no firing squad.

The White Terror, winging its way over the land, looked down on La Grange, hovered a moment, then gave an angry hoot of frustration and flew away to seek its victims elsewhere.

It is true that he helped overthrow Napoleon's government, but without having any clear idea of what kind of government would follow it. He was as much opposed to the Bourbons as he was to Napoleon. Is there anything to be gained by exchanging one brand of tyranny for another?

Napoleon, with all his faults, possessed ability of a high order, while Louis XVIII had no ability of any order, high or low. Both were self-seeking, brazen adventurers—and that applies to Louis XVIII, despite his heritage, family claims and what not as definitely as it does to Napoleon. It is a well-demonstrated principle of human experience that it is impossible to accomplish anything constructive with a fool at the head of affairs, while one may deal intelligently with a clever and able rascal.

2

In 1818 Lafayette entered the Legislative Assembly again as a deputy, elected by the voters of the department of the Sarthe.

Brand Whitlock says,* "The election of Lafayette shook all Europe." I do not agree with Mr. Whitlock. It takes a lot of shaking to shake all Europe. He says further:

The government had done its best to defeat him; its agents swarmed over the department of Sarthe, and when the result was announced at Paris, there was consternation at the Tuileries; Louis XVIII could not hide his disappointment and chagrin, and through his *entourage* there ran a shiver of fear, as though Lafayette were about to plunge France back into revolution, and they would all be obliged to take once more to the dreary road of exile.

I think the extract from Mr. Whitlock's biography which I have just quoted is an overstatement. Most decidedly. The king and his advisers must have known that although Lafayette was a good starter he was a poor finisher. His tendency was to abandon the effort before its conclusion or to get it bungled up in such a fashion that nobody could make head or tail of it. He dreamed of a perfect civilization, but he had no practicable plan to achieve it.

In the Chamber he joined the Liberal Left. During the debates

* Brand Whitlock, *Lafayette*, Vol. II, p. 187.

LAFAYETTE

After the portrait by Ary Scheffer. The original of this picture hangs in the House of Representatives in Washington.

he was usually silent, not because of lack of interest but simply because he was not an orator, and he knew it. Nevertheless, his influence was strong, both in and out of the Legislative Assembly. After his years of retirement he had become again one of the great figures of French political life.

The White Terror was over; men were more at ease in expressing their opinions; the crushed Liberals and even the Bonapartists were coming out of their mental hiding places. The court "viewed with alarm" the resurrection of liberalism. Too many Liberals were being sent to the Chamber of Deputies. Therefore the royalists proposed a number of laws which would restrict further the right of suffrage and the freedom of the press.

The reactionaries formed a bloc to prevent Henri Grégoire, a newly elected member, from taking his seat in the Chamber. Grégroire had served in the States-General and in the Convention. He had voted for the deposition of Louis XVI, but not for the sentence of death. He was a "radical republican" and had been in the past a bitter opponent of Lafayette, who was a republican but not a "radical" one. Between these two terms there was a vast difference of definition. During the Revolution the radicals planned to change the entire governmental structure. They were not Communists but their ideas ran—part of the way—along lines closely parallel to those of the modern Communist. Lafayette, to the infinite disgust of the radicals, was a republican who stood for a constitutional king, restricted suffrage and property rights.

Then, after the flow of years, Henri Grégoire was elected to the Chamber of Deputies. The reactionaries proposed to exclude him on the ground that he was a "regicide." Lafayette rose to defend the right of his former opponent to take his seat in the Chamber. This was in December, 1819. He spoke for hours, with violent interruptions and execrations from the Right, until two o'clock in the morning.

But without avail; the exclusion of Grégoire was voted.

While these ideas and animosities were seething a most unfortunate event occurred. The Duc de Berri, son of Monsieur, Comte d'Artois, was stabbed and killed on the evening of February 13, 1820. He had gone to the opera with his wife. They left before the performance was over. As de Berri was helping the duchess enter their carriage he was stabbed by a man whose name was Louvel, a workman in a saddlemaking establishment. De Berri was taken back into the theater, laid on a couch, and died before morning, surrounded by physicians, courtiers and nurses. The king arrived just before he died. One of the curious features of this scene is that Louvel, the assassin, was strapped against a wall in the death chamber all the time and saw his victim expire.

The assassination of de Berri, deplorable as it was, fell into the hands of the reactionaries like a gift of God. It had about the same effect on the solid, respectable people of France as the assassination of Abraham Lincoln had on the people of the North at the close of the Civil War, though de Berri was certainly not a Lincoln in thought or deed. Just as the inveterate haters of the Confederacy in Lincoln's time sought to prove that the president's assassin—John Wilkes Booth—was inspired, bribed and encouraged by southern rebels, so did the stubborn royalists of France in 1820 seek to prove a connection between the stabbing of the Duc de Berri and the growing spirit of liberalism. Louvel was kept alive for months, with daily inquisitions to determine who had encouraged him. Nothing came of it; he was a raving maniac, and knew nothing except that he was in misery and want and thought the royalist government was responsible for his condition. So he was put to death.

There was then, however, a good excuse for further repressions of free speech, free assembly and individual liberty. A counterrevolution began, encouraged by the frightened group in the Tuileries.

Secret societies of liberty lovers, with grips, passwords and all the other esoteric mummery, came into being. Lafayette joined some of them. One of these organizations was his own creation. It was called *Les Amis de la Liberté de la Presse*—and this society, financed (probably) by Lafayette, was a disturbing force in French affairs for a little while. Of course, its activities soon became known. It is impossible to preserve the secrecy of any association which has many members. There were spies.

In the Chamber Lafayette met the issue fearlesly. He said, in a speech:

The Revolution is the victory of right over privilege; it is the emancipation and development of the human faculties, the restoration of the peoples; and that is so true that the friends of liberty have always been, and still are, hated by the opponents of the Revolution in proportion to the efforts they have made to prevent it from being soiled by crime and disfigured by excess.

The banker Laffitte, who was a friend of Lafayette, said—not then, but later, "You are a statue in search of a pedestal, and you would let a scaffold serve for it."

Lafayette made no answer to that remark, but he did say in the midst of his family, "I have had a long life, and I think I might worthily finish my career on the scaffold as a sacrifice to liberty."

Did he really mean that, or was it merely a piece of rhetoric? I, for one, am convinced that he meant it sincerely. He was over sixty, and most intelligent men past the age of sixty care little or nothing for life. They have seen too much, have learned too much, and are thoroughly disillusioned. One has to die anyway, so why not die for the sake of a just cause?

The Friends of the Freedom of the Press, most of whom were young students, hatched a harebrained scheme. They decided to seize the partially dismantled fortress of Vincennes—near Paris— and set up a provisional government with Lafayette at its head. Then all the free spirits, the liberty-loving citizens, the democratic elements of the French nation, would rally around them and France would soon shake off the shackles of the Bourbon kings.

The plan was preposterous, obviously. One is struck by its similarity in idea to that of John Brown's seizure of Harpers Ferry in 1859, whereby he expected to arouse the slave population of the southern states. The attack on Vincennes was to be made during the night of August 19, 1820. Six hundred students were to form the attacking party. The young men, awaiting the signal, sat up in taverns and in their friends' homes, drinking and carousing. The police knew of the plot—knew it better, indeed, than many of those engaged in it—so around midnight they arrested the leaders and the valorous escapade died at birth. Lafayette was not molested. He was such a big fish that the procureur-général was afraid to tackle him, but he did say that the real leader was not among the young men caught in the net, but "a general famous in the history of our first revolution."

3

Now comes the story of Lafayette and the Carbonari, a much more serious organization than the adolescent Friends of the Freedom of the Press.

The Carbonari began in Italy. It was a secret society with a republican purpose, which may be concisely stated as a plan to rid the world of kings and despots of all descriptions and build up a brotherhood of man on the ruins of empires. A rather large program as one may readily perceive.

It was brought to France in 1821 by some Frenchmen who had joined the order in Italy. Though the first organizers of the French Carbonari were obscure men, they managed to bring the society to the attention of Lafayette and his son George. Both joined, and Lafayette soon became the head man and director of the society's activities. All the ritual and ceremony which had appealed to the Italian imagination was discarded. A candidate for membership was required only to take an oath of secrecy, to subscribe to the general purpose of the order, and to keep in his home—ready for use—a musket and fifty cartridges. Thus constituted, the Carbonari became a formidable revolutionary force. Members were enrolled so rapidly that before the end of 1821 lodges had been established in nearly every large town in France.*

It was what we in America today call a "white-collar" organization. Workmen and peasants were not asked to join. The membership was made up chiefly of lawyers, journalists, ex-army officers, professors, executives and businessmen. Much secret effort was made to foment disaffection in the army. Failure to get the workers into the Carbonari was a grave error. The land swarmed with the veteran soldiers of Bonaparte, but only their officers were accepted as members. This is just another manifestation of Lafayette's lifelong distrust of the common people. Nearly all the young men who had engaged in the frustrated plot to seize Vincennes joined the society, and it was said that the membership amounted to forty thousand before the end of the year 1821.

It was not possible to conceal the existence of the Carbonari, nor its purpose, which was to expel the Bourbons, establish a con-

* John R. Hall, *The Bourbon Restoration*, p. 294.

stitutional monarchy, and put the Duc d'Orléans on the throne.*
Moreover, Lafayette was known to be one of its leaders. What a
curious state of affairs! The royal government knew what was going
on and was unable, or unwilling, to suppress the movement in its
formative stages.

In whispered secrecy the uprising was planned to take place
late in December, 1821. The 29th regiment was stationed at Belfort
in Alsace. Some of its officers belonged to the Carbonari, and they
thought they could manage the regiment. The blow was to be struck
on the night of December 29th, but the conspirators were to wait
until Lafayette arrived and gave the signal.

A first-class mess was made of the whole affair. Lafayette was
not there on December 29th. He did not leave La Grange until
Christmas Day and the roads were so bad that he did not reach
the neighborhood of Belfort until New Year's Day, 1822. Two men
awaited him on the road, outside the town. They stopped his carriage and told him that the uprising had failed. A sergeant had
revealed the plot to the commanding officer and the leaders of the
Carbonari were prisoners.

Lafayette turned around at once and drove to the home of a
friend who lived in the neighborhood. As an excuse for his presence
so near the scene of the mutiny it was announced that he was merely
visiting his friend, and that he was unaware of the insurrectionary
scheme. Probably no one was deceived by such a transparent falsehood.

Revolts had been planned to take place simultaneously in the
garrisons at Marseilles, Toulon, Saumur and La Rochelle. All of
them failed. Four sergeants of the La Rochelle garrison—all of them
members of the Carbonari—were brought to Paris to be tried on a
charge of treason. Lafayette was greatly disturbed by the plight of
these four men. He blamed himself; they had simply followed his
instructions. They were kept in the Conciergerie for months awaiting trial, and were questioned daily in an endeavor to learn the extent of the conspiracy and the names of its leaders, but nothing of
importance was disclosed by the sergeants. Lafayette spent a small
fortune in a secret effort to have them released, but without avail.

Two officers, General Bertron and Lieutenant Colonel Caron,

* This Duc d'Orléans was the son of Philippe Egalité, who was guillotined during
the Revolution. He lived in Paris at the Palais Royal.

accused of having taken part in the conspiracy, were put on trial at Poitiers. The prosecuting attorney was very anxious to connect Lafayette and some of his friends—among them Benjamin Constant, Laffitte, General Foy and Jacques Manuel—with the plot.

One of those called up for examination at this trial was a member of the Carbonari named Baudrillet. In reply to a leading question suddenly thrown at him he admitted that he had gone to Paris for an interview with Lafayette, and had been told what to do. That reply was received with great pleasure on the part of the prosecution, for it seemed to lead directly to the chief conspirator. But before the next question was put Baudrillet had recovered his poise. Asked to describe Lafayette, the witness said that he was a small, potbellied man with black whiskers. A man of about forty-five. That was his story and he stuck to it through a maze of adroit cross-examination. The court finally put an end to the examination by deciding that somebody had impersonated General Lafayette.

The two officers—Bertron and Caron—were convicted and guillotined.

Word came to Lafayette that the governor of the prison in which the four sergeants were held would connive at their escape if he were given enough money to make a fresh start in another country. The governor's salary was twenty thousand francs a year, and no doubt he expected about two hundred thousand francs as a bribe —that is to say, his salary for ten years.

But only sixty thousand francs could be raised, of which sum two-thirds was contributed by Lafayette. The governor of the prison pretended to accept, but he notified the police. Just as the money was being counted out to him the police appeared. The money was seized and there was a pretense of putting the jailer under arrest. No one could be found who would acknowledge ownership of the money, so—presumably—it was turned over to the government after the jailer and the police had taken out of it as much as they dared to take.

The four sergeants were eventually brought to trial, found guilty and executed. Thus came to an end the violent revolutionary activities of the Carbonari, though the society existed as a political force for years thereafter. It was connected, in some degree of kinship, with the Italian and French Freemasons, though the Masons formed only a minor part of its membership. Lafayette was at that time a member of the Masonic order. He had joined as a young man in France, and not in America, though it has been frequently asserted that he became a Mason while he was serving in Washington's army. (For this information I am grateful to Judge Walter P. Gardner, of Jersey City, who has gone thoroughly into the matter.)*

4

When Napoleon was finally suppressed and sent in lonely exile to St. Helena the European powers, inspired by the Czar of Russia, formed what is known in history as the Holy Alliance, which— expressed in simple terms—was a treaty that bound all the rulers in a fraternal brotherhood. The purpose of the alliance was to put down by co-operative force any republican uprising wherever it might occur in Europe. The "holy" part of it is fully explained in the wording of the document. It was saturated with religious mysticism on the theory that the sovereigns of Europe had the sanction of God. Any attempt to overthrow them was therefore an attack on the sanctity and dignity of the Ruler of the Universe.

Do not laugh at this nonsense; it was powerfully effective for about a generation.

In the face of it the people of Spain overturned the corrupt government of Ferdinand VII in 1822. The deposed king called upon France for aid, and the French government responded liberally. Ten million francs were voted to defray the expenses of a military invasion of Spain, and an army under the command of the Duc d'Angoulême was sent to that distressed land for the purpose of putting Ferdinand VII back on his throne.

The measure was not carried unanimously, by any means. The Liberals in the Chamber of Deputies, including Lafayette, voted against it. The chief of the objectors was Jacques Manuel, an intimate friend of Lafayette, and one of the secret leaders of the Carbonari. In a fiery speech before the Chamber he declared that the government of Ferdinand VII was atrocious, and that France was degrading herself by taking his part. He could not finish his speech

* There is hardly any valid relationship—except in form and ceremony—between the European Masons of a hundred or more years ago and the Masonic order as it now exists in America. The American Masons are fraternal organizations only, without a political objective. The European Masons in Lafayette's time were liberals in politics and anti-Catholic.

because of the uproar and the denunciations that came from the royalist side. On March 3, 1823, he was expelled from the Chamber after a three-hour debate which had the dignity of a cat-fight.

Lafayette, shouting above the tumult, said, "We all adhere to what M. Manuel has declared to you! We make common cause with him."

Next day the Liberal deputies, Lafayette at their head, entered the Chamber in a compact body. Manuel was among them. He took his seat quietly. The presiding officer asked him to retire, which he refused to do. He said, "I will yield only to force." The sergeant at arms read an order of expulsion to him which hardly anyone heard as that official was so nervous that he could hardly speak. Manuel refused to budge.

Then the National Guard was sent for, and a detachment came in. Lafayette, founder of the National Guard, rose and confronted them. Despite all the changes of revolutions and dynasties, he was still their patron saint. He exclaimed that he was ashamed of the National Guard; that he would not have believed that the Guard could demean itself to the point of attacking the representatives of the nation. Crestfallen, the Guard detachment went out.

The *gendarmes*—the Paris police—were more amenable. They were sent for. They dragged out Manuel and threw him in the street. Lafayette arose with sixty-three of his Liberal colleagues and departed also. The space they had occupied in the Chamber was left blank and empty.

The Liberal deputies never returned. In February, 1824, his term having expired, Lafayette was a candidate for re-election. The court party decided to defeat him at all cost—and they succeeded in doing so. For weeks before the election their agents swarmed in his district, offering bribes and emoluments. For a time his career as a legislator was over.

5

There was published in England, in 1821, a book about America, the author of which was Frances Wright. The title of the book was *Views of Society and Manners in America*. It was the outcome of Miss Wright's observations of the American people made close at hand during a long sojourn in the United States.

Lafayette read the book, was much impressed by it, and wrote to Miss Wright a letter of appreciation in which he said that he would like to meet her. She dropped whatever she was doing and came speedily to La Grange, where she arrived in September, 1821. She remained there, off and on, for nearly three years, assisting Lafayette in the preparation of his *Mémoires,* and in other matters that contributed to his joy and comfort.

Frances Wright—usually called "Fanny"—was an orphan daughter of a Scottish merchant who had amassed considerable wealth during his mercantile career. His fortune was left to Fanny and her sister Camilla. Miss Wright was considered a wealthy woman. She had reached the age of twenty-six when she met Lafayette.

Fanny Wright was a pronounced radical. Lillian Symes, in her informative book, *Rebel America,* says that Miss Wright was "one of the most brilliant women of the nineteenth century." Very likely she was, but she came too soon, long before the day of "emancipated" women; therefore a great many people considered her an eccentric person. There was a streak of hysteria in her make-up, or so it seems. But that is not surprising. It is a common trait, today as well as then, of both women and men who hope for great careers. Such people display an unwarranted vehemence of assertion in respect to vast, complicated social questions which cannot be solved except by time, patience and common sense. They are one-idea people. Every objection to the dominating idea is thrown aside, not because they have a deliberate intention to ignore facts and opinions, but because they think the adverse opinions have no value and are not worth considering.

Miss Wright, in the 1820's, is described by her contemporaries as "beautiful and slender," but she paid little or no attention to such extraneous charms. She was distinctly intellectual, eager, forceful and fiery. Among her admirers was Jeremy Bentham, the aged English philosopher, who wrote that "She is the sweetest and strongest mind that ever was cased in a female body." High praise, indeed.

She captured Lafayette at once after she had met him. He had never seen a woman like her. All the women he had ever met were either la-da-da, smelling-salts swooners; or social climbers; or those whose whole purpose in life was to marry a successful man—or a rich one at any rate; or high-toned prostitutes; or mental viragos like Mme. de Staël; or quiet, demure *chatelaines* who were always thinking of the children's whooping cough or the best way to get rid of moths.

Frances Wright was quite different from all those. She could slam her feminine fist down on Lafayette's desk and say things that startled him. Her ideas were not new. For years the same notions had floated around him in a nebulous fog. But she knew how to express them with astonishing clarity and brilliance.

Her dominating idea, to which she gave all her thought and energy, was to free the human race; to establish freedom from the tyranny of inherited power, money and superstition. She envisaged a coming generation that would have no masters. All would work cheerfully for the love of occupation. Men would be honest, just and generous because there would be no incentive to act in any other fashion. No one would be considered better than anyone else for the reason that all would be doing their best, in a small or large way.

It is a noble conception. But, considered as a practicable working plan, it appears to be somewhat defective. May I set forth some of its defects, as I see them?

In the first place, mankind does not want to be free. Certainly, men say that they want freedom, but they do not mean what they say. If you insist that men want to be free you are simply flying in the face of historical facts. Men have always fought freedom with the ferocity of tigers. When they find themselves suddenly free— and that has happened—they begin immediately to create dictators, tyrants and political bosses.

Fanny Wright knew all that, but she thought that these conditions—and others like them—were social diseases which might readily be cured. Her persistent effort was to make men free.

One must admit that the word "freedom" has a pleasant sound, and everyone is for it verbally. If you doubt it just go out and ask the first fifty people you meet in the street if they want to be free, and you will find that there will not be a single adverse vote. But the word "freedom" has hundreds of meanings. A biologist, working unprofitably on a line of biological research without adequate laboratory facilities and pestered by debt, has certainly a different idea of freedom from that of a twenty-year-old girl who is in rebellion against the restrictions imposed by her parents.

Like all abstract words, such as "virtue," "honor," "diligence," "honesty," the word "freedom" supplants realities. That is one of the vices of language, and probably an incurable one.

There was no love affair between Lafayette and Frances Wright. I use the phrase "love affair" here in its sexual sense. But she was certainly in love with him—and he was in love with her—in the father-daughter meaning of the word. In a letter written to her on April 26, 1824, when she had gone back to England for a while, he addressed her as *"ma bien aimée, adorée Fanny, la tendre fille de mon choix."* Do not take those tender words too literally. He had had much amatory experience, and in writing to women, or speaking to them, there was without doubt a reverberation of reminiscence. It meant nothing special; he was just being agreeable.

Fanny was equally affectionate in her letters to Lafayette. On July 18, 1822, when he was in Paris attending a session of the Chamber, she wrote to him from La Grange:

My beloved and honored friend—tomorrow I shall have a letter from you, *n'est-ce pas?* In truth I do not know what to make of myself without my paternal friend. I look round for you, listen for your foot, and your voice twenty times a day, but I look and listen in vain. . . .

I do not ask if you sometimes think of me. I know you do—very, very often—even while you are looking at M. de Peyronnet. My friend, my father, and if there be a word more expressive of love, and reverence, and adoration I would fain use it. I am only half alive when away from you. You see you spoilt me. In truth you have been and are too good to me. You must continue to love me, however, in spite of my little worthiness, for in truth I love you very, very much. I have nothing as you see to tell you except this, and as you knew it before was it worth the writing?

I put my arms around the neck of my paternal friend and ask his blessing.

When Fanny arrived at La Grange the Carbonari movement was occupying Lafayette's time, and taking most of his available money. It suited her precisely; as a radical and revolutionary she became his willing and industrious assistant, without pay.

She did not make an overpowering hit with Lafayette's daughters—Anastasie and Virginie. Fanny let it be known that she wanted to be adopted as a daughter of Lafayette. His own daughters were not enthusiastic over that proposal. As time went on she assumed, more and more, the responsibility for running the household. She was no longer a guest, but a fixture. Her popularity with Lafayette's children dropped slowly until it hovered around zero. Probably she never knew that. She was busy from morning to night with the general's *Mémoires*, his correspondence, his political plots.*

Waterman says that "the position which Miss Wright occupied at La Grange became, in the spring of 1824, an impossible one."

* The best book in Miss Wright is by William Randall Waterman, and the title is simply *Frances Wright*. It was published in 1924. Few people have ever heard of it. Vivid, well-written, interesting. It ought to be reprinted.

CHAPTER XXXIII

LAST VISIT TO AMERICA

I

FOR YEARS Lafayette's American friends, with whom he carried on a voluminous correspondence, had urged him to make another visit to the United States. He had long been eager to go but was deterred by the confused state of affairs in France.

In the spring of 1824 came a resolution from Congress inviting him to visit this country as a guest of the American nation, and there was a letter from President Monroe. An American frigate was to be placed at his disposal for the voyage. He made up his mind to undertake the long-deferred trip, but at the same time he decided to decline the American warship, as he felt that an arrival in such state would give an undesirable tone of pomp and formality to what he hoped would be just a pleasant, chatty tour among his American friends.

He dallied over the proposed trip for several months, and people—in Europe and America—wondered why he did not go, since he had accepted the invitation. Vincent Nolte offers an explanation in his *Memoirs of a Merchant*. He knew Lafayette well, and was in Paris with him during the spring and early summer of 1824. He says that it was a question of debts, and he quotes Lafayette as saying:

I have here in Paris debts to the amount of one hundred thousand francs which must be paid before I dare go to another quarter of the world. I could procure the money here if I would give a mortgage upon my estate of La Grange, but it is the heritage of my children—it belonged to my wife, and now is theirs.

These debts were paid by a loan to Lafayette—according to Nolte—made by three persons: James Brown, American minister to France; a Dutchman whose name was Kock; and Jean François Girod, a citizen of New Orleans, who was at that time in France.

Frances Wright wanted to accompany him to America, and he liked the idea. Both go together. Miss Wright had been to America in 1818, and had met many prominent persons. The Lafayette family received this proposal with gloomy faces and sour looks. What would the American people think if he—one of their revered heroes—came across the Atlantic with a good-looking young woman as a companion?

The solidarity of the family is a fixed institution in France. Its potent influence on French life is almost incomprehensible to Americans. There are family conferences on almost everytihng that has even a remote bearing on the family's relation to the community—conferences on proposed marriages, politics, education, property, care of dependent relatives, behavior in public. Although Lafayette was the head of his family—its honored chief—his doings were nevertheless subject to inquiry and comment. The family vetoed his plan to take Miss Wright to America as a member of his party. Of course, their verdict was not binding on Lafayette, and he was free to disregard it, but he felt a moral constraint against a course of action which his children so thoroughly disapproved.

Lafayette fell ill immediately, took to bed, and ceased making plans for the American journey. In a few days his daughters changed their minds. Miss Wright ought to go on the trip, they said, but not on the same vessel. Then it would be all right. He shook his head. It had already been settled that she was not to go. No, the subject was closed, and he was a sick man. Maybe he would not go to America at all. Then they urged him to take Miss Wright; they begged him to take Miss Wright. Being wealthy, she was abundantly able to pay her own expenses, they said, and what was to prevent her from going, anyway? Nothing at all, one had to admit. So it was arranged that Miss Wright would meet him in America. Very soon thereafter he recovered his health and went about making his plans for the voyage.

On July 12, 1824, he sailed from Havre on the *Cadmus,* an American merchant vessel, accompanied by his son, George Washington Lafayette; Levasseur, his secretary; and Bastien, his valet. He reached New York on August 14th, almost exactly forty years since his last visit to the United States.

Forty years is only a second on the great clock of the universe but it is a long, long time in the life of any man. Lafayette, at the age of sixty-seven, must have felt incredibly old when his ship anchored in New York harbor on that bright sunlit day in August, 1824. When he had been here before the French Revolution was still in the future. Now it was only a memory. Napoleon had never been heard of, but he, too, had come and gone; had lived his astonishing and dramatic career, only to come to an end on a bleak rock in the Atlantic. In 1784 Lafayette's three children were prattling infants; now they were sedate people of middle age with children of their own.

The United States, when Lafayette had traveled over the country in 1784, had been a strip of seaboard communities, facing the Atlantic. Forty years later its vast dominion extended westward to the Rocky Mountains, and from the Great Lakes to the Gulf of Mexico, and the population of the country had increased from 3,000,000 to 10,000,000.

August 14th was a Saturday. Late that afternoon the *Cadmus* anchored off Staten Island. Next morning a son of Daniel D. Tompkins, then Vice-President of the United States, came aboard and brought an invitation for Lafayette and party to be his father's guests until Monday at his home on Staten Island. Lafayette was puzzled by this kindly invitation; he thanked the young man and said that no doubt the people in the city were expecting him to land there, so he had better not stop just then. The young man explained the situation. A great reception had been prepared for Lafayette in New York, but as this was Sunday, the reception committee did not wish "to desecrate the Sabbath," so the ovation had been postponed until Monday. In perplexed wonderment Lafayette listened to the explanation. "Desecrating the Sabbath" to receive a guest of the nation! In France Sunday would be the very day selected for the purpose, for the reason that everyone would be at leisure and be able to do justice to the occasion. So he went ashore with young Mr. Tompkins and was a guest of the vice-president until Monday morning.

In that era most of the states had Sunday statutes which were rigidly enforced by fines and imprisonment. No travel on the roads was permitted except for the purpose of going to church or to call a doctor. The streets of the large cities, such as New York, Philadelphia and Boston, were as silent as a cemetery; the houses were shuttered, all the shops were closed. There were no Sunday newspapers, or bathing beaches or picnics. From Saturday evening until Monday morning the American nation sank into silence and was supposed to be communing with God.

2

On Monday morning the cannon were booming and the vibrant echoes of the guns tingled in the air. There was little work done in New York that day. The downtown streets were packed with people. It was long past noon when Lafayette came shore at the Battery. For a short time there was a tense silence. The people were so awe-struck and filled with emotion that they could only stand and gaze. They beheld an old man, tall for a Frenchman, limping on a cane. He wore nankeen trousers and a blue coat. No decorations, medals or gold lace. Simply dressed. They noted his shock of blond hair— it was a wig, but they did not know it—and his fine, fearless eyes. He was as straight as a pine. His presence carried the quality of command. When he spoke to those around him he made quick, commanding gestures, like those of men who are accustomed to being obeyed.

Numerous know-it-alls in the crowd said to their neighbors, "You see he limps. That comes from the wound he got at the battle of the Brandywine." People believed them, and for months during his stay in America he had to explain, again and again, that he had fallen down a flight of steps.

For a moment the crowd at the Battery gazed without voice, as quiet as mice, then came a roar of cheering which spread to the people on Broadway and other streets. The remote multitudes had not yet seen Lafayette, but they knew from the cheering that he had landed at the Battery. In a space cleared and kept open by troops he met the dignitaries, the big men, said a few words and was escorted to an open barouche which moved slowly, surrounded by the Lafayette Guards, to the City Hall.

That evening many a man in New York said to his children, "I saw Lafayette today; I saw him with my own eyes; I was within ten feet of him. Remember that, never forget it. When you grow up you can tell your own children that their grandfather looked at Lafayette. He limps; he is still suffering from the wound that he got at some battle in the Revolutionary War. Speaking of men —there you have a real man. I never saw before such confidence and courage on a human countenance."

We Americans, from head to heel, are hero worshipers. We are proud of it and do not intend to apologize to anybody. We may kill our demigods with kindness, but our intentions are good, just the same.

Lafayette could stand any amount of popular ovations, speech-making, band-playing, processions, handshaking, banquets and flag-waving. For fifteen months he circled around the country, and when he finally departed for home he was as chipper and spry as a youth of twenty-five. As the white sails of his Europe-bound ship sank below the horizon the American people crept home. Their throats were hoarse from yelling; they were almost bent double with fatigue. Now that he was gone with the love and blessing of everybody, the American nation resolved to take a good, long rest.

Has Lafayette's reception ever been exceeded or equaled by that of any other visiting foreigner? The answer is No.

On that first day in New York he was conducted to the City Hall, and there he remained for two hours shaking hands with men and women who passed in line before him. Quarters were provided for him at the City Hotel, but they were not private, although they were supposed to be. From morning until midnight people swarmed in his rooms, drinking and eating and talking.

Charles Floyd, grandfather of Senator William Gibbs McAdoo, commanded Lafayette's guard of honor while the distinguished gentleman was in New York City. Floyd was then an officer in the Marine Corps. In a letter written at that time to his family in Georgia, he said:

> The Marquis has strong features, is a tall man, and dresses in a plain blue coat, yellow nankeen pantaloons and buff vest. His manner is plain and dignified. . . .
>
> If Monsieur lives until the fuss is over he will be completely soaked with wine and cocktails of every description.

One of his callers in New York was Francis Huger whom he had not seen in thirty years, since that day in 1795 when Huger attempted to help him escape from Olmütz.

On this occasion he remained only four days in New York. He departed for Boston on Friday, August 20th. His route had been announced and a sort of time schedule made up but, owing to the ovations everywhere on the road the cavalcade of carriages and horsemen ran far behind its timetable. At Saugatuck—now called Westport—in Connecticut the militia had waited since noon to fire a salute. When Lafayette had not arrived at ten o'clock at night the soldier boys went home. Fairfield was reached at ten-thirty. Since seven o'clock a gorgeous dinner had been waiting. The young ladies of the village had arranged the decorations, which must have been wonderful, as a news chronicler of the time wrote that "the table was like a bed of some fairy enchanted garden, so entirely did the decorations overshadow and conceal the rich collation beneath." I doubt that the concealment of food by heaped-up flowers was really appreciated by Lafayette, but in a spirit of courtesy he "expressed his gratification at this specimen of female taste."

That night he slept at Bridgeport.

At every village he was greeted by the people and had to stay awhile. The larger towns had put up arches with "Welcome Lafayette" on them. The veterans of the Revolution—many of them were men in their eighties—hobbled forward to meet him and talk of the old fighting days. He remembered all of them, even if he had never seen them before, but for the moment could not recall their names.

At New Haven an ancient Colonel Talmadge came forward. He was one of the few people whom Lafayette recognized at sight. He embraced Colonel Talmadge. The colonel, wandering in a maze of senile reminiscences, said to the awe-struck onlookers that he had seen the marquis dismount from his horse and, at the head of his troops, ford the Schuylkill on two cold nights in succession.

The truth is that Lafayette did ford the Schuylkill twice, before and after the battle of Barren Hill. The water was not cold; both occasions were in the warm month of May, 1778. The crossing of the river did not take place, at either time, at night, but in the afternoon, and Lafayette did not dismount from his horse. Why should he have walked on foot across the river when he had a horse to ride? Otherwise, with these slight corrections, the veteran's account was entirely correct.

Lafayette accepted the story and patted the colonel's shoulder. I wonder if it would not have been better for him, in the long run, if he had remained in America and become a politician after the American Revolution instead of going back to France?

His route was through Saybrook; then he crossed into Rhode Island, stopped at Providence a few hours and from there went on to

Boston. He arrived in Boston on Tuesday, August 24th, five days on the road from New York.

Three thousand school children stood on Boston Common to greet him. One little miss ran to his carriage and put a wreath on his head. He took up the child and kissed her; then he set her down and took off the wreath. All through his trip through the northern and eastern states he was pestered by wreaths. He did not want any wreaths; he detested them, yet at the same time he wanted to be polite about it.

He was received in the Senate Chamber in Boston—in formal fashion. Governor Eustis made a welcoming address, but broke down in the middle of it, with tears in his voice. A stolid nonemotional secretary read the remainder of the address from the governor's manuscript. Lafayette responded in English. I believe I have said somewhere in this book that Lafayette always spoke English with an accent which sometimes made his speech unintelligible, although he understood our language perfectly when he heard it spoken. The French, unless they learn English as children, seem to have much difficulty in adapting their vocal cords to our accented syllables and the sound of th.

Anyway, that Boston audience understood him. Some of them complimented him on his ability to speak our language. "Why shouldn't I?" he said. "I am an American who has just returned from a long trip to Europe."

Seven days in Boston, and then the procession of carriages went on its way to Newburyport, to Marblehead, to Portsmouth in New Hampshire. In one carriage were some Boston notables; in another were four New York City aldermen, appointed by the mayor to make the New England trip as a courtesy to the marquis. George Washington Lafayette was also there. He appears to have been a sort of general manager of arrangements, fixing the hours of departure and arrival. He was always busy with maps, measuring and calculating. Levasseur, the marquis's secretary was a member of the Carbonari. He had been an officer in the 29th Regiment at Belfort at the time of the projected uprising. Soon afterward he resigned his commission and entered Lafayette's service. It was his duty to attend to the correspondence. He made a prodigious mass of notes which were to become the basis of a very readable book about the trip. (A. Levasseur: *Lafayette en Amérique en* 1824-25.) Bastien, the general's valet, at first could not speak a word of English, which was a handicap. George Lafayette, who spoke English perfectly, usually interpreted for him.

The people in the line of carriages were not alone in their progress. They were accompanied by mounted militia from one town to another; also by many citizens on horseback or in vehicles. Even in the little villages the music of poorly trained bands smote the ear. At night there were bonfires on the hills and in the village squares. Collations were provided at every stop. Almost any other man would have died under such popular pressure; or, if he survived, would have hated crowds to the end of his days. But Lafayette loved people.

After the visit to Portsmouth the procession turned back to Boston, then to Worcester and Hartford, where Governor Wolcott "took him for a delightful visit to the Asylum for the Deaf and Dumb"—so says the chronicle of his travels. I cannot think of anything less delightful to Lafayette than the spending of an afternoon with a group of deaf and dump people. He would have been better pleased, I am sure, to have attended the annual outdoor meeting of the Hartford Old Settlers' Association, with a barbecue and speeches as features of the program.

From Hartford the party went in a steamboat back to New York. As soon as he got on the boat Lafayette went to bed and slept for fifteen hours. Next day was September 6th—his sixty-seventh birthday—and there was much ado about it in New York. The Society of the Cincinnati gave a stupendous banquet in his honor. At his place at the table there was an arch of laurel, from which a stuffed eagle was suspended just over his head.

On September 1th Fanny Wright and her sister Camilla arrived from Europe, and immediately went to see Lafayette. That same afternoon the French citizens living in New York had a banquet in the general's honor.

The banquet was rather an exclusive affair, but a few days later it was followed by a popular fete in Castle Garden. It is written that six thousand people were in the great circular hall when the marquis entered to the strains of "See the Conquering Hero Comes." The building is now occupied by the New York Aquarium, and I must say that I do not see how six thousand people ever found room

in that hall to sit down at the same time unless they sat in one another's laps. On one of the walls was a huge "transparency," all
agleam with lights. It was a picture of the château at La Grange,
and the caption read, "Here Is His Home."

The steamboat *James Kent* was waiting in the river to take him
and his party to Albany. He did not get away from the Castle Garden entertainment until two o'clock in the morning. When he reached
the steamer he found that a large crowd of well-dressed women had
taken possession of the boat and all its staterooms. They could not
be dislodged by persuasion; they insisted on going up the river with
the marquis. So Lafayette, half dead for lack of sleep, sat up on
deck in company with all the other gentlemen. At West Point the
ladies were prevailed upon to go ashore. Miss Wright and her sister
remained on the boat.

At Albany he was received by the governor of the state on a
balcony of the Capitol. While Lafayette was making his speech
some of his admirers, leaning out of an upper window, lowered a
stuffed eagle on a cord. It had a wreath in its beak, and the idea
seems to have been that the eagle would be maneuvered so as to
deposit the wreath on Lafayette's head. "An eagle, descending from
the sky, crowned our hero with a wreath of immortelles." The sentiment was poetic, but by that time Lafayette had been in America
long enough to look out for eagles and wreaths. He stepped aside,
the eagle flopped to the floor, and that part of the display was a
fizzle.

There was only a brief stay in Albany. Back to New York went
the nation's guest, and from there to Philadelphia. On the way he
stopped for a few hours at the estate of Joseph Bonaparte in the
vicinity of Bordentown, New Jersey. The home of Napoleon's
brother was magnificently furnished with the spoils of European
campaigns. He was delighted to see his friend Lafayette.

On September 25th, the day after his departure, the Wright
sisters also left New York for Philadelphia.

Arriving at the outskirts of Philadelphia he found that an immense procession, of the carnival type, was waiting to escort him
into the city. Besides the troops and the carriages of the men of
local celebrity, there were many floats on which the craftsmen of
the city displayed their talents. On them were carpenters, coopers,
bricklayers, tailors, butchers—all at work. One float carried a small

printing press. As it went on its way it was used to print a poem
in honor of Lafayette, which was thrown out in handfuls over the
crowd. The bands played, the people cheered and young girls handed
flowers to Lafayette. But there were no stuffed eagles or wreaths—
an omission in the program of amenities which seems inexplicable.

Among other organizations the Masonic fraternity entertained
Lafayette in Philadelphia, and there is a tradition that he was made
a Mason while he was there. It is wholly unfounded; the general
had been a Mason for more than forty years.

There was a banquet—or large, formal dinner—in his honor
every evening while he was in the city, and a reception every day
at Independence Hall. He shook hands with thousands of people,
and seemed to stand up very well under the ordeal.

Then the honored guest proceeded to Delaware, on October 6,
1824. In Wilmington he went through the usual welcoming ceremonies. Next day he attended the wedding of Charles Irénée—son
of Victor Dupont—to Dorcas Van Dyke. Lafayette gave the bride
away.

The following five days were spent in Baltimore. In Washing-
ton, the next stop in his triumphal pilgrimage, he was invited by
President Monroe to reside in the White House, but the people were
opposed to that arrangement. It would be too exclusive, they said.
The people could not be disregarded, so the marquis went to a suite
of rooms at Gadsby's Hotel, as a guest of the nation. Andrew
Jackson, then a senator from Tennessee, was also living at Gadsby's.
Lafayette and Jackson became close friends.

Soon after arriving in Washington Lafayette called on the
French minister and was received in formal manner, briefly and
coldly. He never went again to the legation nor did he receive an invitation to dinner—or anything else—from the minister. The reputed
explanation of this coldness, not given out then but later, is that
when Lafayette called the news of the death of Louis XVIII had
just arrived, and the legation was in mourning.*

Until the middle of the next February (1825) Lafayette lived
in Washington. He met all the chief government officials and their
wives and every important man in Congress. In October he made a
trip to Yorktown where a celebration had been arranged in com-

* Louis XVIII died September 16, 1824, and was succeeded by the Comte
d'Artois, who bore the title of Charles X.

memoration of the victory of the Americans and the French over the British in 1781. Forty-three years to a day after that historic occurrence Lafayette visited the field where Cornwallis surrendered. He remarked that he remembered all that had happened on that memorable occasion.

After much speechmaking on the battlefield, a General Taylor advanced with a wreath in his hand, and declaimed, "In behalf of all the chivalry of Virginia . . . I place on the head of Major General Lafayette this wreath of double triumph, won by numerous and illustrious acts of martial prowess, and by a life devoted to the happiness of the human race."

Before the wreath could be placed on his head Lafayette seized it with his right hand, held it to his side and, bowing low, declared that he appreciated the compliment. Later on during the proceedings he gave the wreath to an ancient revolutionary colonel and told him to keep it "as our common property."

After leaving Yorktown the marquis went to Monticello to spend a week with the venerable Thomas Jefferson, then in his eighty-first year. They had not met in thirty-five years, and Lafayette was silently shocked at the appearance of his friend. Like John Adams—whom Lafayette had visited while in Boston—Jefferson did not have long to live, and he knew it. Together they went to Charlottesville to look over the new University of Virginia, then in the building stage and not yet ready to receive students.* Jefferson was very proud of the university, as he had a right to be; it was his own creation. The motto of the university, selected by Jefferson, is, "And ye shall know the truth, and the truth shall make you free."

On parting with Jefferson at Monticello, Lafayette promised to return in a few months to say farewell before his final departure for Europe. Before going back to Washington he passed four days at Montpelier with James and Dolly Madison. By the middle of November he was again at Gadsby's Hotel.

Fanny Wright had gone to Washington, of course, and was living there during Lafayette's stay. She saw him daily, and made herself his constant companion, just as she had been at La Grange. There are some indefinable and shadowy reasons for believing that he was beginning to lose interest in her ideas, though he still thought of her with affection. Buzzing in her head were many impracticable

* It was opened in 1825.

schemes for which she hoped to obtain his approval and support. Also she desired ardently to be adopted as his daughter and did not fail to remind him of her wishes. Probably he would have adopted her if he had had no children of his own, but there were Anastasie and Virginie, and he knew very well that they did not want her as an adopted sister; and there was son George, always at his elbow. George looked upon her proposal with a cold and doubtful eye.

On December 9th—the date is still 1824—he was invited to appear before the Senate as a guest of honor. Next day he was a guest of the House of Representatives. All the senators were present again on that occasion. In the gallery reserved for the diplomatic corps every representative of a foreign nation—except the French minister—was present.

A few days later a resolution to give $200,000 and a township of land to Lafayette, in token of the nation's gratitude, was introduced in Congress by Mr. Hayne, of South Carolina. It was known that he was sorely in need of money. The resolution was carried in the Senate unanimously. In the House twenty-six members voted against it—all of them from the northern states. The members of the House who had voted adversely explained that their attitude was not to be considered a reflection on Lafayette personally, but simply as an expression of policy.*

On New Year's Day the two houses of Congress united in giving a gorgeous banquet in his honor. Replying to the speeches, he said in part:

Words are wanting to express all my respect and all my gratitude for the kindness with which you overwhelm me; but I hope you will do justice to the warmth of my American feelings. Permit me to respond to the toast that has just been drunk, by giving you: To the perpetual union of the United States. It has already saved us in the times of storm, one day it will save the world.

His reference to the United States having already "saved us in the times of storm" is rather enigmatic. If America had done anything, up to that time, to save France or Europe, the occurrence is still unknown to historians. More than ninety years later the American nation did set out to make the world safe for democracy. The unfortunate results of that adventure are well known.

* Lafayette invested $120,000 of this gift in 4½ per cent bonds of the United States government. He wrote Jefferson, "My dear friend, I find myself now quite rich."

3

Lafayette's desk at Gadsby's Hotel had been covered for weeks by invitations to visit the southern states. He decided to make a southern tour. The itinerary as worked out, included Charleston, Savannah and Augusta; then he would go across country to New Orleans. From there a river steamer would take him and his party to Pittsburgh. On land again, he was to visit Buffalo and Niagara Falls, then go straight to Boston. He had agreed positively to be in Boston on June 17th—the fiftieth anniversary of the battle of Bunker Hill. He was to lay the cornerstone of the Bunker Hill monument, and a great many people would be sorely disappointed if he failed to appear. It was a tight schedule, and one that required punctual departures, and swift moving. He was informed that the roads were incredibly bad.

On the twenty-third of February, 1825, the Lafayette party left Washington for Norfolk on a river steamer. All the equipment, including horses, were on board. He intended to ride horseback most of the way, but Mrs. Eliza Custis had lent him one of her carriages which he might use when tired of horseback riding.

At the last moment Miss Frances Wright decided not to accompany the party. She had probably been dissuaded by Lafayette. In a letter to Dolly Madison—dated February 23, 1825—Frances Wright said that she was too ill to accept Mrs. Madison's invitation to visit Montpelier, and that she and her sister expected to leave soon for a long journey westward "so as to join our venerable friend, General Lafayette, in New Orleans on April 1st." Whatever her intentions may have been she did not go to New Orleans and did not see the general again until June 17th, in Boston.

The trip was a long series of uproarious demonstrations. The party passed through Raleigh and reached Fayetteville, which bore the name of the marquis, on March 5th. His namesake, which is now a flourishing and busy little city, was in 1825 just one long and muddy street of log cabins, unpainted frame houses and taverns. But it had a mayor. He delivered a droning harangue of welcome while the rain pelted down. The Masonic lodge provided a banquet at which Lafayette proposed a toast: "To Fayetteville! May her growth and prosperity equal the ardent wishes of her homonym!"

No doubt the word "homonym" caused the worthy citizens to pore over the schoolmaster's dictionary the next day.

At Camden, in South Carolina, he laid the cornerstone of a monument to General De Kalb, who had come over from France with him in his faraway youth. Francis Huger joined the party at Columbia and went on to Charleston with Lafayette. He offered part of his gift of $200,000 from Congress to Huger, but the letter declined, with thanks.

The people of Charleston received him in great state. He was met by a troop of cavalry wearing the uniform of the Parisian National Guard. As his carriage rolled up the horsemen drew their sabers and rent the air with a shout of *"Vive Lafayette!"*

He journeyed from Charleston to Savannah by steamboat. More laying of cornerstones, receptions and a banquet. The party embarked on another steamer and proceeded up the yellow, muddy Savannah River to Augusta. After two days in Augusta he appeared to be completely worn out, and on the way to Macon, had a severe attack of vomiting. The roads were execrable. The party pushed through Macon to Montgomery. From that point a steamer conveyed them to Mobile; and another steamer from Mobile to New Orleans.*

When they left New Orleans to go up the Mississippi Lafayette was ill from too much entertainment; he remained in bed for the greater part of the trip. The steamer turned into the Cumberland River and went up to Nashville. There he was met by Andrew Jackson and was a guest at the Hermitage during his few days' stay.

On the way up the Ohio to Louisville an accident occurred which came within a hairbreadth of putting an end to Lafayette's career. During the night the steamer struck a snag and began to sink immediately. In sinking the vessel listed ominously to starboard, so within a short time the deck was as steeply inclined as the roof of a house. The boats were lowered with difficulty, the night was very dark, and it was believed at first that a number of people had lost their lives. But, fortunately, no one was drowned. Most of the passengers and crew were good swimmers, and the river was almost as still as a pond. Nearly all of them, however, lost their

* The Savannah *Georgian* of March 28, 1825, says that during the reception and ceremonies at Milledgeville, where he stopped overnight on his way from Augusta to Macon, "Six pocketbooks were stolen during the ceremonies, one containing $4500."

luggage. It rained during the night. At dawn, when it grew light enough to see, the passengers looked at one another and, in spite of their discomfort, burst into laughter.

It was a motley assemblage. Clothes were sadly lacking. The governor of Tennessee, who was accompanying Lafayette, had lost his wig and his shoes. His head was bald and his feet were bare. Owing to the quick, deft ministrations of Bastien, and George and Levasseur, the marquis was better clothed than most of his fellow passengers. But his luggage was gone, and so was his vast pile of six hundred unanswered letters. He did not mind the loss of the letters, and was rather cheerful about it, as he realized that he had been relieved of the drudgery of replying to them.

At nine o'clock that morning the steamer *Paragon*—one of the finest of the river boats—was seen going down the river from Louisville. Her owner, a Mr. Neilson, was one of the shivering, shipwrecked passengers on the riverbank. He ordered the *Paragon* to turn back. Everybody got aboard and proceeded to Louisville; and, a few days thereafter, the Lafayette party went on to Cincinnati.

Lafayette remained at Cincinnati three days. The usual program was carried out: review of the militia, banquets, toasts, a ball, handshaking; and there was a magnificent display of fireworks on the river. He was delighted with Cincinnati and would have stayed longer if he had had the time.

At the end of May he was at Niagara Falls, hundreds of miles from Boston. He made the journey in fifteen days despite the long string of celebrations on the way. The Lafayette party, travel-worn but in high spirits, reached Boston June 15, 1825.

Bunker Hill Day—June 17th—was at hand. The patriotic societies assembled at the Common, and at ten o'clock the procession began to move toward Bunker Hill. Lafayette, in an open barouche drawn by six white horses, was one of the centers of attraction. It has been said that two hundred thousand people were in the crowd that lined the way.

The orator of the day was Daniel Webster. Most Americans have read his famous Bunker Hill oration; thousands of school children have been required to learn parts of it by heart.

The cornerstone was laid by Lafayette. He wore his Masonic regalia and used a silver trowel. In a flimsily built shed tables were laid for four thousand people. As they dined the bands played patriotic airs, the guns boomed, and there were speeches and toasts. Very pleasing it all was to Lafayette; he was right in his element.

In a letter to the family at La Grange he said it was "one of the most beautiful patriotic fetes ever celebrated. Nothing can compare with it except the Federation of 1790." He wrote further:

Nothing can describe the effect of that republican prayer pronounced before an immense multitude by an aged chaplain who fought at Bunker Hill. . . . We sat down at a table of four thousand covers where I announced that after having celebrated at this first quinquagenary the freedom of the American hemisphere, the toast of the next quinquagenary will be a freed Europe.

That evening there was a reception at the home of Daniel Webster on Summer Street. To provide room for the large number of guests an opening was cut through the wall of the adjoining house. Among the guests at the reception was Fanny Wright; she had gone to Boston to meet Lafayette.

The Duke of Saxe-Weimar, who was then a traveler in America, wrote—as quoted by Waterman—that "this lady with her sister, unattended by a male protector, had roved about the country, in steamboats and stages, that she constantly tagged about after General Lafayette, and whenever the general arrived at any place, Miss Wright was sure to follow the next day; as but little notice had been taken of this lady in Boston, a literary attack was expected from her pen. She is no longer young, and is of tall stature and masculine manners."*

He planned to sail for France on August 13th, on a passenger vessel, but the secretary of war, who was in Boston, informed him that the government intended to place the new frigate *Brandywine* at his disposal for the return voyage. The vessel was not yet ready, and would not be ready until September. Would he wait a few weeks? Lafayette accepted the offer of the government and agreed to defer his departure.

In the course of his tour he had visited all of the twenty-four states with the exception of Maine and Vermont. The citizens of those two states did not like it a bit. Why should he discriminate against Vermont and Maine? There were pressing invitations. The people did not expect him to stay a long time, but just pass through so they could say he had been there.

* Waterman, *Frances Wright,* p. 90. The duke says that Miss Wright was "no longer young." She was only twenty-nine at that time.

He made the trip, and made it in a hurry. On July 3rd he was back in New York, where he remained for ten days, practically in public the whole time. Then the party began its journey to Washington. The temperature was up in the nineties (Fahrenheit), but Lafayette did not appear to mind it.

In Philadelphia he had a long private talk, behind closed doors, with Miss Frances Wright. What he said to her, or she said to him, is unknown, but it is generally believed that he told her definitely that he would not adopt her as a daughter and gave her the reasons for his decision. She left the party at once and was never again on terms of close friendship with Lafayette. Yet we find her a few years later as a guest for a little while at La Grange.

Before leaving Philadelphia he visited the field of the battle of Brandywine. The veterans present were astonished at his clear memory of the movements on the battlefield.

The new president, John Quincy Adams, insisted that Lafayette stay at the White House while the frigate *Brandywine* was being equipped for her voyage to France. President Adams had him protected from callers, but he found that it was a difficult job—that of keeping Lafayette away from his admirers. The marquis had to journey to Virginia to say farewell to Jefferson and Monroe. On September 6, 1825, the president gave a dinner in his honor at the White House. Lafayette was sixty-eight years old on that day. Despite the effort to make the dinner a gay affair, it was rather sad. Everyone there knew that they were saying good-bye forever to the gallant Frenchman whom they all loved.

4

Next day he sailed on the *Brandywine* for Havre. The ship contained a large collection of diverse articles which had been presented to Lafayette during his tour. There were stuffed animals—any number of them—including stuffed eagles. The Americans of that day seem to have gone in for stuffing in a big way. Then there were Indian relics of all kinds—tomahawks, belts of wampum, war bonnets, pipes. A bottle of water from the Erie Canal was there, and one of the candles supposed to have been in the possession of Lord Cornwallis. Furniture of all descriptions, some live snakes, a raccoon, an opossum, and a grizzly bear given by Governor Clarke of Missouri. Models of steam engines occupied much space; there was a clock without springs that ran by water power, and a hydraulic pump.

The voyage to Havre lasted twenty-four days. Lafayette had been away from France fifteen months. A great crowd of his admirers met him on his debarkation. He was escorted to Rouen, where he was a house guest for a day of one of his former Liberal colleagues in the Chamber of Deputies. While they were at dinner many people gathered before the house. They intended to serenade Lafayette, but they were not able to carry out their intention. Mounted gendarmes charged the crowd, trampled down men and women, injured several persons and arrested many.

Lafayette, looking on, said, "I realize that I am back home again."

CHAPTER XXXIV

REVOLUTION OF JULY, 1830

I

THAT the Bourbons were incapable of learning or forgetting is supposed to be well known, so well known indeed that it is embodied in a popular saying. They had static mentalities, and Charles X—the former Comte d'Artois—was even more static than some of his predecessors. The Revolution and everything else that had occurred since 1789 seemed to him to be wholly wrong and out of place in France. Had he possessed the power he would have turned the clock back forty or fifty years.

His supporters consisted almost entirely of former émigrés, stupid reactionary nobles, the Jesuits, the higher clergy and a nondescript collection of government contractors, army officers, useless officials and others who were living at the public expense.

The National Constitution, called the Charter—granted by Louis XVIII in the year 1814—was one of the chief obstacles to the royalist program, but to an American or to a Frenchman of the twentieth century the Charter appears to have been a rather pathetic bulwark of the liberty of a people. It provided for a parliament of two houses. The members of the lower house—the Chamber of Deputies—were elected; those of the upper chamber—the House of Peers—were appointed by the king. Liberal legislation emanating from the Chamber of Deputies could be effectually blocked by the non-concurrence of the Peers.

About two-thirds of the people were excluded from the suffrage. Men without property were not allowed to vote. That provision excluded most workmen and the whole class of agricultural laborers. But the law went even further; small taxpayers were also denied the ballot except in local affairs. To select the deputies there was a system of indirect voting. A citizen did not vote directly for a candidate of his choice, but for a number of electors who were to represent the community in a convention of the district. This meeting, or convention, selected the deputies for the department.

The right to propose new legislation was reserved for the king. But when a royal proposal was once brought into Parliament it might be amended or rejected.

The president of the Chamber of Deputies—corresponding to our American Speaker of the House—was selected by a vote of the Chamber, but the choice had to be approved by the king before it was effective.

The Charter granted freedom of worship. That is one of the cheapest of concessions that autocratic governments make to their people. Frenchmen might be Roman Catholics, Protestants, Mohammedans, or just plain out-and-out atheists.

Free speech and a free press were also guaranteed, but the guarantee had a string attached to it, and the string might be—and was—pulled in now and then. The accounts of Lafayette's journey through the United States were censored so thoroughly that the newspapers contained little more than a record of his arrivals and departures.

Such suppressions invariably encourage an outlaw press, circulating secretly. Through forbidden publications the French people were kept informed as to Lafayette's triumphal progress in our states.

The army was entirely under royal control; officers might be appointed or dismissed at the pleasure of the king. The right to trial by jury was provided by the Charter, but that guarantee of liberty could be set aside in case of public emergency, a vague term which may be defined as any movement opposed to the existing order.

The Charter worked fairly well under Louis XVIII, who was a mild ruler at heart. The White Terror and other iniquities of his reign were carried on against his wishes, but he did not have sufficient strength of will to suppress them. Most of them had been instigated by the Comte d'Artois.

Charles X had plenty of will power, a vast amount of ignorance, an inability to learn, and a thorough conviction that every republican idea in the world was not only evil in principle but also contrary to common sense. Besides these forbidding qualities there was a cruel streak in his make-up.

That psychological combination would have succeeded, in all probability, during the old regime, and Charles X might have gone

LAFAYETTE AS AN OLD MAN

Painted in the garden at La Grange by Mme. Joubert, in 1834, a short time before Lafayette's death.

LAFAYETTE BEING ESCORTED TO THE HOTEL DE VILLE IN PARIS

into the historic past as a worthy successor of Louis XV. But the old regime was long dead, without hope of resuscitation.

During the past ten years, since the downfall of Napoleon, a new Liberal party had grown up in France. It was not merely a nebulous group of doctrinaires and philosophers. Millions of ordinary, insignificant, hard-working Frenchmen had learned to believe in human rights and the abolition of privilege. They were much better informed than the Jacobins and other firebrands of the French Revolution who had struck blindly against an outworn and vicious tyranny. The liberals of the 1820's knew what they were doing; in general they understood well enough the relation of the individual to the state, and that the prosperity of a nation rests upon its workers and creative minds.

In this alignment of forces we see two opposing social systems facing each other in the arena of public affairs. Like gladiators with swords in their hands they circled around cautiously, each hoping to plant a deadly thrust in the body of his opponent. For the whole of the six-year reign of Charles X this duel went on. Owing to indirect voting and more sinister methods of manipulating the ballot, the Liberals were never able to manifest their full strength in the Chamber of Deputies.

The popular dissatisfaction with the ruling powers was economic as well as political. Industry was stagnant, large numbers of people were unemployed. The high tariff policy of the government was destroying trade with other nations. After a hundred years of economic education many of those who had a hand in directing the government were still ignorant of the true nature of foreign trade, and endeavored to arrange matters so that the French would be sellers but not buyers. Consequently, the high tariff.

2

Soon after the accession of Charles X the ministry brought in a proposal for the indemnification of émigrés and others whose estates had been seized by the nation and sold during the Revolution. The measure was enacted; one billion francs was appropriated as a recompense for those who had been despoiled.

Lafayette was paid 325,000 francs for his lost estates, a sum which has been estimated to have been about one-tenth of their actual value.

In 1827 he was elected a deputy from Meaux. In that election the Liberal party, despite the machinations of the royalists, scored a victory. In the new Chamber there was a majority of sixty liberals.

With his election to the Chamber, Lafayette—then a man of seventy—began again to take an active part in political life. During the months when the Chamber was in session he seldom went to La Grange, but lived at his town house, No. 6 Rue d'Anjou Saint-Honoré. Every Tuesday evening he received anyone who cared to drop in. He held on these occasions an "open house," as we call such gatherings in America. I fancy that he got the idea, during his sojourn in the United States, from his friend Andrew Jackson.

The spacious house was filled with republicans. Formal etiquette was laid aside. At the door there was no gold-laced functionary to demand the names of callers. Some came in coaches and some on foot. Most of those who came wanted to talk with others who held the same, or similar, views. They needed the encouragement that grows from companionship in a common cause. But there were others who came merely to eat and drink. Still others came to listen, to scribble down fragments of conversation and report them to the secret police.

Someone told Lafayette that the police had a *dossier* of revolutionary utterances made in his house. He remarked that it was a useless labor, as nothing was said in his house that was not being said every day in public all over France. That was quite true.

A revolt against Charles X and his circle of favorites was developing spontaneously, without a leader or a definite plan of action, long before it came to a head.

With little effort Lafayette could have made himself the acknowledged leader of the movement for the establishment of a republic and the director of its course. At that time—in the late 1820's —he was the most popular man in France among the masses. In the Chamber of Deputies he had made a great and favorable reputation for himself as an advocate of liberalism. He stood for an extension of the suffrage that would give the ballot to every citizen, and he proposed a primary school system financed and directed by the national government that would include every child in France. He was opposed to the indirect method of voting and argued for a system of balloting which would permit voters to indicate directly the candidates of their choice.

In 1829 Lafayette and son George journeyed to Chavaniac. He

had not been there for years, and he wanted to see the place again. His trip, there and back, was a triumphal progress, evidently to his surprise. There were receptions, banquets, music, girls with flowers.

At Brioude, in reply to an address of welcome, he said that, in his early days, "here my eyes opened to the usurpations of privilege and arbitrary authority; before they close forever may they behold my country in full possession of all her rights and in full enjoyment of the benefits of a pure and complete liberty."

Escorted by volunteer troops of horsemen he went here and there in that part of France. Everywhere he was met by cheering crowds. At Lyons, despite the mayor's injunction against assembling to welcome Lafayette, he was met by a multitude. The next day after his arrival—September 6, 1829—was his seventy-second birthday, and the Masonic lodges gave a great banquet in his honor.

His speeches were really incitements to revolution, and the government was greatly displeased by them. But nothing was done by the royal autocratic authority except to dismiss a few minor officials from their posts for having permitted Lafayette to speak.

Everyone who had an intelligent understanding of public affairs knew—or believed implicitly—that the reign of Charles X was drawing to a close. One did not need to be a clairvoyant or peer into magic mirrors and globes of crystal to know that. The French people simply had had enough, and too much, of Charles X, and that is all there was to it. The king and his little coterie were completely out of touch with the national life, and with national problems.

Very few people thought there would be much trouble in deposing him when the time came. But who was to take his place? The republicans believed that France should declare itself a republic, with Lafayette as its first president. The bankers, industrialists, investors in government bonds and the great landowners had a different view of the matter. They, too, realized that Charles X was no longer acceptable to the nation, if he had ever been acceptable, but they had a profound distrust of democracies, of republics. The distant roar of the French Revolution was still resounding in the air. And their distrust of Lafayette as an administrator and possible president was also profound. Many of them considered him just a plain, romantic fool without any real sense of practical values.

Yet it should be understood that even these opponents of a Fayettist republic were not reactionaries in the ordinary meaning of that term. They were "conservative liberals," and they had no desire to turn France back to the feudal regime. The only downright reactionary party consisted of the king, the court officials and some of the peers.

The conservative liberals had in mind—for the future—a kingdom on the English model. That, too, had been the Lafayette ideal for years. Their choice as the future king was fixed on the Duc d'Orléans, the son of Philippe Egalité, who had been guillotined during the Terror.

Let us examine for a moment, with the brief casual glance of one who inspects a railway ticket, the qualifications of Louis Philippe d'Orléans for the high post of king of France. His qualifications should not be disregarded, or treated with contempt. Exile and poverty had taught him a great deal of ordinary common sense. Long ago he had lost, somewhere in his adventures, the high-and-mighty air of the Bourbons who could never get out of their heads the conviction that the whole of France belonged to them by the grace of God.

He was born in Paris in 1773, so at the beginning of the Revolution he had been a mere lad. Like his father, he went over to the side of the Revolution. He became an officer in the revolutionary army, under the title of Duc de Chartres. In 1792 he commanded a brigade at Valmy and Jemappes, and distinguished himself.

When General Dumouriez left his army and fled from France young Louis Philippe went with him. Thereafter, he lived for years in foreign lands, but he refused to take up arms against the French nation. He experienced many ups and downs. The record of his life in the years of exile is still obscure, but it is known that at times he earned his own precarious livelihood. He lived in America for a while, and for many years he was in England. In the course of time he became as English as any foreigner could be. He spoke the English language with ease, he admired the English way of doing things, and he thought the British government was just about perfect.

When Louis XVIII was raised to the throne after the downfall of Napoleon his friendly advisers urged him to invite Louis Philippe, Duc d'Orléans, to return and make his home in Paris. Readers will recall, I am sure, that Louis Philippe was a direct descendant of Louis XIII, through a younger brother of Louis XIV. The Orleans family owned the vast Palais Royal—or had owned it in times past, and it was returned to Louis Philippe. There he resided for fifteen years.

He was a bourgeois prince, not as a matter of pretense or for political reasons, but because he happened to be that kind of person. He went around Paris dressed in a frock coat, a high collar and a huge black cravat. He wore a tall silk hat, and he carried always a tightly rolled umbrella. I suppose he had lived in England so long that he thought it might rain at any moment; so the umbrella. He reminds one of the pictures of Daniel Webster. During the evenings, in dressing gown and slippers, he sat at home, usually, with his wife, playing small games and reading the news of the day.

His father had been a disreputable rake, gambler and keeper of many varieties of women. Louis Philippe was none of that. There was no more to be said in his disfavor than there was to be said against Calvin Coolidge in our American presidential election of 1924. Baffled criticism retired, gnashing its teeth, and picking up little shreds and crumbs of animosity that it found lying along the road.

When the law to recompense the former émigrés for the loss of their property was enacted in 1825, Louis Philippe d'Orléans was the largest beneficiary in the whole of France. He received fourteen million francs.

3

At the opening of Parliament on March 2, 1830, Charles X said, in his address from the throne, that "if culpable actions raise obstacles for my government that I do not wish to anticipate I shall find the force to overcome them."

That statement was, in its way, a declaration of war against the Liberal party. The Liberals were not slow to accept the challenge. In its reply to the king's address the Chamber declared that "the Charter consecrated the right of the country to participate in discussions affecting the public welfare" and that such participation implies a co-operation of the royal government with the wishes of the people. "Our loyalty and devotion force us to say to you that this co-operation does not exist."

On July 27th the *Moniteur,* official publication of the government, printed five royal decrees that came like lightning from a clear sky.

They were an exhibition of almost unbelievable folly. The king decreed:

1. The suspension of the liberty of the press and of free speech.

2. The dissolution of the Chamber of Deputies.

3. The appointment of a number of inflexible reactionaries to high positions in the government.

4. A tightening up of the suffrage in favor of the reactionaries.

5. A convocation of the electoral colleges for the purpose of selecting a new Chamber.

Charles X intended his announcement as the first gun of a coup d'état, but he was far too weak to carry out such a smashing program. The only dynamic effect of the decrees was to arouse all the latent and active revolutionary forces in the kingdom.

The Revolution of 1830, as it is called in historical narrative, was over in four days. There were mobs in the streets, but they were not especially fierce. The paving was torn up here and there and built into barricades, not that there was any great need of them, but it did seem to all concerned that every revolution ought to have its barricades. A few people were killed, but not many.

The Chamber of Deputies met and appointed Lafayette as general in chief of the National Guard. The king, quite too late, recalled and annulled the offensive decrees. The Carbonari, that had been quiescent for years, rose in force and demanded a republic with Lafayette at its head. They were joined by thousands of workmen and students.

The king had lost the support of his own troops, and—it seems —of everybody else. Yet it was all done in a pleasant manner. One wonders why there was such an air of courtesy about it. The answer is, in all probability, that the downfall of the king had been anticipated for several years, and everybody was prepared for it. Moreover, the royal resistance to the people's verdict was negligible.

Lafayette had become the provisional head of the government. On July 31st he announced that the "royal family had ceased to reign."

Then what?

He was surrounded by thousands of his friends and admirers. Charles de Rémusat, one of the editors of the *Globe*, and the husband of one of Lafayette's granddaughters, came to him in the Hôtel de Ville, and said, "You'll have to make a choice. It will be either you as the president of a French republic or the Duc d'Orléans as a new king."

Lafayette did not know what to say. He could not make such a momentous decision. On that Saturday morning—July 31, 1830— soon after he had announced to the world that France had no king one of his callers was William Cabell Rives, the American minister. "What will the American people say," Lafayette asked, "if they learn that we have proclaimed a republic?"

Mr. Rives replied, "They will say that forty years of experience have been lost on the French."

Exactly what Mr. Rives meant by that remark is beyond my comprehension, and I can only guess. The French had never had a republic. Their experience of the past forty years was concerned with dictators, terrorists, and kings; and it had been, on the whole, an unsatisfactory experience all around.

He was certainly wrong in his estimate of what the American people would say in case France became a republic. There cannot be the slightest doubt that they would have celebrated the birth of a French republic from Maine to Florida, and from Maryland to Missouri; and if Lafayette had been at the head of it, as its first president, the American people would have held two celebrations.

Lafayette was capable of leading a popular movement up to a certain point, but when the time came for ultimate and decisive action he would fumble, hesitate and permit the leadership to be taken out of his hands. On these occasions he seemed to wilt and fold up.

> "And thus the native hue of resolution
> Is sicklied o'er with the pale cast of thought,
> And enterprises of great pith and moment,
> With this regard their currents turn awry,
> And lose the name of action."

As a matter of plain and obvious truth one must say that he was not a great leader of men, or of causes. Yet, at the same time, he had a far-reaching influence. He possessed the rare quality of inspiring people, of gaining their loyalty and affection. But he was lacking in the power to control and direct. Yet, let us not forget that he was in his seventy-fourth year in 1830. He was too old to lead a revolution.

The Orleanists had their way. They took the situation away from Lafayette. They surrounded him in a friendly way in the Hôtel de Ville, giving him advice and admonition, while the streets were crowded with cheering men who called on Lafayette to lead them.

In the afternoon of that fateful Saturday, July 31st, after his talk with the American minister, he sent his friend Mathieu Dumas to the Palais Royal, where the Duc d'Orléans sat awaiting the summons. Lafayette's message was that while he preferred a republic he thought, in the circumstances, that a republic would be impracticable, and would the Duc d'Orléans head a constitutional monarchy? The reply was Yes, emphatically.

The reception of the Duc d'Orléans next morning at the Hôtel de Ville was a depressing affair. As the Duke rode along the street, surrounded by a group of friends, he was greeted by a roar of voices —not cheering for the Duc d'Orléans, but for Lafayette. The cheering came from the republicans who had carried on the three days' revolution; the young men who had build the barricades. But they had not risked their lives to put the Duc d'Orléans on the throne. They had hoped to create a republic, with Lafayette as their leader.

The doings on that day were incomprehensible to the ardent republicans. Packed in the Place de Grève, before the Hôtel de Ville, they saw Lafayette, their chief, come out on the balcony with the Duc d'Orléans. He embraced the duke and kissed him on both cheeks. The Duc d'Orléans waved a tricolor flag of the Revolution which someone had placed in his hands. He said something to the effect that he pledged himself to be a people's king. The crowd yelled *"Vive Lafayette!"* with a thin chorus of *"Vive le Duc d'Orléans!"* The workmen and the students, grimy with the dust and dirt of the past few hectic days, felt that—in some mysterious way—they had been let down altogether.

Within a week there was more grumbling. Lafayette announced that the new government was to be "a popular throne surrounded by republican institutions." He went to the Palais Royal and sat for hours in the stuffy rooms of the bourgeois king. Together they worked out a number of concessions to the people.*

These concessions included a new and more liberal constitution, the abolition of a hereditary peerage, universal suffrage without property qualification, a reorganization of the courts, and the popular election of the officials of towns and communes. (Under the preceding regime most of these officials had been appointed by the central government at Paris, as postmasters are in the United States today.)

* Why were they called "concessions?" I do not know. The new king was the recipient of all the concessions, or so it seems. But the published documents state that the Duc d'Orléans had "conceded" this and that.

The Duc d'Orléans, who took the title of Louis Philippe, was not to be called the "King of France," but the "King of the French."

Charles X was still at Rambouillet—one of his châteaux in the country—lingering on with the hope that something would turn up to change the course of events. Nothing did occur, and on August 3rd he departed for England. On the whole it had been a peaceful revolution. The Chamber of Deputies met and declared the throne vacant, then they made Louis Philippe king of the French.

CHAPTER XXXV

THE DEATH OF LAFAYETTE

1

THE SELECTION of an Orleans prince as head of the nation was not popular with the mass of French people. Within a few years there were six attempts to assassinate Louis Philippe.

Without going deep into the complications of French history— for this book is not a history of France—it may be said definitely that the chief defect of the administration of Louis Philippe was that it disregarded almost wholly the condition of the working people. In that era modern capitalism was beginning in France, and by the word "capitalism" I mean the dominating position of money over men.

The millions of French workmen who earned their daily bread by their labor constituted an unorganized mass of workers which had little or nothing to say in making the laws or in shaping the social state. Public affairs were in the hands of the factory owners, the landed proprietors, the bankers and stockjobbers.

2

Louis Philippe was not a royalist in principle, strangely enough, although he belonged to one of the most ancient royal families of Europe. By nature and instinct he was a bourgeois, a member of the middle class. He had more respect for any shrewd, gimlet-eyed rascal who had made a fortune out of underpaid workers in the silk-weaving business than he had for all the economists and philosophers. He was for men "who do things," meaning those who get the better of some-body else. There were democratic phrases on his tongue but in his mind there was a vision of a contented nation of millionaires and laborers. He had no liking for the idle rich. He was no idler himself, and he thought everyone should be usefully employed.

There were strikes and riots in many parts of France. The most violent was that of the workmen of Lyons, who demanded a raise in wages. Their employers agreed to give them the increase in pay, but after the factory hands had gone back to work they failed to carry out their promise. The workmen seized the city of Lyons and were its masters for three days. Marshal Soult—a military gangster who had risen with Napoleon—was sent to Lyons with thirty thousand men to restore order.

It should not have been difficult to establish an orderly state of affairs. All Marshal Soult had to do was to surround the homes of the employers, take them to jail, and imprison them on the ground that they had broken their promises to the workmen. The whole trouble would have been solved in a short time.

But Marshal Soult did not tackle the problem that way at all. He shot down the workmen in the streets and established order.

Soon afterward Saint-Marc-Girardin, a well-known journalist and a royalist, wrote in the *Journal des Débats:*

Modern society will perish through its proletariat if it does not seek through all possible means to give them a share in ownership. I have no taste for a foolish philanthropy; but whoever does not concern himself with the lot of the lower classes is neither a good Christian nor a good citizen.

For a time, for a few months, Lafayette received at least one letter a day from the king. They were letters of affectionate gratitude. In some of these epistles Louis Philippe asked for advice and counsel, but in all of them he expressed his hopes for the good health of the general.

The National Guard, which had been abolished under Charles X, was re-created and Lafayette was made its commander in chief. How tired he must have been. More than half a century had passed since he had formed the National Guard, and there he was again in the same uniform, at the age of seventy-three, at the head of a new National Guard. Many of those who stood before him in the ranks were the grandsons of the men who had belonged to the original National Guard in 1789.

The French had little respect for Louis Philippe. He was the subject of innumerable ridiculous cartoons. The people said his head was shaped like a pear, though the pear shape does not appear in any of the portraits of him that I have seen. They considered him a stupid person. The word *poire*—a pear—passed into current slang, and even today a dull-witted, slow-thinking man in France is called *une poire*.

3

The friendship of Louis Philippe and Lafayette did not last long. It was over before the end of the year 1830. The king resented deeply the stories that were going around about him and Lafayette. He was described as a puppet king, with Lafayette pulling the wires. In a political cartoon—printed in a Belgian newspaper but circulated all over France—he was depicted as standing before Lafayette bareheaded, his crown in his hand; and Lafayette was shown saying graciously, "You may keep on your hat."

There was, besides, much difference of opinion between Lafayette and the king. They drifted apart. Lafayette was not welcomed any more as an adviser of the monarch.

On December 24, 1830, the Chamber passed a law abolishing the post of commander of the National Guard, which was placed under command of the minister of the interior. It was done without warning; Lafayette did not know such a law was even being considered. Certainly it must have been done with the connivance—or at the direct instigation—of Louis Philippe, though he wrote the next day to Lafayette that he had known nothing about it until he read an announcement of the act in the official report of the proceedings in the Chamber.

Divested of all formalities and pretenses of courtesy, the action of the deputies of the Christmas Eve of 1830 was a notification to Lafayette that he was no longer needed in French affairs. That was what the government meant, but the National Guard immediately opened a subscription among its members to give him a sword of honor. The *arrondissement* of Meaux, which he represented in the Chamber, had a medallion made in honor of Lafayette. There were Lafayette cockades and many pamphlets in which he was praised. But they were all mere eulogies and epitaphs; wreaths laid on the tombstone of a political career.

Never thereafter did he play any great role in public life. He was still a member of the Chamber of Deputies but too old and too feeble in health to take a prominent part in its proceedings. He was partly deaf and had to hold his hand behind his ear to hear the speeches.

Whenever he rose to speak his discourse was almost always

on the advantages of a French republic on the American model. On January 3, 1834, in the course of a debate with M. de Mornay, he said that he was a disciple of the American school:

A man who had been the friend, the associate, if I may be permitted to speak thus, of Washington, of Franklin, and of Jefferson, to say that the combination that we made, and which we then thought to be in the interest and according to the will of the nation, was the best of republics.

Early in the year 1832 Paris was visited by a plague of Asiatic cholera. I know it seems incredible, but it is the truth just the same. The working class *faubourgs* of Saint-Antoine and Saint-Marceau were as filthy as any Chinese city was in the last decade of the nineteenth century. There were thousands of victims; eight hundred and sixty-one died in one day. The physicians had no idea how to treat the disease. Fires were kept burning in the street night and day, under a conviction that the air might be thus purified. People wore masks, or bandages around their mouths, to prevent infection.

The plague spread to the higher classes. General Maximilien Lamarque, aggressive Liberal and intimate friend of Lafayette, died on June 1st. His funeral, which Lafayette attended, was the occasion for a revolutionary demonstration. About one hundred thousand people were in the procession. It halted at the Place de la Bastille and speeches were made there in a pouring rain.

Lafayette had something to say, and said it. Of course, it was on the subject of liberty, which was the only topic on which Lafayette ever spoke in public. It does seem, even to the most kindly commentator, that he might have said something about sanitation and the living conditions of the poor, and the widening gulf between wealth and poverty. However, the speech was received with ebullient enthusiasm, even in the rain, and the crowd yelled *"Vive Lafayette!"* and *"A bas Louis Philippe!"*

Then a wreath was put on his head by someone who stood behind him. Very likely he had thought he was through with wreaths when he had left the United States in 1825. But there was the wreath, on his brow; he snatched it off and threw it on the ground, and then he looked around with an angry stare for the wreath-giver, who was never discovered. No doubt he meant well but he probably was not informed as to Lafayette's aversion to wreaths.

His son George was with him; they decided to go home after the episode of the wreath, but they could not find their carriage. But they did find an empty hack waiting for passengers. They took that and instructed the driver to go to Lafayette's home on the Rue d'Anjou Saint-Honoré. A crowd of students soon took the horses out of the shafts and dragged the vehicle around, here and there. They demanded that he go to the Hôtel de Ville and proclaim a republic, as the wish of the people. Lafayette said to them, "You are not the people, and I must obey my conscience."

While he and George were being dragged along in the little carriage he heard somebody near at hand say: "Let's kill the general and throw him in the river. Everybody would think the government had done it, and then we would have a good reason for revolt."

Eventually he got home, but how miserable he must have felt! He was like an actor who has been too long on the stage and realizes it.

4

One of Lafayette's friends in the Chamber of Deputies was named Dulong. He fought a duel with a General Bugeaud, also a member of the Chamber. George Lafayette was one of Dulong's seconds at this encounter on a misty, cold winter morning. Dulong had the misfortune to be mortally wounded, and he died the next day.

On February 1, 1834, Dulong was buried in the cemetery of Père-Lachaise. Lafayette insisted on walking, lame as he was, in the funeral procession and stood by the grave, bareheaded, while many long-winded speeches were made. When he reached home he was so ill that he had to go to bed at once and summon the physicians. He never recovered from this last illness, although now and then he went out in his carriage.

Dr. Jules Cloquet, who attended Lafayette at that time, wrote something about his final illness in his *Souvenirs de Général Lafayette*, but he did not give any clear description of the disease. He wrote that the general could not urinate, which is, of course, a serious matter. That was overcome, it seems, by very hot baths. Lafayette may have had an urethral stricture, or prostatitis. As to that—who knows? Dr. Cloquet was as squeamish as any Victorian maiden aunt in relation to the hidden parts of the human body. In his account he refers several times to "This organ," but fails to say what organ is meant.

As the spring came, with its warm sunny days, Dr. Cloquet advised him to drive out more and get the air. On an early day in May, 1834, he took a drive in the Bois to visit his granddaughter, Mme. Adolph Périer, was caught in a drenching rain, went home and to bed and never got up again.

The doctor was fussing around with his medicines, and his silly words of encouragement when Lafayette said to him, "You can do nothing for me. Life is going now. It is like the flame of a lamp. When the oil is used up—when there is no more oil—then the flame is out."

Lafayette's life-flame flickered out at dawn on May 20, 1834. He was in his seventy-seventh year.

He was buried in Picpus Cemetery by the side of his wife. On his return from America in 1825 he had brought a large quantity of earth and had it kept so that he might be laid to his eternal rest in American soil. His body lies today in earth that came from his beloved United States.

Lafayette's republican friends planned a great funeral for him, but the government acted at once and forbade any kind of popular demonstration. The military authorities took charge. The funeral cortege was surrounded and almost hidden by troops with fixed bayonets.

"Hide yourselves, Parisians," Armand Carrel wrote. "The funeral of an honest man and a true friend of liberty is passing by."

The End

BIBLIOGRAPHY

BARDOUX, A., *Les dernieres années de Lafayette.* Paris, 1893.

BARTHOU, LOUIS, *Mirabeau.* Paris, 1913.

BEARD, MIRIAM, *A History of the Business Man.* New York, 1938.

BELLOC, HILAIRE, *Robespierre, A Study.* London, 1927.

BLANC, LOUIS, *La Révolution Française* (12 vols.). Paris, 1859.

BLANCHARD, CLAUDE, *Journal de Campagne, guerre d'Amérique.* Paris, 1881.

BROWNING, CHARLES H., *Lafayette's Visit to the United States in 1824–25.* (In the American Historical Register for 1895-1896.)

CHASTELLUX, MARQUIS DE, *Voyages de M. le Marquis de Chastellux dans l'Amérique Septentrionale* (2 vols.). Paris, 1786.

CLARETIE, JULES, *Camille Desmoulins.* Paris, 1908.

CLOQUET, JULES, *Recollections of General Lafayette.*

DONIOL, HENRI DE, *Histoire de la participation de la France à l'établissement des Etats-Unis d'Amérique* (5 vols.). Paris, 1886-1890.

FRIEDENWALD, JULIUS, M.D., *Some Incidents of Medical Interest in the Life of General Lafayette.* New York, 1932.

GEER, WALTER, *The French Revolution: A Historical Sketch.* New York, 1922.

GOTTSCHALK, LOUIS, *Lafayette Comes to America.* Chicago, 1935.

———, *Lafayette Joins the American Army.* Chicago, 1937.

HALE, EDWARD EVERETT, *Franklin in France.* Boston, 1887.

HALL, JOHN R., *The Bourbon Restoration.* Boston, 1909.

HUGER, FRANCIS K., *Statement of the Attempted Rescue of Lafayette from Olmütz.*

JEFFERSON, THOMAS, *Works* (9 vols.). New York, 1854.

JORDAN, ABRAHAM, *Lafayette as a Free-Mason.* (In American Historical Register for 1896.)

KAPP, FREDERICK, *Life of John Kalb.* New York, 1870.

KROPOTKIN, PETER, *The Great French Revolution* (2 vols.). New York, 1927.

"Lafayette, Friend of the Negro," in the *Journal of Negro History,* Vol. XIX. Washington, 1934.

LAFAYETTE, MARQUIS DE, *Mémoires de ma Main* (6 vols.). Paris, 1837-1838.

LASTEYRIE, MADAME DE, *Vie de Madame de Lafayette.* Paris, 1868.

Latzko, Andreas, *Lafayette: A life*. Translation by E. W. Dickes. New York, 1936.

Lenotre, G., *Les Fils de Philippe-Egalité pendant la Terreur*. Paris, 1926.

Letters of Lafayette and Jefferson. With an introduction and notes by Gilbert Chinard. Baltimore, 1929.

Levasseur, A., *Lafayette en Amérique en 1824–25*. Paris, 1829.

Lowell, E. J., *The Eve of the French Revolution*. Boston, 1893.

Lucas-Dubreton, J., *Louis XVIII*. Paris, 1925.

Madelin, Louis, *Figures of the Revolution*. New York, 1929.

———, *La Révolution*. Paris, 1911.

Mathiez, Albert, *The French Revolution*. Translation by Caroline Alison Phillips. New York, 1928.

———, *The Fall of Robespierre*. New York, 1927.

McCabe, Lida Rose, *Ardent Adrienne*. New York, 1930.

Morgan, George, *The True Lafayette*. Philadelphia, 1919.

Morris, Gouverneur, *Diary and Letters* (2 vols.). New York, 1888.

Mosnier, Henri, *Le Château de Chavaniac*. Le Puy, 1883.

Nolte, Vincent, *Memoirs of a Merchant*.

Palmer, John McAuley, *General von Steuben*. New Haven, 1937.

Penman, John S., *Lafayette and Three Revolutions*. Boston, 1929.

Perkins, James B., *France in the American Revolution*. Boston, 1911.

Pontgibaud, Chevalier de, *A French Volunteer in the War of Independence*. Translated by Robert B. Douglas. New York, 1897.

Randolph, Sarah N., *The Domestic Life of Thomas Jefferson*. New York, 1871.

Rivers, John, *Figaro: The Life of Beaumarchais*. London, 1922.

Roverier, A., *Anecdotes sur la Révolution Française*. Paris, 1826.

Sedgwick, Henry Dwight, *Lafayette*. Indianapolis, 1928.

Sherrill, Charles H., *French Memoirs of Eighteenth Century America*. New York, 1915.

Sichel, Edith, *The Household of the Lafayettes*.

Taine, Hippolyte Adolphe, *The Ancient Regime*. (New edition, translation by John Durand.) New York, 1896.

Thomas, Jules, *Correspondance inédite de Lafayette, 1793-1801*. Paris, 1930.

Tower, Charlemagne, *The Marquis de Lafayette in the American Revolution* (2 vols.). Philadelphia, 1895.

Washington, George, *Diaries* (4 vols.). Boston, 1925.

Waterman, William Randall, *Frances Wright*. New York, 1924.

Whitlock, Brand, *Lafayette* (2 vols.). New York, 1930.

INDEX